THE GHOST-DANCE RELIGION
and the
SIOUX OUTBREAK OF 1890

CLASSICS IN ANTHROPOLOGY
Paul Bohannan, Editor

THE GHOST-DANCE RELIGION

and the

SIOUX OUTBREAK OF 1890

By James Mooney
Abridged, with an Introduction
by Anthony F. C. Wallace

THE UNIVERSITY OF CHICAGO PRESS / CHICAGO & LONDON

Originally published as Part 2 of the *Fourteenth Annual Report
of the Bureau of Ethnology to the Secretary of the Smithsonian
Institution, 1892–93* (Washington: Government Printing Office, 1896)

ISBN: 0-226-53516-9 (clothbound); 0-226-53517-7 (paperbound)

Library of Congress Catalog Card Number: 64-24971

The University of Chicago Press, Chicago 60637
The University of Chicago Press, Ltd., London

James Mooney (1861–1921)

and the Study of the Ghost-Dance Religion

James Mooney was one of the most illustrious members of that small band of nineteenth-century ethnologists in the United States whose work with the American Indian laid a foundation for the later development of academic anthropology under the authority of Franz Boas. He belongs with such other self-trained, empirically oriented, and unself-consciously theoretical scholars as D. G. Brinton, L. H. Morgan, J. N. B. Hewitt, O. T. Mason, and J. W. Powell. Mooney contributed to American Indian studies substantial and irreplaceable empirical reports on the traditional culture of the Cherokee and Kiowa, on the population of tribal groups in North America at first contact, and—most importantly—on the Ghost dance. In the Ghost-dance study, which is republished in this volume, Mooney not only provided a vivid and detailed account of a major revitalization movement, but also recognized—albeit in a crudely classificatory way—the essential similarity in process between this one Indian nativistic movement and the many comparable efforts at cultural renewal among other peoples, both primitive and civilized. He recognized, in other words, the pan-human characteristics of the type of event; later scholars have used his insights and his empirical description to develop more detailed theories.

PERSONAL LIFE

Mooney was born in 1861, in a small country town in Indiana, of Irish immigrant parents; in 1897 he married Ione Lee Gaut, of Tennessee, and by her had six children; he died in 1921. In his middle years he was described as "... a small, agile man with long dark-brown hair and large gray eyes." While a youth in the public schools of Richmond, he developed an intense interest in the American Indians, and after spending a few years as a schoolteacher and newspaperman in Indiana, he went to Washington, D.C., to promote a romantic private ambition: to go to Brazil to study the Indian tribes. While in Washington, he met Major John Wesley Powell, who had just founded the Bureau of American Ethnology. Powell appointed him ethnologist in 1885, and from this date until his death Mooney worked for the Bureau in the office and in the field, dividing his time between ethnohistorical library researches and extended visits to the Indian Territory and to reservations. He was also active in preparing Indian exhibits for the famous "expositions" of the period and became one of the founding members of the American Anthropological Association. Mooney's major monographic writings are listed below.

Mooney's capacity to empathize with Indian aspirations for a better, nativistically oriented way of life—particularly as it was expressed so dramatically in the Ghost dance—was no doubt a function more of certain personal sentiments than of theoretical orientation. He was passionately devoted to Irish causes and undertook to promote the interests of Irishmen, in America and in the old country, by active participation in various nativistic enterprises. At the age of eighteen, he helped to organize and direct the Land League in Indiana, and he served as president of the Gaelic Society of Washington from its founding in 1907 until 1910. He wrote articles on traditional Irish customs. He favored deeply the Irish home rule and republican movements, and (despite his own personal religious loyalty to Catholicism) vigorously opposed the conservative role of the Catholic hierarchy in regard to Irish nationalism; he even came to sympathize with socialism as a political philosophy.

Thus in his approach to the Ghost dance and to the Peyote religion, which he supported against criticism in his testimony before a congressional committee—and on which he left an unpublished manuscript—Mooney brought with him a personally experienced model of this type of event, a model which included an awareness of ancient glories, of a sense of wrong and deprivation, and a dream of a golden age returned.[1]

MOONEY'S MAJOR MONOGRAPHIC PUBLICATIONS

A complete bibliography of Mooney's writings, exclusive of posthumous works, is to be found in his obituary in the *American Anthropologist*, XXIV (1922), 209–14.

1885 *Linguistic Families of the Indian Tribes North of Mexico, with Provisional List of the Publications of the Principal Tribal Names and Synonyms.* Miscellaneous Publications of the Bureau of American Ethnology, 55 pp.

1891 *Sacred Formulas of the Cherokee.* Seventh Annual Report of the Bureau of American Ethnology, pp. 301–97.

1894 *Siouan Tribes of the East.* Bulletin 22 of the Bureau of American Ethnology, 101 pp.

1896 *The Ghost-dance Religion and the Sioux Outbreak of 1890.* Fourteenth Annual Report of the Bureau of American Ethnology, Part 2, pp. 641–1110.

1898 *Calendar History of the Kiowa Indians.* Seventeenth Annual Report of the Bureau of American Ethnology, Part 1, pp. 129–445.

---

[1] I am indebted to Dr. Henry Collins, of the Bureau of American Ethnology, for making available to me unpublished materials from the files of the Bureau containing information on Mooney's life.

1900 *Myths of the Cherokee.* Nineteenth Annual Report of the Bureau of American Ethnology, Part 1, pp. 3–548.

1907 *The Cheyenne Indians.* Memoirs of the American Anthropological Association, I, 357–478.

1928 *The Aboriginal Population of America North of Mexico.* Smithsonian Miscellaneous Collections, LXXX, 1–40.

MOONEY'S DESCRIPTION OF THE GHOST DANCE

James Mooney had been a professional ethnologist for only five years when the Ghost dance began, in 1890, to attract public attention. It was at just this time, too, that the last frontier was officially closed, and the frontier phase of American history came to an end. There were many Indians still unreconciled to reservation life; there were still an Indian Territory and a Territory of Oklahoma, but as yet no state of Oklahoma, and the Indian Territory was largely governed by Indians; there were still vivid memories, on both sides, of Custer's Last Stand, of the bloody Sioux uprising in Minnesota, and of other recent Indian wars. But even the Sioux of South Dakota, among whom the Ghost dance was to become the spark of the last Indian war, were making progress in "civilization": they were joining Christian churches, dividing into "progressive" and "conservative" factions, establishing family farms, keeping large herds of cattle, establishing a profitable freight business, sending some of their children to school, and appearing on "Wild West" shows instead of on the warpath. Indians in reservations across the country were sending one another letters by U.S. Post, and making use of the railroads for visiting. And white people across the country were beginning to regard the Indians less as dangerous foreigners than as a difficult but segregated minority.

The interest in the Ghost dance of the Bureau of American Ethnology was thus precipitated not by a policy of interest in nativistic movements but by the agitation aroused in the government and in the popular press concerning the possibility of an "Indian Outbreak" among the Sioux. Mooney was dispatched to investigate this new, and threatening, religion among the Sioux—and other affected tribes—and to report his findings. As I have remarked, it is a fortunate coincidence that Mooney himself was motivated by some of the same nativistic sentiments that inspired the Sioux dancers and the Sioux political conservatives. Thus Mooney was able to take seriously not only the personal tragedy of the Indian men, women, and children who were killed and wounded by Army regulars at the battle of Wounded Knee, but also the faith of the Ghost-dancers, whose religious passion inspired a reckless disrespect both for bureaucracy and bullets.

Mooney's view of the Ghost dance, and of its tragic denouement among the Sioux, was, inevitably, somewhat restricted. His work is incomplete and, occasionally, in error. He mistakes, for instance, the father of Wovoka, the 1890 Ghost-dance prophet, for another man who actually launched the earlier Ghost dance of 1870. And he grossly underestimates not only the importance of the 1870 Ghost dance as a forerunner of the events of 1890 but also the significance of beliefs concerning the return of the dead, traditionally so important among the Paviotso and their northern neighbors, in the genesis of both Ghost-dance movements. It has become apparent, as a result of later researches, that in the culture area of the Rocky Mountain plateau there had existed for many generations— probably predating the arrival of white men—a belief in the eventual return of the dead, encouraged by dances and by the influence of shamans. This belief made locally plausible the revelations of the two Paviotso prophets Tavibo and Wovoka (of 1870 and 1890, respectively) that the dead were soon to return and that the white people and their culture were at the same time to be destroyed by a natural cataclysm. Although the 1870 doctrine was disseminated primarily among the California tribes and that of 1890 was principally spread among the tribes to the east, the two movements were closely similar in doctrine and practice.

Mooney also was not in a position to recognize all the cultural factors affecting the acceptability, or non-acceptability, of the new religion. Although the doctrine was sufficiently abstract to allow for a wide variety of local interpretations—after all, the return of the Indian ancestors and their customs meant a return of a plurality of cultures—it was effectively barred from any people (such as the Navaho) to whom the very idea of ghosts, and any talk of their revival, was offensive. And finally, the simple limitation of time made it impossible for Mooney to trace the subsequent evolution of Ghost-dance doctrine among the various peoples whom it had just begun to affect during his period of observation.

Thus a thorough understanding of the Ghost dance as a cultural phenomenon requires consultation of later works as well as Mooney's, works written after ethnographic and historical studies of the Paviotso, the Klamath, the Sioux, and other tribes became available. It is remarkable, indeed, that so early a student was able to accomplish so much under such extraordinary difficulties.

SOME MAJOR WRITINGS ON THE GHOST DANCE
PUBLISHED SINCE 1896

ABERLE, DAVID F. "The Prophet Dance and Reactions to White Contact," *Southwestern Journal of Anthropology*, XV (1959), 74–83.

BAILEY, PAUL. *Wovoka, the Indian Messiah*. Los Angeles: Westernlore Press, 1957.

DuBois, CORA. "The 1870 Ghost Dance," University of California, *Anthropological Records*, Vol. III (1939), No. 1.

GAYTON, A. H. "The Ghost Dance of 1870 in South-Central California," *University of California Publications in American Archaeology and Ethnology*, XXVIII (1930), 57–82.

HILL, W. W. "The Navaho Indians and the Ghost Dance of 1890," *American Anthropologist*, XL (1944), 523–27.

LESSER, ALEXANDER. "Cultural Significance of the Ghost Dance," *American Anthropologist*, XXXV (1933), 108–15.

———. *The Pawnee Ghost Dance Hand Game: A Study of Cultural Change*. New York: Columbia University Press, 1933.

MILLER, DAVID H. *Ghost Dance*. New York: Duell, Sloan & Pearce, 1959.

NASH, PHILLEO. "The Place of Religious Revivalism in the Formation of the Intercultural Community on Klamath Reservation." *In* Fred Eggan (ed.), *Social Anthropology of North American Indian Tribes*, pp. 375–442. Chicago: University of Chicago Press, 1955.

SPIER, LESLIE. "The Ghost Dance of 1870 among the Klamath of Oregon," *University of Washington Publications in Anthropology*, II (1927), 39–56.

———. *The Prophet Dance of the Northwest and Its Derivatives: The Source of the Ghost Dance*. American Anthropological Association, General Series in Anthropology, No. 1, 1935.

STRONG, WILLIAM DUNCAN. "The Occurrence and Wider Implications of a 'Ghost Cult' on the Columbia River Suggested by Carvings in Wood, Bone and Stone," *American Anthropologist*, XLV (1945), 244–61.

UTLEY, ROBERT M. *The Last Days of the Sioux Nation*. New Haven: Yale University Press, 1963.

VESTAL, STANLEY. *New Sources of Indian History, 1850–1891: The Ghost Dance— the Prairie Sioux, a Miscellany*. Norman: University of Oklahoma Press, 1934.

MOONEY'S CONTRIBUTION TO THE THEORY
OF NATIVISTIC MOVEMENTS

Mooney recognized that the Ghost dance was the same kind of event as many another ecstatic religious movement, not only among American Indians, but around the world. He regarded as similar the prophetic roles of Joan of Arc, Mohammed, and Wovoka. Thus Mooney anticipated those later formulations which posit an essential processual similarity in revolutionary religious movements diverse in form and philosophical basis. Furthermore, Mooney regarded such movements as adaptive responses of peoples to intolerable stresses laid upon them by poverty and oppression. In this restricted sense, he was an early proponent of the "cultural deprivation" school of thought, which interests itself in the function of such movements as more or less effective expressions of social dissatisfaction. In these senses, Mooney foreshadows later theorists.

But Mooney was not primarily a theoretician. He did not attempt a subclassification of revitalization movements; he did not clearly distinguish between absolute deprivation and relative deprivation (in an absolutist economic sense, the Sioux may actually have been in better circumstances than some of the tribes who took far less interest in the Ghost dance); and he did not have sufficient information to explore the determinants of the acceptability of the Ghost-dance doctrine in varying cultural contexts. Thus the second origin of the Ghost dance among the

Paviotso was undoubtedly a function, not only of the deprivation level of this group, but also of the prior occurrence of a Ghost dance which itself was grounded in what Spier (1935) has called the "Prophet Dance" of the Northwest. The rejection of the Ghost dance by the Navaho was a function not of deprivation level but of the Navaho avoidance of mentioning the dead (Hill, 1944). Furthermore, because of the early date of publication, Mooney was unable to incorporate information on the later fate of the Ghost dance: its survival among the Pawnee as the vehicle for a more general nativistic revival, its transformation into the Earth Lodge and Bole Maru cults in the Northwest, etc. These later findings bear on the theoretical issues of the viability and institutionalization of reform movements.

SOME THEORETICAL AND COMPARATIVE STUDIES OF REVITALIZATION MOVEMENTS

BARBER, BERNARD. "Acculturation and Messianic Movements," *American Sociological Review*, I (1941), 663–69.

BARNETT, H. G. *Indian Shakers*. Carbondale: Southern Illinois University Press, 1957.

CANTRIL, HADLEY. *Psychology of Social Movements*. New York: John Wiley & Sons, Inc., 1944.

LINTON, RALPH. "Nativistic Movements," *American Anthropologist*, XLV (1943), 230–40.

RELANDER, CLICK. *Drummers and Dreamers: The Story of Smowhalla the Prophet*. Caldwell, Idaho: Caxton Printers, 1956.

WALLACE, ANTHONY F. C. "Revitalization Movements," *American Anthropologist*, LVIII (1956), 264–81.

WALLIS, WILSON D. *Messiahs: Their Role in Civilization*. Washington, D.C.: American Council of Public Affairs, 1943.

WORSLEY, PETER. *The Trumpet Shall Sound*. London: MacGibbon & Kee, 1957.

THE EDITING OF MOONEY'S GHOST DANCE

In the preparation of this edited edition of Mooney's classic study, I decided to cut two kinds of text material: first, Mooney's more or less incomplete descriptions of other religious movements (all of which have had more thorough chroniclers since him), together with most of his theoretical remarks, which are summarized simply and forcefully in the introductory paragraph of the book; and, second, the glossaries of various Indian languages which he attached to the tribe-by-tribe accounts of Ghost-dance rituals and songs. Otherwise, the book stands as Mooney wrote it—the classic study of an American Indian revitalization movement.

ANTHONY F. C. WALLACE
University of Pennsylvania

Preface

In the fall of 1890 the author was preparing to go to Indian Ter
ritory, under the auspices of the Bureau of Ethnology, to continue
researches among the Cherokee, when the Ghost dance began to attract
attention, and permission was asked and received to investigate that
subject also among the wilder tribes in the western part of the territory. Proceeding directly to the Cheyenne and Arapaho, it soon
became evident that there was more in the Ghost dance than had
been suspected, with the result that the investigation, to which it
had been intended to devote only a few weeks, has extended over a
period of more than three years, and might be continued indefinitely,
as the dance still exists (in 1896) and is developing new features at
every performance. The uprising among the Sioux in the meantime
made necessary also the examination of a mass of documentary material
in the files of the Indian Office and the War Department bearing on
the outbreak, in addition to the study in the field of the strictly religious features of the dance.

The first visit of about four months (December, 1890–April, 1891)
was made to the Arapaho, Cheyenne, Kiowa, Comanche, Apache, Caddo,
and Wichita, all living near together in the western part of what was
then Indian Territory, but is now Oklahoma. These tribes were all
more or less under the influence of the new religion. The principal
study was made among the Arapaho, who were the most active propa-
gators of the "Messiah" doctrine among the southern tribes and are
especially friendly and cordial in disposition.

On returning to Washington, the author received a commission to
make an ethnologic collection for the World's Columbian Exposition,
and, selecting the Kiowa for that purpose as a representative prairie
tribe, started out again almost immediately to the same field. This
trip, lasting three months, gave further opportunity for study of the
Ghost dance among the same tribes. After returning and attending
to the labeling and arranging of the collection, a study was made of all
documents bearing on the subject in possession of the Indian Office and

the War Department. Another trip was then made to the field for the purpose of investigating the dance among the Sioux, where it had attracted most attention, and among the Paiute, where it originated. On this journey the author visited the Omaha, Winnebago, Sioux of Pine Ridge, Paiute, Cheyenne, and Arapaho; met and talked with the messiah himself, and afterward, on the strength of this fact, obtained from the Cheyenne the original letter containing his message and instructions to the southern tribes. This trip occupied about three months.

A few months later, in the summer of 1892, another journey was made to the West, in the course of which the southern tribes and the Sioux were revisited, and some time was spent in Wyoming with the Shoshoni and northern Arapaho, the latter of whom were perhaps the most earnest followers of the messiah in the north. This trip consumed four months. After some time spent in Washington in elaborating notes already obtained, a winter trip (1892–93) was made under another commission from the World's Fair to the Navaho and the Hopi or Moki, of New Mexico and Arizona. Although these tribes were not directly concerned in the Ghost dance, they had been visited by apostles of the new doctrine, and were able to give some account of the ceremony as it existed among the Havasupai or Cohonino and others farther to the west. On the return journey another short stay was made among the Kiowa and Arapaho. In the summer of 1893 a final visit, covering a period of five months, was made to the western tribes of Oklahoma, bringing the personal observation and study of the Ghost dance down to the beginning of 1894.

The field investigation therefore occupied twenty-two months, involving nearly 32,000 miles of travel and more or less time spent with about twenty tribes. To obtain exact knowledge of the ceremony, the author took part in the dance among the Arapaho and Cheyenne. He also carried a kodak and a tripod camera, with which he made photographs of the dance and the trance both without and within the circle. Several months were spent in consulting manuscript documents and printed sources of information in the departments and libraries at Washington, and correspondence was carried on with persons in various parts of the country who might be able to give additional facts. From the beginning every effort was made to get a correct statement of the subject. Beyond this, the work must speak for itself.

As the Ghost dance doctrine is only the latest of a series of Indian religious revivals, and as the idea on which it is founded is a hope common to all humanity, considerable space has been given to a discussion of the primitive messiah belief and of the teachings of the various Indian prophets who have preceded Wovoka, together with brief sketches of several Indian wars belonging to the same periods.

In the songs the effort has been to give the spirit and exact rendering, without going into analytic details. The main purpose of the work is not linguistic, and as nearly every tribe concerned speaks a different language from all the others, any close linguistic study must be left to the philologist who can afford to devote a year or more to an individual tribe. The only one of these tribes of which the author claims intimate knowledge is the Kiowa.

Acknowledgments are due the officers and members of the Office of Indian Affairs and the War Department for courteous assistance in obtaining documentary information and in replying to letters of inquiry; to Mr De Lancey W. Gill and Mr J. K. Hillers and their assistants of the art and photographic divisions of the United States Geological Survey; to Mr A. R. Spofford, Librarian of Congress; to Mr F. V. Coville, botanist, Agricultural Department; Honorable T. J. Morgan, former Commissioner of Indian Affairs; Major J. W. Mac-Murray, first artillery, United States Army; Dr Washington Matthews, surgeon, United States Army; Captain H. L. Scott, seventh cavalry, United States Army; Captain J. M. Lee, ninth infantry, United States Army; Captain E. L. Huggins, second cavalry, United States Army, of the staff of General Miles; the late Captain J. G. Bourke, third cavalry, United States Army; Captain H. G. Browne, twelfth infantry, United States Army; Judge James Wickersham, Tacoma, Washington; Dr George Bird Grinnell, editor of "Forest and Stream," New York city; Mr Thomas V. Keam and the late A. M. Stephen, Keams Canyon, Arizona; Rev. H. R. Voth, Oraibi, Arizona; General L. W. Colby, Washington, District of Columbia; Mr D. B. Dyer, Augusta, Georgia; Rev. Myron Eells, Tacoma, Washington; Mr Emile Berliner and the Berliner Gramophone Company, for recording, and Professors John Philip Sousa and F. W. V. Gaisberg, for arranging the Indian music; W. S. Godbe, Bullionville, Nevada; Miss L. McLain, Washington City; Addison Cooper, Nashville, Tennessee; Miss Emma C. Sickels, Chicago; Professor A. H. Thompson, United States Geological Survey, Washington; Mrs L. B. Arnold, Standing Rock, North Dakota; Mr C. H. Bartlett, South Bend, Indiana; Dr T. P. Martin, Taos, New Mexico, and to the following Indian informants and interpreters: Philip Wells, Louis Menard, Ellis Standing Bear, American Horse, George Sword, and Fire Thunder, of Pine Ridge, South Dakota; Henry Reid, Rev. Sherman Coolidge, Norcok, Sage, and Sharp Nose, of Fort Washakie, Wyoming; Charley Sheep of Walker river, Nevada; Black Coyote, Sitting Bull, Black Short Nose, George Bent, Paul Boynton, Robert Burns, Jesse Bent, Clever Warden, Grant Left-hand, and the Arapaho police at Darlington, Oklahoma; Andres Martinez, Belo Cozad, Paul Setkopti, Henry Poloi, Little Bow, William Tivis, George Parton, Towakoni Jim, Robert Dunlap, Kichai, John Wilson, Tama, Igiagyahona, Deoñ, Mary Zotom, and Eliza Parton of Anadarko, Oklahoma.

Say, shall not I at last attain
Some height, from whence the Past is clear,
In whose immortal atmosphere
I shall behold my dead again?

Bayard Taylor

For the fires grow cold and the dances fail,
And the songs in their echoes die;
And what have we left but the graves beneath,
And, above, the waiting sky?

The Song of the Ancient People

My Father, have pity on me!
I have nothing to eat,
I am dying of thirst—
Everything is gone!

Arapho Ghost Song

Contents

Illustrations

IPPEWA

MENOMINEE

IROQUOIS

THE
NDIAN
RRITORY

CHEROKEE

LOCATION OF SELECTED INDIAN RESERVATIONS
IN THE UNITED STATES IN 1890

APPROXIMATE AREA OF THE GHOST DANCE

0   100   200   300   400

SCALE OF MILES

Introduction

The wise men tell us that the world is growing happier—that we live longer than did our fathers, have more of comfort and less of toil, fewer wars and discords, and higher hopes and aspirations. So say the wise men; but deep in our own hearts we know they are wrong. For were not we, too, born in Arcadia, and have we not—each one of us—in that May of life when the world was young, started out lightly and airily along the path that led through green meadows to the blue mountains on the distant horizon, beyond which lay the great world we were to conquer? And though others dropped behind, have we not gone on through morning brightness and noonday heat, with eyes always steadily forward, until the fresh grass began to be parched and withered, and the way grew hard and stony, and the blue mountains resolved into gray rocks and thorny cliffs? And when at last we reached the toilsome summits, we found the glory that had lured us onward was only the sunset glow that fades into darkness while we look, and leaves us at the very goal to sink down, tired in body and sick at heart, with strength and courage gone, to close our eyes and dream again, not of the fame and fortune that were to be ours, but only of the old-time happiness that we have left so far behind.

As with men, so is it with nations. The lost paradise is the world's dreamland of youth. What tribe or people has not had its golden age, before Pandora's box was loosed, when women were nymphs and dryads and men were gods and heroes? And when the race lies crushed and groaning beneath an alien yoke, how natural is the dream of a redeemer, an Arthur, who shall return from exile or awake from some long sleep to drive out the usurper and win back for his people what they have lost. The hope becomes a faith and the faith becomes the creed of priests and prophets, until the hero is a god and the dream a religion, looking to some great miracle of nature for its culmination and accomplishment. The doctrines of the Hindu avatar, the Hebrew Messiah, the Christian millennium, and the Hesûnanin of the Indian Ghost dance are essentially the same, and have their origin in a hope and longing common to all humanity.

CHAPTER I

Wovoka the Messiah

When the sun died, I went up to heaven and saw God and all the people who had died a long time ago. God told me to come back and tell my people they must be good and love one another, and not fight, or steal, or lie. He gave me this dance to give to my people.—Wovoka.

About 1870 a prophet appeared among the Paiute in Nevada. As most Indian movements are unknown to the whites at their inception, the date is variously put from 1869 to 1872. He is said to have been the father of the present "messiah," who has unquestionably derived many of his ideas from him, and lived, as does his son, in Mason valley, about 60 miles south of Virginia City, not far from Walker River reservation. In talking with his son, he said that his father's name was Tä'vibo or "White man, and that he was a *capita* (Spanish, *capitan*) or petty chief, but not a prophet or preacher, although he used to have visions and was invulnerable. From concurrent testimony of Indians and white men, however, there seems to be no doubt that he did preach and prophesy and introduce a new religious dance among his people, and that the doctrine which he promulgated and the hopes which he held out twenty years ago were the foundation on which his son has built the structure of the present messiah religion. He was visited by Indians from Oregon and Idaho, and his teachings made their influence felt among the Bannock and Shoshoni, as well as among all the scattered bands of the Paiute, to whom he continued to preach until his death a year or two later. (*G. D., 1 and 2; A. G. O., 1; Phister, 1.*)

Captain J. M. Lee, Ninth infantry, formerly on the staff of General Miles, was on duty in that neighborhood at the time and gives the following account of the prophet and his doctrines in a personal letter to the author:

I was on Indian duty in Nevada in 1869, 1870, and 1871. When visiting Walker Lake reservation in 1869–70, I became acquainted with several superstitious beliefs then prevailing among the Paiute Indians. It was a rough, mountainous region roundabout, and mysterious happenings, according to tradition, always occurred when the prophet or medicine-men went up into the mountains and there received their revelations from the divine spirits. In the earlier part of the sixties the whites began to come in and appropriate much of the Indian country in Nevada, and in the usual course it turned out that the medicine-men or prophets were looked to for relief. The most influential went up alone into the mountain and there met the Great Spirit. He brought back with him no tablets of stone, but he was a messenger of good tidings to the effect that within a few moons there was to be a great upheaval or earthquake. All the improvements of the whites—all their houses, their goods, stores, etc.—would remain, but the whites would be swallowed up, while the Indians would be saved and permitted to enjoy the earth and all the fullness thereof, including anything left by the wicked whites. This revelation was duly proclaimed by the prophet, and attracted a few believers, but the doubting skeptics were too many, and they ridiculed the idea that the white men would fall into the holes and be swallowed up while the Indians would not. As the prophet could not enforce his belief, he went up into the mountain again and came back with a second revelation, which was that when the great disaster came, all, both Indians and whites, would be swallowed up or overwhelmed, but that at the end of three days (or a few days) the Indians would be resurrected in the flesh, and would live forever to enjoy the earth, with plenty of game, fish, and pine nuts, while their enemies, the whites, would be destroyed forever. There would thus be a final and eternal separation between Indians and whites.

This revelation, which seemed more reasonable, was rather popular for awhile, but as time wore along faith seemed to weaken and the prophet was without honor even in his own country. After much fasting and prayer, he made a third trip to the mountain, where he secured a final revelation or message to the people. The divine spirit had become so much incensed at the lack of faith in the prophecies, that it was revealed to his chosen one that those Indians who believed in the prophecy would be resurrected and be happy, but those who did not believe in it would stay in the ground and be damned forever with the whites.

It was not long after this that the prophet died, and the poor miserable Indians worried along for nearly two decades, eating grasshoppers, lizards, and fish, and trying to be civilized until the appearance of this new prophet Quoit-tsow, who is said to be the son, either actual or spiritual, of the first one.

Additional details are given in the following interesting extract from a letter addressed to the Commissioner of Indian Affairs, under date of November 19, 1890, by Mr Frank Campbell, who has an intimate acquaintance with the tribe and was employed in an official capacity on the reservation at the time when Tävibo first announced the new revelation. It would appear from Mr Campbell's statement that under the new dispensation both races were to meet on a common level, and, as this agrees with what Professor Thompson, referred to later on, afterward found among the eastern Paiute, it is probable that the original doctrine had been very considerably modified since its first promulgation a few years before.

Eighteen years ago I was resident farmer on Walker Lake Indian reserve, Nevada. I had previously been connected with the Indian service at the reserve for ten years, was familiar with the Paiute customs, and personally acquainted with all the Indians in that region. In 1872 an Indian commenced preaching a new religion at that reserve that caused a profound sensation among the Paiute. For several months I was kept in ignorance of the cause of the excitement—which was remarkable, considering the confidence they had always reposed in me. They no doubt expected me to ridicule the sayings of the new messiah, as I had always labored among them to break down their superstitious beliefs. When finally I was made acquainted with the true facts of the case, I told them the preachings of Waugh-zee-waugh-ber were good and no harm could come from it. Indian emissaries visited the reserve from Idaho, Oregon, and other places, to investigate the new religion. I visited the Indian camp while the prophet was in a trance and remained until he came to. In accordance with instructions, the Indians gathered around him and joined in a song that was to guide the spirit back to the body. Upon reanimation he gave a long account of his visit in the spirit to the Supreme Ruler, who was then on the way with all the spirits of the departed dead to again reside upon this earth and change it into a paradise. Life was to be eternal, and no distinction was to exist between races.

This morning's press dispatches contain an account of Porcupine's visit to Walker lake . . . that proves to me that the religion started at Walker lake eighteen years ago is the same that is now agitating the Indian world. There is nothing in it to cause trouble between whites and Indians unless the new Messiah is misquoted and his doctrine misconstrued. I left Walker Lake reserve in June, 1873, and at the time supposed this craze would die out, but have several times since been reminded by Nevada papers and letters that it was gradually spreading. (*G. D., 3.*)

The name given by Campbell certainly does not much resemble Tävibo, but it is quite possible that the father, like the son, had more than one name. It is also possible that "Waughzeewaughber" was not the prophet described by Captain Lee, but one of his disciples who had taken up and modified the original doctrine. The name Tävibo refers to the east (*tävänagwat*) or place where the sun (*täbi*) rises. By the cognate Shoshoni and Comanche the whites are called *Taivo*.

From oral information of Professor A. H. Thompson, of the United States Geological Survey, I learn some particulars of the advent of the new doctrine among the Paiute of southwestern Utah. While his party was engaged in that section in the spring of 1875, a great excitement was caused among the Indians by the report that two mysterious beings with white skins (it will be remembered that the father of Wovoka was named Tävibo or "white man") had appeared among the Paiute far to the west and announced a speedy resurrection of all the dead Indians, the restoration of the game, and the return of the old-time primitive life. Under the new order of things, moreover, both races alike were to be white. A number of Indians from Utah went over into Nevada, where they met others who claimed to have seen these mysterious visitors farther in the west. On their return to Utah they brought back with them the ceremonial of the new belief, the chief part of the ritual being a dance performed at night in a circle, with no fire in the center, very much as in the modern Ghost dance.

It is said that the Mormons, who hold the theory that the Indians are the descendants of the supposititious "ten lost tribes," cherish, as a part of their faith, the tradition that some of the lost Hebrew emigrants are still ice-bound in the frozen north, whence they will one day emerge to rejoin their brethren in the south. When the news of this Indian revelation came to their ears, the Mormon priests accepted it as a prophecy of speedy fulfillment of their own traditions, and Orson Pratt, one of the most prominent leaders, preached a sermon, which was extensively copied and commented on at the time, urging the faithful to arrange their affairs and put their houses in order to receive the long-awaited wanderers.

According to the statement of the agent then in charge at Fort Hall, in Idaho, the Mormons at the same time—the early spring of 1875— sent emissaries to the Bannock, urging them to go to Salt Lake City to be baptized into the Mormon religion. A large number accepted the invitation without the knowledge of the agent, went down to Utah, and were there baptized, and then returned to work as missionaries of the new faith among their tribes. As an additional inducement, free rations were furnished by the Mormons to all who would come and be baptized, and "they were told that by being baptized and going to church the old men would all become young, the young men would never be sick, that the Lord had a work for them to do, and that they were the chosen people of God to establish his kingdom upon the earth," etc. It is also asserted that they were encouraged to resist the authority of the government. (*Comr., 2.*) However much of truth there may be in these reports, and we must make considerable allowance for local prejudice, it is sufficiently evident that the Mormons took an active interest in the religious ferment then existing among the neighboring tribes and helped to give shape to the doctrine which crystallized some years later in the Ghost dance.

When Tävibo, the prophet of Mason valley, died, about 1870, he left a son named Wovoka, "The Cutter," about 14 years of age. The prophetic claims and teachings of the father, the reverence with which he was regarded by the people, and the mysterious ceremonies which were doubtless of frequent performance in the little tulé wikiup at home must have made early and deep impression on the mind of the boy, who seems to have been by nature of a solitary and contemplative disposition, one of those born to see visions and hear still voices.

The physical environment was favorable to the development of such a character. His native valley, from which he has never wandered, is a narrow strip of level sage prairie some 30 miles in length, walled in by the giant sierras, their sides torn and gashed by volcanic convulsions and dark with gloomy forests of pine, their towering summits white with everlasting snows, and roofed over by a cloudless sky whose blue infinitude the mind instinctively seeks to penetrate to far-off worlds beyond. Away to the south the view is closed in by the sacred mountain of the Paiute, where their Father gave them the first fire and taught them their few simple arts before leaving for his home in the upper regions of the Sun-land. Like the valley of Rasselas, it seems set apart from the great world to be the home of a dreamer.

The greater portion of Nevada is an arid desert of rugged mountains and alkali plains, the little available land being confined to narrow mountain valleys and the borders of a few large lakes. These tracts are occupied by scattered ranchmen engaged in stock raising, and as the white population is sparse, Indian labor is largely utilized, the Paiute being very good workers. The causes which in other parts of the country have conspired to sweep the Indian from the path of the white man seem inoperative here, where the aboriginal proprietors are regarded rather as peons under the protection of the dominant race, and are allowed to set up their small camps of tulé lodges in convenient out-of-the-way places, where they spend the autumn and winter in hunting, fishing, and gathering seeds and piñon nuts, working at fair wages on ranches through spring and summer. In this way young Wovoka became attached to the family of a ranchman in Mason valley, named David Wilson, who took an interest in him and bestowed on him the name of Jack Wilson, by which he is commonly known among the whites. From his association with this family he gained some knowledge of English, together with a confused idea of the white man's

Fig. 1.—Wovoka

theology. On growing up he married, and still continued to work for Mr Wilson, earning a reputation for industry and reliability, but attracting no special notice until nearly 30 years of age, when he announced the revelation that has made him famous among the tribes of the west.

Following are the various forms of his name which I have noticed: Wo′voka, or Wü′voka, which I have provisionally rendered "Cutter," derived from a verb signifying "to cut;" Wevokar, Wopokahte, Kwohitsauq, Cowejo, Koit-tsow, Kvit-Tsow, Quoitze Ow, Jack Wilson, Jackson Wilson, Jack Winson, John Johnson. He has also been confounded with Bannock Jim, a Mormon Bannock of Fort Hall reservation, Idaho, and with Johnson Sides, a Paiute living near Reno, Nevada, and bitterly opposed to Wovoka. His father's name, Tävibo, has been given also as Waughzeewaughber. It is not quite certain that the Paiute prophet of 1870 was the father of Wovoka. This is stated to have been the case by one of Captain Lee's informants (*A. G. O., 4*) and by Lieutenant Phister (*Phister, 2*). Wovoka himself says that his father did not preach, but was a "dreamer" with supernatural powers. Certain it is that a similar doctrine was taught by an Indian living in the same valley in Wovoka's boyhood. Possibly the discrepancy might be explained by an unwillingness on the part of the messiah to share his spiritual honors.

In proportion as Wovoka and his doctrines have become subjects of widespread curiosity, so have they become subjects of ignorant misrepresentation and deliberate falsification. Different writers have made him a Paiute, a half-blood, and a Mormon white man. Numberless stories have been told of the origin and character of his mission and the day predicted for its final accomplishment. The most mischievous and persistent of these stories has been that which represents him as preaching a bloody campaign against the whites, whereas his doctrine is one of peace, and he himself is a mild tempered member of a weak and unwarlike tribe. His own good name has been filched from him and he has been made to appear under a dozen different cognomens, including that of his bitterest enemy, Johnson Sides. He has been denounced as an impostor, ridiculed as a lunatic, and laughed at as a pretended Christ, while by the Indians he is revered as a direct messenger from the Other World, and among many of the remote tribes he is believed to be omniscient, to speak all languages, and to be invisible to a white man. We shall give his own story as told by himself, with such additional information as seems to come from authentic sources.

Notwithstanding all that had been said and written by newspaper correspondents about the messiah, not one of them had undertaken to find the man himself and to learn from his own lips what he really taught. It is almost equally certain that none of them had even seen a Ghost dance at close quarters—certainly none of them understood its meaning. The messiah was regarded almost as a myth, something intangible, to be talked about but not to be seen. The first reliable information as to his personality was communicated by the scout, Arthur Chapman, who, under instructions from the War Department, visited the Paiute country in December, 1890, and spent four days at Walker lake and Mason valley, and in the course of an interview with Wovoka obtained from him a detailed statement similar in all essentials to that which I obtained later on. (*Sec. War, 3.*)

After having spent seven months in the field, investigating the new religion among the prairie tribes, particularly the Arapaho, and after having examined all the documents bearing on the subject in the files of the Indian Office and War Department, the author left Washington in November, 1891, to find and talk with the messiah and to gather additional material concerning the Ghost dance. Before starting, I had written to the agent in charge of the reservation to which he was attached for information in regard to the messiah (Jack Wilson) and the dance, and learned in reply, with some surprise, that the agent had never seen him. The surprise grew into wonder when I was further informed that there were "neither Ghost songs, dances, nor ceremonials" among the Paiute.[1] This was discouraging, but not entirely convincing, and I set out once more for the west. After a few days with the Omaha and Winnebago in Nebraska, and a longer stay with the Sioux at Pine Ridge, where traces of the recent conflict were still fresh on every hand, I crossed over the mountains and finally arrived at Walker Lake reservation in Nevada.

On inquiry I learned that the messiah lived, not on the reservation, but in Mason valley, about 40 miles to the northwest. His uncle, Charley Sheep, lived near the agency, however, so I sought him out and made his acquaintance. He spoke tolerable—or rather intolerable—English, so that we were able to get along together without an interpreter, a fact which brought us into closer sympathy, as an interpreter is generally at best only a necessary evil. As usual, he was very suspicious at first, and inquired minutely as to my purpose. I explained

[1] The letter is given as a sample of the information possessed by some agents in regard to the Indians in their charge:

"UNITED STATES INDIAN SERVICE,
"*Pyramid Lake, Nevada Agency, October 12, 1891.*

"JAMES MOONEY, Esq.,
   "*Bureau of Ethnology.*

"MY DEAR SIR: Your letter of September 24 in regard to Jack Wilson, the 'Messiah,' at hand and duly noted. In reply will say that his Indian name is Ko-wee-jow ('Big belly'). I do not know as it will be possible to get a photo of him. I never saw him or a photo of him. He works among the whites about 40 miles from my Walker Lake reserve, and never comes near the agency when I visit it. My headquarters are at Pyramid lake, about 70 miles north of Walker. I am pursuing the course with him of nonattention or a silent ignoring. He seems to think, so I hear, that I will arrest him should he come within my reach. I would give him no such notoriety. He, like all other prophets, has but little honor in his own country. He has been visited by delegations from various and many Indian tribes, which I think should be discouraged all that is possible. Don't know what the 'Smoholler' religion, you speak of, is. He speaks English well, but is not educated. He got his doctrine in part from contact, living in and with a religious family. There are neither ghost songs, dances, nor ceremonials among them about my agencies. Would not be allowed. I think they died out with 'Sitting Bull.' This is the extent of the information I can give you.
   "Very respectfully, yours,
                    C. C. WARNER, *United States Indian Agent.*"

Here is an agent who has under his special charge and within a few miles of his agency the man who has created the greatest religious ferment known to the Indians of this generation, a movement which had been engrossing the attention of the newspaper and magazine press for a year, yet he has never seen him; and while the Indian Office, from which he gets his commission, in a praiseworthy effort to get at an understanding of the matter, is sending circular letters broadcast to the western agencies, calling for all procurable information in regard to the messiah and his doctrines, he "pursues the course of nonattention." He has never heard of the Smohalla religion of the adjacent northern tribes, although the subject is repeatedly mentioned in the volumes of the Indian Commissioner's report from 1870 to 1879, which were, or should have been, on a shelf in the office in which the letter was written. He asserts that there are no ghost songs, dances, or ceremonies among his Indians, although these things were going on constantly and had been for at least three years, and only a short time before a large delegation from beyond the mountains had attended a Ghost dance near Walker lake which lasted four days and nights. Chapman in 1890, and the author in 1891, saw the cleared grounds with the willow frames where these dances were being held regularly at short intervals. I found the ghost songs familiar to all the Indians with whom I talked, and had no special trouble to find the messiah and obtain his picture. The peaceful character of the movement is sufficiently shown by the fact that while the eastern papers are teeming with rumors of uprising and massacre, and troops are being hurried to the front, the agent at the central point of the disturbance seems to be unaware that there is anything special going on around him and can "silently ignore" the whole matter.

to him that I was sent out by the government to the various tribes to study their customs and learn their stories and songs; that I had obtained a good deal from other tribes and now wanted to learn some songs and stories of the Paiute, in order to write them down so that the white people could read them. In a casual way I then offered to show him the pictures of some of my Indian friends across the mountains, and brought out the photos of several Arapaho and Cheyenne who I knew had recently come as delegates to the messiah. This convinced him that I was all right, and he became communicative. The result was that we spent about a week together in the wikiups (lodges of tulé rushes), surrounded always by a crowd of interested Paiute, discussing the old stories and games, singing Paiute songs, and sampling the seed mush and roasted piñon nuts. On one of these occasions, at night, a medicine-man was performing his incantations over a sick child on one side of the fire while we were talking on the other. When the ice was well thawed, I cautiously approached the subject of the ghost songs and dance, and, as confidence was now established, I found no difficulty in obtaining a number of the songs, with a description of the ceremonial. I then told Charley that, as I had taken part in the dance, I was anxious to see the messiah and get from him some medicine-paint to bring back to his friends among the eastern tribes. He readily agreed to go with me and use his efforts with his nephew to obtain what was wanted.

It is 20 miles northward by railroad from Walker River agency to Wabuska, and 12 miles more in a southwesterly direction from there to the Mason valley settlement. There we met a young white man named Dyer, who was well acquainted with Jack Wilson, and who also spoke the Paiute language, and learned from him that the messiah was about 12 miles farther up the valley, near a place called Pine Grove. Enlisting his services, with a team and driver, making four in all, we started up toward the mountain. It was New Year's day of 1892, and there was deep snow on the ground, a very unusual thing in this part of the country, and due in this instance, as Charley assured us, to the direct agency of Jack Wilson. It is hard to imagine anything more monotonously unattractive than a sage prairie under ordinary circumstances unless it be the same prairie when covered by a heavy fall of snow, under which the smaller clumps of sagebrush look like prairie-dog mounds, while the larger ones can hardly be distinguished at a short distance from wikiups. However, the mountains were bright in front of us, the sky was blue overhead, and the road was good under foot.

Soon after leaving the settlement we passed the dance ground with the brush shelters still standing. We met but few Indians on the way. After several miles we noticed a man at some distance from the road with a gun across his shoulder. Dyer looked a moment and then exclaimed, " I believe that's Jack now!" The Indian thought so, too, and pulling up our horses he shouted some words in the Paiute

FIG. 2.—Winter view in Mason valley, showing snow-covered sagebrush

language. The man replied, and sure enough it was the messiah, hunting jack rabbits. At his uncle's call he soon came over.

As he approached I saw that he was a young man, a dark full-blood, compactly built, and taller than the Paiute generally, being nearly 6 feet in height. He was well dressed in white man's clothes, with the broad-brimmed white felt hat common in the west, secured on his head by means of a beaded ribbon under the chin. This, with a blanket or a robe of rabbit skins, is now the ordinary Paiute dress. He wore a good pair of boots. His hair was cut off square on a line below the base of the ears, after the manner of his tribe. His countenance was open and expressive of firmness and decision, but with no marked intellectuality. The features were broad and heavy, very different from the thin, clear-cut features of the prairie tribes.

As he came up he took my hand with a strong, hearty grasp, and inquired what was wanted. His uncle explained matters, adding that I was well acquainted with some of his Indian friends who had visited him a short time before, and was going back to the same people. After some deliberation he said that the whites had lied about him and he did not like to talk to them; some of the Indians had disobeyed his instructions and trouble had come of it, but as I was sent by Washington and was a friend of his friends, he would talk with me. He was hunting now, but if we would come to his camp that night he would tell us about his mission.

With another hand-shake he left us, and we drove on to the nearest ranch, arriving about dark. After supper we got ready and started across country through the sagebrush for the Paiute camp, some miles away, guided by our Indian. It was already night, with nothing to be seen but the clumps of snow-covered sagebrush stretching away in every direction, and after traveling an hour or more without reaching the camp, our guide had to confess that he had lost the trail. It was two years since he had been there, his sight was failing, and, with the snow and the darkness, he was utterly at a loss to know his whereabouts.

To be lost on a sage plain on a freezing night in January is not a pleasant experience. There was no road, and no house but the one we had left some miles behind, and it would be almost impossible to find our way back to that through the darkness. Excepting for a lantern there was no light but what came from the glare of the snow and a few stars in the frosty sky overhead. To add to our difficulty, the snow was cut in every direction by cattle trails, which seemed to be Indian trails, and kept us doubling and circling to no purpose, while in the uncertain gloom every large clump of sagebrush took on the appearance of a wikiup, only to disappoint us on a nearer approach. With it all, the night was bitterly cold and we were half frozen. After vainly following a dozen false trails and shouting repeatedly in hope of hearing an answering cry, we hit on the expedient of leaving the Indian with the wagon, he being the oldest man of the party, while the rest of us each took a different direction from the central point, following the cattle tracks in the snow and calling to each other at short intervals, in order that we might not become lost from one another. After going far enough to know that none of us had yet struck the right trail, the wagon was moved up a short distance and the same performance was repeated. At last a shout from our driver brought us all together. He declared that he had heard sounds in front, and after listening a few minutes in painful suspense we saw a shower of sparks go up into the darkness and knew that we had struck the camp. Going back to the wagon, we got in and drove straight across to the spot, where we found three or four little wikiups, in one of which we were told the messiah was awaiting our arrival.

On entering through the low doorway we found ourselves in a circular lodge made of bundles of tulé rushes laid over a framework of poles, after the fashion of the thatched roofs of Europe, and very similar to the grass lodges of the Wichita. The lodge was only about 10 feet in diameter and about 8 feet in height, with sloping sides, and was almost entirely open above, like a cone with the top cut off, as in this part of the country rain or snow is of rare occurrence. As already remarked, the deep snow at the time was something unusual. In the center, built directly on the ground, was a blazing fire of sagebrush, upon which fresh stalks were thrown from time to time, sending up a shower of sparks into the open air. It was by this means that we had been guided to the camp. Sitting or lying around the fire were half a dozen Paiute, including the messiah and his family, consisting of his young wife, a boy about 4 years of age, of whom he seemed very fond, and an infant. It was plain that he was a kind husband and father, which was in keeping with his reputation among the whites for industry and relia- bility. The only articles in the nature of furniture were a few grass woven bowls and baskets of various sizes and patterns. There were no Indian beds or seats of the kind found in every prairie tipi, no raw- hide boxes, no toilet pouches, not even a hole dug in the ground for the fire. Although all wore white men's dress, there were no pots, pans, or other articles of civilized manufacture, now used by even the most primitive prairie tribes, for, strangely enough, although these Paiute are practically farm laborers and tenants of the whites all around them, and earn good wages, they seem to covet nothing of the white man's, but spend their money for dress, small trinkets, and ammunition for hunting, and continue to subsist on seeds, piñon nuts, and small game, lying down at night on the dusty ground in their cramped wikiups, destitute of even the most ordinary conveniences in use among other tribes. It is a curious instance of a people accepting the inevitable while yet resisting innovation.

Wovoka received us cordially and then inquired more particularly as to my purpose in seeking an interview. His uncle entered into a detailed explanation, which stretched out to a preposterous length, owing to a peculiar conversational method of the Paiute. Each statement by the older man was repeated at its close, word for word and sentence by sentence, by the other, with the same monotonous inflection. This done, the first speaker signified by a grunt of approval that it had been correctly repeated, and then proceeded with the next statement, which was duly repeated in like manner. The first time I had heard two old men conversing together in this fashion on the reservation I had supposed they were reciting some sort of Indian litany, and it required several such experiences and some degree of patience to become used to it.

At last he signified that he understood and was satisfied, and then in answer to my questions gave an account of himself and his doctrine, a great part of the interpretation being by Dyer, with whom he seemed to be on intimate terms. He said he was about 35 years of age, fixing the date from a noted battle[1] between the Paiute and the whites near Pyramid lake, in 1860, at which time he said he was about the size of his little boy, who appeared to be of about 4 years. His father, Tävibo, "White Man," was not a preacher, but was a *capita* (from the Spanish *capitan*) or petty chief, and was a dreamer and invulnerable. His own proper name from boyhood was Wovoka or Wüvoka, "The Cutter," but a few years ago he had assumed the name of his paternal grandfather, Kwohitsauq, or "Big Rumbling Belly." After the death of his father he had been taken into the family of a white farmer, David Wilson, who had given him the name of Jack Wilson, by which he is commonly known among the whites. He thus has three distinct names, Wovoka, Kwohitsauq, and Jack Wilson. He stated positively that he was a full-blood, a statement borne out by his appearance. The impression that he is a half-blood may have arisen from the fact that his father's name was "White Man" and that he has a white man's name. His followers, both in his own and in all other tribes, commonly refer to him as "our father." He has never been away from Mason valley and speaks only his own Paiute language, with some little knowledge of English. He is not acquainted with the sign language, which is hardly known west of the mountains.

When about 20 years of age, he married, and continued to work for Mr Wilson. He had given the dance to his people about four years before, but had received his great revelation about two years previously. On this occasion "the sun died" (was eclipsed) and he fell asleep in the

---

[1] This battle, probably the most important conflict that ever occurred between the Paiute and the whites, was fought in April, 1860, near the present agency at Pyramid lake and about 8 miles from Wadsworth, Nevada. Some miners having seized and forcibly detained a couple of Indian women, their husbands raised a party and rescued tnem, without, however, inflicting any punishment on the guilty ones. This was considered an "Indian outrage" and a strong body of miners collected and marched toward Pyramid lake to wipe out the Indian camp. The Paiute, armed almost entirely with bows and arrows, surprised them in a narrow pass at the spot indicated, with the result that the whites were defeated and fled in disorder, leaving nearly fifty dead on the field. The whole affair in its causes and results was most discreditable to the whites.

daytime and was taken up to the other world. Here he saw God, with all the people who had died long ago engaged in their oldtime sports and occupations, all happy and forever young. It was a pleasant land and full of game. After showing him all, God told him he must go back and tell his people they must be good and love one another, have no quarreling, and live in peace with the whites; that they must work, and not lie or steal; that they must put away all the old practices that savored of war; that if they faithfully obeyed his instructions they would at last be reunited with their friends in this other world, where there would be no more death or sickness or old age. He was then given the dance which he was commanded to bring back to his people. By performing this dance at intervals, for five consecutive days each time, they would secure this happiness to themselves and hasten the event. Finally God gave him control over the elements so that he could make it rain or snow or be dry at will, and appointed him his deputy to take charge of affairs in the west, while "Governor Harrison" would attend to matters in the east, and he, God, would look after the world above. He then returned to earth and began to preach as he was directed, convincing the people by exercising the wonderful powers that had been given him.

In 1890 Josephus, a Paiute informant, thus described to the scout Chapman the occasion of Wovoka's first inspiration: "About three years ago Jack Wilson took his family and went into the mountains to cut wood for Mr Dave Wilson. One day while at work he heard a great noise which appeared to be above him on the mountain. He laid down his ax and started to go in the direction of the noise, when he fell down dead, and God came and took him to heaven." Afterward on one or two other occasions "God came and took him to heaven again." Wovoka also told Chapman that he had then been preaching to the Indians about three years. In our conversation he said nothing about a mysterious noise, and stated that it was about two years since he had visited heaven and received his great revelation, but that it was about four years since he had first taught the dance to his people. The fact that he has different revelations from time to time would account for the discrepancy of statement.

He disclaimed all responsibility for the ghost shirt which formed so important a part of the dance costume among the Sioux; said that there were no trances in the dance as performed among his people—a statement confirmed by eye-witnesses among the neighboring ranchmen—and earnestly repudiated any idea of hostility toward the whites, asserting that his religion was one of universal peace. When questioned directly, he said he believed it was better for the Indians to follow the white man's road and to adopt the habits of civilization. If appearances are in evidence he is sincere in this, for he was dressed in a good suit of white man's clothing, and works regularly on a ranch, although living in a wikiup. While he repudiated almost everything for which he had been held responsible in the east, he asserted positively that he had been to the spirit world and had been given a revelation and message from God himself, with full control over the elements. From his uncle I learned that Wovoka has five songs for making it rain, the first of which brings on a mist or cloud, the second a snowfall, the third a shower, and the fourth a hard rain or storm, while when he sings the fifth song the weather again becomes clear.

I knew that he was holding something in reserve, as no Indian would unbosom himself on religious matters to a white man with whom he had not had a long and intimate acquaintance. Especially was this true in view of the warlike turn affairs had taken across the mountains. Consequently I accepted his statements with several grains of salt, but on the whole he seemed to be honest in his belief and his supernatural claims, although, like others of the priestly function, he occasionally resorts to cheap trickery to keep up the impression as to his miraculous powers. From some of the reports he is evidently an expert sleight-of-hand performer. He makes no claim to be Christ, the Son of God, as has been so often asserted in print. He does claim to be a prophet who has received a divine revelation. I could not help feeling that he was sincere in his repudiation of a number of the wonderful things attributed to him, for the reason that he insisted so strongly on other things fully as trying to the faith of a white man. He made no argument and advanced no proofs, but said simply that he had been with God, as though the statement no more admitted of controversy than the proposition that 2 and 2 are 4. From Mr J. O. Gregory, formerly employed at the agency, and well acquainted with the prophet, I learned that Wovoka had once requested him to draw up and forward to the President a statement of his supernatural claims, with a proposition that if he could receive a small regular stipend he would take up his residence on the reservation and agree to keep Nevada people informed of all the latest news from heaven and to furnish rain whenever wanted. The letter was never forwarded.

From a neighboring ranchman, who knew Wovoka well and sometimes employed him in the working season, I obtained a statement which seems to explain the whole matter. It appears that a short time before the prophet began to preach he was stricken down by a severe fever, during which illness the ranchman frequently visited and ministered to him. While he was still sick there occurred an eclipse of the sun, a phenomenon which always excites great alarm among primitive peoples. In their system the sun is a living being, of great power and beneficence, and the temporary darkness is caused by an attack on him by some supernatural monster which endeavors to devour him, and will succeed, and thus plunge the world into eternal night unless driven off by incantations and loud noises. On this occasion the Paiute were frantic with excitement and the air was filled with the noise of shouts and wailings and the firing of guns, for the purpose of frightening off the monster that threatened the life of their god. It was now, as Wovoka stated, "when the sun died," that he went to sleep in the day-time and was taken up to heaven. This means simply that the excite-ment and alarm produced by the eclipse, acting on a mind and body already enfeebled by sickness, resulted in delirium, in which he imag-ined himself to enter the portals of the spirit world. Constant dwelling on the subject in thought by day and in dreams by night would effect and perpetuate the exalted mental condition in which visions of the imagination would have all the seeming reality of actual occurrences. To those acquainted with the spiritual nature of Indians and their implicit faith in dreams all this is perfectly intelligible. His frequent trances would indicate also that, like so many other religious ecstatics, he is subject to cataleptic attacks.

I have not been able to settle satisfactorily the date of this eclipse. From inquiry at the Nautical Almanac office I learn that solar eclipses visible in Nevada and the adjacent territory from 1884 to 1890 occurred as follows: 1884, October 18, partial; 1885, March 16, partial; 1886, March 5, partial; 1887, none; 1888, none; 1889, January 1, total or par-tial; 1890, none. The total eclipse of January 1, 1889, agrees best with his statement to me on New Year's night, 1892, that it was about two years since he had gone up to heaven when the sun died. It must be noted that Indians generally count years by winters instead of by series of twelve calendar months, a difference which sometimes makes an apparent discrepancy of nearly a year.

In subsequent conversations he added a few minor details in regard to his vision and his doctrine. He asked many questions in regard to the eastern tribes whose delegates had visited him, and was pleased to learn that the delegates from several of these tribes were my friends. He spoke particularly of the large delegation—about twelve in number—from the Cheyenne and Arapaho, who had visited him the preceding summer and taken part in the dance with his people. Nearly all the members of this party were personally known to me, and the leader, Black Coyote, whose picture I had with me and showed to him, had been my principal instructor in the Ghost dance among the Arapaho. While this fact put me on a more confidential footing with Wovoka, it also proved of great assistance in my further investigation on my return to the prairie tribes, as, when they were satisfied from my statements and the specimens which I had brought back that I had indeed seen and talked with the messiah, they were convinced that I was earnestly desirous of understanding their religion aright, and from that time spoke freely and without reserve.

I had my camera and was anxious to get Wovoka's picture. When the subject was mentioned, he replied that his picture had never been made; that a white man had offered him five dollars for permission to take his photograph, but that he had refused. However, as I had been sent from Washington especially to learn and tell the whites all about him and his doctrine, and as he was satisfied from my acquaintance with his friends in the other tribes that I must be a good man, he would allow me to take his picture. As usual in dealing with Indians, he wanted to make the most of his bargain, and demanded two dollars and a half for the privilege of taking his picture and a like sum for each one of his family. I was prepared for this, however, and refused to pay any such charges, but agreed to give him my regular price per day for his services as informant and to send him a copy of the picture when finished. After some demur he consented and got ready for the operation by knotting a handkerchief about his neck, fastening an eagle feather at his right elbow, and taking a wide brim sombrero upon his knee. I afterward learned that the feather and sombrero were important parts of his spiritual stock in trade. After taking his picture I obtained from him, as souvenirs to bring back and show to my Indian friends in Indian Territory, a blanket of rabbit skins, some piñon nuts, some tail feathers of the magpie, highly prized by the Paiute for ornamentation, and some of the sacred red paint, endowed with most miraculous powers, which plays so important a part in the ritual of the Ghost-dance religion. Then, with mutual expressions of good will, we parted, his uncle going back to the reservation, while I took the train for Indian Territory.

As soon as the news of my arrival went abroad among the Cheyenne and Arapaho on my return, my friends of both tribes came in, eager to hear all the details of my visit to the messiah and to get my own impressions of the man. In comparing notes with some of the recent delegates I discovered something of Wovoka's hypnotic methods, and incidentally learned how much of miracle depends on the mental receptivity of the observer.

The Cheyenne and Arapaho, although for generations associated in the most intimate manner, are of very different characters. In religious matters it may be said briefly that the Arapaho are devotees and prophets, continually seeing signs and wonders, while the Cheyenne are more skeptical. In talking with Tall Bull, one of the Cheyenne delegates and then captain of the Indian police, he said that before leaving they had asked Wovoka to give them some proof of his supernatural powers. Accordingly he had ranged them in front of him, seated on the ground, he sitting facing them, with his sombrero between and his eagle feathers in his hand. Then with a quick movement he had put his hand into the empty hat and drawn out from it "something black." Tall Bull would not admit that anything more had happened, and did not seem to be very profoundly impressed by the occurrence, saying that he thought there were medicine-men of equal capacity among the Cheyenne. In talking soon afterward with Black Coyote, one of the Arapaho delegates and also a police officer, the same incident came up, but with a very different sequel. Black Coyote told how they had seated themselves on the ground in front of Wovoka, as described by Tall Bull, and went on to tell how the messiah had waved his feathers over his hat, and then, when he withdrew his hand, Black Coyote looked into the hat and there "saw the whole world." The explanation is simple. Tall Bull, who has since been stricken with paralysis, was a jovial, light-hearted fellow, fond of joking and playing tricks on his associates, but withal a man of good hard sense and dis- posed to be doubtful in regard to all medicine-men outside of his own tribe. Black Coyote, on the contrary, is a man of contemplative dispo- sition, much given to speculation on the unseen world. His body and arms are covered with the scars of wounds which he has inflicted on himself in obedience to commands received in dreams. When the first news of the new religion came to the southern tribes, he had made a long journey, at his own expense, to his kindred in Wyoming, to learn the doctrine and the songs, and since his return had been drilling his people day and night in both. Now, on his visit to the fountain head of inspiration, he was prepared for great things, and when the messiah performed his hypnotic passes with the eagle feather, as I have so often witnessed in the Ghost dance, Black Coyote saw the whole spirit world where Tall Bull saw only an empty hat. From my knowledge of the men, I believe both were honest in their statements.

As a result of the confidence established between the Indians and myself in consequence of my visit to the messiah, one of the Cheyenne delegates named Black Sharp Nose, a prominent man in his tribe, soon after voluntarily brought down to me the written statement of the doc- trine obtained from the messiah himself, and requested me to take it back and show it to Washington, to convince the white people that there was nothing bad or hostile in the new religion. The paper had been written by a young Arapaho of the same delegation who had learned some English at the Carlisle Indian school, and it had been taken down on the spot from the dictation of the messiah as his mes- sage to be carried to the prairie tribes. On the reverse page of the paper the daughter of Black Sharp Nose, a young woman who had also some school education, had written out the same thing in somewhat better English from her father's dictation on his return. No white man had any part, directly or indirectly, in its production, nor was it orig- inally intended to be seen by white men. In fact, in one part the mes- siah himself expressly warns the delegates to tell no white man.

CHAPTER II

The Doctrine of the Ghost Dance

You must not fight. Do no harm to anyone. Do right always.—*Wovoka.*

The great underlying principle of the Ghost dance doctrine is that the time will come when the whole Indian race, living and dead, will be reunited upon a regenerated earth, to live a life of aboriginal happiness, forever free from death, disease, and misery. On this foundation each tribe has built a structure from its own mythology, and each apostle and believer has filled in the details according to his own mental capacity or ideas of happiness, with such additions as come to him from the trance. Some changes, also, have undoubtedly resulted from the transmission of the doctrine through the imperfect medium of the sign language. The differences of interpretation are precisely such as we find in Christianity, with its hundreds of sects and innumerable shades of individual opinion. The white race, being alien and secondary and hardly real, has no part in this scheme of aboriginal regeneration, and will be left behind with the other things of earth that have served their temporary purpose, or else will cease entirely to exist.

All this is to be brought about by an overruling spiritual power that needs no assistance from human creatures; and though certain medicine-men were disposed to anticipate the Indian millennium by preaching resistance to the further encroachments of the whites, such teachings form no part of the true doctrine, and it was only where chronic dissatisfaction was aggravated by recent grievances, as among the Sioux, that the movement assumed a hostile expression. On the contrary, all believers were exhorted to make themselves worthy of the predicted happiness by discarding all things warlike and practicing honesty, peace, and good will, not only among themselves, but also toward the whites, so long as they were together. Some apostles have even thought that all race distinctions are to be obliterated, and that the whites are to participate with the Indians in the coming felicity; but it seems unquestionable that this is equally contrary to the doctrine as originally preached.

Different dates have been assigned at various times for the fulfillment of the prophecy. Whatever the year, it has generally been held, for very natural reasons, that the regeneration of the earth and the renewal of all life would occur in the early spring. In some cases July, and particularly the 4th of July, was the expected time. This, it may be noted, was about the season when the great annual ceremony of the sun dance formerly took place among the prairie tribes. The messiah himself has set several dates from time to time, as one prediction after another failed to materialize, and in his message to the Cheyenne and Arapaho, in August, 1891, he leaves the whole matter an open question. The date universally recognized among all the tribes immediately prior to the Sioux outbreak was the spring of 1891. As springtime came and passed, and summer grew and waned, and autumn faded again into winter without the realization of their hopes and longings, the doctrine gradually assumed its present form—that some time in the unknown future the Indian will be united with his friends who have gone before, to be forever supremely happy, and that this happiness may be anticipated in dreams, if not actually hastened in reality, by earnest and frequent attendance on the sacred dance.

On returning to the Cheyenne and Arapaho in Oklahoma, after my visit to Wovoka in January, 1892, I was at once sought by my friends of both tribes, anxious to hear the report of my journey and see the sacred things that I had brought back from the messiah. The Arapaho especially, who are of more spiritual nature than any of the other tribes, showed a deep interest and followed intently every detail of the nar-rative. As soon as the news of my return was spread abroad, men and women, in groups and singly, would come to me, and after grasping my hand would repeat a long and earnest prayer, sometimes aloud, some-times with the lips silently moving, and frequently with tears rolling down the cheeks, and the whole body trembling violently from stress of emotion. Often before the prayer was ended the condition of the devo-tee bordered on the hysterical, very little less than in the Ghost dance itself. The substance of the prayer was usually an appeal to the messiah to hasten the coming of the promised happiness, with a peti-tion that, as the speaker himself was unable to make the long journey, he might, by grasping the hand of one who had seen and talked with the messiah face to face, be enabled in his trance visions to catch a glimpse of the coming glory. During all this performance the bystand-ers awaiting their turn kept reverent silence. In a short time it became very embarrassing, but until the story had been told over and over again there was no way of escape without wounding their feelings. The same thing afterward happened among the northern Arapaho in Wyoming, one chief even holding out his hands toward me with short exclamations of *hŭ! hŭ! hŭ!* as is sometimes done by the devotees about a priest in the Ghost dance, in the hope, as he himself explained, that he might thus be enabled to go into a trance then and there. The hope, however, was not realized.

After this preliminary ordeal my visitors would ask to see the things which I had brought back from the messiah—the rabbit-skin robes, the piñon nuts, the gaming sticks, the sacred magpie feathers, and, above all, the sacred red paint. This is a bright-red ocher, about the color of brick dust, which the Paiute procure from the neighborhood of their sacred eminence, Mount Grant. It is ground, and by the help of water is made into elliptical cakes about 6 inches in length. It is the principal paint used by the Paiute in the Ghost dance, and small portions of it are given by the messiah to all the delegates and are carried back by them to their respective tribes, where it is mixed with larger quantities of their own red paint and used in decorating the faces of the participants in the dance, the painting being solemnly performed for each dancer by the medicine-man himself. It is believed to ward off sickness, to contribute to long life, and to assist the mental vision in the trance. On the battlefield of Wounded Knee I have seen this paint smeared on the posts of the inclosure about the trench in which are buried the Indians killed in the fight. I found it very hard to refuse the numerous requests for some of the paint, but as I had only one cake myself I could not afford to be too liberal. My friends were very anxious to touch it, however, but when I found that every man tried to rub off as much of it as possible on the palms of his hands, afterward smearing this dust on the faces of himself and his family, I was obliged in self-defense to put it entirely away.

The piñon nuts, although not esteemed so sacred, were also the subject of reverent curiosity. One evening, by invitation from Left Hand, the principal chief of the Arapaho, I went over to his tipi to talk with him about the messiah and his country, and brought with me a quantity of the nuts for distribution. On entering I found the chief and a number of the principal men ranged on one side of the fire, while his wife and several other women, with his young grandchildren, completed the circle on the other. Each of the adults in turn took my hand with a prayer, as before described, varying in length and earnestness according to the devotion of the speaker. This ceremony consumed a considerable time. I then produced the piñon nuts and gave them to Left Hand, telling him how they were used as food by the Paiute. He handed a portion to his wife, and before I knew what was coming the two arose in their places and stretching out their hands toward the northwest, the country of the messiah, made a long and earnest prayer aloud that *Hesúnanin*, "Our Father," would bless themselves and their children through the sacred food, and hasten the time of his coming. The others, men and women, listened with bowed heads, breaking in from time to time with similar appeals to "the Father." The scene was deeply affecting. It was another of those impressive exhibitions of natural religion which it has been my fortune to witness among the Indians, and which throw light on a side of their character of which the ordinary white observer never dreams. After the prayer the nuts were carefully divided among those present, down to the youngest infant, that all might taste of what to them was the veritable bread of life.

As I had always shown a sympathy for their ideas and feelings, and had now accomplished a long journey to the messiah himself at the cost of considerable difficulty and hardship, the Indians were at last fully satisfied that I was really desirous of learning the truth concerning their new religion. A few days after my visit to Left Hand, several of the delegates who had been sent out in the preceding August came down to see me, headed by Black Short Nose, a Cheyenne. After preliminary greetings, he stated that the Cheyenne and Arapaho were now convinced that I would tell the truth about their religion, and as they loved their religion and were anxious to have the whites know that it was all good and contained nothing bad or hostile they would now give me the message which the messiah himself had given to them, that I might take it back to show to Washington. He then took from a beaded pouch and gave to me a letter, which proved to be the message or statement of the doctrine delivered by Wovoka to the Cheyenne and Arapaho delegates, of whom Black Short Nose was one, on the occasion of their last visit to Nevada, in August, 1891, and written down on the spot, in broken English, by one of the Arapaho delegates, Casper Edson, a young man who had acquired some English education by several years' attendance at the government Indian school at Carlisle, Pennsylvania. On the reverse page of the paper was a duplicate in somewhat better English, written out by a daughter of Black Short Nose, a school girl, as dictated by her father on his return. These letters contained the message to be delivered to the two tribes, and as is expressly stated in the text were not intended to be seen by a white man. The daughter of Black Short Nose had attempted to erase this clause before her father brought the letter down to me, but the lines were still plainly visible. It is the genuine official statement of the Ghost-dance doctrine as given by the messiah himself to his disciples. It is reproduced here in duplicate and verbatim, just as received, with a translation for the benefit of those not accustomed to Carlisle English. In accordance with the request of the Indians, I brought the original to Washington, where it was read by the Indian Commissioner, Honorable T. J. Morgan, after which I had two copies made, giving one to the commissioner and retaining the other myself, returning the original to its owner, Black Short Nose.

The Messiah Letter (Arapaho version)

What you get home you make dance, and will give you the same. when you dance four days and in night one day, dance day time, five days and then fift, will wash five for every body. He likes you flok you give him good many things, he heart been satting feel good. After you get home, will give good cloud, and give you chance to make you feel good. and he give you good spirit. and he give you al a good paint.

You folks want you to come in three [months] here, any tribs from there. There will be good bit snow this year. Sometimes rain's, in fall, this year some rain, never give you any thing like that. grandfather said when he die never no cry. no hurt anybody. no fight, good behave always, it will give you satisfaction, this young man, he is a good Father and mother, dont tell no white man. Jueses was on ground, he just like cloud. Every body is alive again, I dont know when they will [be] here, may be this fall or in spring.

Every body never get sick, be young again,—(if young fellow no sick any more,) work for white men never trouble with him until you leave, when it shake the earth dont be afraid no harm any body.

You make dance for six ᵂᵉᵉᵏˢ night, and put you foot [food?] in dance to eat for every body and wash in the water. that is all to tell, I am in to you. and you will received a good words from him some time, Dont tell lie.

The Messiah Letter (Cheyenne version)

When you get home you have to make dance. You must dance four nights and one day time. You will take bath in the morning before you go to yours homes, for every body, and give you all the same as this. Jackson Wilson likes you all, he is glad to get good many things. His heart satting fully of gladness, after you get home, I will give you a good cloud and give you chance to make you feel good. I give you a good spirit, and give you all good paint, I want you people to come here again, want them in three months any tribs of you from there. There will be a good deal snow this year. Some time rains, in fall this year some rain, never give you any thing like that, grandfather, said, when they were die never cry, no hurt any body, do any harm for it, not to fight. Be a good behave always. It will give a satisfaction in your life. This young man is a good father and mother. Do not tell the white people about this, Juses is on the ground, he just like cloud. Every body is a live again. I don't know when he will be here, may be will be this fall or in spring. When it happen it may be this. There will be no sickness and return to young again. Do not refuse to work for white man or do not make any trouble with them until you leave them. When the earth shakes do not be afraid it will not hurt you. I want you to make dance for six weeks. Eat and wash good clean yourselves [The rest of the letter had been erased].

The Messiah Letter (free Rendering)

When you get home you must make a dance to continue five days. Dance four successive nights, and the last night keep up the dance until the morning of the fifth day, when all must bathe in the river and then disperse to their homes. You must all do in the same way.

I, Jack Wilson, love you all, and my heart is full of gladness for the gifts you have brought me. When you get home I shall give you a good cloud [rain?] which will make you feel good. I give you a good spirit and give you all good paint. I want you to come again in three months, some from each tribe there [the Indian Territory].

There will be a good deal of snow this year and some rain. In the fall there will be such a rain as I have never given you before.

Grandfather [a universal title of reverence among Indians and here meaning the messiah] says, when your friends die you must not cry. You must not hurt anybody or do harm to anyone. You must not fight. Do right always. It will give you satisfaction in life. This young man has a good father and mother. [Possibly this refers to Casper Edson, the young Arapaho who wrote down this message of Wovoka for the delegation].

Do not tell the white people about this. Jesus is now upon the earth. He appears like a cloud. The dead are all alive again. I do not know when they will be here; maybe this fall or in the spring. When the time comes there will be no more sickness and everyone will be young again.

Do not refuse to work for the whites and do not make any trouble with them until you leave them. When the earth shakes [at the coming of the new world] do not be afraid. It will not hurt you.

I want you to dance every six weeks. Make a feast at the dance and have food that everybody may eat. Then bathe in the water. That is all. You will receive good words again from me some time. Do not tell lies.

Every organized religion has a system of ethics, a system of mythology, and a system of ritual observance. In this message from the high priest of the Ghost dance we have a synopsis of all three. With regard to the ritual part, ceremonial purification and bathing have formed a part in some form or other of every great religion from the beginning of history, while the religious dance dates back far beyond the day when the daughter of Saul "looked through a window and saw King David leaping and dancing before the Lord." The feasting enjoined is a part of every Indian ceremonial gathering, religious, political, or social. The dance is to continue four successive nights, in accord with the regular Indian system, in which *four* is the sacred number, as *three* is in Christianity. In obedience to this message the southern prairie tribes, after the return of the delegation in August, 1891, ceased to hold frequent one-night dances at irregular intervals as formerly without the ceremonial bathing, and adopted instead a system of four-night dances at regular periods of six weeks, followed by ceremonial bathing on the morning of the fifth day.

The mythology of the doctrine is only briefly indicated, but the principal articles are given. The dead are all arisen and the spirit hosts are advancing and have already arrived at the boundaries of this earth, led forward by the regenerator in shape of cloud-like indistinctness. The spirit captain of the dead is always represented under this shadowy semblance. The great change will be ushered in by a trembling of the earth, at which the faithful are exhorted to feel no alarm. The hope held out is the same that has inspired the Christian for nineteen centuries—a happy immortality in perpetual youth. As to fixing a date, the messiah is as cautious as his predecessor in prophecy, who declares that "no man knoweth the time, not even the angels of God." His weather predictions also are about as definite as the inspired utterances of the Delphian oracle.

The moral code inculcated is as pure and comprehensive in its simplicity as anything found in religious systems from the days of Gautama Buddha to the time of Jesus Christ. " *Do no harm to any one. Do right always.*" Could anything be more simple, and yet more exact and exacting? It inculcates honesty—"*Do not tell lies.*" It preaches good will—"*Do no harm to any one.*" It forbids the extravagant mourning customs formerly common among the tribes—" *When your friends die, you must not cry,*" which is interpreted by the prairie tribes as forbidding the killing of horses, the burning of tipis and destruction of property, the cutting off of the hair and the gashing of the body with knives, all of which were formerly the sickening rule at every death until forbidden by the new doctrine. As an Arapaho said to me when his little boy died, "I shall not shoot any ponies, and my wife will not gash her arms. We used to do this when our friends died, because we thought we would never see them again, and it made us feel bad. But now we know we shall all be united again." If the Kiowa had held to the Ghost-dance doctrine instead of abandoning it as they had done, they would have been spared the loss of thousands of dollars in horses, tipis, wagons, and other property destroyed, with much of the mental suffering and all of the physical laceration that resulted in consequence of the recent fatal epidemic in the tribe, when for weeks and months the sound of wailing went up night and morning, and in every camp men and women could be seen daily, with dress disordered and hair cut close to the scalp, with blood hardened in clots upon the skin, or streaming from mutilated fingers and fresh gashes on face, and arms, and legs. It preaches peace with the whites and obedience to authority until the day of deliverance shall come. Above all, it forbids war— "*You must not fight.*" It is hardly possible for us to realize the tremendous and radical change which this doctrine works in the whole spirit of savage life. The career of every Indian has been the warpath. His proudest title has been that of warrior. His conversation by day and his dreams by night have been of bloody deeds upon the enemies of his tribe. His highest boast was in the number of his scalp trophies, and his chief delight at home was in the war dance and the scalp dance. The thirst for blood and massacre seemed inborn in every man, woman, and child of every tribe. Now comes a prophet as a messenger from God to forbid not only war, but all that savors of war—the war dance, the scalp dance, and even the bloody torture of the sun dance—and his teaching is accepted and his words obeyed by four-fifths of all the warlike predatory tribes of the mountains and the great plains. Only those who have known the deadly hatred that once animated Ute, Cheyenne, and Pawnee, one toward another, and are able to contrast it with their present spirit of mutual brotherly love, can know what the Ghost-dance religion has accomplished in bringing the savage into civilization. It is such a revolution as comes but once in the life of a race.

The beliefs held among the various tribes in regard to the final catastrophe are as fairly probable as some held on the same subject by more orthodox authorities. As to the dance itself, with its scenes of intense excitement, spasmodic action, and physical exhaustion even to unconsciousness, such manifestations have always accompanied religious upheavals among primitive peoples, and are not entirely unknown among ourselves. In a country which produces magnetic healers, shakers, trance mediums, and the like, all these things may very easily be paralleled without going far from home.

In conclusion, we may say of the prophet and his doctrine what has been said of one of his apostles by a careful and competent investigator: "He has given these people a better religion than they ever had before, taught them precepts which, if faithfully carried out, will bring them into better accord with their white neighbors, and has prepared the way for their final Christianization." (*G. D.*, *4*, and *A. G. O. 5*.)

We may now consider details of the doctrine as held by different tribes, beginning with the Paiute, among whom it originated. The best account of the Paiute belief is contained in a report to the War Department by Captain J. M. Lee, who was sent out in the autumn of 1890 to investigate the temper and fighting strength of the Paiute and other Indians in the vicinity of Fort Bidwell in northeastern California. We give the statement obtained by him from Captain Dick, a Paiute, as delivered one day in a conversational way and apparently without reserve, after nearly all the Indians had left the room:

Long time, twenty years ago, Indian medicine-man in Mason's valley at Walker lake talk same way, same as you hear now. In one year, maybe, after he begin talk he die. Three years ago another medicine-man begin same talk. Heap talk all time. Indians hear all about it everywhere. Indians come from long way off to hear him. They come from the east; they make signs. Two years ago me go to Winnemucca and Pyramid lake, me see Indian Sam, a head man, and Johnson Sides. Sam he tell me he just been to see Indian medicine-man to hear him talk. Sam say medicine-man talk this way:

"All Indians must dance, everywhere, keep on dancing. Pretty soon in next spring Big Man [Great Spirit] come. He bring back all game of every kind. The game be thick everywhere. All dead Indians come back and live again. They all be strong just like young men, be young again. Old blind Indian see again and get young and have fine time. When Old Man [God] comes this way, then all the Indians go to mountains, high up away from whites. Whites can't hurt Indians then. Then while Indians way up high, big flood comes like water and all white people die, get drowned. After that water go way and then nobody but Indians everywhere and game all kinds thick. Then medicine-man tell Indians to send word to all Indians to keep up dancing and the good time will come. Indians who don't dance, who don't believe in this word, will grow little, just about a foot high, and stay that way. Some of them will be turned into wood and be burned in fire." That's the way Sam tell me the medicine-man talk. (A. G. O., 6.)

Lieutenant N. P. Phister, who gathered a part of the material embodied in Captain Lee's report, confirms this general statement and gives a few additional particulars. The flood is to consist of mingled mud and water, and when the faithful go up into the mountains, the skeptics will be left behind and will be turned to stone. The prophet claims to receive these revelations directly from God and the spirits of the dead Indians during his trances. He asserts also that he is invulnerable, and that if soldiers should attempt to kill him they would fall down as if they had no bones and die, while he would still live, even though cut into little pieces. (Phister, 3.)

One of the first and most prominent of those who brought the doctrine to the prairie tribes was Porcupine, a Cheyenne, who crossed the mountains with several companions in the fall of 1889, visited Wovoka, and attended the dance near Walker lake, Nevada. In his report of his experiences, made some months later to a military officer, he states that Wovoka claimed to be Christ himself, who had come back again, many centuries after his first rejection, in pity to teach his children. He quotes the prophet as saying:

I found my children were bad, so I went back to heaven and left them. I told them that in so many hundred years I would come back to see my children. At the end of this time I was sent back to try to teach them. My father told me the earth was getting old and worn out and the people getting bad, and that I was to renew everything as it used to be and make it better.

He also told us that all our dead were to be resurrected; that they were all to come back to earth, and that, as the earth was too small for them and us, he would do away with heaven and make the earth itself large enough to contain us all; that we must tell all the people we met about these things. He spoke to us about fighting, and said that was bad and we must keep from it; that the earth was to be all good hereafter, and we must all be friends with one another. He said that in the fall of the year the youth of all good people would be renewed, so that nobody would be more than forty years old, and that if they behaved themselves well after this the youth of everyone would be renewed in the spring. He said if we were all good he would send people among us who could heal all our wounds and sickness by mere touch and that we would live forever. He told us not to quarrel or fight or strike each other, or shoot one another; that the whites and Indians were to be all one people. He said if any man disobeyed what he ordered his tribe would be wiped from the face of the earth; that we must believe everything he said, and we must not doubt him or say he lied; that if we did, he would know it; that he would know our thoughts and actions in no matter what part of the world we might be. (*G. D., 5.*)

Here we have the statement that both races are to live together as one. We have also the doctrine of healing by touch. Whether or not this is an essential part of the system is questionable, but it is certain that the faithful believe that great physical good comes to them, to their children, and to the sick from the imposition of hands by the priests of the dance, apart from the ability thus conferred to see the things of the spiritual world.

Another idea here presented, namely, that the earth becomes old and decrepit, and requires that its youth be renewed at the end of certain great cycles, is common to a number of tribes, and has an important place in the oldest religions of the world. As an Arapaho who spoke English expressed it, " This earth too old, grass too old, trees too old, our lives too old. Then all be new again." Captain H. L. Scott also found among the southern plains tribes the same belief that the rivers, the mountains, and the earth itself are worn out and must be renewed, together with an indefinite idea that both races alike must die at the same time, to be resurrected in new but separate worlds.

The Washo, Pit River, Bannock, and other tribes adjoining the Paiute on the north and west hold the doctrine substantially as taught by the messiah himself. We have but little light in regard to the belief as held by the Walapai, Cohonino, Mohave, and Navaho to the southward, beyond the general fact that the resurrection and return of the dead formed the principal tenet. As these tribes received their knowledge of the new religion directly from Paiute apostles, it is quite probable that they made but few changes in or additions to the original gospel.

A witness of the dance among the Walapai in 1891 obtained from the leaders of the ceremony about the same statement of doctrine already mentioned as held by the Paiute, from whom also the Walapai had adopted many of the songs and ceremonial words used in connection with the dance. They were then expecting the Indian redeemer to appear on earth some time within three or four years. They were particularly anxious to have it understood that their intentions were not hostile toward the whites and that they desired to live in peace with them until the redeemer came, but that then they would be unable to prevent their destruction even if they wished. (*J. F. L., 3.*)

The manner of the final change and the destruction of the whites has been variously interpreted as the doctrine was carried from its original center. East of the mountains it is commonly held that a deep sleep will come on the believers, during which the great catastrophe will be accomplished, and the faithful will awake to immortality on a new earth. The Shoshoni of Wyoming say this sleep will continue four days and nights, and that on the morning of the fifth day all will open their eyes in a new world where both races will dwell together forever. The Cheyenne, Arapaho, Kiowa, and others, of Oklahoma, say that the new earth, with all the resurrected dead from the beginning, and with the buffalo, the elk, and other game upon it, will come from the west and slide over the surface of the present earth, as the right hand might slide over the left. As it approaches, the Indians will be carried upward and alight on it by the aid of the sacred dance feathers which they wear in their hair and which will act as wings to bear them up. They will then become unconscious for four days, and on waking out of their trance will find themselves with their former friends in the midst of all the oldtime surroundings. By Sitting Bull, the Arapaho apostle, it is thought that this new earth as it advances will be preceded by a wall of fire which will drive the whites across the water to their original and proper country, while the Indians will be enabled by means of the sacred feathers to surmount the flames and reach the promised land. When the expulsion of the whites has been accomplished, the fire will be extinguished by a rain continuing twelve days. By a few it is believed that a hurricane with thunder and lightning will come to destroy the whites alone. This last idea is said to be held also by the Walapai of Arizona, who extend its provisions to include the unbelieving Indians as well. (*G. D., 6.*) The doctrine held by the Caddo, Wichita, and Delaware, of Oklahoma, is practically the same as is held by the Arapaho and Cheyenne from whom they obtained it. All these tribes believe that the destruction or removal of the whites is to be accomplished entirely by supernatural means, and they severely blame the Sioux for having provoked a physical conflict by their impatience instead of waiting for their God to deliver them in his own good time.

Among all the tribes which have accepted the new faith it is held that frequent devout attendance on the dance conduces to ward off disease and restore the sick to health, this applying not only to the actual participants, but also to their children and friends. The idea of obtaining temporal blessings as the reward of a faithful performance of religious duties is too natural and universal to require comment. The purification by the sweat-bath, which forms an important preliminary to the dance among the Sioux, while devotional in its purpose, is probably also sanitary in its effect.

Among the powerful and warlike Sioux of the Dakotas, already restless under both old and recent grievances, and more lately brought to the edge of starvation by a reduction of rations, the doctrine speedily assumed a hostile meaning and developed some peculiar features, for which reason it deserves particular notice as concerns this tribe. The earliest rumors of the new messiah came to the Sioux from the more western tribes in the winter of 1888–89, but the first definite account was brought by a delegation which crossed the mountains to visit the messiah in the fall of 1889, returning in the spring of 1890. On the report of these delegates the dance was at once inaugurated and spread so rapidly that in a few months the new religion had been accepted by the majority of the tribe.

Perhaps the best statement of the Sioux version is given by the veteran agent, James McLaughlin, of Standing Rock agency. In an official letter of October 17, 1890, he writes that the Sioux, under the influence of Sitting Bull, were greatly excited over the near approach of a predicted Indian millennium or "return of the ghosts," when the white man would be annihilated and the Indian again supreme, and which the medicine-men had promised was to occur as soon as the grass was green in the spring. They were told that the Great Spirit had sent upon them the dominant race to punish them for their sins, and that their sins were now expiated and the time of deliverance was at hand. Their decimated ranks were to be reinforced by all the Indians who had ever died, and these spirits were already on their way to reinhabit the earth, which had originally belonged to the Indians, and were driving before them, as they advanced, immense herds of buffalo and fine ponies. The Great Spirit, who had so long deserted his red children, was now once more with them and against the whites, and the white man's gunpowder would no longer have power to drive a bullet through the skin of an Indian. The whites themselves would soon be overwhelmed and smothered under a deep landslide, held down by sod and timber, and the few who might escape would become small fishes in the rivers. In order to bring about this happy result, the Indians must believe and organize the Ghost dance.

The agent continues:

It would seem impossible that any person, no matter how ignorant, could be brought to believe such absurd nonsense, but as a matter of fact a great many Indians of this agency actually believe it, and since this new doctrine has been ingrafted here from the more southern Sioux agencies the infection has been wonderful, and so pernicious that it now includes some of the Indians who were formerly numbered with the progressive and more intelligent, and many of our very best Indians appear dazed and undecided when talking of it, their inherent superstition having been thoroughly aroused. (*G. D.*, 7.)

The following extract is from a translation of a letter dated March 30, 1891, written in Sioux by an Indian at Pine Ridge to a friend at Rosebud agency:

And now I will tell another thing. Lately there is a man died and come to life again, and he say he has been to Indian nation of ghosts, and tells us dead Indian nation all coming home. The Indian ghost tell him come after his war bonnet. The Indian (not ghost Indian) gave him his war bonnet and he died again. (*G. D., S.*)

The Sioux, like other tribes, believed that at the moment of the catastrophe the earth would tremble. According to one version the landslide was to be accompanied by a flood of water, which would flow into the mouths of the whites and cause them to choke with mud. Storms and whirlwinds were also to assist in their destruction. The Indians were to surmount the avalanche, probably in the manner described in speaking of the southern tribes, and on reaching the surface of the new earth would behold boundless prairies covered with long grass and filled with great herds of buffalo and other game. When the time was near at hand, they must assemble at certain places of rendezvous and prepare for the final abandonment of all earthly things by stripping off their clothing. In accordance with the general idea of a return to aboriginal habits, the believers, as far as possible, discarded white man's dress and utensils. Those who could procure buckskin—which is now very scarce in the Sioux country—resumed buckskin dress, while the dancers put on " ghost shirts " made of cloth, but cut and ornamented in Indian fashion. No metal of any kind was allowed in the dance, no knives, and not even the earrings or belts of imitation silver which form such an important part of prairie Indian costume. This was at variance with the custom among the Cheyenne and other southern tribes, where the women always wear in the dance their finest belts studded with large disks of German silver. The beads used so freely on moccasins and leggings seem to have been regarded as a substitute for the oldtime wampum and porcupine quill work, and were therefore not included in the prohibition. No weapon of any kind was allowed to be carried in the Ghost dance by any tribe, north or south, a fact which effectually disposes of the assertion that this was another variety of war dance. At certain of the Sioux dances, however, sacred arrows and a sacred bow, with other things, were tied on the tree in the center of the circle.

Valuable light in regard to the Sioux version of the doctrine is obtained from the sermon delivered at Red Leaf camp, on Pine Ridge reservation, October 31, 1890, by Short Bull, one of those who had been selected to visit the messiah, and who afterward became one of the prime leaders in the dance:

My friends and relations: I will soon start this thing in running order. I have told you that this would come to pass in two seasons, but since the whites are interfering so much, I will advance the time from what my father above told me to do, so the time will be shorter. Therefore you must not be afraid of anything. Some of my relations have no ears, so I will have them blown away.

Now, there will be a tree sprout up, and there all the members of our religion and the tribe must gather together. That will be the place where we will see our dead relations. But before this time we must dance the balance of this moon, at the end of which time the earth will shiver very hard. Whenever this thing occurs, I will start the wind to blow. We are the ones who will then see our fathers, mothers, and everybody. We, the tribe of Indians, are the ones who are living a sacred life. God, our father himself, has told and commanded and shown me to do these things.

Our father in heaven has placed a mark at each point of the four winds. First, a clay pipe, which lies at the setting of the sun and represents the Sioux tribe. Second, there is a holy arrow lying at the north, which represents the Cheyenne tribe. Third, at the rising of the sun there lies hail, representing the Arapaho tribe. Fourth, there lies a pipe and nice feather at the south, which represents the Crow tribe. My father has shown me these things, therefore we must continue this dance. If the soldiers surround you four deep, three of you, on whom I have put holy shirts, will sing a song, which I have taught you, around them, when some of them will drop dead. Then the rest will start to run, but their horses will sink into the earth. The riders will jump from their horses, but they will sink into the earth also. Then you can do as you desire with them. Now, you must know this, that all the soldiers and that race will be dead. There will be only five thousand of them left living on the earth. My friends and relations, this is straight and true.

Now, we must gather at Pass creek where the tree is sprouting. There we will go among our dead relations. You must not take any earthly things with you. Then the men must take off all their clothing and the women must do the same. No one shall be ashamed of exposing their persons. My father above has told us to do this, and we must do as he says. You must not be afraid of anything. The guns are the only things we are afraid of, but they belong to our father in heaven. He will see that they do no harm. Whatever white men may tell you, do not listen to them, my relations. This is all. I will now raise my hand up to my father and close what he has said to you through me. (*Short Bull; War, 4.*)

The pipe here referred to is the most sacred thing in Sioux mythology and will be more fully described in treating of the Sioux songs. The sacred object of the Cheyenne is the "medicine arrow," now in the keeping of the band living near Cantonment, Oklahoma. The Crow and Arapaho references are not so clear. The Arapaho are called by the Sioux the "Blue Cloud" people, a name which may possibly have some connection with hail. The sprouting tree at which all the believers must gather refers to the tree or pole which the Sioux planted in the center of the dance circle. The cardinal directions here assigned to the other tribes may refer to their former locations with regard to the Sioux. The Cheyenne and Arapaho, who now live far west and south of the Sioux, originally lived north and east of them, about Red river and the Saskatchewan.

The most noted thing connected with the Ghost dance among the Sioux is the "ghost shirt" which was worn by all adherents of the doctrine—men, women, and children alike. It is described by Captain Sword in his account of the Ghost dance, given in the appendix to this chapter, and will be noticed at length hereafter in treating of the ceremony of the dance. During the dance it was worn as an outside garment, but was said to be worn at other times under the ordinary dress. Although the shape, fringing, and feather adornment were practically the same in every case, considerable variation existed in

Fig. 3.—Sioux ghost shirts from Wounded Knee battlefield

EXPLANATION OF FIGURE 3

The originals of these ghost shirts, now in the National Museum, were taken, by scouts present during the fight, from the bodies of Indians killed at Wounded Knee, and were obtained by the author, at Pine Ridge, from Philip Wells and Louis Menard, mixed-blood interpreters, the former having also been present as interpreter for the Indian scouts during the fight. They are made of coarse white cloth, sewn with sinew. One of the shirts is partially burned, having probably been taken out of one of the tipis overturned and set on fire during the action. Two other ghost shirts, said to be from the same battlefield, are also in the National Museum.

regard to the painting, the designs on some being very simple, while the others were fairly covered with representations of sun, moon, stars, the sacred things of their mythology, and the visions of the trance. The feathers attached to the garment were always those of the eagle, and the thread used in the sewing was always the old-time sinew. In some cases the fringe or other portions were painted with the sacred red paint of the messiah. The shirt was firmly believed to be impenetrable to bullets or weapons of any sort. When one of the women shot in the Wounded Knee massacre was approached as she lay in the church and told that she must let them remove her ghost shirt in order the better to get at her wound, she replied: "Yes; take it off. They told me a bullet would not go through. Now I don't want it any more."

The protective idea in connection with the ghost shirt does not seem to be aboriginal. The Indian warrior habitually went into battle naked above the waist. His protecting "medicine" was a feather, a tiny bag of some sacred powder, the claw of an animal, the head of a bird, or some other small object which could be readily twisted into his hair or hidden between the covers of his shield without attracting attention. Its virtue depended entirely on the ceremony of the consecration and not on size or texture. The war paint had the same magic power of protection. To cover the body in battle was not in accordance with Indian usage, which demanded that the warrior should be as free and unincumbered in movement as possible. The so-called "war shirt" was worn chiefly in ceremonial dress parades and only rarely on the war-path.

Dreams are but incoherent combinations of waking ideas, and there is a hint of recollection even in the wildest visions of sleep. The ghost shirt may easily have been an inspiration from a trance, while the trance vision itself was the result of ideas derived from previous observation or report. The author is strongly inclined to the opinion that the idea of an invulnerable sacred garment is not original with the Indians, but, like several other important points pertaining to the Ghost-dance doctrine, is a practical adaptation by them of ideas derived from contact with some sectarian body among the whites. It may have been suggested by the "endowment robe" of the Mormons, a seamless garment of white muslin adorned with symbolic figures, which is worn by their initiates as the most sacred badge of their faith, and by many of the believers is supposed to render the wearer invulnerable. The Mormons have always manifested a particular interest in the Indians, whom they regard as the Lamanites of their sacred writings, and hence have made special efforts for their evangelization, with the result that a considerable number of the neighboring tribes of Ute, Paiute, Bannock, and Shoshoni have been received into the Mormon church and invested with the endowment robe. (See the appendix to this chapter: "The Mormons and the Indians;" also "Tell It All," by Mrs T. B. H. Stenhouse.) The Shoshoni and northern Arapaho occupy the same reservation in Wyoming, and anything which concerns one tribe is more or less talked of by the other. As the Sioux, Cheyenne, and other eastern tribes make frequent visits to the Arapaho, and as these Arapaho have been the great apostles of the Ghost dance, it is easy to see how an idea borrowed by the Shoshoni from the Mormons could find its way through the Arapaho first to the Sioux and Cheyenne and afterward to more remote tribes. Wovoka himself expressly disclaimed any responsibility for the ghost shirt, and whites and Indians alike agreed that it formed no part of the dance costume in Mason valley. When I first went among the Cheyenne and neighboring tribes of Oklahoma in January, 1891, the ghost shirt had not yet reached them. Soon afterward the first one was brought down from the Sioux country by a Cheyenne named White Buffalo, who had been a Carlisle student, but the Arapaho and Cheyenne, after debating the matter, refused to allow it to be worn in the dance, on the ground that the doctrine of the Ghost dance was one of peace, whereas the Sioux had made the ghost shirt an auxiliary of war. In consequence of this decision such shirts have never been worn by the dancers among the southern tribes. Instead they wear in the dance their finest shirts and dresses of buckskin, covered with painted and beaded figures from the Ghost-dance mythology and the visions of the trance.

The Ghost dance is variously named among the different tribes. In its original home among the Paiute it is called *Nänigükwa*, "dance in a circle" (*nüka*, dance), to distinguish it from the other dances of the tribe, which have only the ordinary up-and-down step without the circular movement. The Shoshoni call it *Tänä'räyün* or *Tämanä'rayära*, which may be rendered "everybody dragging," in allusion to the manner in which the dancers move around the circle holding hands, as children do in their ring games. They insist that it is a revival of a similar dance which existed among them fifty years ago. The Comanche call it *A'p-anĕka'ra*, "the Father's dance," or sometimes the dance "with joined hands." The Kiowa call it *Mânposo'ti guan*, "dance with clasped hands," and the frenzy, *guan â'dalka-i*, "dance craziness." The Caddo know it as *Ă'ă kakĭ'mbawi'ut*, "the prayer of all to the Father," or as the *Nänisana ka au'-shan*, "nänisana dance," from *nänisana*, "my children," which forms the burden of so many of the ghost songs in the language of the Arapaho, from whom they obtained the dance. By the Sioux, Arapaho, and most other prairie tribes it is called the "spirit" or "ghost" dance (Sioux, *Wana'ghi wa'chipi*; Arapaho, *Thigŭ'nawat*), from the fact that everything connected with it relates to the coming of the spirits of the dead from the spirit world, and by this name it has become known among the whites.

APPENDIX

THE MORMONS AND THE INDIANS

   While the Indian excitement was at its height in 1892, a curious pamphlet was published anonymously at Salt Lake City in connection with a proposed series of lectures, from which we make some extracts for the light they give on the Mormon attitude toward the Indians. The pamphlet is headed, "The Mormons have stepped down and out of Celestial Government—the American Indians have stepped up and into Celestial Government." It begins by stating that the Messiah came to His people at the time appointed of the Father—March, 1890—notwithstanding the assertion in the Deseret Evening News, made January, 1892: '1890 has passed, and no Messiah has come.'" It goes on to say:

   "1891 has passed, and no pruning of the vineyard." The vineyard of the Lord is the house of Israel.—Isa. 5: 7. In the part of the vineyard the American Indians, descendants of the righteous branch of Joseph, who were led to the Western Continent or hemisphere—Zion—we find the vine, the stone-power of the Latter Days. Ps. 80.

   The celestial prophet, seer, and revelator, Joseph Smith, jr., prophesied on the 2d of April, 1843, that the Messiah would reveal himself to man in mortality in 1890. Doctrine and Covenants, 130, 15, 17, which reads: "I was once praying very earnestly to know the time of the coming of the Son of Man, when I heard a voice speak the following: 'Joseph, my son, if thou livest until thou art eighty-five years old, thou shalt see the face of the Son of Man.'"

*   *   *   *   *   *   *

   Five years later (than 1882) the sign that was to usher in the work of the Father was given to the American Indians, while March, 1890, witnesses the organization of a church under the restored order, where twelve disciples were chosen and ordained, whose first allegiance is given irrevocably to the Lord God, whereas that of the Celestial Church is given to the government fostering it.

*   *   *   *   *   *   *

   The following seven signs were to precede the fullness of the Gentiles upon the land of America; Zion, the time, place, and parties given with each. [The first, second, and third "signs" are omitted here.]

   4. When the Bible and Book of Mormon become one in the hands of the Messiah. Ezk. 37: 19; III Nephi, 21: 1-7. In 1887, sixty years after the plates were delivered to Joseph Smith, jr., the Book of Mormon in Spanish was delivered to the American Indians, with the promise to those who are identified with the Gentiles that if they will not harden their hearts, but will repent and know the true points of my doctrine they shall be numbered with my covenant people, the Branch of Joseph. Doctrine and Covenant, 19:59–62; 20:8–17; III Nephi, 21:1-7.

   5. The coming of the Messiah. Three years later, March, 1890, the people of God, who were notified by the three Nephites, met at Walkers lake, Esmeralda county, Nevada, where a dispensation of the Celestial kingdom of God—the gospel in the covenant of consecration, a perfect oneness in all things, temporal and spiritual— was given unto them. Twelve disciples were ordained, not by angels or men, but by the Messiah, in the presence of hundreds, representing scores of tribes or nations, who saw his face, heard and understood his voice as on the day of pentecost. Acts 2, also fulfilling sec. 90:9, 10, 11 of Doctrine and Covenant. Ezk. 20:33–37.

6. The Fulness of the Gentiles. In 1492, the Lord God let His vineyard to the nations of the Gentiles, to punish His people the Branch of Joseph for 400 years (Gen. 15: 13), bringing the fulness of the Gentiles the end of their rule over the American Indians. October, 1892, Rom. II: 25–26; Gen. 50: 25; New Trans. Matt. 21: 33–41.

7. The Pruning of the Vineyard. The husbandmen upon this land began the last pruning of the vineyard in 1891. Prominent among which stands our government in fulfilling Matt. 21: 33–41, saying, let us kill the heirs and hold the inheritance, as shown in the massacre of Wounded Knee; the butchery of Sitting Bull; the imprisonment of Short Bull and others; the breaking up of reservations, and the attempts to destroy the treaty stipulations above mentioned by forcing the mark of the Beast, citizenship and statehood, upon the American Indians, which will ultimately terminate in a war of extermination. Isa. 10: 24–27; Dan. 2: 34; Isa. 14: 21.

According to the astronomical, prophetic, and historical evidence found in the Bible, Book of Mormon, and Doctrine and Covenants for the redemption of Zion and the restoration of Israel, there are seven celestial keys of powers to be used which can not be handled by apostles, prophets, or angels. They can only be handled by the Messiah and his Father.

* * * * * * *

2. The key of power that restores the heirs, the American Indians, to their own lands consecrating to them the wealth of the Gentiles.

3. The key of power that turns away ungodliness from Jacob (the American Indians) enabling them to build the temple on the spot pointed out by the finger of God (Independence, Jackson County, Missouri), on which the true sign of Israel is to rest, the glory of the living God of the Hebrews, the cloud by day and the pillar of fire by night by the close of this generation, 1896.

* * * * * * *

On and after July 10, 1892, free lectures illustrated by figures, will be given weekly, on Sunday, Monday, and Tuesday, from 6.30 to 8.30 p. m. (weather permitting), at the book stand in the Nineteenth Ward, opposite Margett's Brewery, No. 312 North Second West.

First. On the coming of the Messiah to the Hebrews, at the sacrifice of Esau, near the close of the 400-year bondage of Jacob in the morning of the Abrahamic Covenant, B. C. 1491.

Second. On the coming of the Messiah to the Jews, at the Meridian sacrifice of Jacob at the close of the last 1921 years of the covenant, the year one A. D.

Third. On the coming of the Messiah to the American Indians, the remnants, at the evening sacrifice of Esau, near the expiration of the evening bondage of Jacob of 400 years, 1892, in the last 430 years of the covenant.

PORCUPINE'S ACCOUNT OF THE MESSIAH

The following statement was made to Major Carroll, in command of Camp Crook, at Tongue River agency, Montana, June 15, 1890, and transmitted through the War Department to the Indian Office:

In November last [1889] I left the reservation with two other Cheyennes. I went through [Fort] Washakie and took the Union Pacific railroad at Rawlins. We got on early in the morning about breakfast, rode all day on the railroad, and about dark reached a fort [Bridger?]. I stayed there two days, and then took a passenger train, and the next morning got to Fort Hall. I found some lodges of Snakes and Bannocks there. I saw the agent here, and he told me I could stay at the agency, but the chief of the Bannocks who was there took me to his camp near by. The Bannocks told me they were glad to see a Cheyenne and that we ought to make a treaty with the Bannocks.

The chief told me he had been to Washington and had seen the President, and that we ought all to be friends with the whites and live at peace with them and with each other. We talked these matters over for ten days. The agent then sent for me and some of the Bannocks and Shoshones, and asked me where I was going. I told him I was just traveling to meet other Indians and see other countries; that my people were at peace with the whites, and I thought I could travel anywhere I wished. He asked me why I did not have a pass. I said because my agent would not give me one. He said he was glad to see me anyhow, and that the whites and Indians were all friends. Then he asked me where I wanted a pass to. I told him I wanted to go further and some Bannocks and Shoshones wanted to go along. He gave passes—five of them—to the chiefs of the three parties. We took the railroad to a little town near by, and then took a narrow-gauge road. We went on this, riding all night at a very fast rate of speed, and came to a town on a big lake [Ogden or Salt Lake City]. We stayed there one day, taking the cars at night, rode all night, and the next morning about 9 oclock saw a settlement of Indians. We traveled south, going on a narrow-gauge road. We got off at this Indian town. The Indians here were different from any Indians I ever saw. The women and men were dressed in white people's clothes, the women having their hair banged. These Indians had their faces painted white with black spots. We stayed with these people all day. We took the same road at night and kept on. We traveled all night, and about day-light we saw a lot of houses, and they told us there were a lot more Indians there; so we got off, and there is where we saw Indians living in huts of grass [tulé?]. We stopped here and got something to eat. There were whites living near by. We got on the cars again at night, and during the night we got off among some Indians, who were fish-eaters [Paiute]. We stayed among the Fish-eaters till morning, and then got into a wagon with the son of the chief of the Fish-eaters, and we arrived about noon at an agency on a big river. There was also a big lake near the agency.

The agent asked us where we were from and said we were a long ways from home, and that he would write to our agent and let him know we were all right. From this agency we went back to the station, and they told us there were some more Indians to the south. One of the chiefs of the Fish-eaters then furnished us with four wagons. We traveled all day, and then came to another railroad. We left our wagons here and took the railroad, the Fish-eaters telling us there were some more Indians along the railroad who wanted to see us. We took this railroad about 2 oclock and about sun down got to another agency, where there were more Fish-eaters. [From diagrams drawn and explanations given of them in addition to the foregoing, there seems to be no doubt that the lakes visited are Pyramid and Walker lakes, western Nevada, and the agencies those of the same name.]

They told us they had heard from the Shoshone agency that the people in this country were all bad people, but that they were good people there. All the Indians from the Bannock agency down to where I finally stopped danced this dance [refer-ring to the late religious dances at the Cheyenne agency], the whites often dancing it themselves. [It will be recollected that he traveled constantly through the Mormon country.] I knew nothing about this dance before going. I happened to run across it, that is all. I will tell you about it. [Here all the Indian auditors removed their hats in token that the talk to follow was to be on a religious subject.] I want you all to listen to this, so that there will be no mistake. There is no harm in what I am to say to anyone. I heard this where I met my friends in Nevada. It is a wonder you people never heard this before. In the dance we had there [Nevada] the whites and Indians danced together. I met there a great many kinds of people, but they all seemed to know all about this religion. The people there seemed all to be good. I never saw any drinking or fighting or bad conduct among them. They treated me well on the cars, without pay. They gave me food without charge, and I found that this was a habit among them toward their neighbors. I thought it strange that the people there should have been so good, so different from those here.

What I am going to say is the truth. The two men sitting near me were with me, and will bear witness that I speak the truth. I and my people have been living in ignorance until I went and found out the truth. All the whites and Indians are brothers, I was told there. I never knew this before.

The Fish-eaters near Pyramid lake told me that Christ had appeared on earth again. They said Christ knew he was coming; that eleven of his children were also coming from a far land. It appeared that Christ had sent for me to go there, and that was why unconsciously I took my journey. It had been foreordained. Christ had summoned myself and others from all heathen tribes, from two to three or four from each of fifteen or sixteen different tribes. There were more different languages than I ever heard before and I did not understand any of them. They told me when I got there that my great father was there also, but did not know who he was. The people assembled called a council, and the chief's son went to see the Great Father [messiah], who sent word to us to remain fourteen days in that camp and that he would come to see us. He sent me a small package of something white to eat that I did not know the name of. There were a great many people in the council, and this white food was divided among them. The food was a big white nut. Then I went to the agency at Walker lake and they told us Christ would be there in two days. At the end of two days, on the third morning, hundreds of people gathered at this place. They cleared off a place near the agency in the form of a circus ring and we all gathered there. This space was perfectly cleared of grass, etc. We waited there till late in the evening anxious to see Christ. Just before sundown I saw a great many people, mostly Indians, coming dressed in white men's clothes. The Christ was with them. They all formed in this ring around it. They put up sheets all around the circle, as they had no tents. Just after dark some of the Indians told me that the Christ [Father] was arrived. I looked around to find him, and finally saw him sitting on one side of the ring. They all started toward him to see him. They made a big fire to throw light on him. I never looked around, but went forward, and when I saw him I bent my head. I had always thought the Great Father was a white man, but this man looked like an Indian. He sat there a long time and nobody went up to speak to him. He sat with his head bowed all the time. After awhile he rose and said he was very glad to see his children. "I have sent for you and am glad to see you. I am going to talk to you after awhile about your relatives who are dead and gone. My children, I want you to listen to all I have to say to you. I will teach you, too, how to dance a dance, and I want you to dance it. Get ready for your dance and then, when the dance is over, I will talk to you." He was dressed in a white coat with stripes. The rest of his dress was a white man's except that he had on a pair of moccasins. Then he commenced our dance, everybody joining in, the Christ singing while we danced. We danced till late in the night, when he told us we had danced enough.

The next morning, after breakfast was over, we went into the circle and spread canvas over it on the ground, the Christ standing in the midst of us. He told us he was going away that day, but would be back that next morning and talk to us.

In the night when I first saw him I thought he was an Indian, but the next day when I could see better he looked different. He was not so dark as an Indian, nor so light as a white man. He had no beard or whiskers, but very heavy eyebrows. He was a good-looking man. We were crowded up very close. We had been told that nobody was to talk, and even if we whispered the Christ would know it. I had heard that Christ had been crucified, and I looked to see, and I saw a scar on his wrist and one on his face, and he seemed to be the man. I could not see his feet. He would talk to us all day.

That evening we all assembled again to see him depart. When we were assembled, he began to sing, and he commenced to tremble all over, violently for a while, and then sat down. We danced all that night, the Christ lying down beside us apparently dead.

The next morning when we went to eat breakfast, the Christ was with us. After breakfast four heralds went around and called out that the Christ was back with us and wanted to talk with us. The circle was prepared again. The people assembled, and Christ came among us and sat down. He said he wanted to talk to us again and for us to listen. He said: "I am the man who made everything you see around you. I am not lying to you, my children. I made this earth and everything on it. I have been to heaven and seen your dead friends and have seen my own father and mother. In the beginning, after God made the earth, they sent me back to teach the people, and when I came back on earth the people were afraid of me and treated me badly. This is what they did to me [showing his scars]. I did not try to defend myself. I found my children were bad, so went back to heaven and left them. I told them that in so many hundred years I would come back to see my children. At the end of this time I was sent back to try to teach them. My father told me the earth was getting old and worn out, and the people getting bad, and that I was to renew everything as it used to be, and make it better."

He told us also that all our dead were to be resurrected; that they were all to come back to earth, and that as the earth was too small for them and us, he would do away with heaven, and make the earth itself large enough to contain us all; that we must tell all the people we meet about these things. He spoke to us about fighting, and said that was bad, and we must keep from it; that the earth was to be all good hereafter, and we must all be friends with one another. He said that in the fall of the year the youth of all the good people would be renewed, so that nobody would be more than 40 years old, and that if they behaved themselves well after this the youth of everyone would be renewed in the spring. He said if we were all good he would send people among us who could heal all our wounds and sickness by mere touch, and that we would live forever. He told us not to quarrel, or fight, nor strike each other, nor shoot one another; that the whites and Indians were to be all one people. He said if any man disobeyed what he ordered, his tribe would be wiped from the face of the earth; that we must believe everything he said, and that we must not doubt him, or say he lied; that if we did, he would know it; that he would know our thoughts and actions, in no matter what part of the world we might be.

When I heard this from the Christ, and came back home to tell it to my people, I thought they would listen. Where I went to there were lots of white people, but I never had one of them say an unkind word to me. I thought all of your people knew all of this I have told you of, but it seems you do not.

Ever since the Christ I speak of talked to me I have thought what he said was good. I see nothing bad in it. When I got back, I knew my people were bad, and had heard nothing of all this, so I got them together and told them of it and warned them to listen to it for their own good. I talked to them for four nights and five days. I told them just what I have told you here today. I told them what I said were the words of God Almighty, who was looking down on them. I wish some of you had been up in our camp here to have heard my words to the Cheyennes. The only bad thing that there has been in it at all was this: I had just told my people that the Christ would visit the sins of any Indian upon the whole tribe, when the recent trouble [killing of Ferguson] occurred. If any one of you think I am not telling the truth, you can go and see this man I speak of for yourselves. I will go with you, and I would like one or two of my people who doubt me to go with me.

The Christ talked to us all in our respective tongues. You can see this man in your sleep any time you want after you have seen him and shaken hands with him once. Through him you can go to heaven and meet your friends. Since my return I have seen him often in my sleep. About the time the soldiers went up the Rosebud I was lying in my lodge asleep, when this man appeared and told me that the Indians had gotten into trouble, and I was frightened. The next night he appeared to me and told me that everything would come out all right.

THE GHOST DANCE AMONG THE SIOUX

The following was written originally in the Teton Dakota dialect by George Sword, an Ogalala Sioux Indian, formerly captain of the Indian police at Pine Ridge agency and now judge of the Indian court. It was translated by an Indian for Miss Emma C. Sickels and is published by her courtesy. The copy of the original Sioux manuscript is in the archives of the Bureau of Ethnology:

In the story of ghost dancing, the Ogalala heard that the Son of God was truly on earth in the west from their country. This was in the year 1889. The first people knew about the messiah to be on earth were the Shoshoni and Arapaho. So in 1889 Good Thunder with four or five others visited the place where Son of God said to be. These people went there without permission. They said the messiah was there at the place, but he was there to help the Indians and not the whites; so this made the Indians happy to find out this. Good Thunder, Cloud Horse, Yellow Knife, and Short Bull visited the place again in 1890 and saw the messiah. Their story of visit to the messiah is as follows:

"From the country where the Arapaho and Shoshoni we start in the direction of northwest in train for five nights and arrived at the foot of the Rocky mountains. Here we saw him and also several tribes of Indians. The people said that the messiah will come at a place in the woods where the place was prepare for him. When we went to the place a smoke descended from heaven to the place where he was to come. When the smoke disappeared, there was a man of about forty, which was the Son of God. The man said:

"'My grandchildren! I am glad you have come far away to see your relatives. This are your people who have come back from your country.' When he said he want us to go with him, we looked and we saw a land created across the ocean on which all the nations of Indians were coming home, but, as the messiah looked at the land which was created and reached across the ocean, again disappeared, saying that it was not time for that to take place. The messiah then gave to Good Thunder some paints—Indian paint and a white paint—a green grass [sagebrush twigs?]; and said, 'My grandchildren, when you get home, go to farming and send all your children to school. And on way home if you kill any buffalo cut the head, the tail, and the four feet and leave them, and that buffalo will come to live again. When the soldiers of the white people chief want to arrest me, I shall stretch out my arms, which will knock them to nothingness, or, if not that, the earth will open and swallow them in. My father commanded me to visit the Indians on a purpose. I have came to the white people first, but they not good. They killed me, and you can see the marks of my wounds on my feet, my hands, and on my back. My father has given you life—your old life—and you have come to see your friends, but you will not take me home with you at this time. I want you to tell when you get home your people to follow my examples. Any one Indian does not obey me and tries to be on white's side will be covered over by a new land that is to come over this old one. You will, all the people, use the paints and grass I give you. In the spring when the green grass comes, your people who have gone before you will come back, and you shall see your friends then, for you have come to my call.'"

The people from every tipi send for us to visit them. They are people who died many years ago. Chasing Hawk, who died not long ago, was there, and we went to his tipi. He was living with his wife, who was killed in war long ago. They live in a buffalo skin tipi—a very large one—and he wanted all his friends to go there to live. A son of Good Thunder who died in war long ago was one who also took us to his tipi so his father saw him. When coming we come to a herd of buffaloes. We killed one and took everything except the four feet, head, and tail, and when we came a little ways from it there was the buffaloes come to life again and went off. This was one of the messiah's word came to truth. The messiah said, "I will short your journey when you feel tired of the long ways, if you call upon me." This we did when we were tired. The night came upon us, we stopped at a place, and we called upon the messiah to help us, because we were tired of long journey. We went to sleep and in the morning we found ourselves at a great distance from where we stopped.

The people came back here and they got the people loyal to the government, and those not favor of the whites held a council. The agent's soldiers were sent after them and brought Good Thunder and two others to the agency and they were confined to the prison. They were asked by the agent and Captain Sword whether they saw the Son of God and whether they hold councils over their return from visit, but Good Thunder refused to say "yes." They were confined in the prison for two days, and upon their promising not to hold councils about their visit they were released. They went back to the people and told them about their trouble with the agent. Then they disperse without a council.

In the following spring the people at Pine Ridge agency began to gather at the White Clay creek for councils. Just at this time Kicking Bear, from Cheyenne River agency, went on a visit to the Arapaho and said that the Arapaho there have ghost dancing. He said that people partaking in dance would get crazy and die, then the messiah is seen and all the ghosts. When they die they see strange things, they see their relatives who died long before. They saw these things when they died in ghost dance and came to life again. The person dancing becomes dizzy and finally drop dead, and the first thing they saw is an eagle comes to them and carried them to where the messiah is with his ghosts. The man said this:

The persons in the ghost dancing are all joined hands. A man stands and then a woman, so in that way forming a very large circle. They dance around in the circle in a continuous time until some of them become so tired and overtired that they became crazy and finally drop as though dead, with foams in mouth all wet by perspiration. All the men and women made holy shirts and dresses they wear in dance. The persons dropped in dance would all lie in great dust the dancing make. They paint the white muslins they made holy shirts and dresses out of with blue across the back, and alongside of this is a line of yellow paint. They also paint in the front part of the shirts and dresses. A picture of an eagle is made on the back of all the shirts and dresses. On the shoulders and on the sleeves they tied eagle feathers. They said that the bullets will not go through these shirts and dresses, so they all have these dresses for war. Their enemies weapon will not go through these dresses. The ghost dancers all have to wear eagle feather on head. With this feather any man would be made crazy if fan with this feather. In the ghost dance no person is allow to wear anything made of any metal, except the guns made of metal is carry by some of the dancers. When they come from ghosts or after recovery from craziness, they brought meat from the ghosts or from the supposed messiah. They also brought water, fire, and wind with which to kill all the whites or Indians who will help the chief of the whites. They made sweat house and made holes in the middle of the sweat house where they say the water will come out of these holes. Before they begin to dance they all raise their hands toward the northwest and cry in supplication to the messiah and then begin the dance with the song, "*Ate misunkala ceya omani-ye,*" etc.

SELWYN'S INTERVIEW WITH KUWAPI

On November 21, 1890, it was reported to Agent E. W. Foster, in charge of Yankton agency, South Dakota, that an Indian named Kuwapi, from Rosebud agency, was on the reservation teaching the doctrine and ceremony of the Ghost dance. He at once had the man arrested by a force in charge of William T. Selwyn, a full-blood Yankton Sioux, who had received a fair education under the patronage of a gentleman in Philadelphia, and who had for several years been employed in various capacities at different Sioux agencies. Selwyn had recently come from Pine Ridge, where he had learned and reported to Agent Gallagher something of the religious excitement among the western Sioux, and had afterward repeated this information to the agent at Yankton. While Kuwapi was in his custody Selwyn questioned him at length concerning the new doctrine, and forwarded the following report (*G. D., Document 36861—1890*) of the interview to Agent Foster:

YANKTON AGENCY, SOUTH DAKOTA,
November 22, 1890.

Colonel E. W. FOSTER,
United States Indian Agent, Yankton Agency, South Dakota.

DEAR SIR: It has been reported here a few days ago that there was an Indian visitor up at White Swan from Rosebud agency who has been telling or teaching the doctrines of the new messiah, and has made some agitation among the people up there. According to the request of Captain Conrad, United States Army, of Fort Randall, South Dakota, and by your order of the 21st instant, I went up to White Swan and have arrested the wanted man (Kuwapi, or One they chased after). On my way to the agency with the prisoner I have made little interview with him on the subject of the new messiah. The following are the facts which he corroborated concerning the new messiah, his laws and doctrines to the Indians of this continent:

Q. Do you believe in the new messiah?—A. I somewhat believe it.

Q. What made you believe it?—A. Because I ate some of the buffalo meat that he (the new messiah) sent to the Rosebud Indians through Short Bull.

Q. Did Short Bull say that he saw the living herd of roaming buffaloes while he was with the son of the Great Spirit?—A. Short Bull told the Indians at Rosebud that the buffalo and other wild game will be restored to the Indians at the same time when the general resurrection in favor of the Indians takes place.

Q. You said a "general resurrection in favor of the Indians takes place;" when or how soon will this be?—A. The father sends word to us that he will have all these caused to be so in the spring, when the grass is knee high.

Q. You said "father;" who is this father?—A. It is the new messiah. He has ordered his children (Indians) to call him "father."

Q. You said the father is not going to send the buffalo until the resurrection takes place. Would he be able to send a few buffaloes over this way for a sort of a sample, so as to have his children (Indians) to have a taste of the meat?—A. The father wishes to do things all at once, even in destroying the white race.

Q. You said something about the destroying of the white race. Do you mean to say that all mankind except the Indians will be killed?—A. Yes.

Q. How, and who is going to kill the white people?—A. The father is going to cause a big cyclone or whirlwind, by which he will have all the white people to perish.

Q. If it should be a cyclone or whirlwind, what are we going to do to protect ourselves?—A. The father will make some kind of provisions by which we will be saved.

Q. You said something about the coming destruction on the white people by your father. Supposing your father is sick, tired out, forget, or some other accidental cause by which he should not be able to accomplish his purpose, what would be the case about the destroying of the white people?—A. There is no doubt about these things, as the miracle performer or the father is going to do just as what he said he would do.

Q. What other object could you come to by which you are led to believe that there is such a new messiah on earth at present?—A. The ghost dancers are fainted whenever the dance goes on.

Q. Do you believe that they are really fainted?—A. Yes.

Q. What makes you believe that the dancers have really fainted?—A. Because when they wake or come back to their senses they sometimes bring back some news from the unknown world, and some little trinkets, such as buffalo tail, buffalo meat, etc.

Q. What did the fainted ones see when they get fainted?—A. They visited the happy hunting ground, the camps, multitudes of people, and a great many strange people.

Q. What did the ghost or the strange people tell the fainted one or ones?—A. When the fainted one goes to the camp, he is welcomed by the relatives of the visitor (the fainted one), and he is also invited to several feasts.

Q. Were the people at Rosebud agency anxiously waiting or expecting to see all of their dead relatives who have died several years ago?—A. Yes.

Q. We will have a great many older folks when all the dead people come back, would we not?—A. The visitors all say that there is not a single old man nor woman in the other world—all changed to young.

Q. Are we going to die when the dead ones come back?—A. No; we will be just the same as we are today.

Q. Did the visitor say that there is any white men in the other world?—A. No; no white people.

Q. If there is no white people in the other world, where did they get their provisions and clothing?—A. In the other world, the messenger tells us that they have depended altogether for their food on the flesh of buffalo and other wild game; also, they were all clad in skins of wild animals.

Q. Did the Rosebud agency Indians believe the new messiah, or the son of the Great Spirit?—A. Yes.

Q. How do they show that they have a believe in the new messiah?—A. They show themselves by praying to the father by looking up to heaven, and call him "father," just the same as you would in a church.

Q. Have you ever been in a church?—A. No.

Q. Do you faithfully believe in the new messiah?—A. I did not in the first place, but as I became more acquainted with the doctrines of the new messiah that I really believe in him.

Q. How many people at Rosebud, in your opinion, believe this new messiah?—A. Nearly every one.

Q. Did you not the Rosebud people prepare to attack the white people this summer? While I was at Pine Ridge agency this summer the Oglalla Sioux Indians say they will resist against the government if the latter should try to put a stop to the messiah question. Did your folks at Rosebud say the same thing?—A. Yes.

Q. Are they still preparing and thinking to attack the white people should the government send our soldiers with orders to put a stop to your new business of the messiah?—A. I do not know, but I think that the Wojaji band at Rosebud agency will do some harm at any time.

Q. You do not mean to say that the Rosebud Indians will try and cause an outbreak?—A. That seems to be the case.

Q. You said something about the "son of the Great Spirit," or "the father." What do you mean by the son of the Great Spirit?—A. This father, as he is called, said himself that he is the son of the Great Spirit.

Q. Have you talked to or with any Indian at White Swan about the new messiah, his laws and doctrines, or have you referred this to anyone while there?—A. I have told a few of them. I did not voluntarily express my wish for them to know and follow the doctrines of the new messiah.

Q. Yes, but you have explained the matter to the Indians, did you not?—A. Yes, I have.

Q. Do the Yankton Indians at White Swan believe in your teaching of the new messiah?—A. I did not intend to teach them, but as I have been questioned on the subject, that I have said something about it.

Q. Did any of them believe in you?—A. Some have already believed it, and some of them did not believe it.

Q. Those that have believed in you must be better men than the others, are they not?—A. I do not know.

Q. Do you intend to introduce the doctrines of the new messiah from Rosebud to this agency as a missionary of the gospel?—A. No, I did not.

Q. What brings you here, then?—A. I have some relatives here that I wanted to see, and this was the reason why I came here.

Q. Where does this new messiah question originate?   I mean from the first start of it.—A. This has originated in White mountains.

Q. Where is this White mountain?—A. Close to the big Rocky mountains, near the country that belong to the Mexicans.

Q. Do you think that there will be a trouble in the west by next spring?—A. Yes.

Q. What makes you think so?—A. Because that is what I have heard people talk of.

This is all that I have questioned Kuwapi on the subject of the new messiah.

Respectfully, your obedient servant,

WILLIAM T. SELWYN.

CHAPTER III

The Ghost Dance West of the Rockies

The first Ghost dance on Walker Lake reservation took place in January, 1889, about a mile above the railroad bridge near the agency. Wovoka's preaching had already been attracting general attention among his own people for some months. It is said that six Apache attended this first dance, but the statement is improbable, as this would imply that they had made a journey of 600 miles through a desert country to see a man as yet unknown outside of his own tribe. From this time, however, his fame went abroad, and another large dance in the same vicinity soon after was attended by a number of Ute from Utah. The Ute are neighbors of the Paiute on the east, as the Bannock are on the north, and these tribes were naturally the first to hear of the new prophet and to send delegates to attend the dance. The doctrine spread almost simultaneously to all the scattered bands of Paiute in Nevada, Oregon, and adjacent sections.

In its essential features the Ghost dance among the Paiute as conducted by the messiah himself was practically the same as among the majority of the prairie tribes, as will later be described. The Sioux, Kiowa, and perhaps some other tribes, however, danced around a tree or pole set up in the center of the ring, differing in this respect from the Paiute, as well as from the Cheyenne, Arapaho, Caddo, and others. No fire was allowed within the ring by any of the prairie tribes among whom the subject was investigated, but among the Paiute it seems that fires were built either within the circle or close to it. When I visited the messiah in January, 1892, deep snow was on the ground, which had caused the temporary suspension of dancing, so that I had no opportunity of seeing the performance there for myself. I saw, however, the place cleared for the dance ground—the same spot where the large delegation from Oklahoma had attended the dance the preceding summer—at the upper end of Mason valley. A large circular space had been cleared of sagebrush and leveled over, and around the circumference were the remains of the low round structures of willow branches which had sheltered those in attendance. At one side, within the circle, was a larger structure of branches, where the messiah gave audience to the delegates from distant tribes, and, according to their statements, showed them the glories of the spirit world through the medium of hypnotic trances. The Paiute always dance five nights, or perhaps more properly four nights and the morning of the fifth day, as enjoined by the messiah on the visiting delegates, ending the performance with a general shaking and waving of blankets, as among the prairie tribes, after which all go down and bathe in the nearest stream. The shaking of the blankets dispels all evil influences and drives sickness and disease away from the dancers. There is no previous consecration of the ground, as among the Arapaho, and no preliminary sweat bath, as among the Sioux. The sweat bath seems to be unknown to the Paiute, who are preeminently a dirty people, and I saw no trace of sweat-house frames at any of their camps. Nakash, the Arapaho who visited the messiah in 1889 and first brought the dance to the eastern tribes, confirmed the statements of the Paiute and ranchmen that there were no trances in the Paiute Ghost dance.

Besides the dance ground in Mason valley, where the messiah himself generally presided, there were several others on Walker River reservation, although, if we are to believe the agent, no Ghost dances were ever held on either reservation.

The following extract from Porcupine's account of his visit to the messiah in the fall of 1889 (see page 37) gives some idea of the Paiute Ghost dance and throws light on the cataleptic peculiarities of the messiah:

I went to the agency at Walker lake, and they told us Christ would be there in two days. At the end of two days, on the third morning, hundreds of people gathered at this place. They cleared off a place near the agency in the form of a circus ring and we all gathered there. This space was perfectly cleared of grass, etc. We waited there till late in the evening, anxious to see Christ. Just before sundown I saw a great many people, mostly Indians, coming dressed in white men's clothes. The Christ was with them. They all formed in this ring in a circle around him. They put up sheets all around the circle, as they had no tents. Just after dark some of the Indians told me that the Christ (father) was arrived. I looked around to find him, and finally saw him sitting on one side of the ring. They all started toward him to see him. They made a big fire to throw light on him. I never looked around, but went forward, and when I saw him I bent my head. . . . He sat there a long time and nobody went up to speak to him. He sat with his head bowed all the time. After awhile he rose and said he was very glad to see his children. "I have sent for you and am glad to see you. I am going to talk to you after awhile about your relatives who are dead and gone. My children, I want you to listen to all I have to say to you. I will teach you, too, how to dance a dance, and I want you to dance it. Get ready for your dance, and then when the dance is over I will talk to you." He was dressed in a white coat with stripes. The rest of his dress was a white man's, except that he had on a pair of moccasins. Then he commenced our dance, everybody joining in, the Christ singing while we danced. We danced till late in the night; then he told us we had danced enough.

The next morning after breakfast was over, we went into the circle and spread canvas over it on the ground, the Christ standing in the midst of us. He told us he was going away that day, but would be back the next morning and talk to us. . . . He had no beard or whiskers, but very heavy eyebrows. He was a good-looking man. We were crowded up very close. We had been told that nobody was to talk, and that even if we whispered the Christ would know it. . . . He would talk to us all day.

That evening we all assembled again to see him depart. When we were assembled he began to sing, and he commenced to tremble all over violently for a while and then sat down. We danced all that night, the Christ lying down beside us apparently dead.

The next morning when we went to eat breakfast, the Christ was with us. After breakfast four heralds went around and called out that the Christ was back with us and wanted to talk with us. The circle was prepared again. The people assembled, and Christ came among us and sat down. (*G. D., 9.*)

We come now to the other tribes bordering on the Paiute. First in order are the Washo, a small band dwelling on the slopes of the sierras in the neighborhood of Carson, Nevada, and speaking a peculiar language of unknown affinity. They are completely under the domination of the Paiute. They had no separate dance, but joined in with the nearest camps of Paiute and sang the same songs. Occupying practically the same territory as the Paiute, they were among the first to receive the new doctrine.

Farther to the south, in California, about Bridgeport and Mono lake and extending across to the westward slope of the sierras, are several small Shoshonean bands closely akin to the Paiute and known locally as the "Diggers." The Paiute state that bands of these Indians frequently came up and participated in the dance on the reservation. They undoubtedly had their own dances at home also.

According to the statement of the agent in charge of the Mission Indians in southern California in 1891, the doctrine reached them also, and the medicine-men of Potrero began to prophesy the destruction of the whites and the return of Indian supremacy. Few believed their predictions, however, until rumors brought the news of the overflow of Colorado river and the birth of "Salton sea" in the summer of 1891. Never doubting that the great change was near at hand, the frightened Indians fled to the mountains to await developments, but after having gone hungry for several days the millennial dawn seemed still as far away as ever, and they returned to their homes with disappointment in their hearts. Although the agent mentions specifically only the Indians of Potrero, there can be no doubt that the inhabitants of the other Mission rancherias in the vicinity were also affected, and we are thus enabled to fix the boundary of the messiah excitement in this direction at the Pacific ocean. (*Comr., 27.*)

In northern California the new doctrine was taken up late in 1890 by the Pit River Indians, a group of tribes constituting a distinct linguistic stock and scattered throughout the whole basin of Pit river, from Goose lake to the Sacramento, which may have formed the boundary of the Ghost-dance movement in this direction. (*A. G. O., 7.*) As a number of these Indians are living also on Round Valley reservation in California, it is possible that the doctrine may have reached there also. Having obtained the dance ritual directly from the Paiute, their neighbors on the east, the ceremony and belief were probably the same with both tribes.

So far as can be learned from the reports of agents, and from the statement of Wovoka himself, the dance was never taken up by the Indians of Hoopa Valley reservation in California; of Klamath, Siletz,

Grande Ronde, or Umatilla reservations in Oregon; by any of the tribes in Washington; by those of Lapwai or Cœur d'Alêne reservations in Idaho; or on Jocko reservation in Montana. Wovoka stated that he had been visited by delegates from Warmspring agency, in Oregon, who also had taken part in the dance, but these may have been some of the Paiute living on that reservation. The small band of Paiute living with the Klamath probably also attended the dance at some time.[1]

A single Nez Percé visited the messiah, but the visit had no effect on his tribe at home. In a general way it may be stated that the doctrine of the Ghost dance was never taken up by any tribes of the Salishan or Shahaptian stocks, occupying practically the whole of the great Columbia basin. This is probably due to the fact that the more important of these tribes have been for a long time under the influence of Catholic or other Christian missionaries, while most of the others are adherents of the Smohalla or the Shaker doctrine.

Of the tribes southward from the Paiute, according to the best information obtainable, the Ghost dance never reached the Yuma, Pima, Papago, Maricopa, or any of the Apache bands in Arizona or New Mexico, neither did it affect any of the Pueblo tribes except the Taos, who performed the dance merely as a pastime. As before stated, it is said that six Apache attended the first large dance at Walker lake in 1889. This seems improbable, but if true it produced no effect on any part of the tribe at large. Later on the Jicarilla Apache, in northern New Mexico, may have heard of it through the southern Ute, but, so far as is known officially, neither of these tribes ever engaged in the dance. The agent of the Jicarilla states that the tribe knew nothing of the doctrine until informed of it by himself. (*G. D., 10.*) It seems never to have been taken up by the Mescalero Apache in southern New Mexico, although they are in the habit of making frequent visits to the Kiowa, Comanche, Apache, and other Ghost-dancing tribes of Oklahoma. The agent of the Mohave states officially that these Indians knew nothing about it, but this must be a mistake, as there is constant communication between the Mohave and the southern Paiute, and, according to Wovoka's statement, Mohave delegates attended the dance in 1890, while the 700 Walapai and Chemehuevi associated with the Mohave are known to have been devoted adherents of the doctrine.

The dance was taken up nearly simultaneously by the Bannock, Shoshoni, Gosiute, and Ute in the early part of 1889. All these tribes are neighbors (on the east) of the Paiute and closely cognate to them, the Bannock particularly having only a slight dialectal difference of language, so that communication between them is an easy matter. The

---

[1] Hoopa Valley, Siletz, and Grande Ronde reservations are occupied by the remnants of a number of small tribes. Klamath reservation is occupied by the Klamath, Modoc, and Paiute. On Umatilla reservation are the Cayuse, Umatilla, and Wallawalla. The Nez Percé are at Lapwai to the number of over 1,800. On the Cœur d'Alêne reservation are the Cœur d'Alênes, Kutenai, Pend d'Oreilles, and part of the Spokan. On Jocko reservation in Montana are the Flatheads, Kutenai, and a part of the Pend d'Oreilles. Warmspring reservation in Oregon is occupied by the Warmspring, Wasco, Tenino, Paiute, and John Day Indians.

Bannock are chiefly on Fort Hall and Lemhi reservations in Idaho. The Shoshoni are on the Western Shoshone (Duck Valley) reservation in Nevada, on Fort Hall and Lemhi reservations in Idaho, and on Wind River reservation in Wyoming. The Ute are on Uintah and Uncompahgre reservations in Utah, and on the Southern Ute reservation in Colorado. There are also a considerable number of Bannock and Shoshoni not on reservations. The Ute of Utah sent delegates to the messiah soon after the first Ghost dance in January, 1889, but it is doubtful if the southern Ute in Colorado were engaged in the dance. Although aware of the doctrine, they ridiculed the idea of the dead returning to earth. (*G. D., 11.*)

In regard to the dance among the Shoshoni and Paiute on the Western Shoshoni reservation, in Nevada and Idaho, their agent writes, under date of November 8, 1890:

> The Indians of this reservation and vicinity have just concluded their second medicine dance, the previous one having taken place in August last. They are looking for the coming of the Indian Christ, the resurrection of the dead Indians, and the consequent supremacy of the Indian race. Fully one thousand people took part in the dance. While the best of order prevailed, the excitement was very great as morning approached. When the dancers were worn out mentally and physically, the medicine-men would shout that they could see the faces of departed friends and relatives moving about the circle. No pen can paint the picture of wild excitement that ensued. All shouted in a chorus, Christ has come, and then danced and sung until they fell in a confused and exhausted mass on the ground. . . . I apprehend no trouble beyond the loss of time and the general demoralizing effect of these large gatherings of people. Several of the leading men have gone to Walker lake to confer with a man who calls himself Christ. Others have gone to Fort Hall to meet Indians from Montana and Dakota, to get the news from that section. In fact, the astonishing part of the business is the fact that all the Indians in the country seem to possess practically the same ideas and expect about the same result. (*G. D., 12.*)

On December 6 he writes that another Ghost dance had then been in progress for six days, and that the Indians had announced their intention to dance one week in each month until the grass grew, at which time the medicine-men had told them the messiah would come, bringing with him all their dead friends. (*G. D., 13.*) This dance, however, was attended by a much smaller number of Indians, and skeptics had already arisen among them to scoff at the new believers. The leaven was working, and only a little shrewd diplomacy was needed to turn the religious scale, as is shown by an extract from a third letter, dated January 10, 1891, from which it would seem that Agent Plumb is a man of practical common sense, as likewise that Esau was not the only one who would sell his birthright for a mess of pottage:

> Christmas day was the day set for commencing another dance. On learning this, I told the Indians that it was my intention to give them all a big feast and have a general holiday on Christmas, but that I would not give them anything if they intended to dance. I told them they could play all of their usual games, in fact, have a good time, but that dancing was forbidden. I showed them how continued dancing at various Sioux agencies had ended in soldiers being sent to stop them. I stated the case as clearly as I could; the Indians debated it two days, and then

reported that while they hoped their dead friends would come back, and believed that dancing would help to bring them, yet they were friends of the government, and friends of the whites, and my friends, and would not hold any more resurrection dances without my consent. Up to this date they have kept their word. I have no hope of breaking up their dances altogether, but I have strong hopes of controlling them. (*G. D., 14.*)

The Bannock and Shoshoni of Fort Hall reservation in Idaho have served as the chief medium of the doctrine between the tribes west of the mountains and those of the plains. Situated almost on the summit of the great divide, they are within easy reach of the Paiute to the west, among whom the dance originated, and whose language the Bannock speak, while at no great distance to the east, on Wind River reservation in Wyoming, the remaining Shoshoni are confederated with the Arapaho, who have been from the first the great apostles of the doctrine among the prairie tribes. There is constant visiting back and forth between the tribes of these two reservations, while the four railroads coming in at Fort Hall, together with the fact of its close proximity to the main line of the Union Pacific, tend still more to make it a focus and halting point for Indian travel. Almost every delegation from the tribes east of the mountains stopped at this agency to obtain the latest news from the messiah and to procure interpreters from among the Bannock to accompany them to Nevada. In a letter of November 26, 1890, to the Indian Commissioner, the agent in charge states that during the preceding spring and summer his Indians had been visited by representatives from about a dozen different reservations. In regard to the dance and the doctrine at Fort Hall, he also says that the extermination and resurrection business was not a new thing with his tribes by any means, but had been quite a craze with them every few years for the last twenty years or more, only varying a little according to the whim of particular medicine-men. (*G. D., 15.*) This may have referred to the doctrine already mentioned as having been taught by Tävibo.

Early in 1889 a Bannock from Fort Hall visited the Shoshoni and Arapaho of Wind River reservation in Wyoming and brought them the first knowledge of the new religion. He had just returned from a visit to the Paiute country, where he said he had met messengers who had told him that the dead people were coming back, and who had commanded him to go and tell all the tribes. "And so," said the Shoshoni, "he came here and told us all about it." Accordingly, in the summer of that year a delegation of five Shoshoni, headed by Täbinshi, with Nakash ("Sage"), an Arapaho, visited the messiah of Mason valley, traveling most of the way by railroad and occupying several days in the journey. They attended a Ghost dance, which, according to their accounts, was a very large one, and after dancing all night were told by the messiah that they would meet all their dead in two years from that time at the turning of the leaves, i. e., in the autumn of 1891. They were urged to dance frequently, "because the dance moves the dead." One of the Shoshoni delegates understood the Bannock and Paiute language and interpreted for the rest. The information was probably conveyed by the Shoshoni to the Arapaho through the medium of the sign language.

In accord with the report of the delegates, on their return home the Shoshoni and Arapaho at once began to dance. A year later, in the fall of 1890, a dense smoke from forest fires in the mountains drifted down and obscured the air in the lower country to such an extent that horses were lost in the haze. This was regarded by the Indians as an indication of the approach of the great change, and the dance was continued with increased fervor, but at last the atmosphere began to clear and the phenomenon ended as it had begun—in smoke. The dance was kept up, however, without abatement for another year, until the predicted time had come and gone, when the Shoshoni—who seem to share the skeptical nature of their southern kinsmen, the Comanche— concluded that they had been deceived, and abandoned the dance. The Arapaho, who have greater faith in the unseen things of the spirit world, kept it up, and were still dancing when I visited them in the summer of 1892. A part of the Arapaho, headed by their chief, Black Coal, and encouraged by the Catholic missionaries, had steadily opposed the dance from the first. After considerable discussion of the matter it was decided, on Black Coal's proposition, to send another delegation to the messiah, under the guidance of Yellow Eagle, a graduate of a government Indian school, to learn as to the truth or falsity of the new doctrine. They returned early in 1891 and reported against the movement. Their report confirmed the doubters in their skepticism, but produced little effect on the rest of the tribe.

When I visited Wind River reservation in Wyoming in June, 1892, the agent in charge informed me that there was no Ghost dancing on his reservation; that he had explained how foolish it was and had strictly forbidden it, and that in consequence the Indians had abandoned it. However, he expressed interest in my investigation, and as the Arapaho, with whom I had most to do, were then camped in a body a few miles up in the mountains cutting wood, he very kindly furnished a conveyance and camping outfit, with two of the agency employees— a clerk and an interpreter—to take me out. It appeared afterward that the escort had received instructions of their own before starting. Having reached the camp and set up our tent, the Arapaho soon came around to get acquainted, over a pipe and a cup of coffee; but, in answer to questions put by one of my companions, a white man, who assumed the burden of the conversation, it seemed that the Indians had lost all interest in the dance. In fact, some of them were so ignorant on the subject that they wanted to know what it meant.

After trying in vain to convince me that it was useless to waste time further with the Indians, the clerk started back again after supper, satisfied that that part of the country was safe so far as the Ghost dance was concerned. By this time it was dark, and the Indians invited the interpreter and myself to come over to a tipi about half a mile away, where we could meet all the old men. We started, and had gone but a short distance when we heard from a neighboring hill the familiar measured cadence of the ghost songs. On turning with a questioning look to my interpreter—who was himself a half-blood—he quietly said: "Yes; they are dancing the Ghost dance. That's something I have never reported, and I never will. It is their religion and they have a right to it." Not wishing to be an accomplice in crime, I did not go over to the dance; but it is needless to state that the old men in the tipi that night, and for several successive nights thereafter, knew all about the songs and ceremonies of the new religion. As already stated, the Shoshoni had really lost faith and abandoned the dance.

Among the Shoshoni the dance was performed around a small cedar tree, planted in the ground for that purpose. Unlike the Sioux, they hung nothing on this tree. The men did not clasp each other's hands, but held on to their blankets instead; but a woman standing between two men took hold of their hands. There was no preliminary medicine ceremony. The dance took place usually in the morning, and at its close the performers shook their blankets in the air, as among the Paiute and other tribes, before dispersing. However novel may have been the doctrine, the Shoshoni claim that the Ghost dance itself as performed by them was a revival of an old dance which they had had fully fifty years before.

The selection of the cedar in this connection is in agreement with the general Indian idea, which has always ascribed a mystic sacredness to that tree, from its never-dying green, which renders it so conspicuous a feature of the desert landscape; from the aromatic fragrance of its twigs, which are burned as incense in sacred ceremonies; from the durability and fine texture of its wood, which makes it peculiarly appropriate for tipi poles and lance shafts; and from the dark-red color of its heart, which seems as though dyed in blood. In Cherokee myth the cedar was originally a pole, to the top of which they fastened the fresh scalps of their enemies, and the wood was thus stained by the blood that trickled slowly down along it to the ground. The Kiowa also selected a cedar for the center of their Ghost-dance circle.

We go back now to the southern tribes west of the mountains. Some time in the winter of 1889–90 Paiute runners brought to the powerful tribe of the Navaho, living in northern New Mexico and Arizona, the news of the near advent of the messiah and the resurrection of the dead. They preached and prophesied for a considerable time, but the Navaho were skeptical, laughed at the prophets, and paid but little attention to the prophesies. (*Matthews, 1.*) According to the official report for 1892, these Indians, numbering somewhat over 16,000 souls, have, in round numbers, 9,000 cattle, 119,000 horses, and 1,600,000

sheep and goats; and, as suggested by Dr Matthews, the authority on
that tribe, it may be that, being rich in herds and wealth of silver, they
felt no special need of a redeemer.   While with the Navaho in the winter of 1892–93 I made inquiry in various parts of their wide-extended
territory, but could not learn that the Ghost dance had ever been

Fig. 4.—Navaho Indians

performed among them, and it was evident that in their case the doctrinal seed had fallen on barren ground.

Before visiting the tribe, I had written for information to Mr A. M.
Stephen, of Keams Cañon, Arizona, since deceased, who had studied
the Navaho and Hopi for years and spoke the Navaho language
fluently. I quote from him on the subject. It may be noted that

Keams Cañon is about 125 miles northwest of Fort Wingate, the point from which Dr Matthews writes, and nearer by that much to the Paiute, Cohonino, and Walapai, all of whom have accepted the new religion. Mr Stephen states that some time in February or March, 1890, he first heard rumors among the Navaho that "the old men long dead" had returned to some foreign tribes in the north or east, the vague far away. The intelligence was brought to the Navaho either by the Ute or Paiute, or both. The rumor grew and the idea became commonly current among the Navaho that the mythic heroes were to return and that under their direction they were to expel American and Mexican and restrict the Zuñi and Hopi close to their villages, and, in fact, to reestablish their old domain from San Francisco mountains to Santa Fé. (*Stephen, 1.*) On November 22, 1891, he further writes:

While out this last time I camped over night with some Navajo friends, and over a pipe brought up the messiah topic. This family belongs to the Bitter-Water gens, and this is the gist of what I got from them: A Pah-ute came to a family of their gens living near Navajo mountain and told them that *Na'-Keh-tkla-i* was to return from the under world and bring back all the Tinneh (Navajo) he had killed. *Na'-keh-tkla-i* (i. e., "foreigner with white foot sole") in the long ago had a puma and a bear. These were his pets. He would call puma from the east and bear from the west, and just before dawn they met in the center. Thus they met four times. On the fourth meeting puma reached back with his forepaw and plucked his mane, tossing the hair aloft, and for every hair a Tinneh died. This fatal sorcery continued for a long time, and great numbers were killed. Now, the Pah-ute said, this sorcerer was to return, and would call his pets, and they would come east and west, and following their trail would be all the people whose death they had caused. These Navajo said they had heard of other Pah-ute prophecies a year or more ago, all to the effect that long dead people were to return alive from the under world. These resurrected ones were also to bring back the departed game, and the Tinneh would again dominate the region. But, said my informant, *datsaigi yelti,* "it is worthless talk." (*Stephen, 2.*)

In connection with hypnotism as seen in the Ghost dance, Dr Matthews states that in one curious Navaho ceremony he has several times seen the patient hypnotized or pretend to be hypnotized by a character dressed in evergreens. The occurrence of the hypnotic trance is regarded as a sign that the ceremony has been effective. If the trance does not occur, some other ceremony must be tried. (*Matthews, 2.*)

West of the Navaho in northeastern Arizona live the Hopi, or Moki, a Pueblo tribe occupying several villages on the tops of nearly inaccessible mesas. In July, 1891, four of these Indians, while on a visit to the Cohonino, living farther to the west, first heard of the new doctrine and witnessed a Ghost dance, as will be described hereafter. They brought back the news to their people, but it made no impression on them and the matter was soon forgotten. (*Stephen, 3.*) In this connection Mr Stephen states, in response to a letter of inquiry, that although he does not recollect any Hopi myth concerning rejuvenation of the world and reunion with the resurrected dead on this earth, yet the doctrine of a reunion with the revivified dead in the under world is a commonly accepted belief of the Hopi. They have also a curious myth of a fair-hair god and a fair-skin people who came up from the under world with the Hopi, and who then left them with a promise to return. This suggests the idea of a messiah, but Mr Stephen has not yet been able to get the myth in its entirety. He does not think it derived from

Fig. 5.—Vista in the Hopi pueblo of Walpi

any corrupt source, however, through Spanish or other missionaries, as the allusions are all of archaic tendency. (*Stephen, 4.*)

The Cohonino or Havasupai are a small tribe occupying the canyon of Cataract creek, an affluent of the Colorado, in northern Arizona, about 120 miles west of the Hopi, with whom they have a considerable trade in buckskins and mesquite bread. They probably obtained the doctrine and the dance directly from the Paiute to the northward. Our only knowledge of the Cohonino dance is derived through Hopi informants, and as the two tribes speak languages radically different the ideas conveyed were neither complete nor definite, but it is evident that the general doctrine was the same, although the dance differed in some respects from that of the other tribes.

We quote again from Stephen's letter of November 22, 1891:

During a quiet interval, in one of the kivas I found the Hopi who brought the tidings of the resurrection to his people. His name is Pütci and his story is very meager and confused. He went on a customary trading visit to the Cojonino in their home at Cataract creek, and I could not determine just when. The chief of the Cojonino is named Navajo, and when Pütci got there, Navajo had but lately returned from a visit to the westward. He had been with the Walapai, the Mohave, and perhaps still farther west, and had been gone nearly three months. He told his people a vague mystic story that he had heard during his travels, to the effect that the long-time dead people of the Antelope, Deer, and Rabbit [Antelope, Deer, etc, are probably Cohonino gentes—J. M.] were to come back and live in their former haunts; that they had reached to a place where were the people of the Puma, the Wolf, and the Bear; that this meeting delayed the coming, but eventually all these people would appear, and in the sequence here related. Pütci was accompanied by three other Hopi, and they said they did not very well understand this strange story. While they were stopping in Cataract cañon a one-night dance was held by the Cojonino, at which these Hopi were present. During the night a long pole, having the tail of an eagle fastened to the end, was brought out and securely planted in the ground, and the dancers were told by their shamans that anyone who could climb this pole and put his mouth on the tail would see his dead mother (maternal ancestor). One man succeeded in climbing it and laid his mouth on the feathers, and then fell to the bottom in a state of collapse. They deemed him dead, but before dawn he recovered and then said that he had seen his dead mother and several other dead ancestors, who told him they were all on their way back. The Hopi on their return home related these marvels, but apparently it made little impression, and it was only with difficulty I could gather the above meager details.

Through the kindness of Mr Thomas V. Keam, trader for the Hopi and Navaho, we get a revision of Pütci's story. Pütci states that in July, 1891, he with three other Hopi went on a visit to the Cohonino to trade for buckskins. When they arrived in the vicinity of the Cohonino camp, they were met by one of the tribe, who informed the visitors that all the Indians were engaged in a very important ceremony, and that before they could enter the camp they must wash their bodies and paint them with white clay. Accordingly, when this had been done, they were escorted to the camp and introduced to the principal chief and headmen, all of whom they found engaged in washing their heads, decorating themselves, and preparing for the ceremony, which took place on a clear space near the camp late in the afternoon. Here a very tall straight pole had been securely fastened upright in the ground. At the top were tied two eagle-tail feathers. A circle was formed around this pole by the Indians, and, after dancing around it until almost dark, one of the men climbed the pole to the top, and remained

there until exhausted, when he would slide to the ground, clinging
insensible to the pole. After remaining in this state for some time, the
medicine-men resuscitated him. On recovery he stood up and told them
he had been into another world, where he saw all the old men who had
died long ago, and among them his own people. They told him they
would all come back in time and bring the deer, the antelope, and all
other good things they had when they dwelt on this earth. This ceremony lasted four days, including the cleansing and decorating of the
dancers and the climbing of the pole, with an account of what had
been seen by the Indian during the time he was in an apparently life-
less state. Each day the ceremony was attended by the whole tribe.
(*Keam, 1.*) Resuscitation by the medicine-men, as here mentioned, is
something unknown among the prairie tribes, where the unconscious
subject is allowed to lie undisturbed on the ground until the senses
return in the natural way.

Beyond the Cohonino, and extending for about 200 miles along Colorado river on the Arizona side, are the associated tribes of Mohave,
Walapai, and Chemehuevi, numbering in all about 2,800 souls, of
whom only about one-third are on a reservation. The Chemehuevi,
being a branch of the Paiute and in constant communication with
them, undoubtedly had the dance and the doctrine. The Mohave also
have much to do with the Paiute, the two tribes interchanging visits
and mutually borrowing songs and games. They sent delegates to
the messiah and in all probability took up the Ghost dance, in spite of
the agent's statement to the contrary. As only 660 of more than 2,000
Mohave are reported as being on the reservation, the agent may have
a good reason for not keeping fully informed in regard to them.

Concerning the Walapai we have positive information. In September, 1890, the commanding officer at Fort Whipple was informed that a
Paiute from southern Utah was among the Walapai, inciting them to
dance for the purpose of causing hurricanes and storms to destroy the
whites and such Indians as would not participate in the dances. It
was stated also that these dances had then been going on for several
months and were participated in by a large portion of the tribe, and
that each dance lasted four or five nights in succession. On investigation it appeared that this Paiute was one of a party who had come
down and inaugurated the Ghost dance among the Walapai the preceding year. (*G. D., 17.*)

We find an account of the Walapai Ghost dance in a local paper a
year later. The article states that all the songs were in the language of
the Paiute, from whom the doctrine had originally come. The Walapai version of the doctrine has been already noted. The dance itself,
and the step, as here described, are essentially the same as among other
tribes. Each dance lasted five nights, and on the last night was kept
up until daylight. Just before daylight on the morning of the last night
the medicine men ascended a small butte, where they met and talked

with the expected god, and on coming down again delivered his message to the people. The dance was held at irregular intervals, according to the instructions received on the butte by the medicine-men.

The dance place was a circular piece of ground a hundred feet in diameter, inclosed by a fence of poles and bushes, and surrounded by high mountain walls of granite, which reflected the light from half a dozen fires blazing within the circle. The dancers, to the number of 200, clad in white robes with fancy trimmings, their faces and hair painted white in various decorative designs, moved slowly around in a circle, keeping time with a wild chant, while 200 more stood or crouched around the fires, awaiting their turn to participate. The dancers faced toward the center, each holding the hands of the ones next to him and joining in the chant in unison. The dust issued in clouds from beneath their feet, and with the dust and exertion together the performers were soon exhausted and dropped out, when others took their places. After each circuit they rested a few minutes and then started round again. At each circuit a different chant was sung, and thus the dance continued until midnight, when, with a loud clapping of hands, it ended, and the people separated and went to their homes. Throughout the performance two or three chiefs or medicine-men were constantly going about on the outside of the circle to preserve order and reprimand any merriment, one of them explaining to the visitors that, as this was a religious ceremony, due solemnity must be observed. (*F. L. J., 2.*)

CHAPTER IV

The Ghost Dance East of the Rockies—
among the Sioux

In 1889 the Ogalala heard that the son of God had come upon earth in the west. They said the Messiah was there, but he had come to help the Indians and not the whites, and it made the Indians happy to hear this.—*George Sword.*

They signed away a valuable portion of their reservation, and it is now occupied by white people, for which they have received nothing. They understood that ample provision would be made for their support; instead, their supplies have been reduced and much of the time they have been living on half and two-thirds rations. Their crops, as well as the crops of white people, for two years have been almost a total failure. The disaffection is widespread, especially among the Sioux, while the Cheyennes have been on the verge of starvation and were forced to commit depredations to sustain life. These facts are beyond question, and the evidence is positive and sustained by thousands of witnesses.—*General Miles.*

Among the tribes east of the mountains and north of Oklahoma, it appears from official documents in the Indian Office and from other obtainable information that the Ghost dance and the doctrine, if known at all, were never accepted by the Blackfeet of Montana; the Ojibwa of Turtle mountain and Devils lake in North Dakota, or by the rest of the tribe farther to the east in Minnesota, Wisconsin, and Michigan; the Omaha, Winnebago, and Ponka in Nebraska; the small band of Sauk and Fox in Iowa; the still smaller band of Sauk and Fox, the Potawatomi, Kickapoo, Iowa, and Ojibwa in northeastern Kansas; or by the Sioux of Devils lake in North Dakota, Lake Traverse (Sisseton agency) and Flandreau in South Dakota, and Santee agency in Nebraska. All or most of these Sioux belong to the Santee or eastern division of the tribe, and have long been under civilizing influences. According to official statements the dance was not taken up by any of the Sioux of Crow Creek or Yankton agencies in South Dakota, but they were certainly more or less affected by it, as they knew all about it and are in constant communication with the wilder bands of Sioux which were concerned in the outbreak. I was informed by the Omaha and Winnebago in 1891 that they had been told of the new messiah by visiting Sioux from Pine Ridge agency in April, 1890, and later on by other Sioux from Yankton agency, but had put no faith in the story, and had never organized a Ghost dance. According to the agent in charge, the Crow of Montana were not affected. This, if true, is remarkable, in view of the fact that the Crow are a large tribe and comparatively primitive, and have living near them the wildest of the Ghost-dancing tribes, the northern Cheyenne especially occupying practically the same reservation. It is possible that their experience in the Sword-bearer affair in 1887, already mentioned, had a tendency to weaken their faith in later prophets. Dr George Bird Grinnell, a competent authority, states, in reply to a personal letter, that nothing was known about the dance by the Blackfeet of Montana or by the Blackfeet, Sarsi, or Plains Cree on the Canadian side of the boundary line.

Within the same general region, east of the Rocky mountains and north of Oklahoma, the doctrine and the dance were accepted by the Asiniboin (Fort Belknap and Fort Peck agencies), Grosventres (Arapaho subtribe, Fort Belknap agency), northern Cheyenne of Montana; the Arikara, Grosventres (Minitari), and Mandan of Fort Berthold agency, North Dakota; the Shoshoni and northern Arapaho on Wind River reservation in Wyoming, as already mentioned; and by the great body of the Sioux, at Fort Peck agency (Yanktonais), Montana, and at Standing Rock, Cheyenne River, Lower Brulé, Pine Ridge, and Rosebud agencies in North Dakota and South Dakota. The whole number of Sioux concerned was about 20,000, of whom 16,000 belonged to the Teton division, among the wildest and most warlike of all the western tribes. A few Cheyenne are also associated with the Sioux at Pine Ridge.

The northern Arapaho and the Shoshoni of Wyoming were the medium by which the doctrine of the new messiah was originally communicated to all these tribes. In the spring of 1889, Nakash, "Sage," the Arapaho chief already mentioned, crossed the mountains to investigate the reports of the new religion, and brought back a full confirmation of all that had been told them from the west. A visiting Grosventre, then among the Arapaho, heard the story and brought back the wonderful news to the Grosventres and Asiniboin of Fort Belknap, but although his account was received by some with unquestioning faith, the excitement had in it nothing of a dangerous character. (*G. D.*, *18.*)

In a short time the news spread to the Cheyenne in Montana and the Sioux of the Dakotas, and in the fall of 1889 delegates from these two tribes arrived at Fort Washakie to learn more about the messiah in the west. The principal Cheyenne delegate was Porcupine, while Short Bull and Kicking Bear were the leaders of the Sioux party. After hearing the statements of the Arapaho and Shoshoni, it was decided that some of the Cheyenne should return and report to their tribe, while Porcupine and one or two others, with the Sioux delegates, several Shoshoni, and the Arapaho, Sitting Bull, and Friday, should go to Nevada, interview the messiah himself, and learn the whole truth of the matter. Accordingly, about November, 1889, Porcupine and his companions left Fort Washakie in Wyoming for Fort Hall reservation in Idaho, where they met the Shoshoni and Bannock and were well received and entertained by them. The tribes at this place were firm believers in the new doctrine, and Porcupine states that from there on to the end of the journey all the Indians they met were dancing the Ghost dance. After stopping a few days at Fort Hall, they went on again, accompanied by several Bannock and Shoshoni, and going rapidly by railroad soon found themselves in the country of the Paiute, and after stopping at one or two camps arrived at the agency at Pyramid lake. Here the Paiute furnished them conveyances and guides to the other agency farther south at Walker river. Porcupine is our principal authority for the events of the trip, and although he claims that he undertook this journey of a thousand miles without any definite purpose or destination in view, it is evident enough from his own narrative that he left Wyoming with the fixed intention of verifying the rumors of a messiah. He has much to say of the kindness of the whites they met west of the mountains, who, it will be remembered, were largely Mormons, who have always manifested a special interest in the Indians. He also states that many of the whites took part with the Indians in the dance.

They were now in the messiah's country. "The Fisheaters, near Pyramid lake, told me that Christ had appeared on earth again. They said Christ knew he was coming; that eleven of his children were also coming from a far land. It appeared that Christ had sent for me to go there, and that was why, unconsciously, I took my journey. It had been foreordained. Christ had summoned myself and others from all heathen tribes. There were more different languages than I had ever heard before, and I did not understand any of them." The delegation of which Porcupine was a member was probably the one mentioned by the agent in charge at Pyramid lake as having arrived in the spring of 1890, and consisting of thirty-four Indians of different tribes. (*G. D., 19.*)

In a few days preparations were made for a great dance near Walker lake, with all the delegates from the various tribes and hundreds of Indians in attendance. They danced two nights or longer, the messiah himself—Wovoka—coming down from his home in Mason valley to lead the ceremony. After the dance Wovoka went into a trance, and on awaking announced to those assembled that he had been to the other world and had seen the spirits of their dead friends and of his own father and mother, and had been sent back to teach the people. According to Porcupine he claimed to be the returned Christ and bore on his body the scars of the crucifixion. He told them that the dead were to be resurrected, and that as the earth was old and worn out it would be renewed as it used to be and made better; that when this happened the youth of everyone would be renewed with each return of spring, and that they would live forever; that there would be universal peace, and that any tribe that refused his message would be destroyed from the face of the earth.

It was early in the spring of 1890 when Porcupine and his Cheyenne companions returned to their tribe at Tongue River agency in Montana with the news of the appearance of the messiah. A council was called and Porcupine made a full report of the journey and delivered the divine message, talking five days in succession. The report aroused the wildest excitement among the Cheyenne, and after several long debates on the subject the Ghost dance was inaugurated at the various camps in accordance with the instructions from beyond the mountains. In June the matter came to the attention of the military officer on the reservation, who summoned Porcupine before him and obtained from him a full account of the journey and the doctrine.   (See page 37.) Porcupine insisted strongly on the sacred character of the messiah and his message, and challenged any doubters to return with him to Nevada and investigate for themselves. He claimed also that the messiah could speak all languages. As a matter of fact, Wovoka speaks only his native Paiute and a little English, but due allowance must be made for the mental exaltation of the narrator.

Grinnell states that the failure of certain things to happen according to the predictions of the messiah, in September, 1890, caused a temporary loss of faith on the part of the Cheyenne, but that shortly afterward some visiting Shoshoni and Arapaho from Wyoming reported that in their journey as they came over they had met a party of Indians who had been dead thirty or forty years, but had been resurrected by the messiah, and were now going about as if they had never died. It is useless to speculate on the mental condition of men who could seriously report or believe such things; but, however that may be, the result was that the Cheyenne returned to the dance with redoubled fervor. (*J. F. L.*, *5*.)

The Sioux first heard of the messiah in 1889. According to the statement of Captain George Sword, of that tribe, the information came to the Ogalala (Sioux of Pine Ridge) in that year, through the Shoshoni and Arapaho. Later in the same year a delegation consisting of Good Thunder and several others started out to the west to find the messiah and to investigate the truth of the rumor. On their return they announced that the messiah had indeed come to help the Indians, but not the whites. Their report aroused a fervor of joyful excitement among the Indians and a second delegation was sent out in 1890, consisting of Good Thunder, Cloud Horse, Yellow Knife, and Short Bull. They confirmed the report of the first delegation, and on this assurance the Ghost dance was inaugurated among the Sioux at Pine Ridge in the spring of 1890.

The matter is stated differently and more correctly by William Selwyn, an educated Sioux, at that time employed as postmaster at Pine Ridge. He says there was some talk on the subject by Indians from western tribes who visited the agency in the fall of 1888 (?), but that it did not excite much attention until 1889, when numerous letters concerning the new messiah were received by the Indians at Pine Ridge from tribes in Utah, Wyoming, Montana, Dakota, and Oklahoma. As Selwyn was postmaster, the Indians who could not read usually brought their letters to him to read for them, so that he was thus in position to get accurate knowledge of the extent and nature of the excitement. It may be remarked here that, under present conditions, when the various tribes are isolated upon widely separated reservations, the Ghost dance could never have become so widespread, and would probably have died out within a year of its inception, had it not been for the efficient aid it received from the returned pupils of various eastern government schools, who conducted the sacred correspondence for their friends at the different agencies, acted as interpreters for the delegates to the messiah, and in various ways assumed the leadership and conduct of the dance.

In the fall of 1889, at a council held at Pine Ridge by Red Cloud, Young Man Afraid, Little Wound, American Horse, and other Sioux chiefs, a delegation was appointed to visit the western agencies to learn more about the new messiah. The delegates chosen were Good Thunder, Flat Iron, Yellow Breast, and Broken Arm, from Pine Ridge; Short Bull and another from Rosebud, and Kicking Bear from Cheyenne River agency. They started on their journey to the west, and soon began to write from Wyoming, Utah, and beyond the mountains, confirming all that had been said of the advent of a redeemer. They were gone all winter, and their return in the spring of 1890 aroused an intense excitement among the Sioux, who had been anxiously awaiting their report. All the delegates agreed that there was a man near the base of the Sierras who said that he was the son of God, who had once been killed by the whites, and who bore on his body the scars of the crucifixion. He had now returned to punish the whites for their wickedness, especially for their injustice toward the Indians. With the coming of the next spring (1891) he would wipe the whites from the face of the earth, and would then resurrect all the dead Indians, bring back the buffalo and other game, and restore the supremacy of the aboriginal race. He had before come to the whites, but they had rejected him. He was now the God of the Indians, and they must pray to him and call him "father," and prepare for his awful coming. Selwyn's account of this delegation, which was accompanied by representatives of several other tribes, including Porcupine the Cheyenne, and Sitting Bull the Arapaho, agrees with the statements of the Arapaho as given in chapter XIV. Three of the Sioux delegates found their way to Umatilla reservation in Oregon and remained there several days discussing the new doctrine. (*Comr., 30—Dorchester, 529.*)

The delegates made their report at Pine Ridge in April, 1890. A council was at once called to discuss the matter, but Selwyn informed the agent, Colonel Gallagher, who had Good Thunder and two others arrested and imprisoned. They were held in confinement two days, but refused to talk when questioned. The intended council was not held, but soon afterward Kicking Bear returned from a visit to the northern Arapaho in Wyoming with the news that those Indians were already dancing, and could see and talk with their dead relatives in the trance. The excitement which the agent had thought to smother by the arrest of the leaders broke out again with added strength. Red Cloud himself, the great chief of the Ogalala, declared his adhesion to the new doctrine and said his people must do as the messiah had commanded. Another council was called on White Clay creek, a few miles from Pine Ridge agency, and the Ghost dance was formally inaugurated among the Sioux, the recent delegates acting as priests and leaders of the ceremony.

As the result of all he could learn, Selwyn, in November, 1890, warned the agent in charge of Yankton agency that the Indians intended a general outbreak in the spring. Six months earlier, and before Porcupine's statement had been made to the officer at Camp Crook, a letter dated May 29, 1890, had been addressed to the Interior Department from a citizen of Pierre, South Dakota, stating that the Sioux, or a portion of them, were secretly planning for an outbreak in the near future. This was the first intimation of trouble ahead. (*G. D.*, *20*.)

Wonderful things were said of the messiah by the returned delegates. It was claimed that he could make animals talk and distant objects appear close at hand, and that he came down from heaven in a cloud. He conjured up before their eyes a vision of the spirit world, so that when they looked they beheld an ocean, and beyond it a land upon which they saw "all the nations of Indians coming home," but as they looked the vision faded away, the messiah saying that the time had not yet come. Curiously enough, although he came to restore the old life, he advised his hearers to go to work and to send their children to school. Should the soldiers attempt to harm him, he said he need only stretch out his arms and his enemies would become powerless, or the ground would open and swallow them. On their way home if they should kill a buffalo—the messiah had evidently not read Allen's monograph—they must cut off its head and tail and feet and leave them on the ground and the buffalo would come to life again. They must tell their people to follow his instructions. Unbelievers and renegade Indians would be buried under the new earth which was to come upon the old. They must use the sacred red and white paint and the sacred grass (possibly sagebrush) which he gave them, and in the spring, when the green grass came, their people who were gone before would return, and they would see their friends again.

Now comes the most remarkable part, quoting from the statement given to Captain Sword:

The people from every tipi send for us to visit them; they are people who died many years ago. Chasing Hawk, who died not long ago, was there and we went to his tipi. He was living with his wife, who was killed in war long ago. They live in a buffalo skin tipi—a very large one—and he wanted all his friends to go there to live. A son of Good Thunder, who died in war long ago, was one who also took us to his tipi, so his father saw him. When coming we come to a herd of buffaloes. We killed one and took everything except the four feet, head, and tail, and when we came a little ways from it there was the buffaloes come to life again and went off. This was one of the messiah's word came to truth. The messiah said, "I will short your journey when you feel tired of the long ways, if you call upon me." This we did when we were tired. The night came upon us, we stopped at a place and we called upon the messiah to help us because we were tired of long journey. We went to sleep and in the morning we found ourselves at a great distance from where we stopped.

It is useless to assert that these men, who had been selected by the chiefs of their tribe to investigate and report upon the truth or falsity of the messiah rumors, were all liars, and that all the Cheyenne, Arapaho, and other delegates who reported equally wonderful things were liars likewise. They were simply laboring under some strange psychologic influence as yet unexplained. The story of the revivified buffalo became so widely current as to form the subject of a Kiowa ghost song.

Having mentioned some characteristics of the Ghost dance west of the Rockies, we shall notice here some of the peculiar features of the dance as it existed among the Sioux. The ceremony will be described in detail later on.

Before going into the dance the men, or at least the leaders, fasted for twenty-four hours, and then at sunrise entered the sweat-house for the religious rite of purification preliminary to painting themselves for the dance. The sweat-house is a small circular framework of willow branches driven into the ground and bent over and brought together at the top in such a way that when covered with blankets or buffalo robes the structure forms a diminutive round-top tipi just high enough to enable several persons to sit or to stand in a stooping posture inside. The doorway faces the east, as is the rule in Indian structures, and at the distance of a few feet in front of the doorway is a small mound of earth, on which is placed a buffalo skull, with the head turned as if looking into the lodge. The earth of which the mound is formed is taken from a hole dug in the center of the lodge. Near the sweat-house, on the outside, there is frequently a tall sacrifice pole, from the top of which are hung strips of bright-colored cloth, packages of tobacco, or other offerings to the deity invoked by the devotee on any particular occasion.

The sweat bath is in frequent use, both as a religious rite of purification and as a hygienic treatment. Like everything else in Indian life, even the sanitary application is attended with much detail of religious ceremony. Fresh bundles of the fragrant wild sage are strewn upon the ground inside of the sweat-house, and a fire is kindled outside a short distance away. In this fire stones are heated by the medicine-men, and when all is ready the patient or devotee, stripped to the breech-cloth, enters the sweat-house. The stones are then handed in to him by the priests by means of two forked sticks, cut especially for the purpose, and with two other forked sticks he puts the stones into the hole already mentioned as having been dug in the center of the lodge. Water is then passed in to him, which he pours over the hot stones until the whole interior is filled with steam; the blankets are pulled

Fig. 6.—Sioux sweat-house and sacrifice pole

tight to close every opening, and he sits in this aboriginal Turkish bath
until his naked body is dripping with perspiration. During this time
the doctors outside are doing their part in the way of praying to the
gods and keeping up the supply of hot stones and water until in their
estimation he has been sufficiently purified, physically or morally, when
he emerges and resumes his clothing, sometimes first checking the
perspiration and inducing a reaction by a plunge into the neighboring
stream. The sweat bath in one form or another was common to almost
every tribe in the United States, but as an accompaniment to the Ghost
dance it seems to have been used only by the Sioux. It may have been
used in this connection among the Shoshoni or northern Cheyenne, but
was not among any of the tribes of the southern plains. The Ghost-
dance sweat-house of the Sioux was frequently made sufficiently large
to accommodate a considerable number of persons standing inside at
the same time.

After the sweating ceremony the dancer was painted by the medicine-
men who acted as leaders, of whom Sitting Bull was accounted the
greatest among the Sioux. The design and color varied with the individual, being frequently determined by a previous trance vision of
the subject, but circles, crescents, and crosses, representing respectively
the sun, the moon, and the morning star, were always favorite figures
upon forehead, face, and cheeks. As this was not a naked dance, the
rest of the body was not usually painted. After the painting the
dancer was robed in the sacred ghost shirt already described. This
also was painted with symbolic figures, among which were usually
represented sun, moon, or stars, the eagle, magpie, crow, or sage-hen,
all sacred to the Ghost dance among the Sioux. In connection with the
painting the face and body were rubbed with the sweet-smelling vernal
grass (*Hierochloe*), used for this purpose by many of the prairie tribes,
and sometimes also burned as incense in their sacred ceremonies or
carried as a perfume in small pouches attached to the clothing.

The painting occupied most of the morning, so that it was about noon
before the participants formed the circle for the dance. Among the
Sioux, unlike the southern and western tribes generally, a small tree
was planted in the center of the circle, with an American flag or colored
streamers floating from the top. Around the base of this tree sat the
priests. At a great dance at No Water's camp on White river near Pine
Ridge, shortly before the arrival of the troops, a young woman standing within the circle gave the signal for the performance by shooting
into the air toward the cardinal points four sacred arrows, made after
the old primitive fashion with bone heads, and dipped in the blood of a
steer before being brought to the dance. These were then gathered up
and tied to the branches of the tree, together with the bow, a gaming
wheel and sticks, and a peculiar staff or wand with horns. (See Figs.
38, 39.) Another young woman, or the same one, remained standing
near the tree throughout the dance, holding a sacred redstone pipe

stretched out toward the west, the direction from which the messiah was to appear.

At the beginning the performers, men and women, sat on the ground in a large circle around the tree. A plaintive chant was then sung, after which a vessel of some sacred food was passed around the circle until everyone had partaken, when, at a signal by the priests, the dancers rose to their feet, joined hands, and began to chant the opening song and move slowly around the circle from right to left. The rest of the performance, with its frenzies, trances, and recitals of visions, was the same as with the southern tribes, as will be described in detail hereafter. Like these tribes also, the Sioux usually selected Sunday, the great medicine day of the white man, for the ceremony.

We come now to the Sioux outbreak of 1890, but before going into the history of this short but costly war it is appropriate to state briefly the causes of the outbreak. In the documentary appendix to this chapter these causes are fully set forth by competent authorities—civilian, military, missionary, and Indian. They may be summarized as (1) unrest of the conservative element under the decay of the old life, (2) repeated neglect of promises made by the government, and (3) hunger.

The Sioux are the largest and strongest tribe within the United States. In spite of wars, removals, and diminished food supply since the advent of the white man, they still number nearly 26,000. In addition to these there are about 600 more residing in Canada. They formerly held the headwaters of the Mississippi, extending eastward almost to Lake Superior, but were driven into the prairie about two centuries ago by their enemies, the Ojibwa, after the latter had obtained firearms from the French. On coming out on the buffalo plains they became possessed of the horse, by means of which reinforcement to their own overpowering numbers the Sioux were soon enabled to assume the offensive, and in a short time had made themselves the undisputed masters of an immense territory extending, in a general way, from Minnesota to the Rocky mountains and from the Yellowstone to the Platte. A few small tribes were able to maintain their position within these limits, but only by keeping close to their strongly built permanent villages on the Missouri. Millions of buffalo to furnish unlimited food supply, thousands of horses, and hundreds of miles of free range made the Sioux, up to the year 1868, the richest and most prosperous, the proudest, and withal, perhaps, the wildest of all the tribes of the plains.

In that year, in pursuance of a policy inaugurated for bringing all the plains tribes under the direct control of the government, a treaty was negotiated with the Sioux living west of the Missouri by which they renounced their claims to a great part of their territory and had " set apart for their absolute and undisturbed use and occupation "— so the treaty states—a reservation which embraced all of the present state of South Dakota west of Missouri river. At the same time agents were appointed and agencies established for them; annuities and rations, cows, physicians, farmers, teachers, and other good things were promised them, and they agreed to allow railroad routes to be surveyed and built and military posts to be established in their territory and neighborhood. At one stroke they were reduced from a free nation to dependent wards of the government. It was stipulated also that they should be allowed to hunt within their old range, outside the limits of the reservation, so long as the buffalo abounded—a proviso which, to the Indians, must have meant forever.

The reservation thus established was an immense one, and would have been ample for all the Sioux while being gradually educated toward civilization, could the buffalo have remained and the white man kept away. But the times were changing. The building of the railroads brought into the plains swarms of hunters and emigrants, who began to exterminate the buffalo at such a rate that in a few years the Sioux, with all the other hunting tribes of the plains, realized that their food supply was rapidly going. Then gold was discovered in the Black hills, within the reservation, and at once thousands of miners and other thousands of lawless desperadoes rushed into the country in defiance of the protests of the Indians and the pledges of the government, and the Sioux saw their last remaining hunting ground taken from them. The result was the Custer war and massacre, and a new agreement in 1876 by which the Sioux were shorn of one-third of their guaranteed reservation, including the Black hills, and this led to deep and widespread dissatisfaction throughout the tribe. The conservatives brooded over the past and planned opposition to further changes which they felt themselves unable to meet. The progressives felt that the white man's promises meant nothing.

On this point Commissioner Morgan says, in his statement of the causes of the outbreak:

Prior to the agreement of 1876 buffalo and deer were the main support of the Sioux. Food, tents, bedding were the direct outcome of hunting, and with furs and pelts as articles of barter or exchange it was easy for the Sioux to procure whatever constituted for them the necessaries, the comforts, or even the luxuries of life. Within eight years from the agreement of 1876 the buffalo had gone and the Sioux had left to them alkali land and government rations. It is hard to overestimate the magnitude of the calamity, as they viewed it, which happened to these people by the sudden disappearance of the buffalo and the large diminution in the numbers of deer and other wild animals. Suddenly, almost without warning, they were expected at once and without previous training to settle down to the pursuits of agriculture in a land largely unfitted for such use. The freedom of the chase was to be exchanged for the idleness of the camp. The boundless range was to be abandoned for the circumscribed reservation, and abundance of plenty to be supplanted by limited and decreasing government subsistence and supplies. Under these circumstances it is not in human nature not to be discontented and restless, even turbulent and violent. (*Comr., 28.*)

It took our own Aryan ancestors untold centuries to develop from savagery into civilization. Was it reasonable to expect that the Sioux could do the same in fourteen years?

The white population in the Black hills had rapidly increased, and it had become desirable to open communication between eastern and western Dakota. To accomplish this, it was proposed to cut out the heart of the Sioux reservation, and in 1882, only six years after the Black hills had been seized, the Sioux were called on to surrender more territory. A commission was sent out to treat with them, but the price offered—only about 8 cents per acre—was so absurdly small, and the methods used so palpably unjust, that friends of the Indians interposed and succeeded in defeating the measure in Congress. Another agreement was prepared, but experience had made the Indians suspicious, and it was not until a third commission went out, under the chairmanship of General Crook, known to the Indians as a brave soldier and an honorable man, that the Sioux consented to treat. (*Welsh, 1.*) The result, after much effort on the part of the commission and determined opposition by the conservatives, was another agreement, in 1889, by which the Sioux surrendered one-half (about 11,000,000 acres) of their remaining territory, and the great reservation was cut up into five smaller ones, the northern and southern reservations being separated by a strip 60 miles wide.

Then came a swift accumulation of miseries. Dakota is an arid country with thin soil and short seasons. Although well adapted to grazing it is not suited to agriculture, as is sufficiently proven by the fact that the white settlers in that and the adjoining state of Nebraska have several times been obliged to call for state or federal assistance on account of failure of crops. To wild Indians hardly in from the warpath the problem was much more serious. As General Miles points out in his official report, thousands of white settlers after years of successive failures had given up the struggle and left the country, but the Indians, confined to reservations, were unable to emigrate, and were also as a rule unable to find employment, as the whites might, by which they could earn a subsistence. The buffalo was gone. They must depend on their cattle, their crops, and the government rations issued in return for the lands they had surrendered. If these failed, they must starve. The highest official authorities concur in the statement that all of these did fail, and that the Indians were driven to outbreak by starvation. (See appendix to this chapter.)

In 1888 their cattle had been diminished by disease. In 1889 their crops were a failure, owing largely to the fact that the Indians had been called into the agency in the middle of the farming season and kept there to treat with the commission, going back afterward to find their fields trampled and torn up by stock during their absence. Then followed epidemics of measles, grippe, and whooping cough, in rapid succession and with terribly fatal results. Anyone who understands the Indian character needs not the testimony of witnesses to know the mental effect thus produced. Sullenness and gloom, amounting almost to despair, settled down on the Sioux, especially among the wilder portion. "The people said their children were all dying from the face of the earth, and they might as well be killed at once." Then came another entire failure of crops in 1890, and an unexpected reduction of rations, and the Indians were brought face to face with starvation. They had been expressly and repeatedly told by the commission that their rations would not be affected by their signing the treaty, but immediately on the consummation of the agreement Congress cut down their beef rations by 2,000,000 pounds at Rosebud, 1,000,000 at Pine Ridge, and in less proportion at other agencies. Earnest protest against this reduction was made by the commission which had negotiated the treaty, by Commissioner Morgan, and by General Miles, but still Congress failed to remedy the matter until the Sioux had actually been driven to rebellion. As Commissioner Morgan states, "It was not until January, 1891, *after the troubles*, that an appropriation of $100,000 was made by Congress for additional beef for the Sioux." The protest of the commission, a full year before the outbreak, as quoted by Commissioner Morgan (see page 74), is strong and positive on this point.

Commissioner Morgan, while claiming that the Sioux had before been receiving more rations than they were justly entitled to according to their census number, and denying that the reduction was such as to cause even extreme suffering, yet states that the reduction was especially unwise at this juncture, as it was in direct violation of the promises made to the Indians, and would be used as an argument by those opposed to the treaty to show that the government cared nothing for the Indians after it had obtained their lands. It is quite possible that the former number of rations was greater than the actual number of persons, as it is always a difficult matter to count roving Indians, and the difficulties were greater when the old census was made. The census is taken at long intervals and the tendency is nearly always toward a decrease. Furthermore, it has usually been the policy with agents to hold their Indians quiet by keeping them as well fed as possible. On the other hand, it must be remembered that the issue is based on the weight of the cattle as delivered at the agency in the fall, and that months of exposure to a Dakota winter will reduce this weight by several hundred pounds to the animal. The official investigation by Captain Hurst at Cheyenne River agency shows conclusively that the essential food items of meat, flour, and coffee were far below the amount stipulated by the treaty. (See page 82.)

In regard to the effect of this food deficiency Bishop Hare says: "The people were often hungry and, the physicians in many cases said, died, when taken sick, not so much from disease as for want of food." General Miles says: "The fact that they had not received sufficient food is admitted by the agents and the officers of the government who have had opportunities of knowing," and in another place he states that in spite of crop failures and other difficulties, after the sale of the reservation "instead of an increase, or even a reasonable supply for their support, they have been compelled to live on half and two-thirds rations and received nothing for the surrender of their lands." The testimony from every agency is all to the same effect.

There were other causes of dissatisfaction, some local and others general and chronic, which need not be detailed here. Some of these are treated in the documents appended to this chapter. Prominent among them were the failure of Congress to make payment of the money due the Sioux for the lands recently ceded, or to have the new lines surveyed promptly so that the Indians might know what was still theirs and select their allotments accordingly; failure to reimburse the friendly Indians for horses confiscated fourteen years before; the tardy arrival of annuities, consisting largely of winter clothing, which according to the treaty were due by the 1st of August, but which seldom arrived until the middle of winter; the sweeping and frequent changes of agency employees from the agent down, preventing anything like a systematic working out of any consistent policy, and almost always operating against the good of the service, especially at Pine Ridge, where so brave and efficient a man as McGillycuddy was followed by such a one as Royer—and, finally, the Ghost dance.

The Ghost dance itself, in the form which it assumed among the Sioux, was only a symptom and expression of the real causes of dissatisfaction, and with such a man as McGillycuddy or McLaughlin in charge at Pine Ridge there would have been no outbreak, in spite of broken promises and starvation, and the Indians could have been controlled until Congress had afforded relief. That it was not the cause of the outbreak is sufficiently proved by the fact that there was no serious trouble, excepting on the occasion of the attempt to arrest Sitting Bull, on any other of the Sioux reservations, and none at all among any of the other Ghost-dancing tribes from the Missouri to the Sierras, although the doctrine and the dance were held by nearly every tribe within that area and are still held by the more important. Among the Paiute, where the doctrine originated and the messiah has his home, there was never the slightest trouble. It is significant that Commissioner Morgan in his official statement of the causes of the outbreak places the "messiah craze" eleventh in a list of twelve, the twelfth being the alarm created by the appearance of troops. The Sioux outbreak of 1890 was due entirely to local grievances, recent or long standing. The remedy and preventive for similar trouble in the future is sufficiently indicated in the appended statements of competent authorities.

APPENDIX—CAUSES OF THE OUTBREAK

COMMISSIONER MORGAN'S STATEMENT

[*From the Report of the Commissioner of Indian Affairs for 1891, Vol. I, 132-135.*]

In stating the events which led to this outbreak among the Sioux, the endeavor too often has been merely to find some opportunity for locating blame. The causes are complex, and many are obscure and remote. Among them may be named the following:

First. A feeling of unrest and apprehension in the mind of the Indians has naturally grown out of the rapid advance in civilization and the great changes which this advance has necessitated in their habits and mode of life.

Second. Prior to the agreement of 1876 buffalo and deer were the main support of the Sioux. Food, tents, bedding were the direct outcome of hunting, and, with furs and pelts as articles of barter or exchange, it was easy for the Sioux to procure whatever constituted for them the necessaries, the comforts, or even the luxuries of life. Within eight years from the agreement of 1876 the buffalo had gone, and the Sioux had left to them alkali land and government rations. It is hard to overestimate the magnitude of the calamity, as they viewed it, which happened to these people by the sudden disappearance of the buffalo and the large diminution in the numbers of deer and other wild animals. Suddenly, almost without warning, they were expected at once and without previous training to settle down to the pursuits of agriculture in a land largely unfitted for such use. The freedom of the chase was to be exchanged for the idleness of the camp. The boundless range was to be abandoned for the circumscribed reservation, and abundance of plenty to be supplanted by limited and decreasing government subsistence and supplies. Under these circumstances it is not in human nature not to be discontented and restless, even turbulent and violent.

Third. During a long series of years, treaties, agreements, cessions of land and privileges, and removals of bands and agencies have kept many of the Sioux, particularly those at Pine Ridge and Rosebud, in an unsettled condition, especially as some of the promises made them were fulfilled tardily or not at all. (A brief history of negotiations with the Sioux was given in my letter of December 24, 1890, to the Department, which will be found in the appendix, page 182.)

Fourth. The very large reduction of the great Sioux reservation, brought about by the Sioux commission through the consent of the large majority of the adult males, was bitterly opposed by a large, influential minority. For various reasons, they regarded the cession as unwise, and did all in their power to prevent its consummation, and afterwards were constant in their expressions of dissatisfaction and in their endeavors to awaken a like feeling in the minds of those who signed the agreement.

Fifth. There was diminution and partial failure of the crops for 1889, by reason of their neglect by the Indians, who were congregated in large numbers at the council with the Sioux commission, and a further diminution of ordinary crops by the drought of 1890. Also, in 1888, the disease of black leg appeared among the cattle of the Indians.

Sixth. At this time, by delayed and reduced appropriations, the Sioux rations were temporarily cut down. Rations were not diminished to such an extent as to bring the Indians to starvation or even extreme suffering, as has been often reported; but short rations came just after the Sioux commission had negotiated the agreement for the cession of lands, and, as a condition of securing the signatures of the majority, had assured the Indians that their rations would be continued unchanged. To this matter the Sioux commission called special attention in their report dated December 24, 1889, as follows:

"During our conference at the different agencies we were repeatedly asked whether the acceptance or rejection of the act of Congress would influence the action of the government with reference to their rations, and in every instance the Indians were assured that subsistence was furnished in accordance with former treaties, and that signing would not affect their rations, and that they would continue to receive them as provided in former treaties. Without our assurances to this effect it would have been impossible to have secured their consent to the cession of their lands. Since our visit to the agencies it appears that large reductions have been made in the amounts of beef furnished for issues, amounting at Rosebud to 2,000,000 pounds and at Pine Ridge to 1,000,000 pounds, and lesser amounts at the other agencies. This action of the Department, following immediately after the successful issue of our negotiations, can not fail to have an injurious effect. It will be impossible to convince the Indians that the reduction is not due to the fact that the government, having obtained their land, has less concern in looking after their material interests than before. It will be looked upon as a breach of faith and especially as a violation of the express statements of the commissioners. Already this action is being used by the Indians opposed to the bill, notably at Pine Ridge, as an argument in support of the wisdom of their opposition."

In forwarding this report to Congress the Department called special attention to the above-quoted statements of the commission and said: "The commission further remarks that as to the quality of the rations furnished there seems to be no just cause for complaint, but that it was particularly to be avoided that there should be any diminution of the rations promised under the former treaties at this time, as the Indians would attribute it to their assent to the bill. Such diminution certainly should not be allowed, as the government is bound in good faith to carry into effect the former treaties where not directly and positively affected by the act, and if under the provisions of the treaty itself the ration is at any time reduced, the commissioners recommend that the Indians should be notified before spring opens, so that crops may be cultivated. It is desirable that the recent reduction made should be restored, as it is now impossible to convince the Indians that it was not due to the fact that the government, having obtained their lands, had less concern in looking after their material interests."

Notwithstanding this plea of the commission and of the Department, the appropriation made for the subsistence and civilization of the Sioux for 1890 was only $950,000, or $50,000 less than the amount estimated and appropriated for 1888 and 1889, and the appropriation not having been made until August 19, rations had to be temporarily purchased and issued in limited quantities pending arrival of new supplies to be secured from that appropriation. It was not until January, 1891, after the troubles, that an appropriation of $100,000 was made by Congress for additional beef for the Sioux.

Seventh. Other promises made by the Sioux commission and the agreement were not promptly fulfilled; among them were increase of appropriations for education, for which this office had asked an appropriation of $150,000; the payment of $200,000 in compensation for ponies taken from the Sioux in 1876 and 1877; and the reimbursement of the Crow Creek Indians for a reduction made in their per capita allowance of land, as compared with the amount allowed other Sioux, which called for an appropriation of $187,039. The fulfillment of all these promises except the last named was contained in the act of January 19, 1891.

Eighth. In 1889 and 1890 epidemics of la grippe, measles, and whooping cough, followed by many deaths, added to the gloom and misfortune which seemed to surround the Indians.

Ninth. The wording of the agreement changed the boundary line between the Rosebud and Pine Ridge diminished reservations and necessitated a removal of a portion of the Rosebud Indians from the lands which, by the agreement, were included in the Pine Ridge reservation to lands offered them in lieu thereof upon the diminished Rosebud reserve. This, although involving no great hardship to any considerable number, added to the discontent.

Tenth. Some of the Indians were greatly opposed to the census which Congress ordered should be taken. The census at Rosebud, as reported by Special Agent Lea and confirmed by a special census taken by Agent Wright, revealed the somewhat startling fact that rations had been issued to Indians very largely in excess of the number actually present, and this diminution of numbers as shown by the census necessitated a diminution of the rations, which was based, of course, upon the census.

Eleventh. The Messiah craze, which fostered the belief that "ghost shirts" would be invulnerable to bullets, and that the supremacy of the Indian race was assured, added to discontent the fervor of fanaticism and brought those who accepted the new faith into the attitude of sullen defiance, but defensive rather than aggressive.

Twelfth. The sudden appearance of military upon their reservation gave rise to the wildest rumors among the Indians of danger and disaster, which were eagerly circulated by disaffected Indians and corroborated by exaggerated accounts in the newspapers, and these and other influences connected with and inseparable from military movements frightened many Indians away from their agencies into the bad lands and largely intensified whatever spirit of opposition to the government existed

EX-AGENT McGILLYCUDDY'S STATEMENT

[*Letter of Dr V. T. McGillycuddy, formerly agent at Pine Ridge, written in reply to inquiry from General L. W. Colby, commanding Nebraska state troops during the outbreak, and dated January 15, 1891. From article on "The Sioux Indian War of 1890–91," by General L. W. Colby, in Transactions and Reports of the Nebraska State Historical Society, III, 1892, pages 176–180.*]

SIR: In answer to your inquiry of a recent date, I would state that in my opinion to no one cause can be attributed the recent so-called outbreak on the part of the Sioux, but rather to a combination of causes gradually cumulative in their effect and dating back through many years—in fact to the inauguration of our practically demonstrated faulty Indian policy.

There can be no question but that many of the treaties, agreements, or solemn promises made by our government with these Indians have been broken. Many of them have been kept by us technically, but as far as the Indian is concerned have been misunderstood by him through a lack of proper explanation at time of signing, and hence considered by him as broken.

It must also be remembered that in all of the treaties made by the government with the Indians, a large portion of them have not agreed to or signed the same. Noticeably was this so in the agreement secured by us with them the summer before last, by which we secured one-half of the remainder of the Sioux reserve, amounting to about 16,000 square miles. This agreement barely carried with the Sioux nation as a whole, but did not carry at Pine Ridge or Rosebud, where the strong majority were against it; and it must be noted that wherever there was the strongest opposition manifested to the recent treaty, there, during the present trouble, have been found the elements opposed to the government.

The Sioux nation, which at one time, with the confederated bands of Cheyennes and Arapahos, controlled a region of country bounded on the north by the Yellowstone, on the south by the Arkansas, and reaching from the Missouri river to the Rocky mountains, has seen this large domain, under the various treaties, dwindle down to their now limited reserve of less than 16,000 square miles, and with the land has disappeared the buffalo and other game. The memory of this, chargeable by them to the white man, necessarily irritates them.

There is back of all this the natural race antagonism which our dealings with the aborigine in connection with the inevitable onward march of civilization has in no degree lessened. It has been our experience, and the experience of other nations, that defeat in war is soon, not sooner or later, forgotten by the coming generation, and as a result we have a tendency to a constant recurrence of outbreak on the part of the weaker race. It is now sixteen years since our last war with the Sioux in 1876—a time when our present Sioux warriors were mostly children, and therefore have no memory of having felt the power of the government. It is but natural that these young warriors, lacking in experience, should require but little incentive to induce them to test the bravery of the white man on the war path, where the traditions of his people teach him is the only path to glory and a chosen seat in the "happy hunting grounds." For these reasons every precaution should be adopted by the government to guard against trouble with its disastrous results. Have such precautions been adopted? Investigation of the present trouble does not so indicate.

Sitting Bull and other irreconcilable relics of the campaign of 1876 were allowed to remain among their people and foment discord. The staple article of food at Pine Ridge and some of the other agencies had been cut down below the subsisting point, noticeably the beef at Pine Ridge, which from an annual treaty allowance of 6,250,000 pounds gross was cut down to 4,000,000 pounds. The contract on that beef was violated, insomuch as that contract called for northern ranch beef, for which was substituted through beef from Texas, with an unparalleled resulting shrinkage in winter, so that the Indians did not actually receive half ration of this food in winter—the very time the largest allowance of food is required. By the fortunes of political war, weak agents were placed in charge of some of the agencies at the very time that trouble was known to be brewing. Noticeably was this so at Pine Ridge, where a notoriously weak and unfit man was placed in charge. His flight, abandonment of his agency, and his call for troops have, with the horrible results of the same, become facts in history.

Now, as for facts in connection with Pine Ridge, which agency has unfortunately become the theater of the present "war," was there necessity for troops? My past experience with those Indians does not so indicate. For seven long years, from 1879 to 1886, I, as agent, managed this agency without the presence of a soldier on the reservation, and none nearer than 60 miles, and in those times the Indians were naturally much wilder than they are to-day. To be sure, during the seven years we occasionally had exciting times, when the only thing lacking to cause an outbreak was the calling for troops by the agent and the presence of the same. As a matter of fact, however, no matter how much disturbed affairs were, no matter how imminent an outbreak, the progressive chiefs, with their following, came to the front enough in the majority, with the fifty Indian policemen, to at once crush out all attempts at rebellion against the authority of the agent and the government.

Why was this? Because in those times we believed in placing confidence in the Indians; in establishing, as far as possible, a home-rule government on the reservation. We established local courts, presided over by the Indians, with Indian juries; in fact, we believed in having the Indians assist in working out their own salvation. We courted and secured the friendship and support of the progressive and orderly element, as against the mob element. Whether the system thus inaugurated was practicable, was successful, comparison with recent events will decide.

When my Democratic successor took charge in 1886, he deemed it necessary to make general changes in the system at Pine Ridge, i. e., a Republican system. All white men, half-breeds, or Indians who had sustained the agent under the former administration were classed as Republicans and had to go. The progressive chiefs, such as Young Man Afraid, Little Wound, and White Bird, were ignored, and the backing of the element of order and progress was alienated from the agent and the government, and in the place of this strong backing that had maintained order for seven years was substituted Red Cloud and other nonprogressive chiefs, sustainers of the ancient tribal system.

If my successor had been other than an amateur, or had had any knowledge or experience in the inside Indian politics of an Indian tribe, he would have known that if the element he was endeavoring to relegate to the rear had not been the balance of power, I could not for seven years have held out againt the mob element which he now sought to put in power. In other words, he unwittingly threw the balance of power at Pine Ridge against the government, as he later on discovered to his cost. When still later he endeavored to maintain order and suppress the ghost dance, the attempt resulted in a most dismal failure.

The Democratic agent was succeeded in October last by the recently removed Republican agent, a gentleman totally ignorant of Indians and their peculiarities; a gentleman with not a qualification in his make-up calculated to fit him for the position of agent at one of the largest and most difficult agencies in the service to manage; a man selected solely as a reward for political services. He might possibly have been an average success as an Indian agent at a small, well-regulated agency. He endeavored to strengthen up matters, but the chiefs and leaders who could have assisted him in so doing had been alienated by the former agent. They virtually said among themselves, "We, after incurring the enmity of the bad element among our people by sustaining the government, have been ignored and ill-treated by that government, hence this is not our affair." Being ignorant of the situation, he had no one to depend on. In his first clash with the mob element he discovered that the Pine Ridge police, formerly the finest in the service, were lacking in discipline and courage, and, not being well supplied with those necessary qualities himself, he took the bluff of a mob for a declaration of war, abandoned his agency, returned with troops—and you see the result.

As for the ghost dance, too much attention has been paid to it. It was only the symptom or surface indication of deep-rooted, long-existing difficulty; as well treat the eruption of smallpox as the disease and ignore the constitutional disease.

As regards disarming the Sioux, however desirable it may appear, I consider it neither advisable nor practicable. I fear that it will result as the theoretical enforcement of prohibition in Kansas, Iowa, and Dakota; you will succeed in disarming the friendly Indians, because you can, and you will not so succeed with the mob element, because you can not. If I were again to be an Indian agent and had my choice, I would take charge of 10,000 armed Sioux in preference to a like number of disarmed ones; and, furthermore, agree to handle that number, or the whole Sioux nation, without a white soldier.

Respectfully, etc, V. T. McGILLYCUDDY.

P. S.—I neglected to state that up to date there has been neither a Sioux outbreak nor war. No citizen in Nebraska or Dakota has been killed, molested, or can show the scratch of a pin, and no property has been destroyed off the reservation.

STATEMENT OF GENERAL MILES

[*From the Report of the Secretary of War for 1891, Vol. I, pp, 133, 134, and 149. He enumerates specific causes of complaint at each of the principal Sioux agencies, all of whic! causes may be summarized as hunger and unfulfilled promises.*]

Cause of Indian dissatisfaction.—The causes that led to the serious disturbance of the peace in the northwest last autumn and winter were so remarkable that an explanation of them is necessary in order to comprehend the seriousness of the situation. The Indians assuming the most threatening attitude of hostility were the Cheyennes and Sioux. Their condition may be stated as follows: For several years following their subjugation in 1877, 1878, and 1879 the most dangerous element of the Cheyennes and the Sioux were under military control. Many of them were disarmed and dismounted; their war ponies were sold and the proceeds returned to them in domestic stock, farming utensils, wagons, etc. Many of the Cheyennes, under the charge of military officers, were located on land in accordance with the laws of Congress, but after they were turned over to civil agents and the vast herds of buffalo and large game had been destroyed their supplies were insufficient, and they were forced to kill cattle belonging to white people to sustain life.

The fact that they had not received sufficient food is admitted by the agents and the officers of the government who have had opportunities of knowing. The majority of the Sioux were under the charge of civil agents, frequently changed and often inexperienced. Many of the tribes became rearmed and remounted. They claimed that the government had not fulfilled its treaties and had failed to make large enough appropriations for their support; that they had suffered for want of food, and the evidence of this is beyond question and sufficient to satisfy any unprejudiced intelligent mind. The statements of officers, inspectors, both of the military and the Interior departments, of agents, of missionaries, and civilians familiar with their condition, leave no room for reasonable doubt that this was one of the principal causes. While statements may be made as to the amount of money that has been expended by the government to feed the different tribes, the manner of distributing those appropriations will furnish one reason for the deficit.

The unfortunate failure of the crops in the plains country during the years of 1889 and 1890 added to the distress and suffering of the Indians, and it was possible for them to raise but very little from the ground for self-support; in fact, white settlers have been most unfortunate, and their losses have been serious and universal throughout a large section of that country. They have struggled on from year to year; occasionally they would raise good crops, which they were compelled to sell at low prices, while in the season of drought their labor was almost entirely lost. So serious have been their misfortunes that thousands have left that country within the last few years, passing over the mountains to the Pacific slope or returning to the east of the Missouri or the Mississippi.

The Indians, however, could not migrate from one part of the United States to another; neither could they obtain employment as readily as white people, either upon or beyond the Indian reservations. They must remain in comparative idleness and accept the results of the drought—an insufficient supply of food. This created a feeling of discontent even among the loyal and well disposed and added to the feeling of hostility of the element opposed to every process of civilization.

Reports forwarded by Brigadier-General Ruger, commanding Department of Dakota, contained the following:

The commanding officer at Fort Yates, North Dakota, under date of December 7, 1890, at the time the Messiah delusion was approaching a climax, says, in reference to the disaffection of the Sioux Indians at Standing Rock agency, that it is due to the following causes:

(1) Failure of the government to establish an equitable southern boundary of the Standing Rock agency reservation.

(2) Failure of the government to expend a just proportion of the money received from the Chicago, Milwaukee and St. Paul railroad company, for right of way privileges, for the benefit of the Indians of said agency. Official notice was received October 18, 1881, by the Indian agent at the Standing Rock agency, that the said railroad company had paid the government under its agreement with the Sioux Indians, for right of way privileges, the sum of $13,911. What additional payments, if any, have been made by the said railroad company, and what payments have been made by the Dakota Central railroad company, the records of the agency do not show. In 1883, and again in 1885, the agent, upon complaints made by the Indians, wrote to the Commissioner of Indian Affairs, making certain recommendations as regards the expenditure of the money received from the said railroad company, but was in each instance informed that until Congress took action with respect to the funds referred to nothing could be done. No portion of the money had been expended up to that time (December, 1890) for the benefit of the Indians of the agency, and frequent complaints had been made to the agent by the Indians because they had received no benefits from their concessions to the said railroad companies.

(3) Failure of the government to issue the certificates of title to allotments, as required by article 6 of the treaty of 1868.

(4) Failure of the government to provide the full allowance of seeds and agricultural implements to Indians engaged in farming, as required in article 8, treaty of 1868.

(5) Failure of the government to issue to such Indians the full number of cows and oxen provided in article 10, treaty of 1876.

(7) Failure of the government to issue to the Indians the full ration stipulated in article 5, treaty of 1876. (For the fiscal year beginning July 1, 1890, the following shortages in the rations were found to exist: 485,275 pounds of beef [gross], 761,212 pounds of corn, 11,937 pounds of coffee, 281,712 pounds of flour, 26,234 pounds of sugar, and 39,852 pounds of beans. Although the obligations of the government extend no further than furnishing so much of the ration prescribed in article 5 as may be necessary for the support of the Indians, it would seem that, owing to the almost total failure of crops upon the Standing Rock reservation for the past four years, and the absence of game, the necessity for the issue of the full ration to the Indians here was never greater than at the present time—December, 1890.)

(8) Failure of the government to issue to the Indians the full amount of annuity supplies to which they were entitled under the provisions of article 10, treaty of 1868.

(9) Failure of the government to have the clothing and other annuity supplies ready for issue on the first day of August of each year. Such supplies have not been ready for issue to the Indians, as a rule, until the winter season is well advanced. (After careful examination at this agency, the commanding officer is convinced that not more than two-thirds of the supplies provided in article 10 have been issued there, and the government has never complied with that provision of article 10 which requires the supplies enumerated in paragraphs 2, 3, and 4 of said article to be delivered on or before the first day of August of each year. Such supplies for the present fiscal year, beginning July 1, 1890, had not yet reached (December, 1890) the nearest railway station, about 60 miles distant, from which point they must, at this season of the year, be freighted to this agency in wagons. It is now certain that the winter will be well advanced before the Indians at this agency receive their annual allowance of clothing and other annuity supplies.)

(10) Failure of the government to appropriate money for the payment of the Indians for the ponies taken from them, by the authority of the government, in 1876.

In conclusion, the commanding officer says: "It, however, appears from the foregoing, that the government has failed to fulfill its obligations, and in order to render the Indians law-abiding, peaceful, contented, and prosperous it is strongly recommended that the treaties be promptly and fully carried out, and that the promises made by the commission in 1889 be faithfully kept."

[*The reports from Pine Ridge, Rosebud, Cheyenne River, and Yankton agencies are of similar tenor. Following are two telegrams sent from the field by General Miles at the beginning of the trouble.*]

RAPID CITY, SOUTH DAKOTA, *December 19, 1890.*

Senator DAWES,
    Washington, District of Columbia:

You may be assured of the following facts that can not be gainsaid:

First. The forcing process of attempting to make large bodies of Indians self-sustaining when the government was cutting down their rations and their crops almost a failure, is one cause of the difficulty.

Second. While the Indians were urged and almost forced to sign a treaty presented to them by the commission authorized by Congress, in which they gave up a valuable portion of their reservation which is now occupied by white people, the government has failed to fulfill its part of the compact, and instead of an increase or even a reasonable supply for their support, they have been compelled to live on half and two-thirds rations, and received nothing for the surrender of their lands, neither has the government given any positive assurance that they intend to do any differently with them in the future.

Congress has been in session several weeks and could, if it were disposed, in a few hours confirm the treaties that its commissioners have made with these Indians and appropriate the necessary funds for its fulfillment, and thereby give an earnest of their good faith or intention to fulfill their part of the compact. Such action, in my judgment, is essential to restore confidence with the Indians and give peace and protection to the settlements. If this be done, and the President authorized to place the turbulent and dangerous tribes of Indians under the control of the military, Congress need not enter into details, but can safely trust the military authorities to subjugate and govern, and in the near future make self-sustaining, any or all of the Indian tribes of this country.

RAPID CITY, SOUTH DAKOTA, *December 19, 1890.*

General JOHN M. SCHOFIELD,
  Commanding the Army, Washington, District of Columbia:

Replying to your long telegram, one point is of vital importance—the difficult Indian problem can not be solved permanently at this end of the line. It requires the fulfillment by Congress of the treaty obligations which the Indians were entreated and coerced into signing. They signed away a valuable portion of their reservation, and it is now occupied by white people, for which they have received nothing. They understood that ample provision would be made for their support; instead, their supplies have been reduced, and much of the time they have been living on half and two-thirds rations. Their crops, as well as the crops of the white people, for two years have been almost a total failure. The disaffection is widespread, especially among the Sioux, while the Cheyennes have been on the verge of starvation and were forced to commit depredations to sustain life. These facts are beyond question, and the evidence is positive and sustained by thousands of witnesses. Serious difficulty has been gathering for years. Congress has been in session several weeks and could in a single hour confirm the treaties and appropriate the necessary funds for their fulfillment, which their commissioners and the highest officials of the government have guaranteed to these people, and unless the officers of the army can give some positive assurance that the government intends to act in good faith with these people, the loyal element will be diminished and the hostile element increased. If the government will give some positive assurance that it will fulfill its part of the understanding with these 20,000 Sioux Indians, they can safely trust the military authorities to subjugate, control, and govern these turbulent people, and I hope that you will ask the Secretary of War and the Chief Executive to bring this matter directly to the attention of Congress.

REPORT OF CAPTAIN HURST

(A. G. O. Doc. 6266—1891.)

FORT BENNETT, SOUTH DAKOTA, *January 9, 1891.*

ASSISTANT ADJUTANT-GENERAL,
  Department of Dakota, Saint Paul, Minnesota.

SIR: In compliance with instructions of the department commander—copy attached marked A—I have the honor to submit the following report as the result of my investigations into the matters referred to therein.

I have been at this post continuously since August 6, 1887, and inspector of Indian supplies at the Cheyenne River Indian agency, located here, during that period, and am at the present time.

The Indians of this agency have a standing list of grievances which they present at every opportunity, and talk about in council when they assemble at every monthly ration issue. The Indians most persistent in recounting and proclaiming their grievances are those least willing to help in bettering their condition, and who are opposed to any change or improvement of their old habits and customs, and oppose all progress. Of this class I cite Big Foot's band of irreconcilables—who have now ceased to complain—and those in accord with them. Except in the matter of short rations, the story of their wrongs needs no attention. It commences with a recital of the wrong done them by the white race sharing the earth with them.

The other class, comprising a large majority of Indians of the reservation, have accepted the situation forced upon them, and have been for years bravely struggling in the effort to reconcile themselves to the ways of civilization and moral progress, with a gratifying degree of success. It is this class whose complaints and grievances demand considerate attention. They complain in true Indian style that they only have kept faith in all treaties made with them, and that somehow the treaties when they appeared in print were not in many respects the treaties which they signed.

They complain principally —

(1) That the boundaries of the reservation in the treaty of 1877 are not what they agreed to and thought they were signing on the paper, and they especially emphasize the point that the line of the western boundary should be a *straight line* at the Black Hills, instead of as it appears on the maps.

(2) That they have never received full recompense for the ponies taken from them in 1876.

(3) That the game has been destroyed and driven out of the country by the white people.

(4) That their children are taken from them to eastern schools and kept for years, instead of being educated among them.

(5) That when these eastern graduates return to them with civilized habits, education, and trades, there is no provision made on the reservation for their employment and improvement to the benefit of themselves and their people.

(6) That the agents and employees sent out to them have not all been "good men" and considerate of their (the Indians') interests and welfare.

(7) That the issue of their annuity goods is delayed so late in the winter as to cause them much suffering.

(8) That they are expected to plow the land and raise grain when the climate will not permit them to reap a crop. They think cattle should be issued to them for breeding purposes instead of farming implements for useless labor.

(9) That the rations issued to them are insufficient in quantity and frequently (beef and flour) very poor in quality.

Complaints 2, 3, 4, 5, 7, 8, and 9 are all well founded and justified by the facts in each case, No. 9 especially so, and this through no fault or negligence of the agent. The agent makes his annual estimate for sustenance in kind for the number of people borne on his rolls, based on the stipulated ration in treaty of 1877. This estimate is modified or cut down in the Indian Commissioner's office to meet the requirements of a limited or reduced Congressional appropriation, and when it returns to the agent's hands approved, he finds that he has just so many pounds of beef and flour, etc, placed to his credit for the year, without regard to whether they constitute the full number of treaty rations or not. There is no allowance given him for loss by shrinkage, wastage, or other unavoidable loss, and with the very best efforts and care in the distribution throughout the year of this usually reduced allowance there can not be issued to each Indian his treaty ration nor enough to properly sustain life. As a general thing the Indians of this reservation have been compelled to purchase food according to their means, between ration issues. Those having no means of purchase have suffered.

The half pound of flour called for by the treaty ration could not be issued in full, and the half pound of corn required has never been issued nor anything in lieu of it. In the item of beef but 1 pound was issued instead of the pound and a half called for in the treaty, and during the early spring months, when the cattle on the range are thin and poor, the pound of beef issued to the Indian is but a fraction of the pound issued to him on the agent's returns, and, under the system of purchase in practice until the present fiscal year, must necessarily be so. The agent's purchase of the beef supply on the hoof for the year, under contract, is closed in the month of November, from which time he has to herd them the balance of the year as best he can. He is responsible for the weight they show on the scales when *fat and in prime condition*, so that a steer weighing 1,200 pounds in the fall must represent 1,200 pounds in April, while in fact it may be but skin, horns, and bones, and weigh scarcely 600 pounds, while he has done his best to care for them during the severity of a Dakota winter. The Indians do not understand why they should be made to suffer all this shrinkage and loss, and it is a useless and humiliating attempt to explain. The agent is not to blame. The department of Indian affairs can do only the best it can with a limited and tardy appropriation. The remedy in the matter of food supply seems to be: A sufficient and earlier appropriation of funds. All contracts for the beef supply should call for delivery when required by the agent. The agent should be allowed a percentage of wastage to cover unavoidable loss in issue by shrinkage and wastage. The government should bear this loss and not the Indians.

Complaint 1: No remarks.

Complaint 2: Is before Congress.

Complaint 4: Should be remedied by adequate home schools.

Complaint 5: Suggests its proper remedy.

Complaint 6: No remarks.

Complaint 7: Can be remedied only by earlier appropriations.

Complaint 8: This reservation is not agricultural land. The climate makes it a grazing country. The Indians now can raise cattle successfully and care for them in winter. All attempts at general farming must result in failure on account of climatic conditions.

In connection with complaint 9, I respectfully invite attention to tabular statement accompanying this report, marked B, showing rations as issued up to December 6 in present fiscal year and amount required to make the issues according to article 5, treaty of February 27, 1877, and special attention to columns 6 and 7 therein.

Appended to this report, marked C, is an extract copy of treaties of 1877 and 1868.

In submitting this report, I desire to commend the administration of the affairs of this agency, as it has appeared under my daily observation since August, 1887. So far as this reservation is concerned, the present unrest among the Indians is not attributable to any just cause of complaint against the former or present agent or employees; nor is it due entirely or largely to failure on the part of the government to fulfill treaty obligations.

Very respectfully, your obedient servant,

J. H. HURST,
Captain, Twelfth Infantry, Commanding Post.

APPENDIX C.—EXTRACT COPY—TREATIES OF 1877 AND 1868

TREATY OF 1877

ARTICLE 3. The said Indians also agree that they will hereafter receive all annuities provided by the said treaty of 1868, and all subsistence and supplies which may be provided for them under the present or any future act of Congress, at such points and places on the said reservation and in the vicinity of the Missouri river as the President of the United States shall designate.

ARTICLE 5. In consideration of the foregoing cession of territory and rights, and upon full compliance with each and every obligation assumed by the said Indians, the United States agree to provide all necessary aid to assist the said Indians in the work of civilization; to furnish to them schools and instruction in mechanical and agricultural arts, as provided for by the treaty of 1868. Also to provide the said Indians with subsistence consisting of a ration for each individual of a pound and a half of beef (or in lieu thereof, one-half pound of bacon), one-half pound of flour, and one-half pound of corn; and for every one hundred rations, four pounds of coffee, eight pounds of sugar, and three pounds of beans, or in lieu of said articles the equivalent thereof, in the discretion of the Commissioner of Indian Affairs. Such rations, or so much thereof as may be necessary, shall be continued until the Indians are able to support themselves. Rations shall in all cases be issued to the head of each separate family; and whenever schools shall have been provided by the government for said Indians, no rations shall be issued for children between the ages of six and fourteen years (the sick and infirm excepted), unless such children shall regularly attend school. Whenever the said Indians shall be located upon lands which are suitable for cultivation, rations shall be issued only to the persons and families of those persons who labor (the aged, sick, and infirm excepted); and as an incentive to industrious habits the Commissioner of Indian Affairs may provide that persons be furnished in payment for their labor such other necessary articles as are requisite for civilized life. . . .

ARTICLE 8. The provisions of the said treaty of 1868, except as herein modified, shall continue in full force. . . .

ARTICLE 8. When the head of a family or lodge shall have selected lands in good faith and received a certificate therefor and commenced farming in good faith, he is to receive not to exceed one hundred dollars for the first year in seeds and agricultural implements, and for a period of three years more not to exceed twenty-five dollars in seeds and implements.

ARTICLE 10. In lieu of all sums of money or other annuities provided to be paid to the Indians herein named under any treaty or treaties heretofore made, the United States agrees to deliver at the agency house on the reservation herein named on (or before) the first day of August of each year for thirty years, the following articles, to wit:

For each male person over fourteen years of age, a suit of good, substantial woolen clothing, consisting of coat, pantaloons, flannel shirt, hat, and a pair of home-made socks.

For each female over twelve years of age, a flannel skirt or the goods necessary to make it, a pair of woolen hose, twelve yards of calico, and twelve yards of cotton domestics.

For the boys and girls under the ages named, such flannel and cotton goods as may be needed to make each a suit aforesaid, with a pair of hose for each. And in addition to the clothing herein named, the sum of ten dollars for each person entitled to the beneficial effects of this treaty, shall be annually appropriated for a period of thirty years, while such persons roam and hunt, and twenty dollars for each person who engages in farming, to be used by the Secretary of the Interior in the purchase of such articles as from time to time the condition and necessities of the Indians may indicate to be proper. And if within thirty years at any time it shall appear that the amount of money needed for clothing, under this article, can be appropriated to better uses for the Indians named herein, Congress may, by law, change the appropriation to other purposes, but in no event shall the amount of the appropriation be withdrawn or discontinued for the period named.

Article 10 further stipulates that each lodge or family who shall commence farming shall receive within sixty days thereafter one good American cow and one good well-broken pair of American oxen.

Extract from tabular statement, showing articles of subsistence received or to be received, rations as issued up to date, and amount required to make the issues according to Article 5 of treaty of February 27, 1877, in fiscal year 1891—At Cheyenne River agency, Fort Bennett, South Dakota.

3	5	7
Name of articles.	Quantity allowed to 100 rations up to date.	Quantity per 100 rations as allowed per treaty 1877.
	Pounds.	*Pounds.*
Bacon	3	16⅔
Beans.............................	3	3
Baking powder	1½	....
Beef, gross......................	a 100	b 100
Coffee............................	2½–3	4
Flour	45	50
Sugar............................	4¾	8
Salt..............................	1	....
Soap.............................	2	....
Mess pork	3	....
Hard bread (in lieu of bacon)	25	....
Corn (in lieu of flour)	None.	50

a Net.   b Net, or 150 without bacon.

Rations as fixed by treaty of 1877: 1½ pounds beef or ½ pound bacon; ½ pound flour and ½ pound corn; 4 pounds coffee, 8 pounds sugar, and 3 pounds beans to every 100 rations; "or, in lieu of said articles, the equivalent thereof, in the discretion of the Commissioner of Indian Affairs."

STATEMENT OF AMERICAN HORSE

[*Delivered in council at Pine Ridge agency to Agent Royer, and forwarded to the Indian Office, November 27, 1890. G. D. Doc. 37002—1890.*]

American Horse, Fast Thunder, Spotted Horse, Pretty Back, and Good Lance present, with American Horse as spokesman:

"I think the late Sioux commissioners (General Crook, Major Warner, and Governor Foster) had something to do with starting this trouble. I was speaker for the whole tribe. In a general council I signed the bill (the late Sioux bill) and 580 signed with me. The other members of my band drew out and it divided us, and ever since

these two parties have been divided.   The nonprogressive started the ghost dance to
draw from us.   We were made many promises, but have never heard from them since.
The Great Father says if we do what he directs it will be to our benefit; but instead
of this they are every year cutting down our rations, and we do not get enough to
keep us from suffering.   General Crook talked nice to us; and after we signed the
bill they took our land and cut down our allowance of food.   The commission made
us believe that we would get full sacks if we signed the bill, but instead of that our
sacks are empty.   We lost considerable property by being here with the commissioners last year, and have never got anything for it.   Our chickens were all stolen, our
cattle some of them were killed, our crops were entirely lost by us being absent
here with the Sioux commission, and we have never been benefited one bit by the
bill; and, in fact, we are worse off than we were before we signed the bill.   We
are told if we do as white men we will be better off, but we are getting worse off
every year.

"The commissioners promised the Indians living on Black Pipe and Pass creeks
that if they signed the bill they could remain where they were and draw their
rations at this agency, showing them on the map the line, and our people want them
here, but they have been ordered to move back to Rosebud agency.   This is one of
the broken promises.   The commission promised to survey the boundary line, and
appropriate $1,000 for the purpose, but it has not been done.   When we were at
Washington, the President, the Secretary of the Interior, and the Commissioner all
promised us that we would get the million pounds of beef that were taken from us,
and I heard the bill appropriating the money passed Congress, but we never got the
beef.   The Commissioner refused to give it to us.   American Horse, Fast Thunder,
and Spotted Horse were all promised a spring wagon each, but they have never
heard anything of it.   This is another broken promise."

In forwarding the report of the council, the agent says: "After American Horse
was through talking, I asked the other men present if his statement voiced their
sentiments and they all answered, Yes."

STATEMENT OF BISHOP HARE

[*Bishop W. H. Hare is the veteran Episcopal missionary bishop among the Sioux.   The following
extracts are from a communication by him to Secretary Noble, dated January 7, 1891.   G. D. Doc.
2440—1891.*]

The evidence compels the conclusion that, among the Pine Ridge Indians at least,
hunger has been an important element in the causes of *discontent* and *insubordination.*
In the farming season of 1889 [July] the Indians were all called into the agency and
kept there for a month by the Sioux commission.   During their absence their cattle
broke into their fields and trod down, or ate up, their crops.   The Indians reaped
practically nothing.   In the year 1890, drought, the worst known for many years,
afflicted the western part of South Dakota, and the Indian crops were a total failure.
There is ample evidence that, during this period, the rations issued lasted, even
when carefully used, for only two-thirds the time for which they were intended.   To
add to their distress, this period, 1889 and 1890, was marked by extraordinary misfortune.   The measles prevailed with great virulence in 1889, the grippe in 1890.
Whooping cough also attacked the children.   The sick died from want.   In this
statement Inspector Gardiner, Dr McGillycuddy, late agent, Miss Elaine Goodale, who
has been in the camps a good deal, the missionary force, and many others whose
testimony is of the highest value because of their character and their knowledge of
the situation, all agree.   .   .   .

The time seemed now to have come to take a further step and divide the Great
Sioux reservation up into separate reserves for each important tribe, and to open the
surplus land to settlement.   The needs of the white population, with their business
and railroads, and the welfare of the Indians, seemed alike to demand this.   Commissioners were therefore sent out to treat with the people for the accomplishment

of this end, and an agreement which, after much debate, had won general approval was committed to them for presentation to the Indians. The objections of the Indians to the bill, however, were many and they were ardently pressed. Some preferred their old life, the more earnestly because schools and churches were sapping and undermining it. Some wished delay. All complained that many of the engagements solemnly made with them in former years when they had surrendered valued rights had been broken, and here they were right. They suspected that present promises of pay for their lands would prove only old ones in a new shape (when milch cows were promised, cows having been promised in previous agreements, the Indians exclaimed, "There's that same old cow"), and demanded that no further surrender should be expected until former promises had been fulfilled. They were assured that a new era had dawned, and that all past promises would be kept. So we all thought. The benefits of the proposed agreement were set before them, and verbal promises, over and above the stipulations of the bill, were made, that special requests of the Indians would be met. The Indians have no competent representative body. The commissioners had to treat at each agency with a crowd, a crowd composed of full-bloods, half-breeds, and squaw men, a crowd among whom all sorts of sinister influences and brute force were at work. Commissioners with such a business in hand have the devil to fight, and can fight him, so it often seems, only with fire, and many friends of the Indians think that in this case the commission, convinced that the acceptance of the bill was essential, carried persuasion to the verge of intimidation. I do not blame them if they sometimes did. The wit and patience of an angel would fail often in such a task.

But the requisite number, three-fourths of the Indians, signed the bill, and expectation of rich and prompt rewards ran high. The Indians understand little of the complex forms and delays of our government. Six months passed, and nothing came. Three months more, and nothing came. A bill was drawn up in the Senate under General Crook's eye and passed, providing for the fulfillment of the promises of the commission, but it was pigeon-holed in the House. But in the midst of the winter's pinching cold the Indians learned that the transaction had been declared complete and half of their land proclaimed as thrown open to the whites. Surveys were not promptly made; perhaps they could not be, and no one knew what land was theirs and what was not. The very earth seemed sliding from beneath their feet. Other misfortunes seemed to be crowding on them. On some reserves their rations were being reduced, and lasted, even when carefully husbanded, but one-half the period for which they were issued. (The amount of beef *bought* for the Indians is not a fair criterion of the amount he *receives*. A steer will lose 200 pounds or more of its flesh during the course of the winter.) In the summer of 1889 all the people on the Pine Ridge reserve, men, women, and children, were called in from their farms to the agency to treat with the commissioners and were kept there a whole month, and, on returning to their homes, found that their cattle had broken into their fields and trampled down or eaten up all their crops. This was true in a degree elsewhere. In 1890 the crops, which promised splendidly early in July, failed entirely later, because of a severe drought. The people were often hungry, and, the physicians in many cases said, died when taken sick, not so much from disease as for want of food. (This is doubtless true of all the poor—the poor in our cities and the poor settlers in the west.)

No doubt the people could have saved themselves from suffering if industry, economy, and thrift had abounded; but these are just the virtues which a people merging from barbarism lack. The measles prevailed in 1889 and were exceedingly fatal. Next year the grippe swept over the people with appalling results. Whooping cough followed among the children. Sullenness and gloom began to gather, especially among the heathen and wilder Indians. A witness of high character told me that a marked discontent amounting almost to despair prevailed in many quarters. The people said their children were all dying from diseases brought by the whites, their race was perishing from the face of the earth, and they might as well be killed at once. Old chiefs and medicine men were losing their power. Withal new ways were prevailing more and more which did not suit the older people. The old ways which they loved were passing away. In a word, all things were against them, and to add to the calamity, many Indians, especially the wilder element, had nothing to do but to brood over their misfortunes. While in this unhappy state, the story of a messiah coming, with its ghost dance and strange hallucinations, spread among the heathen part of the people. . . .

But these things we do want. A profound conviction in the mind not only of a few, but of the *people*, that the Indian problem is worth attending to. Next, that the officials placed in charge of the difficult Indian problem should be protected from the importunity of hungry politicians, and that the employees in the Indian country, agents, teachers, farmers, carpenters, should not be changed with every shuffling of the political cards. The abuse here has been shameful. Next, that Congress, especially the House of Representatives, shall consider itself bound in honor to make provision for the fulfillment of promises made to the Indians by commissioners duly appointed and sent to the Indians by another branch of the government. The evils which have arisen from a violation of this comity have been most serious. Next, that testimony regarding Indian affairs should not be swallowed until careful inquiry has been made as to the disinterestedness of the witness. An honest man out here burns with indignation when he reads in the papers that so and so, represented as being fully informed on the whole question, affirms that Indians have no grievances and ought to receive no quarter, when he knows that the lots which the witness owns in a town near the Indian country would no longer be a drug in the market if Indians could be gotten out of the way. Next, let it be remembered that the crisis has lifted evils in the Indian country up to the light, and left the good things in the shade. But the good things are real and have shown their vigor under trial. There is no reason for losing faith or courage. Let all kind and honest men unite with the higher officials of the government, all of whom, I believe, mean well, in a spirit of forbearance toward each other, of willingness to learn, and of mutual helpfulness, to accomplish the results which they all desire.

CHAPTER V

The Sioux Outbreak—Sitting Bull and Wounded Knee

We were made many promises, but have never heard from them since. — *American Horse.*

Congress has been in session several weeks and could, if it were disposed, in a few hours confirm the treaty that its commissioners have made with these Indians, and appropriate the necessary funds for their fulfillment, and thereby give an earnest of good faith or intention to fulfill their part of the compact. Such action in my judgment is essential to restore confidence with the Indians and give peace and protection to the settlements. — *General Miles.*

Approximate cost of outbreak in one month: Forty-nine whites and others on the government side, and three hundred Indians, killed; $1,200,000 expense to government and individuals.

Short Bull and the other Sioux delegates who had gone to see the messiah in the fall of 1889 returned in March, 1890. Short Bull, on Rosebud reservation, at once began to preach to his people the doctrine and advent of the messiah, but desisted on being warned to stop by Agent Wright. (*Comr.*, *29.*) The strange hope had taken hold of the Indians however, and the infection rapidly, although quietly, spread among all the wilder portion of the tribe. The first warning of trouble ahead came in the shape of a letter addressed to Secretary Noble by Charles L. Hyde, a citizen of Pierre, South Dakota, under date of May 29, 1890, in which he stated that he had trustworthy information that the Sioux, or a part of them, were secretly planning an outbreak in the near future. His informant appears to have been a young half-blood from Pine Ridge, who was at that time attending school in Pierre, and was in correspondence with his Indian relatives at home. (*G. D.*, *20.*) The letter was referred to the Commissioner of Indian Affairs, who forwarded a copy of it to the agents of the several western Sioux reservations, with a request for further information. They promptly and unanimously replied that there was no ground for apprehension, that the Indians were peaceably disposed, and that there was no undue excitement beyond that occasioned by the rumors of a messiah in the west. This excitement they thought would continue to increase as the predicted time drew near, and would die a natural death when the prophecy failed of its fulfillment.

All the agents are positive in the opinion that at this time, about the middle of June, 1890, the Indians had no hostile intentions. McLaughlin, the veteran agent of Standing Rock, who probably knew the Sioux better than any other white man having official relations with them, states that among his people there was nothing in word or action to justify such a suspicion, and that he did not believe such an imprudent step was seriously contemplated by any of the tribe, and concludes by saying that he has every confidence in the good intentions of the Sioux as a people, that they would not be the aggressors in any hostile act, and that if justice were only done them no uneasiness need be entertained. He complains, however, of the evil influence exercised by Sitting Bull and a few other malcontents attached to his agency and advises their removal from among the Indians. Wright, at Rosebud, also advised the removal of Crow Dog and some other mischief-makers. These men had led the opposition to the late treaty and to every advance

Fig. 7.—A Sioux warrior—Weasel Bear

of civilization, by which they felt their former influence undermined, and between them and the progressive party there was uncompromising hostility. (*G. D.*, *21.*) Although the trouble did come six months later, it is sufficiently evident that at this time there was no outbreak intended. Certain it is that the Sioux as a tribe—25,000 strong—did not engage in the outbreak, and in view of all the circumstances it will hardly be claimed that they were deliberate aggressors.

The first mutterings of dissatisfaction came from Pine Ridge. This is the largest of the Sioux agencies, having 6,000 of the wildest and most warlike of the tribe, largely under the influence of the celebrated chief Red Cloud, the twin spirit of Sitting Bull in wily disposition and hatred of the white man. It is the most remote from the white settlements along Missouri river, and joins Rosebud reservation, with 4,000 more Sioux of about the same condition and temper, thus making a compact body of 10,000 of the most warlike Indians of the plains. Above all other reservations in the United States this was the very one where there was most urgent and obvious necessity for efficient and vigorous administration and for prompt and honest fulfillment of pledges.

From 1879 to 1886 this agency was in charge of Dr V. T. McGillycuddy, a man of unflinching courage, determined will, and splendid executive ability. Taking charge of these Indians when they had come in fresh from the warpath, he managed them, as he himself says, for seven years without the presence of a soldier on the reservation, and with none nearer than 60 miles. Relying on the Indians themselves, he introduced the principle of home rule by organizing a force of 50 Indian police, drilled in regular cavalry and infantry tactics. With these he was able to thwart all the mischievous schemes of Red Cloud, maintain authority, and start the Indians well on the road to civilization.

Then came a political change of administration, with a resulting train of changes all through the service. Out of 58 Indian agents more than 50 were removed and new men appointed. Some of these appointments were for the better, but the general result was bad, owing mainly to the inexperience of the new officials. In the meantime commissioners were negotiating with the Sioux for a further cession of lands, which was finally effected in spite of the opposition of a large part of the tribe, especially of those under the influence of Red Cloud and Sitting Bull at Pine Ridge and Standing Rock. Then rations were reduced and the Indians began to suffer and, consequently, to be restless, their unrest being intensified but not caused by the rumors of a messiah soon to appear to restore the former conditions. According to the official statement of General Brooke, the beef issue at Pine Ridge was reduced from 8,125,000 pounds in 1886 to 4,000,000 pounds in 1889, a reduction of more than one-half in three years. (*War, 5.*) In April, 1890, Gallagher, the agent then in charge, informed the Department that the monthly beef issue was only 205,000 pounds, whereas the treaty called for 470,400. He was informed that it was better to issue half rations all the time than to issue three-fourths or full rations for two months and none for the rest of the year. From other sources also the warning now came to the Department that the Sioux of Pine Ridge were becoming restless from hunger. (*G. D., 22.*) Repeated representations failed to bring more beef, and at last in the summer of 1890 the Indians at Pine Ridge made the first actual demonstration by refusing to accept the deficient issue and making threats against the agent. They were finally persuaded to take the beef, but Agent Gallagher, finding that the dissatisfaction was growing and apparently without remedy, resigned, and his successor took charge in the beginning of October, 1890.

By this time the Ghost dance was in full progress among the western Sioux and was rapidly spreading throughout the tribe. The principal

FIG. 8.—Red Cloud

dance ground on Pine Ridge reservation was at No Water's camp on White Clay creek, about 20 miles from the agency. At a great Ghost dance held here about the middle of June the ghost shirts were worn probably for the first time. (*Comr.,30.*) In August about 2,000 Indians had assembled for a dance at the same rendezvous, when Agent Gallagher sent out several police with orders to the dancers to quit and go home. They refused to do so, and the agent himself went out with more police to enforce the order. On repeating his demand a number of the warriors leveled their guns toward him and the police, and told him that they were ready to defend their religion with their lives. Under the circumstances the agent, although known to be a brave man, deemed it best to withdraw and the dance went on. (*Comr., 31; G. D., 23.*)

On Rosebud reservation, which adjoins Pine Ridge on the east and is occupied by the turbulent and warlike Brulés, the warning given to Short Bull had such an effect that there was no open manifestation until September, when the Ghost dance was inaugurated at the various camps under the leadership of Short Bull the medicine-man, Crow Dog, and Two Strike. Agent Wright, then in charge, went out to the Indians and told them the dance must be stopped, which was accordingly done. He expressly states that no violence was contemplated by the Indians, and that no arms were carried in the dance, but that he forbade it on account of its physical and mental effect on the participants and its tendency to draw them from their homes. In some way a rumor got among the Indians at this time that troops had arrived on the reservation to attack them, and in an incredibly short time every Indian had left the neighborhood of the agency and was making preparations to meet the enemy. It was with some difficulty that Agent Wright was able to convince them that the report was false and persuade them to return to their homes. Soon afterward circumstances obliged him to be temporarily absent, leaving affairs in the meantime in charge of a special agent. The Indians took advantage of his absence to renew the Ghost dance and soon defied control. The agent states, however, that no Indians left the agency until the arrival of the troops, when the leaders immediately departed for Pine Ridge, together with 1,800 of their followers. (*G. D., 24; Comr., 32.*)

On October 9 Kicking Bear of Cheyenne River agency, the chief high priest of the Ghost dance among the Sioux, went to Standing Rock by invitation of Sitting Bull and inaugurated the dance on that reservation at Sitting Bull's camp on Grand river. The dance had begun on Cheyenne river about the middle of September, chiefly at the camps of Hump and Big Foot. On learning of Kicking Bear's arrival, Agent McLaughlin sent a force of police, including two officers, to arrest him and put him off the reservation, but they returned without executing the order, both officers being in a dazed condition and fearing the power of Kicking Bear's "medicine." Sitting Bull, however, had promised that his visitors would go back to their own reservation, which they did a day or two later, but he declared his intention to continue the dance, as they had received a direct message from the spirit world through Kicking Bear that they must do so to live. He promised that he would suspend the dance until he could come and talk the matter over with the agent, but this promise he failed to keep. Considering Sitting Bull the leader and instigator of the excitement on the reservation, McLaughlin again advised his removal, and that of several other mischief makers, and their confinement in some military prison at a distance. (*G. D., 25.*)

The two centers of excitement were now at Standing Rock reservation, where Sitting Bull was the open and declared leader, and at Pine Ridge, where Red Cloud was a firm believer in the new doctrine, although perhaps not an instigator of direct opposition to authority. At Rosebud the movement had been smothered for the time by the prompt action of Agent Wright, as already described. At the first-named reservation McLaughlin met the emergency with bravery and ability reinforced by twenty years of experience in dealing with Indians, and, while recommending the removal of Sitting Bull, expressed confidence in his own ability to allay the excitement and suppress the dance. At Pine Ridge, however, where the crisis demanded a man of most positive character—somebody of the McGillycuddy stamp—Gallagher had resigned and had been succeeded in October by D. F. Royer, a person described as "destitute of any of those qualities by which he could justly lay claim to the position—experience, force of character, courage, and sound judgment." (*Welsh, 2.*) This appears in every letter and telegram sent out by him during his short incumbency, and is sufficiently evidenced in the name by which the Sioux soon came to know him, Lakota Kokipa-Koshkala, "Young-man-afraid-of-Indians." Before he had been in charge a week, he had so far lost control of his Indians as to allow a half dozen of them to release and carry off a prisoner named Little, whom the police had arrested and brought to the agency. On October 12 he reported that more than half of his 6,000 Indians were dancing, and that they were entirely beyond the control of the police, and suggested that it would be necessary to call out the military. (*G. D., 26.*)

About the same time Agent Palmer at Cheyenne River reported to the Department that Big Foot's band (afterward engaged at Wounded Knee) was very much excited over the coming of the messiah, and could not be kept by the police from dancing. In reply, both agents were instructed to use every prudent measure to stop the dance and were told that military assistance would be furnished if immediate need should arise. (*L. B., 1.*) Instructions were also sent to agents in Nevada to warn the leaders of the dance in that quarter to desist. A few days later the agent at Cheyenne River had a talk with the dancers, and so far convinced them of the falsity of their hopes that he was able to report that the excitement was dying out, but recommended the removal of Hump, as a leader of the disaffection. (*G. D., 27.*)

By the advice of the Department, Royer had consulted General Miles, at that time passing on his way to the west, as to the necessity for troops, and, after hearing a full statement, the general expressed the opinion that the excitement would die out of itself. The next day the general had a talk with the Indians, who informed him that they intended to continue the dance. He gave them some good advice and told them that they must stop. Had the matter rested here until the words of the commanding officer could have been deliberated in their minds—for the mental process of an Indian can not well be hurried— all might have been well. Unfortunately, however, the agent, now thoroughly frightened, wrote a long letter to the Department on October 30, stating that the only remedy for the matter was the use of military, and that about 600 or 700 troops would be necessary. On November 11 he telegraphed for permission to come to Washington to "explain," and was refused. Then came other telegraphic requests, at the rate of one every day, for the same permission, all of which were refused, with pointed intimation that the interests of the service required that the agent should remain at his post of duty. Finally the matter was reported by the Indian Office to the War Department, and on November 15 Royer was instructed to report the condition of affairs to the commander of the nearest military post, Fort Robinson, Nebraska. On the same day he had telegraphed that the Indians were wild and crazy and that at least a thousand soldiers were needed. The agent at Rosebud also now reported that his Indians were beyond control by the police. Special agents were sent to both agencies and confirmed the reports as to the alarming condition of affairs. The agent at Crow Creek and Lower Brulé agency reported at the same time that his Indians were under good control and that the police were sufficient for all purposes. (*G. D., 28; L. B., 2.*)

On the last day of October, Short Bull, one of those who had been to see the messiah, made an address to a large gathering of Indians near Pine Ridge, in which he said that as the whites were interfering so much in the religious affairs of the Indians he would advance the time for the great change and make it nearer, even within the next month. He urged them all to gather in one place and prepare for the coming messiah, and told them they must dance even though troops should surround them, as the guns of the soldiers would be rendered harmless and the white race itself would soon be annihilated. (See his speech, page 30.)

Soon afterward, McLaughlin personally visited Sitting Bull at his camp on Grand river and attempted to reason with the Indians on the absurdity of their belief. In reply, Sitting Bull proposed that they should both go with competent attendants to the country of the messiah and see and question him for themselves, and rest the truth or falsity of the new doctrine on the result. The proposition was not accepted. (*G. D., 29.*) There can be no question that the leaders of the Ghost dance among the Sioux were fully as much deceived as their followers.

As the local agents had declared the situation beyond their control, the War Department was at last called on and responded. On November 13 the President had directed the Secretary of War to assume a military responsibility to prevent an outbreak (*G. D., 30*), and on November 17 troops, under command of General John R. Brooke, were ordered to the front. The general plan of the campaign was under the direction of General Nelson A. Miles, in command of the military department of the Missouri. On November 19 the first troops arrived at Pine Ridge from Fort Robinson, Nebraska, and were speedily reinforced by others. Within a few days there were at Pine Ridge agency, under immediate command of General Brooke, eight troops of the Seventh cavalry, under Colonel Forsyth; a battalion of the Ninth cavalry (colored), under Major Henry; a battalion of the Fifth artillery, under Captain Capron, and a company of the Eighth infantry and eight companies of the Second infantry, under Colonel Wheaton. At Rosebud were two troops of the Ninth cavalry, with portions of the Eighth and Twenty-first infantry, under Lieutenant-Colonel Poland. Between Rosebud and Pine Ridge were stationed seven companies of the First infantry, under Colonel Shafter. West and north of Pine Ridge were stationed portions of the First, Second, and Ninth cavalry, under command of Colonel Tilford and Lieutenant-Colonel Sanford. Farther west, at Buffalo Gap, on the railroad, were stationed three troops from the Fifth and Eighth cavalry, under Captain Wells. Farther north on the railroad, at Rapid City, was Colonel Carr with six troops of the Sixth cavalry. Along the south fork of Cheyenne river Lieutenant-Colonel Offley took position with seven companies of the Seventeenth infantry, and east of him was stationed Lieutenant-Colonel Sumner with three troops of the Eighth cavalry, two companies of the Third infantry, and Lieutenant Robinson's company of Crow Indian scouts. Small garrisons were also stationed at Forts Meade, Bennett, and Sully. Most of the force was placed in position between the Indians now gathering in the Bad Lands, under Short Bull and Kicking Bear, and the scattered settlements nearest them. Seven companies of the Seventh infantry, under Colonel Merriam, were also placed along Cheyenne river to restrain the Indians of Cheyenne River and Standing Rock reservations. In a short time there were nearly 3,000 troops in the field in the Sioux country. General Miles established his headquarters at Rapid City, South Dakota, close to the center of disturbance. (*War, 6.*) On December 1 the Secretary of the Interior directed that the agents be instructed to obey and cooperate with the military officers in all matters looking to the suppression of an outbreak. (*G. D., 31.*)

Upon the first appearance of the troops a large number of Indians of Rosebud and Pine Ridge, led by Short Bull, Kicking Bear, and others, left their homes and fled to the rough broken country known as the Bad Lands, northwest of White river in South Dakota, on the edge

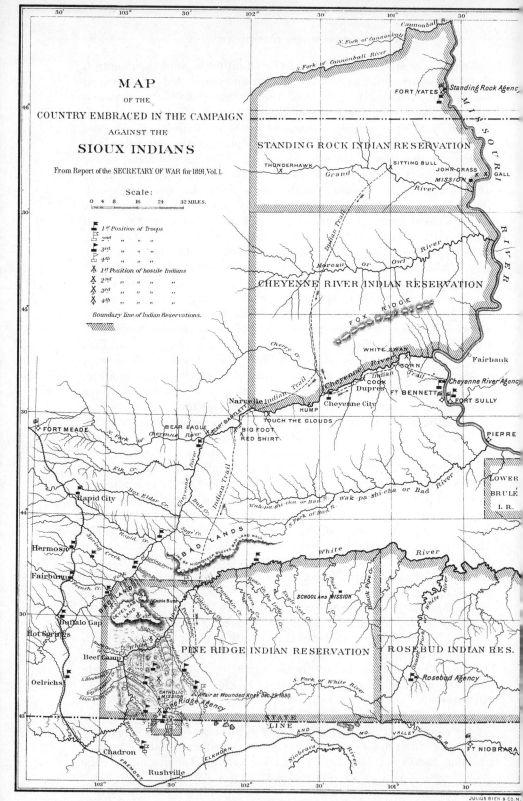

Fig. 9

of Pine Ridge reservation and about 50 miles northwest of the agency. In their flight they destroyed the houses and other property of the friendly Indians in their path and compelled many to go with them. They succeeded also in capturing a large portion of the agency beef herd. Others rapidly joined them until soon a formidable body of

Fig. 10.—Short Bull

3,000 Indians had gathered in the Bad Lands, where, protected by the natural fastnesses and difficulties of the country, their future intentions became a matter of anxious concern to the settlers and the authorities.

From the concurrent testimony of all the witnesses, including Indian Commissioner Morgan and the Indians themselves, this flight to the

Bad Lands was not properly a hostile movement, but was a stampede caused by panic at the appearance of the troops. In his official report Commissioner Morgan says:

> When the troops reached Rosebud, about 1,800 Indians—men, women, and children—stampeded toward Pine Ridge and the Bad Lands, destroying their own property before leaving and that of others en route.

After the death of Sitting Bull he says:

> Groups of Indians from the different reservations had commenced concentrating in the Bad Lands, upon or in the vicinity of the Pine Ridge reservation. Killing of cattle and destruction of other property by these Indians, almost entirely within the limits of Pine Ridge and Rosebud reservations, occurred, but no signal fires were built, no warlike demonstrations were made, no violence was done to any white settlers, nor was there any cohesion or organization among the Indians themselves. Many of them were friendly Indians who had never participated in the ghost dance. but had fled thither from fear of soldiers, in consequence of the Sitting Bull affair or through the overpersuasion of friends. The military gradually began to close in around them and they offered no resistance, and a speedy and quiet capitulation of all was confidently expected. (*Comr., 33.*)

The Sioux nation numbers over 25,000, with between 6,000 and 7,000 warriors. Hardly more than 700 warriors were concerned altogether, including those of Big Foot's band and those who fled to the Bad Lands. None of the Christian Indians took any part in the disturbance.

While it is certain that the movement toward the Bad Lands with the subsequent events were the result of panic at the appearance of the troops, it is equally true that the troops were sent only on the request of the civilian authorities. On this point General Miles says: "Not until the civil agents had lost control of the Indians and declared themselves powerless to preserve peace, and the Indians were in armed hostility and defiance of the civil authorities, was a single soldier moved from his garrison to suppress the general revolt." (*War, 7.*) Throughout the whole trouble McGillycuddy at Standing Rock consistently declared his ability to control his Indians without the presence of troops.

In accord with instructions from the Indian Office, the several agents in charge among the Sioux had forwarded lists of disturbers whom it would be advisable to arrest and remove from among the Indians, using the military for the purpose if necessary. The agents at the other reservations sent in all together the names of about fifteen subjects for removal, while Royer, at Pine Ridge, forwarded as a "conservative estimate" the names of sixty-four. Short Bull and Kicking Bear being in the Bad Lands, and Red Cloud being now an old man and too politic to make much open demonstration, the head and front of the offenders was Sitting Bull, the irreconcilable; but McLaughlin, within whose jurisdiction he was, in a letter of November 22, advised that the arrest be not attempted until later in the season, as at the date of writing the weather was warm and pleasant—in other words, favorable to the Indians in case they should make opposition. (*G. D., 32.*) The worst element had withdrawn to the Bad Lands, where they were making no hostile demonstrations, but were apparently badly frightened and awaiting developments to know whether to come in and surrender or to continue to retreat. The dance had generally been discontinued on the reservations, excepting at Sitting Bull's camp on Grand river and

Fig. 11.—Kicking Bear

Big Foot's camp on Cheyenne river. The presence of troops had stopped the dances near the agencies, and the Secretary of the Interior, in order to allay the dissatisfaction, had ordered that the full rations due under the treaty should be issued at all the Sioux agencies, which at the same time were placed under the control of the military. (*G.*

D., 33; L. B., 3.)   Such were the conditions on the opening of December, 1890.   Everything seemed to be quieting down, and it was now deemed a favorable time to forestall future disturbance by removing the ringleaders.

Agent McLaughlin at Standing Rock had notified the Department some weeks before that it would be necessary to remove Sitting Bull and several others at no distant day to put an end to their harmful influence among the Sioux, but stated also that the matter should not be precipitated, and that when the proper time came he could accomplish the undertaking with his Indian police without the aid of troops. As soon as the War Department assumed control of the Sioux agencies, it was determined to make an attempt to secure Sitting Bull by military power.   Accordingly, orders were given to the noted scout, William F. Cody, better known as Buffalo Bill, who was well acquainted with Sitting Bull and was believed to have influence with him, to proceed to Standing Rock agency to induce him to come in, with authority to make such terms as might seem necessary, and, if unsuccessful, to arrest him and remove him from his camp to the nearest post, Fort Yates.   Cody arrived at Fort Yates on November 28, and was about to undertake the arrest, when his orders were countermanded at the urgent remonstrance of Agent McLaughlin, who represented that such a step at that particular time was unwise, as military interference was liable to provoke a conflict, in which the Indians would have the advantage, as the warm weather was in their favor.   He insisted that there was no immediate danger from the dancing, and that at the proper time—when the weather grew colder—he could take care of Sitting Bull and the other disturbers whose removal he advised with the aid of the Indian police, whom, in all his years of service, he had always found equal to the emergency.   The attempt was accordingly postponed.   In the meantime Sitting Bull had promised to come into the agency to talk over the situation with the agent, but failed to keep his engagement.   A close watch was kept over his movements and the agent was instructed to make no arrests except by authority from the military or the Secretary of the Interior.   (*G. D., 34.*)

There is no question that Sitting Bull was plotting mischief.   His previous record was one of irreconcilable hostility to the government, and in every disturbance on the reservation his camp had been the center of ferment.   It was at his camp and on his invitation that Kicking Bear had organized the first Ghost dance on the reservation, and the dance had been kept up by Sitting Bull ever since in spite of the repeated remonstrance of the agent.   At the same time the turbulent followers of the medicine-man took every opportunity to insult and annoy the peaceable and progressive Indians who refused to join them until these latter were forced to make complaint to the agent.   In October, while the dance was being organized at his camp, Sitting Bull had deliberately broken the "pipe of peace" which he had kept

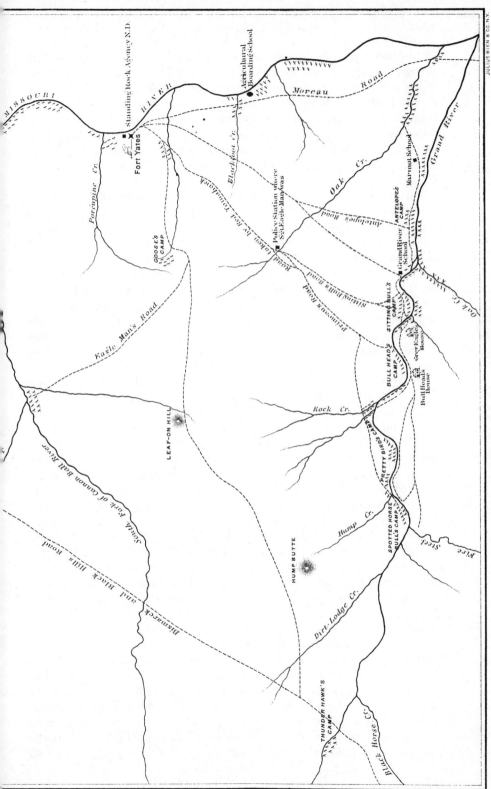

FIG. 12.—Standing Rock agency and vicinity

in his house since his surrender in 1881, and when asked why he had broken it, replied that he wanted to die and wanted to fight. From that time he discontinued his regular visits to the agency. It became known that he contemplated leaving the reservation to visit the other leaders of dissatisfaction at the southern Sioux agencies, and to frustrate such an attempt the agent had gradually increased the number of police in the neighborhood of his camp, and had arranged for speedy information and prompt action in case of any sudden move on his part. (*G. D., 35.*)

Foreseeing from the active movements of the military that the arrest of Sitting Bull was liable to be ordered at any moment, and fearing that such action might come at an inopportune time, and thus result in trouble, McLaughlin made arrangements to have him and several other disturbers arrested by the Indian police on the night of December 6, the weather and other things being then, in his opinion, most favorable for the attempt. On telegraphing to the Indian department, however, for authority, he was directed to make no arrests excepting upon order from the military authorities or the Secretary of the Interior. In reply to a telegram from General Ruger, McLaughlin stated that there was no immediate need of haste, and that postponement was preferable, as the winter weather was cooling the ardor of the dancers.

On December 12 the military order came for the arrest of Sitting Bull. Colonel Drum, in command at Fort Yates, was directed to make it his personal duty to secure him and to call on the agent for assistance and cooperation in the matter. On consultation between the commandant and the agent, who were in full accord, it was decided to make the arrest on the 20th, when most of the Indians would be down at the agency for rations, and there would consequently be less danger of a conflict at the camp. On the 14th, however, late Sunday afternoon, a courier came from Grand river with a message from Mr Carignan, the teacher of the Indian school, stating, on information given by the police, that an invitation had just come from Pine Ridge to Sitting Bull asking him to go there, as God was about to appear. Sitting Bull was determined to go, and sent a request to the agent for permission, but in the meantime had completed his preparations to go anyhow in case permission was refused. With this intention it was further stated that he had his horses already selected for a long and hard ride, and the police urgently asked to be allowed to arrest him at once, as it would be a difficult matter to overtake him after he had once started.

It was necessary to act immediately, and arrangements were made between Colonel Drum and Agent McLaughlin to attempt the arrest at daylight the next morning, December 15. The arrest was to be made by the Indian police, assisted, if necessary, by a detachment of troops, who were to follow within supporting distance. There were already twenty-eight police under command of Lieutenant Bull Head in the immediate vicinity of Sitting Bull's camp on Grand river, about 40 miles southwest of the agency and Fort Yates, and couriers were at once dispatched to these and to others in that direction to concentrate at Sitting Bull's house, ready to make the arrest in the morning. It was then sundown, but with loyal promptness the police mounted their ponies and by riding all night from one station to another assembled a force of 43 trained and determined Indian police, including four volunteers, at the rendezvous on Grand river before daylight. In performing this courier service Sergeant Red Tomahawk covered the distance of 40 miles between the agency and the camp, over an unfamiliar road,

FIG. 13.—Red Tomahawk

in four hours and a quarter; and another, Hawk Man, made 100 miles, by a roundabout way, in twenty-two hours. In the meantime two troops of the Eighth cavalry, numbering 100 men, under command of Captain E. G. Fechét, and having with them a Hotchkiss gun, left Fort Yates at midnight, guided by Louis Primeau, and by a rapid night march arrived within supporting distance near Sitting Bull's camp just before daybreak. It was afterward learned that Sitting Bull, in anticipation of such action, had had a strong guard about his house for his protection for several nights previous, but on this particular night the

Indians had been dancing until nearly morning, and the house was consequently left unguarded.

At daybreak on Monday morning, December 15, 1890, the police and volunteers, 43 in number, under command of Lieutenant Bull Head, a cool and reliable man, surrounded Sitting Bull's house. He had two log cabins, a few rods apart, and to make sure of their man, eight of the police entered one house and ten went into the other, while the rest remained on guard outside. They found him asleep on the floor in the larger house. He was aroused and told that he was a prisoner and must go to the agency. He made no objection, but said "All right; I will dress and go with you." He then sent one of his wives to the other house for some clothes he desired to wear, and asked to have his favorite horse saddled for him to ride, which was done by one of the police. On looking about the room two rifles and several knives were found and taken by the police. While dressing, he apparently changed his mind and began abusing the police for disturbing him, to which they made no reply While this was going on inside, his followers, to the number of perhaps 150, were congregating about the house outside and by the time he was dressed an excited crowd of Indians had the police entirely surrounded and were pressing them to the wall. On being brought out, Sitting Bull became greatly excited and refused to go, and called on his followers to rescue him. Lieutenant Bull Head and Sergeant Shave Head were standing on each side of him, with Second Sergeant Red Tomahawk guarding behind, while the rest of the police were trying to clear the way in front, when one of Sitting Bull's followers, Catch-the-Bear, fired and shot Lieutenant Bull Head in the side. Bull Head at once turned and sent a bullet into the body of Sitting Bull, who was also shot through the head at the same moment by Red Tomahawk. Sergeant Shave Head was shot by another of the crowd, and fell to the ground with Bull Head and Sitting Bull. Catch-the-Bear, who fired the first shot, was immediately shot and killed by Alone Man, one of the police, and it became a desperate hand-to-hand fight of less than 43 men against more than a hundred. The trained police soon drove their assailants into the timber near by, and then returned and carried their dead and wounded into the house and held it for about two hours, until the arrival of the troops under Captain Fechét, about half past seven. The troops had been notified of the perilous situation of the police by Hawk Man, who had volunteered to carry the information from Sitting Bull's camp. He succeeded in getting away, assisted by Red Tomahawk, although so closely pursued that several bullets passed through his clothing. In spite of the efforts of the hostiles, the police also held possession of the corral, which Sitting Bull had filled with horses in anticipation of his flight. When the cavalry came in sight over a hill, about 1,500 yards distant from the camp, the police at the corral raised a white flag to show where they were, but the troops, mistaking them for hostiles, fired two shells at them from the Hotchkiss, when Sergeant Red Tomahawk, who had taken command after the wounding of his superior officers, paraded his men in line and then rode out alone with a white flag to meet the troops. On the approach of the soldiers Sitting Bull's warriors fled up Grand river a short distance and then turned south across the prairie toward Cherry creek and Cheyenne river. Not wishing to create such a panic among them as to drive them into the hostile camp in the Bad Lands, Captain Fechét pursued them only a short distance and then left them to be handled by the other detachments in that direction. Their wives and families, their property and their dead, were left behind in the flight.

Fig. 14.—Sitting Bull the Sioux medicine man

As soon as possible Captain Fechét also sent word to them by some Indian women to return to their homes and they would not be molested. To further reassure them, the troops at once began their march back to the post. As a result of this sensible policy, very few of the Sitting Bull band joined the hostiles. They had made no resistance to the troops, but fled immediately on their appearance.

The fight lasted only a few minutes, but with terribly fatal result. Six policemen were killed or mortally wounded, including the officers Bull Head and Shave Head, and one other less seriously wounded. The hostiles lost eight killed, including Sitting Bull and his son Crow

Foot, 17 years of age, with several wounded. During the fight the
women attacked the police with knives and clubs, but notwithstanding
the excitement the police simply disarmed them and put them in one
of the houses under guard.

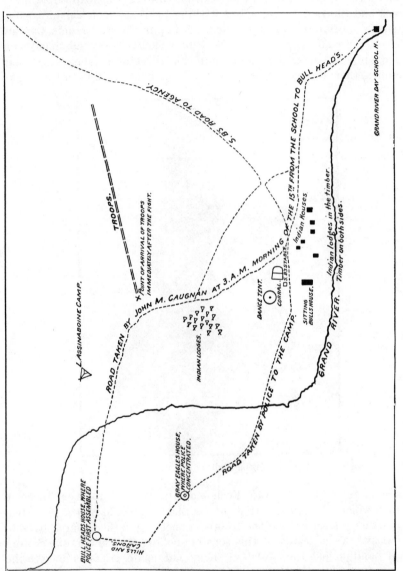

FIG. 15.—Sketch of the country of the Sitting Bull fight, December 15, 1890

The warmest praise is given the Indian police for their conduct on
this occasion by those who are most competent to judge. Some who
thus faced death in obedience to orders had near relatives among those
opposed to them. Agent McLaughlin in one official letter says that he

can not too strongly commend their splendid courage and ability in the action, and in another letter says: "The details of the battle show that the Indian police behaved nobly and exhibited the best of judgment and bravery, and a recognition by the government for their services on this occasion is richly deserved. . . . I respectfully urge that the Interior Department cooperate with the War Department in obtaining Congressional action which will secure to these brave survivors and to the families of the dead a full and generous reward." Colonel Drum, under whose orders the arrest was made, after stating that Sitting Bull was not hurt until he began struggling to escape and until one of the police had been shot, adds: "It is also remarkable that no squaws or children were hurt. The police appear to have constantly warned the other Indians to keep away, until they were forced to fight in self-defense. It is hardly possible to praise their conduct too highly." Notwithstanding the recommendation of the Commissioner of Indian Affairs, Congress has taken no action in recognition of their services on this occasion.

Before the action orders had been sent to the police to have with them a wagon, in order to convey Sitting Bull quickly away from the camp, so as to avoid trouble, but in the excitement of preparation this was overlooked. The police returned to the agency late in the afternoon, bringing with them their dead and wounded, together with two prisoners and the body of Sitting Bull, which was turned over to the military authorities at Fort Yates. The four dead policemen were buried at the agency next day with military honors. Bull Head and Shave Head died in the hospital soon afterward, with the consolation of having their friends around them in their last moments. The agent states that the large majority of the Indians were loyal to the government, and expressed satisfaction at what they considered the termination of the disturbance. Couriers were again sent after the fleeing Indians by McLaughlin, warning them to return to the agency, where they would be safe, or suffer the consequences if found outside the reservation. Within a few days nearly 250 had come in and surrendered, leaving only about one-third still out. Most of these soon afterward surrendered with Hump on Cherry creek, while the remainder, about 50, joined Big Foot or went on to Pine Ridge. (*G. D., 36; War, 8.*)

Thus died Tata'nka I'yota'nke, Sitting Bull, the great medicine-man of the Sioux, on the morning of December 15, 1890, aged about 56 years. He belonged to the Uncpapa division of the Teton Sioux. Although a priest rather than a chief, he had gained a reputation in his early years by organizing and leading war parties, and became prominent by his participation in the battle of Little Bighorn, in Montana, on June 25, 1876, by which Custer's command was wiped out of existence. Being pursued by General Terry, Sitting Bull and his band made their escape northward into Canada, where they remained until 1881, when he surrendered, through the mediation of the Canadian authorities, on a promise of pardon. To obtain subsistence while in Canada, his people had been obliged to sell almost all they possessed, including their fire-arms, so that they returned to their old homes in an impoverished condition. After confinement as a prisoner of war until 1883, Sitting Bull took up his residence on Grand river, where he remained until he met his death. Here he continued to be the leader of the opposition to civilization and the white man, and his camp became the rallying point for the dissatisfied conservative element that clung to the old order of things, and felt that innovation meant destruction to their race. For seven years he had steadily opposed the treaty by which the great Sioux reservation was at last broken up in 1889. After the treaty had been signed by the requisite number to make it a law, he was asked by a white man what the Indians thought about it. With a burst of pas-sionate indignation he replied, "Indians! There are no Indians left now but me." However misguided he may have been in thus continu-ing a losing fight against the inevitable, it is possible that from the Indian point of view he may have been their patriot as he was their high priest. He has been mercilessly denounced as a bad man and a liar; but there can be no doubt that he was honest in his hatred of the whites, and his breaking of the peace pipe, saying that he "wanted to fight and wanted to die," showed that he was no coward. But he rep-resented the past. His influence was incompatible with progress, and his death marks an era in the civilization of the Sioux. In the language of General Miles, "His tragic fate was but the ending of a tragic life. Since the days of Pontiac, Tecumseh, and Red Jacket no Indian has had the power of drawing to him so large a following of his race and molding and wielding it against the authority of the United States, or of inspiring it with greater animosity against the white race and civilization." (*War*, *9*.)

On December 18 the Indians who had already fled to the Bad Lands attacked a small party of men on Spring creek of Cheyenne river. Major Tupper with 100 men of Carr's division was sent to their rescue, and a skirmish ensued with the Indians, who were concealed in the bushes along the creek. The government wagons, while crossing the creek, were also attacked by the hostiles, who were finally driven off by reinforcements of cavalry under Captain Wells. On the same date over a thousand Indians returned to Pine Ridge. News was received that there were still about 1,500 fugitives camped on Cheyenne river in the neighborhood of Spring creek. (*Colby*, *1*.)

The most dangerous leader of dissatisfaction in the north after the death of Sitting Bull was considered to be Hump, on Cheyenne River reservation. The agent in charge had long before recommended his removal, but it was thought that it would now be next to impossible to arrest him. Hump with his band of about 400 persons, and Big Foot with nearly as many, had their camps about the junction of Cherry creek and Cheyenne river. For several weeks they had been dancing almost constantly, and were very sullen and apparently very hostile. After serious consideration of the matter, the task of securing Hump was assigned to Captain E. P. Ewers of the Fifth infantry, who had had charge of this chief and his band for seven years and had their full confidence and respect. He was then on duty in Texas, but was ordered forward and reported soon after at Fort Bennett on the border of the reservation. So dangerous was Hump considered to be that the civil agents did not think it possible even for the officer to communicate with him. However, Captain Ewers, without troops and attended only by Lieutenant Hale, at once left the fort and rode out 60 miles to Hump's camp. " Hump at the time was 20 miles away and a runner was sent for him. Immediately upon hearing that Captain Ewers was in the vicinity he came to him and was told that the division commander desired him to take his people away from the hostiles and·bring them to the nearest military post. He replied that if General Miles sent for him, he would do whatever he desired. He immediately brought his people into Fort Bennett and complied with all the orders and instructions given him, and subsequently rendered valuable service for peace. Thus an element regarded as among the most dangerous was removed." After coming into the fort, Hump enlisted as a scout under Captain Ewers, and soon afterward, in connection with the same Lieutenant Hale, proved his loyalty by bringing about the surrender of the Sitting Bull fugitives. Subsequently Captain Ewers further distinguished himself by conducting the northern Cheyenne — who were considered as particularly dangerous, but who regarded Captain Ewers with absolute affection — from Pine Ridge to Tongue river, Montana, a distance of 300 miles, and in the most rigorous of the winter season, without an escort of troops and without the loss of a single life or the commission by an Indian of a single unlawful act. (*War, 10.*)

The Sitting Bull fugitives who had not come in at once had fled southward toward their friends and near relatives of Cheyenne River reservation, and were camped on Cherry creek a few miles above its junction with Cheyenne river at Cheyenne City. As their presence there could serve only to increase the unrest among the other Indians in that vicinity, and as there was great danger that they might attempt to join those already in the Bad Lands, Captain Hurst, of the Twelfth infantry, commanding at Fort Bennett, directed Lieutenant H. E. Hale on December 18 to go out and bring them in. On arriving at Cheyenne City the officer found it deserted, all the citizens excepting one man having fled in alarm a short time before on the report of a half-blood that the Sitting Bull Indians were coming and had sworn to kill the first white man they met. Having succeeded in frightening the whole population, the half-blood himself, Narcisse Narcelle, left at once for the fort.

After some difficulty in finding anyone to assist him, Hale sent a policeman to bring back Narcelle and sent out another Indian to learn the situation and condition of the Indian camp. His only interpreter for the purpose was Mr Angell, the single white man who had remained, and who had learned some of the Sioux language during his residence among them. While thus waiting, a report came that the Indians had raided a ranch about 10 miles up the creek. Not hearing from his scouts, the lieutenant determined to go alone and find the camp, and was just about to start, when Hump, the late dangerous hostile, but now an enlisted scout, rode in with the news that the Sitting Bull Indians were approaching only a short distance away, and armed. Although from the reports there was every reason to believe that they had just destroyed a ranch and were now coming to attack the town, the officer, with rare bravery, kept his determination to go out and meet them, even without an interpreter, in the hope of preventing their hostile purpose. Hump volunteered to go with him. The two rode out together and soon came up with the Indians, who received them in a friendly manner. There were 46 warriors in the party, besides women and children, wagons and ponies. Says the officer: "I appreciated the importance of the situation, but was absolutely powerless to communicate with the Indians. I immediately formed the opinion that they could be easily persuaded to come into the agency if I could but talk with them. While I was trying by signs to make them understand what I wanted, Henry Angell rode into the circle and took his place at my side. This generous man had not liked the idea of my going among these Indians, and from a true spirit of chivalry had ridden over to 'see it out.'" Verily, while such men as Ewers, Hale, and Angell live, the day of chivalry is not gone by.

With Angell's assistance as interpreter, the officer told the Indians that if they would stay where they were for one day, he would go back to the agency and return within that time with the chief (Captain J. H. Hurst) and an interpreter and no soldiers. They replied that they would not move, and, having directed Angell to kill a beef for them, as they were worn-out and well-nigh starving, and leaving Hump with them to reassure them, the lieutenant rode back to Fort Bennett, 40 miles away, notified Captain Hurst, and returned with him, Sergeant Gallagher, and two Indian scouts as interpreters, the next day. Knowing the importance of haste, they started out on this winter ride of 40 miles without blankets or rations.

On arriving Captain Hurst told them briefly what he had come for, and then, being exhausted from the rapid ride, and knowing that an Indian must not be hurried, he ordered some beef and a plentiful supply of tobacco for them, and said that after he and they had eaten and rested they could talk the matter over. In the evening the principal men met him and told him over a pipe that they had left Standing Rock agency forever; that their great chief and friend Sitting Bull had been killed there without cause; that they had come down to talk with their friends on Cherry creek about it, but had found them gone, and were consequently undecided as to what they should do. The captain replied that he had come as a friend; that if they would surrender their arms and go back with him to Fort Bennett, they would be provided for and would not be harmed; that he could make no promises as to their future disposition; that if they chose to join Big Foot's camp, only a few miles up the river, the result would be their certain destruction. After deliberating among themselves until midnight, they came in a body, delivered a number of guns, and said they would go back to the fort. Accordingly they broke camp next morning and arrived at Fort Bennett on December 24. The entire body numbered 221, including 55 belonging on Cherry creek. These last were allowed to join their own people camped near the post. The Sitting Bull Indians, with some others from Standing Rock, numbering 227 in all, were held at Fort Sully, a few miles below Fort Bennett, until the close of the trouble. Thirty-eight others of the Sitting Bull band had joined Big Foot and afterward fled with him. (*War, 11.*)

After the death of Sitting Bull and the enlistment of Hump in the government service, the only prominent leader outside of the Bad Lands who was considered as possibly dangerous was Sitanka or Big Foot, whose village was at the mouth of Deep creek, a few miles below the forks of Cheyenne river. The duty of watching him was assigned to Lieutenant-Colonel E. V. Sumner of the Eighth cavalry, who had his camp just above the forks. Here he was visited by Big Foot and his head men, who assured the officer that they were peaceable and intended to remain quietly at home. Friendly relations continued until the middle of December, when Big Foot came to bid good bye, telling Sumner that his people were all going to the agency to get their annuities. A day or two later the order came to arrest Big Foot and send him as a prisoner to Fort Meade. Believing that the chief was acting in good faith to control his warriors, who might easily go beyond control were he taken from them, Colonel Sumner informed General Miles that the Indians were already on their way to the agency; that if Big Foot should return he (Sumner) would try to get him, and that otherwise he could be arrested at the agency, if necessary. Soon after, however, the report came that Big Foot had stopped at Hump's camp on the way to the agency, to meet the fugitives coming south from Sitting Bull's camp.

On receipt of this information, Sumner at once marched down the river with the intention of stopping Big Foot. When about half way to Hump's camp, Big Foot himself came up to meet him, saying that he was friendly, and that he and his men would obey any orders that the officer might give. He stated that he had with him 100 of his own Indians and 38 from Standing Rock (Sitting Bull's band). When asked why he had received these last, knowing that they were refugees from their reservation, he replied that they were his brothers and relations; that they had come to his people hungry, footsore, and almost naked; and that he had taken them in and fed them, and that no one with a heart could do any less.

Sumner then directed one of his officers, Captain Hennisee, to go to the Indian camp with Big Foot and. bring in all the Indians. That officer started and returned the next day, December 21, with 333 Indians. This large number was a matter of surprise in view of Big Foot's statement shortly before, but it is possible that in speaking of his party he intended to refer only to the warriors. They went into camp as directed, turned out their ponies to graze, and were fed, and on the next morning all started quietly back with the troops. As they had all along appeared perfectly friendly and compliant with every order, no attempt was made to disarm them. On arriving near their own village, however, it became apparent that Big Foot could not control their desire to go to their homes. The chief came frankly to Sumner and said that he himself would go wherever wanted, but that there would be trouble to force the women and children, who were cold and hungry, away from their village. He protested also that they were now at home, where they had been ordered by the government to stay, and that none of them had done anything to justify their removal. As it was evident that they would not go peaceably, Colonel Sumner determined to bring his whole force on the next day to compel them. In the meantime he sent a white man named Dunn, who had a friendly acquaintance with Big Foot, to tell him that the Indians must obey the order to remove. Dunn delivered the message and returned, being followed later by the interpreter, with the statement that the Indians had consented to go to the agency, and would start the next morning, December 23. That evening, however, scouts came in with the word that the Indians had left their village and were going southward. It was at first thought that they intended turning off on another trail to the agency, but instead of doing so they kept on in the direction of Pine Ridge and the refugees in the Bad Lands, taking with them only their ponies and tipi poles.

The cause of this precipitate flight after the promise given by Big Foot is somewhat uncertain. The statement of the interpreter, Felix Benoit, would make it appear that the Indians were frightened by Dunn, who told them that the soldiers were coming in the morning to carry them off and to shoot them if they refused to go. While this doubtless had the effect of alarming them, the real cause of their flight was probably the fact that just at this critical juncture Colonel Merriam was ordered to move with his command up Cheyenne river to join forces with Sumner in compelling their surrender. Such is the opinion of General Ruger, who states officially that "Big Foot and adherents who had joined him, probably becoming alarmed on the movement of Colonel Merriam's command from Fort Bennett and a rumor that Colonel Sumner would capture them, eluded Colonel Sumner's command and started for the Pine Ridge reservation." This agrees with the statement of several of the survivors that they had been frightened from their homes by the news of Merriam's approach. Sumner, in his report, calls attention to the fact that they committed no depredations in their flight, although they passed several ranches and at one time even went through a pasture filled with horses and cattle without attempting to appropriate them. He also expresses the opinion that Big Foot was compelled unwillingly to go with his people. The whole number of fugitives was at least 340, including a few from the bands of Sitting Bull and Hump. Immediately on learning of their flight Colonel Sumner notified General Carr, commanding in the direction of the Bad Lands. (*War, 12.*)

The situation at this crisis is thus summed up by Indian Commissioner Morgan:

Groups of Indians from the different reservations had commenced concentrating in the Bad Lands upon or in the vicinity of the Pine Ridge reservation. Killing of cattle and destruction of other property by these Indians, almost entirely within the limits of Pine Ridge and Rosebud reservations, occurred, but no signal fires were built, no warlike demonstrations were made, no violence was done to any white settler, nor was there cohesion or organization among the Indians themselves. Many of them were friendly Indians, who had never participated in the ghost dance, but had fled thither from fear of soldiers, in consequence of the Sitting Bull affair or through the overpersuasion of friends. The military gradually began to close in around them and they offered no resistance, and a speedy and quiet capitulation of all was confidently expected. (*Comr., 34.*)

Nearly 3,000 troops were now in the field in the Sioux country. This force was fully sufficient to have engaged the Indians with success, but as such action must inevitably have resulted in wholesale killing on both sides, with the prospect of precipitating a raiding warfare unless the hostiles were completely annihilated, it was thought best to bring about a surrender by peaceful means.

The refugees in the Bad Lands who had fled from Pine Ridge and Rosebud had been surrounded on the west and north by a strong cordon of troops, operating under General Brooke, which had the effect of gradually forcing them back toward the agency. At the same time that officer made every effort to expedite the process by creating dissensions in the Indian camp, and trying in various ways to induce them to come in by small parties at a time. To this end the Indians were promised that if they complied with the orders of the military their rights and interests would be protected, so far as it was within the power of the military department to accomplish that result. Although they had about lost confidence in the government, these assurances had a good effect, which was emphasized by the news of the death of Sitting Bull, the arrest of Big Foot, and return of Hump to his agency, and the steady pressure of the troops from behind; and on December 27, 1890, the entire force broke camp and left their stronghold in the Bad Lands and began moving in toward the agency at Pine Ridge. The several detachments of troops followed behind, within supporting distance of one another, and so closely that the fires were still burning in the Indian camps when the soldiers moved in to occupy the same ground. (*War, 13.*)

As early as December 6 a conference had been brought about at Pine Ridge, through the efforts of Father Jutz, the priest of the Catholic mission, between General Brooke and the leading chiefs of both friend-lies and "hostiles." Although no definite conclusion was reached, the meeting was a friendly one, ending with a feast and an Indian dance. The immediate effect was a division in the hostile camp, culminating in a quarrel between the two factions, with the result that Two Strike and his party left the rest and moved in toward the agency, while Short Bull and Kicking Bear retreated farther into the Bad Lands. On learning of this condition of affairs, General Brooke sent out American Horse and Big Road with a large party of warriors to meet Two Strike and go back with him to persuade the others, if possible, to come in. At the same time the troops were moved up to intercept the flight of the hos-tiles. (*Colby, 2; G. D., 37.*)

On Christmas day the Cheyenne scouts, camped on Battle creek north of the Bad Lands, were attacked by a party of hostiles led by Kicking Bear in person. The fight was kept up until after dark, several being killed or wounded on both sides, but the hostiles were finally driven off. (*Colby, 3.*)

But the tragedy was near at hand. Orders had been given to inter-cept Big Foot's party in its flight from Cheyenne river toward the Bad Lands. This was accomplished on December 28, 1890, by Major Whitside of the Seventh cavalry, who came up with him a short dis-tance west of the Bad Lands. Not having succeeded in communicat-ing with the refugees who had fled there and who were already on their way to the agency, Big Foot had made no stop, but continued on also toward Pine Ridge. On sighting the troops he raised a white flag, advanced into the open country, and asked for a parley. This was refused by Major Whitside, who demanded an unconditional surrender, which was at once given, and the Indians moved on with the troops to Wounded Knee creek, about 20 miles northeast of Pine Ridge agency, where they camped as directed by Major Whitside. In order to make assurance complete, General Brooke sent Colonel Forsyth to join Major Whitside with four additional troops of the Seventh cavalry, which, with the scouts under Lieutenant Taylor, made up a force of eight troops of cavalry, one company of scouts, and four pieces of light artil-lery (Hotchkiss guns), with a total force of 470 men, as against a total of 106 warriors then present in Big Foot's band. A scouting party of Big Foot's band was out looking for the camp under Kicking Bear and Short Bull, but as these chiefs, with their followers, were already on their way to the agency, the scouting party was returning to rejoin Big Foot when the fight occurred the next morning. It was the intention of General Miles to send Big Foot and his followers back to their own reservation, or to remove them altogether from the country until the excitement had subsided. (*War*, *14*.)

At this time there were no Indians in the Bad Lands. Two Strike and Crow Dog had come in about a week before and were now camped close to the agency. Kicking Bear and Short Bull, with their follow- ers, had yielded to the friendly persuasions of American Horse, Little Wound, Standing Bear, and others who had gone out to them in the interests of peace, and both parties were now coming in together and had arrived at the Catholic mission, 5 miles from the agency, when the battle occurred.

On the morning of December 29, 1890, preparations were made to disarm the Indians preparatory to taking them to the agency and thence to the railroad. In obedience to instructions the Indians had pitched their tipis on the open plain a short distance west of the creek and surrounded on all sides by the soldiers. In the center of the camp the Indians had hoisted a white flag as a sign of peace and a guarantee of safety. Behind them was a dry ravine running into the creek, and on a slight rise in the front was posted the battery of four Hotchkiss machine guns, trained directly on the Indian camp. In front, behind, and on both flanks of the camp were posted the various troops of cav- alry, a portion of two troops, together with the Indian scouts, being dismounted and drawn up in front of the Indians at the distance of only a few yards from them. Big Foot himself was ill of pneumonia in his tipi, and Colonel Forsyth, who had taken command as senior officer, had provided a tent warmed with a camp stove for his reception.

Shortly after 8 oclock in the morning the warriors were ordered to come out from the tipis and deliver their arms. They came forward and seated themselves on the ground in front of the troops. They were then ordered to go by themselves into their tipis and bring out and surrender their guns. The first twenty went and returned in a short time with only two guns. It seemed evident that they were unwilling to give them up, and after consultation of the officers part of the soldiers were ordered up to within ten yards of the group of war- riors, while another detachment of troops was ordered to search the tipis. After a thorough hunt these last returned with about forty rifles, most of which, however, were old and of little value. The search had consumed considerable time and created a good deal of excitement among the women and children, as the soldiers found it necessary in the process to overturn the beds and other furniture of the tipis and in some instances drove out the inmates. All this had its effect on their husbands and brothers, already wrought up to a high nervous tension and not knowing what might come next. While the soldiers had been looking for the guns Yellow Bird, a medicine-man, had been walking about among the warriors, blowing on an eagle-bone whistle, and urging them to resistance, telling them that the soldiers would become weak and powerless, and that the bullets would be

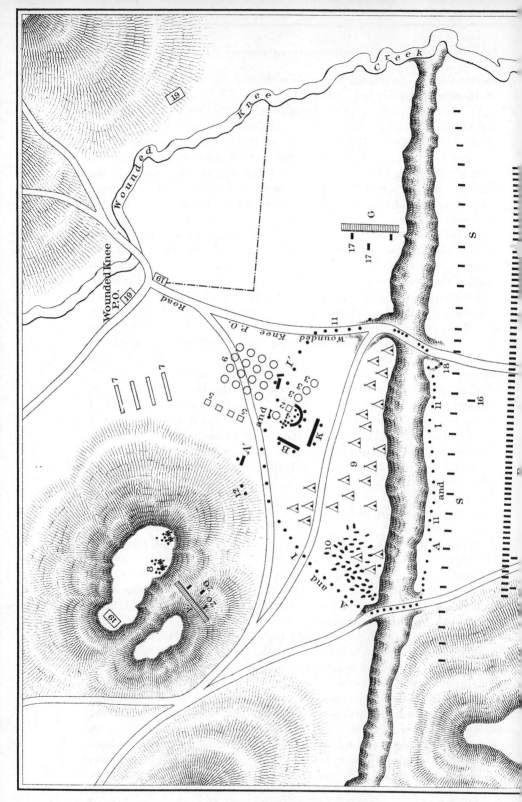

FIG. 16.—Wounded Knee battlefield

EXPLANATION OF FIGURE 16

Compiled from map by Lieutenant T. Q. Donaldson, Seventh United States cavalry, kindly loaned by
Dr J. D. Glennan, United States Army.

A and I. Seventy-six men from A and I troops forming dismounted line of sentinels.

B. Troop B dismounted and in line.

C. Troop C mounted and in line (sorrel troop).

D. Troop D mounted and in line (black troop).

E. Troop E mounted and in line (bay troop).

G. Troop G mounted and in line (gray troop).

K. Troop K dismounted and in line.

S. Indian scouts.

1. Tent from which a hostile warrior shot two soldiers.

2. Tent occupied by Big Foot and his wife and in front of which the former was killed.

3. Tents put up for the use of Big Foot's band.

4. Council ring in or near which were General Forsyth, Major Whitside, Captain Varnum, Captain Hoff, Captain Wallace, Doctor Glennan, Lieutenant Robinson, Lieutenant Nicholson, Lieutenant McCormick, and the reporters.

5. Officers' tents, first battalion.

6. Enlisted mens' tents, first battalion.

7. Bivouac of second battalion on night of December 28, 1890.

8. Four Hotchkiss guns and detachment of First artillery, under Captain Capron, First artillery, and Lieutenant Hawthorne, Second artillery.

9. Indian village.

10. Indian ponies.

11. Dismounted line of sentinels.

12. Captains Ilsley and Moylan.

13. Lieutenants Garlington and Waterman.

14. Captain Godfrey and Lieutenant Tompkins.

15. Captain Jackson and Lieutenant Donaldson.

16. Lieutenant Taylor, Ninth cavalry, commanding Indian scouts (S).

17. Captain Edgerly and Lieutenant Brewer.

18. Captain Nowlan and Lieutenant Gresham.

19. Indian houses.

20. Lieutenants Sickel and Rice.

Just beyond the limit of the map, toward the west, the ravine forms a bend, in which a number of hostiles took refuge, and from which Lieutenant Hawthorne was shot. Captain Wallace was found near the center of the council ring. Big Foot was killed two or three yards in front of his tent. Father Craft was near the center of the ring when stabbed. The Indians broke to the west through B and K troops. While in the council ring all the warriors had on blankets, with their arms, principally Winchester rifles, concealed under them. Most of the warriors, including the medicine-man, were painted and wore ghost shirts.

unavailing against the sacred "ghost shirts," which nearly every one of the Indians wore. As he spoke in the Sioux language, the officers did not at once realize the dangerous drift of his talk, and the climax came too quickly for them to interfere. It is said one of the searchers now attempted to raise the blanket of a warrior. Suddenly Yellow Bird stooped down and threw a handful of dust into the air, when, as if this were the signal, a young Indian, said to have been Black Fox from Cheyenne river, drew a rifle from under his blanket and fired at the soldiers, who instantly replied with a volley directly into the crowd of warriors and so near that their guns were almost touching. From the number of sticks set up by the Indians to mark where the dead fell, as seen by the author a year later, this one volley must have killed nearly half the warriors (Fig. 18). The survivors sprang to their feet, throwing their blankets from their shoulders as they rose, and for a few minutes there was a terrible hand to hand struggle, where every man's thought was to kill. Although many of the warriors had no guns, nearly all had revolvers and knives in their belts under their blankets, together with some of the murderous warclubs still carried by the Sioux. The very lack of guns made the fight more bloody, as it brought the combatants to closer quarters.

At the first volley the Hotchkiss guns trained on the camp opened fire and sent a storm of shells and bullets among the women and children, who had gathered in front of the tipis to watch the unusual spectacle of military display. The guns poured in 2-pound explosive shells at the rate of nearly fifty per minute, mowing down everything alive. The terrible effect may be judged from the fact that one woman survivor, Blue Whirlwind, with whom the author conversed, received fourteen wounds, while each of her two little boys was also wounded by her side. In a few minutes 200 Indian men, women, and children, with 60 soldiers, were lying dead and wounded on the ground, the tipis had been torn down by the shells and some of them were burning above the helpless wounded, and the surviving handful of Indians were flying in wild panic to the shelter of the ravine, pursued by hundreds of maddened soldiers and followed up by a raking fire from the Hotchkiss guns, which had been moved into position to sweep the ravine.

There can be no question that the pursuit was simply a massacre, where fleeing women, with infants in their arms, were shot down after resistance had ceased and when almost every warrior was stretched dead or dying on the ground. On this point such a careful writer as Herbert Welsh says: "From the fact that so many women and children were killed, and that their bodies were found far from the scene of action, and as though they were shot down while flying, it would look as though blind rage had been at work, in striking contrast to the moderation of the Indian police at the Sitting Bull fight when they were assailed by women." (*Welsh, 3.*) The testimony of American Horse and other friendlies is strong in the same direction. (See page

84.) Commissioner Morgan in his official report says that "Most of the men, including Big Foot, were killed around his tent, where he lay sick. The bodies of the women and children were scattered along a distance of two miles from the scene of the encounter." (*Comr.*, *35.*)

This is no reflection on the humanity of the officer in charge. On the contrary, Colonel Forsyth had taken measures to guard against such an occurrence by separating the women and children, as already stated, and had also endeavored to make the sick chief, Big Foot, as comfortable as possible, even to the extent of sending his own surgeon, Dr Glennan, to wait on him on the night of the surrender. Strict orders had also been issued to the troops that women and children were not to be hurt. The butchery was the work of infuriated soldiers whose comrades had just been shot down without cause or warning. In justice to a brave regiment it must be said that a number of the men were new recruits fresh from eastern recruiting stations, who had never before been under fire, were not yet imbued with military discipline, and were probably unable in the confusion to distinguish between men and women by their dress.

After examining all the official papers bearing on the subject in the files of the War Department and the Indian Office, together with the official reports of the Commissioner of Indian Affairs and of the Secretary of War and the several officers engaged; after gathering all that might be obtained from unofficial printed sources and from conversation with survivors and participants in the engagement on both sides, and after going over the battle-ground in company with the interpreter of the scouts engaged, the author arrives at the conclusion that when the sun rose on Wounded Knee on the fatal morning of December 29, 1890, no trouble was anticipated or premeditated by either Indians or troops; that the Indians in good faith desired to surrender and be at peace, and that the officers in the same good faith had made preparations to receive their surrender and escort them quietly to the reservation; that in spite of the pacific intent of Big Foot and his band, the medicine-man, Yellow Bird, at the critical moment urged the warriors to resistance and gave the signal for the attack; that the first shot was fired by an Indian, and that the Indians were responsible for the engagement; that the answering volley and attack by the troops was right and justifiable, but that the wholesale slaughter of women and children was unnecessary and inexcusable.

Authorities differ as to the number of Indians present and killed at Wounded Knee. General Ruger states that the band numbered about 340, including about 100 warriors, but Major Whitside, to whom they surrendered, reported them officially as numbering 120 men and 250 women and children, a total of 370. (*War*, *15; G. D.*, *38.*) This agrees almost exactly with the statement made to the author by Mr Asay, a trader who was present at the surrender. General Miles says that there were present 106 warriors, a few others being absent at the time in

search of the party under Kicking Bear and Short Bull. (*War, 16.*)
Among those who surrendered were about 70 refugees from the bands
of Sitting Bull and Hump. (*G. D., 39.*) No exact account of the dead
could be made immediately after the fight, on account of a second attack
by another party of Indians coming up from the agency. Some of the
dead and wounded left on the field were undoubtedly carried off by
their friends before the burial party came out three days later, and of
those brought in alive a number afterward died of wounds and exposure, but received no notice in the official reports. The Adjutant-
General, in response to a letter of inquiry, states that 128 Indians were
killed and 33 wounded. Commissioner Morgan, in his official report,
makes the number killed 146. (*Comr., 36.*) Both these estimates are
evidently too low. General Miles, in his final report, states that about
200 men, women, and children were killed. (*War, 17.*) General Colby,
who commanded the Nebraska state troops, says that about 100 men
and over 120 women and children were found dead on the field, a total
of about 220. (*Colby, 4.*) Agent Royer telegraphed immediately after
the fight that about 300 Indians had been killed, and General Miles,
telegraphing on the same day, says, "I think very few Indians have
escaped." (*G. D., 40.*) Fifty-one Indians were brought in the same
day by the troops, and a few others were found still alive by the burial
party three days later. A number of these afterward died. No considerable number got away, being unable to reach their ponies after
the fight began. General Miles states that 98 warriors were killed on
the field. (*War, 18.*) The whole number killed on the field, or who
later died from wounds and exposure, was probably very nearly 300.

According to an official statement from the Adjutant-General, 31
soldiers were killed in the battle. About as many more were wounded,
one or two of whom afterward died. All of the killed, excepting
Hospital Steward Pollock and an Indian scout named High Backbone,
belonged to the Seventh cavalry, as did probably also nearly all of the
wounded. The only commissioned officer killed was Captain Wallace.
He received four bullet wounds in his body and finally sank under a
hatchet stroke upon the head. Lieutenant E. A. Garlington, of the
Seventh cavalry, and Lieutenant H. L. Hawthorne, of the Second artillery, were wounded. (*War, 19.*) The last-named officer owed his life
to his watch, which deflected the bullet that otherwise would have
passed through his body.

Below is given a complete list of officers and enlisted men who were
killed, or died of wounds or exposure, in connection with the Sioux
campaign. The statement is contained in an official letter of reply
from the Adjutant-General's office dated May 26, 1894. Unless otherwise noted all were of the Seventh cavalry and were killed on December 29, the date of the battle of Wounded Knee. In addition to these,
two others, Henry Miller, a herder, and George Wilhauer, of the
Nebraska militia, were killed in the same connection. With the 6

Indian police killed in arresting Sitting Bull, this makes a total of 49 deaths on the government side, including 7 Indians and a negro:

Adams, William.

Bone, Albert S. (corporal, died of wounds).

Casey, Edward W. (first lieutenant Twenty-second infantry, January 7).

Coffey, Dora S. (first sergeant).

Cook, Ralph L.

Corwine, Richard W. (sergeant major).

Costello, John.

Cummings, Pierce.

De Vreede, Jan.

Dyer, Arthur C. (sergeant).

Elliott, George (died of wounds, January 13).

Francischetti, Dominic (December 30).

Forrest, Harry R. (corporal).

Frey, Henry.

Grauberg, Herman (died of wounds, December 30).

Haywood, Charles (Ninth cavalry, colored, December 30).

High Backbone (Indian scout).

Hodges, William T. (sergeant).

Howard, Henry (sergeant, died of wounds, January 23).

Johnson, George P.

Kelley, James E.

Kellner, August.

Korn, Gustav (blacksmith).

Logan, James.

McClintock, William F.

McCue, John M.

Mann, James D. (first lieutenant, died of wounds, January 15).

Meil, John W. (killed in railroad accident, January 26).

Mezo, William S.

Murphy, Joseph.

Nettles, Robert H. (sergeant).

Newell, Charles H. (corporal, died of wounds).

Pollock, Oscar (hospital steward).

Regan, Michael.

Reinecky, Frank T.

Schartel, Thomas (First artillery, killed in railroad accident, January 26).

Schwenkey, Philip.

Stone, Harry B. (died of wounds, January 12).

Twohig, Daniel.

Wallace, George B. (captain).

Zehnder, Bernhard (died of wounds).

The heroic missionary priest, Father Craft, who had given a large part of his life to work among the Sioux, by whom he was loved and respected, had endeavored at the beginning of the trouble to persuade the stampeded Indians to come into the agency, but without success, the Indians claiming that no single treaty ever made with them had been fulfilled in all its stipulations. Many of the soldiers being of his own faith, he accompanied the detachment which received the surrender of Big Foot, to render such good offices as might be possible to either party. In the desperate encounter he was stabbed through the lungs, but yet, with bullets flying about him and hatchets and warclubs circling through the air, he went about his work, administering the last religious consolation to the dying until he fell unconscious from loss of blood. He was brought back to the agency along with the other wounded, and although his life was despaired of for some time, he finally recovered. In talking about Wounded Knee with one of the friendly warriors who had gone into the Bad Lands to urge the hostiles to come in, he spoke with warm admiration of Father Craft, and I asked why it was, then, that the Indians had tried to kill him. He replied, " They did not know him. Father Jutz [the priest at the Drexel Catholic mission, previously mentioned] always wears his black robe, but Father Craft on that day wore a soldier's cap and overcoat. If he had worn his black robe, no Indian would have hurt him." On

Fig. 17.—After the battle

MARY IRVIN WRIGHT

inquiring afterward I learned that this was not correct, as Father Craft did have on his priestly robes. From the Indian statement, however, and the well-known affection in which he was held by the Sioux, it is probable that the Indian who stabbed him was too much excited at the moment to recognize him.

The news of the battle was brought to the agency by Lieutenant Guy Preston, of the Ninth cavalry, who, in company with a soldier and an Indian scout, made the ride of 16 or 18 miles in a little over an hour, one horse falling dead of exhaustion on the way. There were then at the agency, under command of General Brooke, about 300 men of the Second infantry and 50 Indian police.

The firing at Wounded Knee was plainly heard by the thousands of Indians camped about the agency at Pine Ridge, who had come in from the Bad Lands to surrender. They were at once thrown into great excitement, undoubtedly believing that there was a deliberate purpose on foot to disarm and massacre them all, and when the fugitives—women and children, most of them—began to come in, telling the story of the terrible slaughter of their friends and showing their bleeding wounds in evidence, the camp was divided between panic and desperation. A number of warriors mounted in haste and made all speed to the battle-ground, only about two hours distant, where they met the troops, who were now scattered about, hunting down the fugitives who might have escaped the first killing, and picking up the dead and wounded. The soldiers were driven in toward the center, where they threw up entrenchments, by means of which they were finally able to repel the attacking party. With the assistance of a body of Indian scouts and police, they then gathered up the dead and wounded soldiers, with some of the wounded Indians and a few other prisoners to the number of 51, and came into the agency. In the meantime the hostiles under Two Strike had opened fire on the agency from the neighboring hills and endeavored to approach, by way of a deep ravine, near enough to set fire to the buildings. General Brooke, desiring to avoid a general engagement, ordered out the Indian police—a splendidly drilled body of 50 brave men—who gallantly took their stand in the center of the agency inclosure, in full view of the hostiles, some of whom were their own relatives, and kept them off, returning the fire of besiegers with such good effect as to kill two and wound several others. The attacking party, as well as those who rode out to help their kinsmen at Wounded Knee, were not the Pine Ridge Indians (Ogalala) but the Brulé from Rosebud under the lead of Two Strike, Kicking Bear, and Short Bull. On the approach of the detachment returning from Wounded Knee almost the entire body that had come in to surrender broke away and fell back to a position on White Clay creek, where the next day found a camp of 4,000 Indians, and including more than a thousand warriors now thoroughly hostile. On the evening of the battle General Miles telegraphed to military headquarters,

"Last night everything looked favorable for getting all the Indians under control; since report from Forsyth it looks more serious than at any other time." (*G. D.*, *41.*) It seemed that all the careful work of the last month had been undone.

At the first indication of coming trouble in November all the outlying schools and mission stations on Pine Ridge reservation had been abandoned, and teachers, farmers, and missionaries had fled to the agency to seek the protection of the troops, all but the members of the Drexel Catholic mission, 5 miles northwest from the agency. Here the two or three priests and five Franciscan sisters remained quietly at their post, with a hundred little children around them, safe in the assurance of the "hostiles" that they would not be molested. While the fighting was going on at Wounded Knee and hundreds of furious warriors were firing into the agency, where the handful of whites were shivering in spite of the presence of troops and police, these gentle women and the kindly old German priest were looking after the children, feeding the frightened fugitive women, and tenderly caring for the wounded Indians who were being brought in from Wounded Knee and the agency. Throughout all these weeks of terror they went calmly about the duties to which they had consecrated their lives, and kept their little flock together and their school in operation, without the presence of a single soldier, completely cut off from the troops and the agency and surrounded by thousands of wild Indians.

Some time afterward, in talking with the Indians about the events of the campaign, the warrior who had spoken with such admiration of Father Craft referred with the same affectionate enthusiasm to Father Jutz, and said that when the infuriated Indians attacked the agency on hearing of the slaughter at Wounded Knee they had sent word to the mission that no one there need be afraid. "We told him to stay where he was and no Indian would disturb him," said the warrior. He told how the priest and the sisters had fed the starving refugees and bound up the wounds of the survivors who escaped the slaughter, and then after a pause he said: "He is a brave man; braver than any Indian." Curious to know why this man had not joined the hostiles, among whom were several of his near relatives, I asked him the question. His reply was simple: "I had a little boy at the Drexel mission. He died and Father Jutz put a white stone over him. That is why I did not join the hostiles."

While visiting Pine Ridge in 1891 I went out to see the Drexel school and found Father John Jutz, a simple, kindly old German from the Tyrol, with one or two other German lay brothers and five Franciscan sisters, Americans. Although but a recent establishment, the school was in flourishing condition, bearing in everything the evidences of orderly industry. Like a true German of the Alps, Father Jutz had already devised a way to make jelly from the wild plums and excellent wine from the chokecherry. While talking, the recess hour arrived and

FIG. 18.—Battlefield of Wounded Knee

a bevy of small children came trooping in, pushing over one another in the effort to get hold of a finger of the good father, or at least to hold on to his robe while he led them into another room where one of the sisters gave to each a ginger cake, hot from the oven. The room was filled with the shouts and laughter of the children and the father explained, "Children get hungry, and we always have some cakes for the little ones at recess. I let the boys be noisy in the playroom as long as they don't fight. It is good for them." Looking at the happy, noisy crowd around the black-gowned missionary and sister, it was easy to see how they had felt safe in the affection of the Indians through all the days and nights when others were trembling behind breastworks and files of soldiers. Referring to what the Indians had told me, I asked Father Jutz if it was true that the hostiles had sent word to them not to be afraid. He replied, "Yes; they had sent word that no one in the mission need be alarmed," and then, with a gentle smile, he added, "But it was never our intention to leave." It was plain enough that beneath the quiet exterior there burned the old missionary fire of Jogues and Marquette.

The conflict at Wounded Knee bore speedy fruit. On the same day, as has been said, a part of the Indians under Two Strike attacked the agency and the whole body of nearly 4,000 who had come in to sur- render started back again to intrench themselves in preparation for renewed hostilities. On the morning of December 30, the next day after the fight, the wagon train of the Ninth cavalry (colored) was attacked within 2 miles of the agency while coming in with supplies. One soldier was killed, but the Indians were repulsed with the loss of several of their number.

On the same day news came to the agency that the hostiles had attacked the Catholic mission 5 miles out, and Colonel Forsyth with eight troops of the Seventh cavalry and one piece of artillery was ordered by General Brooke to go out and drive them off. It proved that the hostiles had set fire to several houses between the mission and the agency, but the mission had not been disturbed. As the troops approached the hostiles fell back, but Forsyth failed to occupy the commanding hills and was consequently surrounded by the Indians, who endeavored to draw him into a canyon and pressed him so closely that he was obliged to send back three times for reinforcements. Major Henry had just arrived at the agency with a detachment of the Ninth cavalry, and on hearing the noise of the firing started at once to the relief of Forsyth with four troops of cavalry and a Hotchkiss gun. On arriving on the ground he occupied the hills and thus succeeded in driving off the hostiles without further casualty, and rescued the Seventh from its dangerous position. In this skirmish, known as the "mission fight," the Seventh lost one officer, Lieutenant Mann, and a private, Dominic Francischetti, killed, and seven wounded. (*War, 20; G. D., 42.*)

The conduct of the colored troops of the Ninth calvary on this occasion deserves the highest commendation. At the time of the battle at Wounded Knee, the day before, they were in the Bad Lands, about 80 or 90 miles out from Pine Ridge, when the order was sent for them to come in to aid in repelling the attack on the agency. By riding all night they arrived at the agency at daylight, together with two Hotchkiss guns, in charge of Lieutenant John Hayden of the First artillery. Hardly had they dismounted when word arrived that their wagon train, coming on behind, was attacked, and they were obliged to go out again to its relief, as already described. On coming in again they lay down to rest after their long night ride, when they were once more called out to go to the aid of the Seventh at the mission. Jumping into the saddle they rode at full speed to the mission, 5 miles out, repelled the hostiles and saved the command, and returned to the agency, after having ridden over 100 miles and fought two engagements within thirty hours. Lieutenant Hayden, with his Hotchkiss, who had come in with them from the Bad Lands, took part also with them in the mission fight.

On the same evening Standing Soldier, an Indian scout, arrived at the agency with a party of 65 Indians, including 18 men. These were a part of Big Foot's or Short Bull's following, who had lost their way during the flight from Cheyenne river and were hunting for the rest of the band when captured by the scouts. They were not aware of the death of Big Foot and the extermination of his band, but after having been disarmed and put under guard they were informed of it, but only in a mild way, in order not to provoke undue excitement. (*G. D.*, *43*.)

Immediately after the battle of Wounded Knee, in consequence of the panic among the frontier settlers of Nebraska, the Nebraska state troops were called out under command of General L. W. Colby. They were stationed at the most exposed points between the settlements and the reservation and remained in the field until the surrender of the hostiles two weeks later. The only casualty among them was the death of private George Wilhauer, who was accidentally shot by a picket. (*Colby, 5.*)

On New Year's day of 1891, three days after the battle, a detachment of troops was sent out to Wounded Knee to gather up and bury the Indian dead and to bring in the wounded who might be still alive on the field. In the meantime there had been a heavy snowstorm, culminating in a blizzard. The bodies of the slaughtered men, women, and children were found lying about under the snow, frozen stiff and covered with blood (Fig. 17). Almost all the dead warriors were found lying near where the fight began, about Big Foot's tipi, but the bodies of the women and children were found scattered along for 2 miles from the scene of the encounter, showing that they had been killed while trying to escape. (*Comr., 37; Colby, 6.*) A number of women and children were found still alive, but all badly wounded or frozen, or both, and most of them died after being brought in. Four babies were found

Fig. 19.—Burying the dead

alive under the snow, wrapped in shawls and lying beside their dead mothers, whose last thought had been of them. They were all badly frozen and only one lived. The tenacity of life so characteristic of wild

FIG. 20.—Survivors of Wounded Knee—Blue Whirlwind and children (1891)

people as well as of wild beasts was strikingly illustrated in the case of these wounded and helpless Indian women and children who thus lived three days through a Dakota blizzard, without food, shelter, or attention to their wounds. It is a commentary on our boasted Christian civilization that although there were two or three salaried missionaries at the agency not one went out to say a prayer over the poor mangled bodies of these victims of war.   The Catholic priests had reasons for not being present, as one of them, Father Craft, was lying in the hospital with a dangerous wound received on the battlefield while bravely administering to the dying wants of the soldiers in the heat of the encounter, and the other, Father Jutz, an old man of 70 years, was at the mission school 5 miles away, still attending to his little flock of 100 children

FIG. 21.—Survivors of Wounded Knee—Marguerite Zitkala-noni (1891)

as before the trouble began, and unaware of what was transpiring at the agency.

A long trench was dug and into it were thrown all the bodies, piled one upon another like so much cordwood, until the pit was full, when the earth was heaped over them and the funeral was complete (Fig. 19). Many of the bodies were stripped by the whites, who went out in order to get the " ghost shirts," and the frozen bodies were thrown into the trench stiff and naked.   They were only dead Indians.   As one of the burial party said, " It was a thing to melt the heart of a man, if it was

FIG. 22.—Grave of the dead at Wounded Knee

of stone, to see those little children, with their bodies shot to pieces, thrown naked into the pit." The dead soldiers had already been brought in and buried decently at the agency. When the writer visited the spot the following winter, the Indians had put up a wire fence around the trench and smeared the posts with sacred red medicine paint (Fig. 22).

A baby girl of only three or four months was found under the snow, carefully wrapped up in a shawl, beside her dead mother, whose body was pierced by two bullets. On her head was a little cap of buckskin,

FIG. 23.—Survivors of Wounded Knee—Jennie Sword (1891)

upon which the American flag was embroidered in bright beadwork. She had lived through all the exposure, being only slightly frozen, and soon recovered after being brought in to the agency. Her mother being killed, and, in all probability, her father also, she was adopted by General Colby, commanding the Nebraska state troops. The Indian women in camp gave her the poetic name of Zitkala-noni, "Lost Bird," and by the family of her adoption she was baptized under the name of Marguerite (Fig. 21). She is now (1896) living in the general's family at Washington, a chubby little girl 6 years of age, as happy with her dolls and playthings as a little girl of that age ought to be.

Another little girl about 5 years of age was picked up on the battle-field and brought in by the Indian police on the afternoon of the fight. She was adopted by George Sword, captain of the Indian police, and is now living with him under the name of Jennie Sword, a remarkably pretty little girl, gentle and engaging in her manners (Fig. 23).

A little boy of four years, the son of Yellow Bird, the medicine-man, was playing on his pony in front of a tipi when the firing began. As

Fig. 24.—Survivors of Wounded Knee—Herbert Zitkalazi (1892)

he described it some time ago in lisping English: "My father ran and fell down and the blood came out of his mouth [he was shot through the head], and then a soldier put his gun up to my white pony's nose and shot him, and then I ran and a policeman got me." As his father was thus killed and his mother was already dead, he was adopted by Mrs Lucy Arnold, who had been a teacher among the Sioux and knew his

family before the trouble began. She had already given him his name, Herbert Zitkælazi, the last word being the Sioux form of his father's name, "Yellow Bird." She brought him back with her to Washington, where he soon learned English and became a general favorite of all who knew him for his affectionate disposition and unusual intelligence, with genuine boyish enthusiasm in all he undertook. His picture here given (Fig. 24) is from a photograph made in Lafayette park, Washington, in 1892. His adopted mother having resumed her school work among his tribe, he is now back with her, attending school under her supervision at Standing Rock, where, as in Washington, he seems to be a natural leader among those of his own age. When we think of these children and consider that only by the merest accident they escaped the death that overtook a hundred other children at Wounded Knee, who may all have had in themselves the same possibilities of affection, education, and happy usefulness, we can understand the sickening meaning of such affairs as the Chivington massacre in Colorado and the Custer fight on the Washita, where the newspaper reports merely that "the enemy was surprised and the Indian camp destroyed."

The Indian scouts at Wounded Knee, like the Indian police at Grand river and Pine Ridge, were brave and loyal, as has been the almost universal rule with Indians when enlisted in the government service, even when called on, as were these, to serve against their own tribe and relatives. The prairie Indian is a born soldier, with all the soldier's pride of loyalty to duty, and may be trusted implicitly after he has once consented to enter the service. The scouts at Wounded Knee were Sioux, with Philip Wells as interpreter. Other Sioux scouts were ranging the country between the agency and the hostile camp in the Bad Lands, and acted as mediators in the peace negotiations which led to the final surrender. Fifty Cheyenne and about as many Crow scouts were also employed in the same section of country. Throughout the entire campaign the Indian scouts and police were faithful and received the warmest commendation of their officers.

On New Year's day, 1891, Henry Miller, a herder, was killed by Indians a few miles from the agency. This was the only noncombatant killed by the Indians during the entire campaign, and during the same period there was no depredation committed by them outside of the reservation. On the next day the agent reported that the school buildings and Episcopal church on White Clay creek had been burned by hostiles, who were then camped to the number of about 3,000 on Grass creek, 15 miles northeast of the agency. They had captured the government beef herd and were depending on it for food. Red Cloud, Little Wound, and their people were with them and were reported as anxious to return, but prevented by the hostile leaders, Two Strike, Short Bull, and Kicking Bear, who threatened to kill the first one who made a move to come in. (*G. D.*, 44.) A few days later a number of

Red Cloud's men came in and surrendered and reported that the old chief was practically a prisoner and wanted the soldiers to come and rescue him from the hostiles, who were trying to force him into the war. They reported further that there was much suffering from cold and hunger in the Indian camp, and that all the Ogalala (Red Cloud's people of Pine Ridge) were intending to come in at once in a body.

On the 3d of January General Miles took up his headquarters at Pine Ridge and directed General Brooke to assume immediate command of the troops surrounding the hostile camp. Brooke's men swung out to form the western and northern part of a circle about the hostiles, cutting them off from the Bad Lands, while the troops under General Carr closed in on the east and northeast in such a way that the Indians were hemmed in and unable to make a move in any direction excepting toward the agency.

On January 3 a party of hostiles attacked a detachment of the Sixth cavalry under Captain Kerr on Grass creek, a few miles north of the agency, but were quickly repulsed with the loss of four of their number, the troops having been reinforced by other detachments in the vicinity. In this engagement the Indian scouts again distinguished themselves. (*War, 21.*) The effect of this repulse was to check the westward movement of the hostiles and hold them in their position along White Clay creek until their passion had somewhat abated.

On January 5 there was another encounter on Wounded Knee creek. A small detachment which had been sent out to meet a supply train coming into the agency found the wagons drawn up in a square to resist an attack made by a band of about 50 Indians. The soldiers joined forces with the teamsters, and by firing from behind the protection of the wagons succeeded in driving off the Indians and killing a number of their horses. The hostiles were reinforced, however, and a hard skirmish was kept up for several hours until more troops arrived from the agency about dark, having been sent in answer to a courier who managed to elude the attacking party. The troops charged on a gallop and the Indians retreated, having lost several killed and wounded, besides a number of their horses. (*Colby, 7.*)

Amid all these warlike alarms the gentle muse Calliope hovered over the field and inspired W. H. Prather, a colored private of troop I of the Ninth cavalry, to the production of the ballad given below, one of the few good specimens of American ballad poetry, and worthy of equal place with "Captain Lovewell's Fight," "Old Quebec," or anything that originated in the late rebellion. It became a favorite among the troops in camp and with the scattered frontiersmen of Dakota and Nebraska, being sung to a simple air with vigor and expression and a particularly rousing chorus, and is probably by this time a classic of the barracks. It is here reproduced verbatim from the printed slip published for distribution among the soldiers during the campaign.

THE INDIAN GHOST DANCE AND WAR

The Red Skins left their Agency, the Soldiers left their Post,
All on the strength of an Indian tale about Messiah's ghost
Got up by savage chieftains to lead their tribes astray;
But Uncle Sam wouldn't have it so, for he ain't built that way.
They swore that this Messiah came to them in visions sleep,
And promised to restore their game and Buffalos a heap,
So they must start a big ghost dance, then all would join their band,
And may be so we lead the way into the great Bad Land.

Chorus :

They claimed the shirt Messiah gave, no bullet could go through,
But when the Soldiers fired at them they saw this was not true.
The Medicine man supplied them with their great Messiah's grace,
And he, too, pulled his freight and swore the 7th hard to face.

About their tents the Soldiers stood, awaiting one and all,
That they might hear the trumpet clear when sounding General call
Or Boots and Saddles in a rush, that each and every man
Might mount in haste, ride soon and fast to stop this devilish band
But Generals great like Miles and Brooke don't do things up that way,
For they know an Indian like a book, and let him have his sway
Until they think him far enough and then to John they'll say,
"You had better stop your fooling or we'll bring our guns to play."

Chorus.—They claimed the shirt, etc.

The 9th marched out with splendid cheer the Bad Lands to explo'e—
With Col. Henry at their head they never fear the foe;
So on they rode from Xmas eve 'till dawn of Xmas day;
The Red Skins heard the 9th was near and fled in great dismay;
The 7th is of courage bold both officers and men,
But bad luck seems to follow them and twice has took them in;
They came in contact with Big Foot's warriors in their fierce might
This chief made sure he had a chance of vantage in the fight.

Chorus.—They claimed the shirt, etc.

A fight took place, 'twas hand to hand, unwarned by trumpet call,
While the Sioux were dropping man by man—the 7th killed them all,
And to that regiment be said "Ye noble braves, well done,
Although you lost some gallant men a glorious fight you've won."
The 8th was there, the sixth rode miles to swell that great command
And waited orders night and day to round up Short Bull's band.
The Infantry marched up in mass the Cavalry's support,
And while the latter rounded up, the former held the fort.

Chorus.—They claimed the shirt, etc.

E battery of the 1st stood by and did their duty well,
For every time the Hotchkiss barked they say a hostile fell.
Some Indian soldiers chipped in too and helped to quell the fray,
And now the campaign's ended and the soldiers marched away.
So all have done their share, you see, whether it was thick or thin,
And all helped break the ghost dance up and drive the hostiles in.
The settlers in that region now can breathe with better grace;
They only ask and pray to God to make John hold his base.

Chorus.—They claimed the shirt, etc.

(W. H. Prather, I, 9th Cavalry).

APPENDIX—THE INDIAN STORY OF WOUNDED KNEE

[*From the Report of the Commissioner of Indian Affairs for 1891, volume 1, pages 179–181. Extracts from verbatim stenographic report of council held by delegations of Sioux with Commissioner of Indian Affairs, at Washington, February 11, 1891.*]

TURNING HAWK, Pine Ridge (Mr Cook, interpreter). Mr Commissioner, my purpose to-day is to tell you what I know of the condition of affairs at the agency where I live. A certain falsehood came to our agency from the west which had the effect of a fire upon the Indians, and when this certain fire came upon our people those who had farsightedness and could see into the matter made up their minds to stand up against it and fight it. The reason we took this hostile attitude to this fire was because we believed that you yourself would not be in favor of this particular mischief-making thing; but just as we expected, the people in authority did not like this thing and we were quietly told that we must give up or have nothing to do with this certain movement. Though this is the advice from our good friends in the east, there were, of course, many silly young men who were longing to become identified with the movement, although they knew that there was nothing absolutely bad, nor did they know there was anything absolutely good, in connection with the movement.

In the course of time we heard that the soldiers were moving toward the scene of trouble. After awhile some of the soldiers finally reached our place and we heard that a number of them also reached our friends at Rosebud. Of course, when a large body of soldiers is moving toward a certain direction they inspire a more or less amount of awe, and it is natural that the women and children who see this large moving mass are made afraid of it and be put in a condition to make them run away. At first we thought that Pine Ridge and Rosebud were the only two agencies where soldiers were sent, but finally we heard that the other agencies fared likewise. We heard and saw that about half our friends at Rosebud agency, from fear at seeing the soldiers, began the move of running away from their agency toward ours (Pine Ridge), and when they had gotten inside of our reservation they there learned that right ahead of them at our agency was another large crowd of soldiers, and while the soldiers were there, there was constantly a great deal of false rumor flying back and forth. The special rumor I have in mind is the threat that the soldiers had come there to disarm the Indians entirely and to take away all their horses from them. That was the oft-repeated story.

So constantly repeated was this story that our friends from Rosebud, instead of going to Pine Ridge, the place of their destination, veered off and went to some other direction toward the "Bad Lands." We did not know definitely how many, but understood there were 300 lodges of them, about 1,700 people. Eagle Pipe, Turning Bear, High Hawk, Short Bull, Lance, No Flesh, Pine Bird, Crow Dog, Two Strike, and White Horse were the leaders.

Well, the people after veering off in this way, many of them who believe in peace and order at our agency, were very anxious that some influence should be brought upon these people. In addition to our love of peace we remembered that many of these people were related to us by blood. So we sent out peace commissioners to the people who were thus running away from their agency.

I understood at the time that they were simply going away from fear because of so many soldiers. So constant was the word of these good men from Pine Ridge agency that finally they succeeded in getting away half of the party from Rosebud, from the place where they took refuge, and finally were brought to the agency at Pine Ridge. Young-Man-Afraid-of-his-Horses, Little Wound, Fast Thunder, Louis Shangreau, John Grass, Jack Red Cloud, and myself were some of these peacemakers.

The remnant of the party from Rosebud not taken to the agency finally reached the wilds of the Bad Lands. Seeing that we had succeeded so well, once more we sent to the same party in the Bad Lands and succeeded in bringing these very Indians out of the depths of the Bad Lands and were being brought toward the agency. When we were about a day's journey from our agency we heard that a certain party of Indians (Big Foot's band) from the Cheyenne River agency was coming toward Pine Ridge in flight.

CAPTAIN SWORD. Those who actually went off of the Cheyenne River agency probably number 303, and there were a few from the Standing Rock reserve with them, but as to their number I do not know. There were a number of Ogalallas, old men and several school boys, coming back with that very same party, and one of the very seriously wounded boys was a member of the Ogalalla boarding school at Pine Ridge agency. He was not on the warpath, but was simply returning home to his agency and to his school after a summer visit to relatives on the Cheyenne river.

TURNING HAWK. When we heard that these people were coming toward our agency we also heard this. These people were coming toward Pine Ridge agency, and when they were almost on the agency they were met by the soldiers and surrounded and finally taken to the Wounded Knee creek, and there at a given time their guns were demanded. When they had delivered them up, the men were separated from their families, from their tipis, and taken to a certain spot. When the guns were thus taken and the men thus separated, there was a crazy man, a young man of very bad influence and in fact a nobody, among that bunch of Indians fired his gun, and of course the firing of a gun must have been the breaking of a military rule of some sort, because immediately the soldiers returned fire and indiscriminate killing followed.

SPOTTED HORSE. This man shot an officer in the army; the first shot killed this officer. I was a voluntary scout at that encounter and I saw exactly what was done, and that was what I noticed; that the first shot killed an officer. As soon as this shot was fired the Indians immediately began drawing their knives, and they were exhorted from all sides to desist, but this was not obeyed. Consequently the firing began immediately on the part of the soldiers.

TURNING HAWK. All the men who were in a bunch were killed right there, and those who escaped that first fire got into the ravine, and as they went along up the ravine for a long distance they were pursued on both sides by the soldiers and shot down, as the dead bodies showed afterwards. The women were standing off at a different place from where the men were stationed, and when the firing began, those of the men who escaped the first onslaught went in one direction up the ravine, and then the women, who were bunched together at another place, went entirely in a different direction through an open field, and the women fared the same fate as the men who went up the deep ravine.

AMERICAN HORSE. The men were separated, as has already been said, from the women, and they were surrounded by the soldiers. Then came next the village of the Indians and that was entirely surrounded by the soldiers also. When the firing began, of course the people who were standing immediately around the young man who fired the first shot were killed right together, and then they turned their guns, Hotchkiss guns, etc., upon the women who were in the lodges standing there under a flag of truce, and of course as soon as they were fired upon they fled, the men fleeing in one direction and the women running in two different directions. So that there were three general directions in which they took flight.

There was a women with an infant in her arms who was killed as she almost touched the flag of truce, and the women and children of course were strewn all along the circular village until they were dispatched. Right near the flag of truce a mother was shot down with her infant; the child not knowing that its mother was dead was still nursing, and that especially was a very sad sight. The women as they were fleeing with their babes were killed together, shot right through, and the women who were very heavy with child were also killed. All the Indians fled in these three directions, and after most all of them had been killed a cry was made that all those who were not killed or wounded should come forth and they would be safe. Little boys who were not wounded came out of their places of refuge, and as soon as they came in sight a number of soldiers surrounded them and butchered them there.

Of course we all feel very sad about this affair. I stood very loyal to the government all through those troublesome days, and believing so much in the government and being so loyal to it, my disappointment was very strong, and I have come to Washington with a very great blame on my heart. Of course it would have been all right if only the men were killed; we would feel almost grateful for it. But the fact of the killing of the women, and more especially the killing of the young boys and girls who are to go to make up the future strength of the Indian people, is the saddest part of the whole affair and we feel it very sorely.

I was not there at the time before the burial of the bodies, but I did go there with some of the police and the Indian doctor and a great many of the people, men from the agency, and we went through the battlefield and saw where the bodies were from the track of the blood.

TURNING HAWK. I had just reached the point where I said that the women were killed. We heard, besides the killing of the men, of the onslaught also made upon the women and children, and they were treated as roughly and indiscriminately as the men and boys were.

Of course this affair brought a great deal of distress upon all the people, but especially upon the minds of those who stood loyal to the government and who did all that they were able to do in the matter of bringing about peace. They especially have suffered much distress and are very much hurt at heart. These peacemakers continued on in their good work, but there were a great many fickle young men who were ready to be moved by the change in the events there, and consequently, in spite of the great fire that was brought upon all, they were ready to assume any hostile attitude. These young men got themselves in readiness and went in the direction of the scene of battle so they might be of service there. They got there and finally exchanged shots with the soldiers. This party of young men was made up from Rosebud, Ogalalla (Pine Ridge), and members of any other agencies that happened to be there at the time. While this was going on in the neighborhood of Wounded Knee — the Indians and soldiers exchanging shots — the agency, our home, was also fired into by the Indians. Matters went on in this strain until the evening came on, and then the Indians went off down by White Clay creek. When the agency was fired upon by the Indians from the hillside, of course the shots were returned by the Indian police who were guarding the agency buildings.

Although fighting seemed to have been in the air, yet those who believed in peace were still constant at their work. Young-Man-Afraid-of-his-Horses, who had been on a visit to some other agency in the north or northwest, returned, and immediately went out to the people living about White Clay creek, on the border of the Bad Lands, and brought his people out. He succeeded in obtaining the consent of the people to come out of their place of refuge and return to the agency. Thus the remaining portion of the Indians who started from Rosebud were brought back into the agency. Mr Commissioner, during the days of the great whirlwind out there, those good men tried to hold up a counteracting power, and that was "Peace." We have now come to realize that peace has prevailed and won the day. While we were engaged in bringing about peace our property was left behind, of course, and most of us have lost everything, even down to the matter of guns with which to kill ducks, rabbits, etc, shotguns, and guns of that order. When Young-Man-Afraid brought the people in and their guns were asked for, both men who were called hostile and men who stood loyal to the government delivered up their guns.

CHAPTER VI

Close of the Outbreak—the Ghost Dance in the South

In the meantime overtures of peace had been made by General Miles to the hostiles, most of whose leaders he knew personally, having received their surrender on the Yellowstone ten years before, at the close of the Custer war. On the urgent representations of himself and others Congress had also appropriated the necessary funds for carrying out the terms of the late treaty, by the disregard of which most of the trouble had been caused, so that the commander was now able to assure the Indians that their rights and necessities would receive attention. They were urged to come in and surrender, with a guaranty that the general himself would represent their case with the government. At the same time they were informed that retreat was cut off and that further resistance would be unavailing. As an additional step toward regaining their confidence, the civilian agents were removed from the several disturbed agencies, which were then put in charge of military officers well known and respected by the Indians. Cheyenne River agency was assigned to Captain J. H. Hurst, and Rosebud agency to Captain J. M. Lee, while Royer, at Pine Ridge, was superseded on January 8 by Captain F. E. Pierce. The last-named officer was afterward relieved by Captain Charles G. Penney, who is now in charge. (*War, 22; Comr., 38; G. D., 45.*)

The friendly overtures made by General Miles, with evidences that the government desired to remedy their grievances, and that longer resistance was hopeless, had their effect on the hostiles. Little Wound, Young-man-afraid-of-his-horses (more properly, "Young-man-of-whose-horses-they-are-afraid), Big Road, and other friendly chiefs, also used their persuasions with such good effect that by January 12 the whole body of nearly 4,000 Indians had moved in to within sight of the agency and expressed their desire for peace. The troops closed in around them, and on the 16th of January, 1891, the hostiles surrendered, and the outbreak was at an end. They complied with every order and direction given by the commander, and gave up nearly 200 rifles, which, with other arms already surrendered, made a total of between 600 and 700 guns, more than had ever before been surrendered by the Sioux at one time. As a further guaranty of good faith, the commander demanded the surrender of Kicking Bear and Short Bull, the principal leaders, with about twenty other prominent warriors, as

hostages. The demand was readily complied with, and the men designated came forward voluntarily and gave themselves up as sureties for
the good conduct of their people. They were sent to Fort Sheridan,
Illinois, near Chicago, where they were kept until there was no further
apprehension, and were then returned to their homes. (*War, 23; Colby,*
8.) After the surrender the late hostiles pitched their camp, numbering in all 742 tipis, in the bottom along White Clay creek, just west of
the agency, where General Miles had supplies of beef, coffee, and sugar
issued to them from the commissary department, and that night they
enjoyed the first full meal they had known in several weeks.

Thus ended the so called Sioux outbreak of 1890–91. It might be
better designated, however, as a Sioux panic and stampede, for, to
quote the expressive letter of McGillycuddy, writing under date of
January 15, 1891, "Up to date there has been neither a Sioux outbreak or war. No citizen in Nebraska or Dakota has been killed,
molested, or can show the scratch of a pin, and no property has been
destroyed off the reservation." (*Colby, 9.*) Only a single noncombatant
was killed by the Indians, and that was close to the agency. The
entire time occupied by the campaign, from the killing of Sitting Bull
to the surrender at Pine Ridge, was only thirty-two days. The late
hostiles were returned to their homes as speedily as possible. The
Brulé of Rosebud, regarded as the most turbulent of the hostiles, were
taken back to the agency by Captain Lee, for whom they had respect,
founded on an acquaintance of several years' standing, without escort
and during the most intense cold of winter, but without any trouble or
dissatisfaction whatever. The military were returned to their usual
stations, and within a few weeks after the surrender affairs at the various agencies were moving again in the usual channel.

An unfortunate event occurred just before the surrender in the killing
of Lieutenant E. W. Casey of the Twenty-second infantry by Plenty
Horses, a young Brulé, on January 7. Lieutenant Casey was in command of a troop of Cheyenne scouts, and was stationed at the mouth
of White Clay creek, charged with the special duty of watching the
hostile camp, which was located 8 miles farther up the creek at No
Water's place. On the day before his death several of the hostiles had
visited him and held a friendly conference. The next morning, in company with two scouts, he went out avowedly for the purpose of observ-
ing the hostile camp more closely. He rode up to within a short distance
of the camp, meeting and talking with several of the Indians on the
way, and had stopped to talk with a half-blood relative of Red Cloud,
when Plenty Horses, a short distance away, deliberately shot him
through the head, and he fell from his horse dead. His body was not
disturbed by the Indians, but was brought in by some of the Cheyenne
scouts soon after. Plenty Horses was arraigned before a United States
court, but was acquitted on the ground that as the Sioux were then at
war and the officer was practically a spy upon the Indian camp, the act

was not murder in the legal sense of the word. Lieutenant Casey had been for a year in charge of the Cheyenne scouts and had taken great interest in their welfare and proficiency, and his death was greatly deplored by the Indians as the insane act of a boy overcome by the excitement of the times. (*War, 24; Comr., 39; Colby, 10; G. D., 46.*)

On January 11 an unprovoked murder was committed on a small party of peaceable Indians on Belle Fourche, or North fork of Cheyenne river, by which the Indians who had come in to surrender were once more thrown into such alarm that for a time it seemed as if serious trouble might result. A party of Ogalala from Pine Ridge, consisting of Few Tails, a kindly, peaceable old man, with his wife, an old woman, and One Feather, with his wife and two children—one a girl about 13 years of age and the other an infant—had been hunting in the Black Hills under a pass from the agency. They had had a successful hunt, and were returning with their two wagons well loaded with meat, when they camped for the night at the mouth of Alkali creek. During the evening they were visited by some soldiers stopping at a ranch a few miles distant, who examined their pass and pronounced it all right. In the morning, after breakfast, the Indians started on again toward the agency, but had gone only a few hundred yards when they were fired upon by a party of white men concealed near the road. The leaders of the whites were three brothers named Culbertson, one of whom had but recently returned from the penitentiary. One of the murderers had visited the Indians in their camp the night before, and even that very morning. At the first fire Few Tails was killed, together with both ponies attached to the wagon. His wife jumped out and received two bullets, which brought her to the ground. The murderers rode past her, however, to get at the other Indian, who was coming up behind in the other wagon with his wife and two children. As soon as he saw his companion killed, One Feather turned his wagon in the other direction, and, telling his wife, who had also been shot, to drive on as fast as she could to save the children, he jumped upon one of the spare ponies and held off the murderers until his family had had time to make some distance. He then turned and joined his family and drove on for some 8 or 10 miles until the pursuers came up again, when he again turned and fought them off, while his wife went ahead with the wagon and the children. The wounded woman bravely drove on, while the two little children lay down in the wagon with their heads covered up in the blankets. As they drove they passed near a house, from which several other shots were fired at the flying mother, when her husband again rode up and kept off the whole party until the wagon could get ahead. Finally, as the ponies were tired out, this heroic man abandoned the wagon and put the two children on one of the spare ponies and his wounded wife and himself upon another and continued to retreat until the whites gave up the pursuit. He finally reached the agency with the wife and children.

The wife of Few Tails, after falling wounded by two bullets beside the wagon in which was her dead husband, lay helpless and probably unconscious upon the ground through all the long winter night until morning, when she revived, and finding one of the horses still alive, mounted it and managed by night to reach a settler's house about 15 miles away. Instead of meeting help and sympathy, however, she was driven off by the two men there with loaded rifles, and leaving her horse in her fright, she hurried away as well as she could with a bullet in her leg and another in her breast, passing by the trail of One Feather's wagon with the tracks of his pursuers fresh behind it, until she came near a trader's store about 20 miles farther south. Afraid to go near it on account of her last experience, the poor woman circled around it, and continued, wounded, cold, and starving as she was, to travel by night and hide by day until she reached the Bad Lands. The rest may be told in her own words:

After that I traveled every night, resting daytime, until I got here at the beef corral. Then I was very tired, and was near the military camp, and early in the morning a soldier came out and he shouted something back, and in a few minutes fifty men were there, and they got a blanket and took me to a tent. I had no blanket and my feet were swelled, and I was about ready to die. After I got to the tent a doctor came in—a soldier doctor, because he had straps on his shoulders—and washed me and treated me well.

A few of the soldiers camped near the scene of the attack had joined in the pursuit at the beginning, on the representations of some of the murderers, but abandoned it as soon as they found their mistake. According to all the testimony, the killing was a wanton, unprovoked, and deliberate murder, yet the criminals were acquitted in the local courts. The apathy displayed by the authorities of Meade county, South Dakota, in which the murder was committed, called forth some vigorous protests. Colonel Shafter, in his statement of the case, concludes, referring to the recent killing of Lieutenant Casey: "So long as Indians are being arrested and held for killing armed men under conditions of war, it seems to me that the white murderers of a part of a band of peaceful Indians should not be permitted to escape punishment." The Indians took the same view of the case, and when General Miles demanded of Young-man-afraid-of-his-horses the surrender of the slayers of Casey and the herder Miller, the old chief indignantly replied: "No; I will not surrender them, but if you will bring the white men who killed Few Tails, I will bring the Indians who killed the white soldier and the herder; and right out here in front of your tipi I will have my young men shoot the Indians and you have your soldiers shoot the white men, and then we will be done with the whole business."

In regard to the heroic conduct of One Feather, the officer then in charge of the agency says: "The determination and genuine courage, as well as the generalship he manifested in keeping at a distance the six men who were pursuing him, and the devotion he showed toward his family, risking his life against great odds, designate him as entitled to a place on the list of heroes." (*War, 25; Comr., 40; G. D., 47.*)

On the recommendation of General Miles, a large delegation of the principal leaders of both friendly and hostile parties among the Sioux was allowed to visit Washington in February, 1891, to present their grievances and suggest remedies for dissatisfaction in the future. Among the principal speakers were: From Pine Ridge, American Horse, Captain George Sword, Big Road, and He Dog; from Rosebud, White Bird and Turning Hawk; from Cheyenne River, Little No Heart and Straight Head; from Standing Rock, John Grass and Mad Bear. The interpreters were Reverend C. S. Cook, David Zephier, Louis Primeau, Louis Richard, Clarence Three Stars, and Louis Shangreau. Their visit was eminently satisfactory and resulted in the inauguration of a more efficient administration of Sioux affairs for the future. Steps were taken to reimburse those whose ponies had been confiscated at the time of the Custer war in 1876, and additional appropriations were made for rations, so that before the end of the year the Indians were receiving half as much more as before the outbreak. (*War, 26.*) On returning to their homes the Indians of the various Sioux agencies went to work in good faith putting in their crops and caring for their stock, and in a short time all further apprehension was at an end.

The discussion of Indian affairs in connection with the outbreak led to the passage by Congress of a bill which enacted that all future vacancies in the office of Indian agent should be filled by military officers selected by the Indian office and detailed for the purpose from the army. At the same time a plan was originated to enlist Indians as a component part of the regular army. Small parties from various tribes had long been attached to various posts and commands in an irregular capacity as scouts. These bodies of scouts were now reduced in number or disbanded altogether, and in their stead were organized Indian troops or companies to be regularly attached to the different cavalry or infantry regiments. In the spring of 1891 officers were sent out to various western reservations, and succeeded in thus recruiting a number of regular troops from among the most warlike of the tribes, a considerable part of these coming from the late hostile Sioux.

Although the campaign lasted only about a month the destruction of life was great, for an Indian war, and the money loss to the government and to individuals was something enormous. Three officers and 28 privates were killed or mortally wounded during the campaign, and 4 officers and 38 privates were less seriously wounded, several of these dying later on. (*War, 27.*) The Indian loss can not be stated exactly. In the arrest of Sitting Bull there were killed or mortally wounded 8 of Sitting Bull's party and 6 police, a total of 14. Those killed in the Wounded Knee fight, or who afterward died of wounds or exposure, numbered, according to the best estimates, at least 250. Those afterward killed in the various small skirmishes, including the Few Tails affair, may have numbered 20 or 30. In all, the campaign cost the lives of 49 whites and others on the government side and about 300 or more Indians.

The direct or incidental expenses of the campaign were as follows: Expenses of the Department of Justice for defending Plenty Horses and prosecuting the murderers of Few Tails, unknown; appropriation by Congress to reimburse Nebraska national guard for expense of service during the campaign, $43,000; paid out under act of Congress to reimburse friendly Indians and other legal residents on the reservations for property destroyed by hostiles, $97,646.85 (*Comr.*, *41*); extra expense of Commissary department of the army, $37,764.69; extra expense of the Medical department of the army, $1,164, besides extra supplies purchased by individuals; extra expenses of Ordnance department of the army, for ammunition, not accounted for; total extra expense of Quartermaster's department of the army, $915,078.81, including $120,634.17 for transportation of troops over bonded railroads. (*A. G. O.*, *8*.) The total expense, public or private, was probably but little short of $1,200,000, or nearly $40,000 per day, a significant commentary on the bad policy of breaking faith with Indians.

According to the report of the agency farmer sent out after the trouble to learn the extent of property of the friendly Indians destroyed by the hostiles on Pine Ridge agency, there were burned 53 Indian dwellings, 1 church, 2 schoolhouses, and a bridge, all on White Clay creek, while nearly every remaining house along the creek had the windows broken out. A great deal of farming machinery and nearly all of the hay were burned, while stoves were broken to pieces and stock killed. A few of the friendly Indians had been so overcome by the excitement that they had burned their own houses and run their machinery down high hills into the river, where it was found frozen in the ice several months later. (*G. D.*, *48*.)

In view of the fact that only one noncombatant was killed and no depredations were committed off the reservation, the panic among the frontier settlers of both Dakotas, Nebraska, and Iowa was something ludicrous. The inhabitants worked themselves into such a high panic that ranches and even whole villages were temporarily abandoned and the people flocked into the railroad cities with vivid stories of murder, scalping, and desolation that had no foundation whatever in fact. A reliable authority who was on the ground shortly after the scare had subsided gives this characteristic instance among others:

In another city, a place of 3,000 inhabitants, 75 miles from any Indians and 150 miles from any hostiles, word came about 2 o'clock Sunday morning for the militia to be in readiness. The company promptly assembled, were instructed and drilled. In an evening church service one of the pastors broke out in prayer: "O Lord, prepare us for what awaits us. We have just been listening to the sweet sounds of praise, but ere the morning sun we may hear the war whoop of the red man." The effect on children and nervous persons may be imagined. The legislature was in session and the impression upon that body was such as to lead it to make an appropriation for the benefit of the state militia at the expense of one to the state agricultural fair. (*Comr.*, *42*.)

The crisis produced the usual crop of patriots, all ready to serve their country—usually for a consideration. Among these was a lady of Utica,

New York, claiming to be of the renowned Iroquois blood, and styling herself the "Doctor Princess Viroqua," who, with her sister "Wynima," wrote to the Indian Office for a commission to go out to try the effect of moral suasion on the belligerent Sioux, representing that by virtue of her descent from a long line of aboriginal princes she would be welcomed with enthusiasm and accomplish her mission of peace. (*G. D., 49.*) As a matter of fact, neither of the names Viroqua or Wynima could be pronounced by a genuine Iroquois knowing only his own tongue, and the second one, Wynima, is borrowed from Meacham's sensational history of the Modoc war in California.

The proprietor of a "wild west" show in New York, signing himself Texas Ben, wrote also volunteering his services and submitting as credentials his museum letter-head, stating that he had served with Quantrell, and had the written indorsement of Cole Younger. An old veteran of the Iowa soldiers' home wrote to Secretary Noble, with a redundance of capitals and much bad spelling, offering his help against the hostiles, saying that he had been "RAZeD" among them and could "ToLK The TUN" and was ready to "Do eneThin FoR mY CuntRY." (*G. D., 50.*)

A band of patriots in Minnesota, whose early education appears to have been somewhat neglected, wrote to the Secretary of the Interior offering to organize a company of 50 men to put down the outbreak, provided the government would look after a few items which they enumerated: "The government to Furnish us with Two good Horses Each a good Winchester Rifle, Two good Cotes Revolvers and give us $300.00 Bounty and say a Salary of Fifty Per Month, Each and our own judgment and we will settel this Indian question For Ever, and Rations and Ammunition. We Should Have in addition to this say Five dollars a Head." (*G. D., 51.*)

A man named Albert Hopkins appeared at Pine Ridge in December, 1890, wearing a blanket and claiming to be the Indian messiah, and announced his intention of going alone into the Bad Lands to the Indians, who were expecting his arrival, with the "Pansy Banner of Peace." His claims were ridiculed by Red Cloud and others, and he was promptly arrested and put off the reservation. However, he was not dead, but only sleeping, and on March, 1893, having come to Washington, he addressed an urgent letter to Secretary Noble requesting official authority to visit the Sioux reservations and to preach to the Indians, stating that "with the help of the Pansy and its motto and manifest teaching, 'Union, Culture, and Peace,' and the star-pansy banner, of which I inclose an illustration, I hope to establish the permanent peace of the border." He signs himself "Albert C. Hopkins, Pres. Pro. tem. The Pansy Society of America."

The letter was referred to the Indian Office, which refused permission. This brought a reply from Hopkins, who this time signs himself "The Indian Messiah," in which he states that as the Indians were expecting the messiah in the spring, "in accordance with the prophecy of Sitting

Bull," it was necessary that he should go to them at once, so that they might "accept the teaching of the pansy and its motto, which now they only partially or very doubtfully accept."

Receiving no answer, he wrote again about the end of March, both to the Secretary and to the Indian Commissioner, stating that messiahs, being human, were subject to human limitations, of which fact the Indians were well aware, but warning these officials that if these limitations were set by the government it would be held responsible for his nonappearance to the Indians, as he had promised, "before the native pansies blossom on the prairies." He ends by stating that he would leave on Easter Sunday for the Sioux country, but as nothing was heard of him later, it is presumed that he succumbed to the limitations. (*G. D.*, *52.*)

The first direct knowledge of the messiah and the Ghost dance came to the northern Arapaho in Wyoming, through Nakash, "Sage," who, with several Shoshoni, visited the messiah in the early spring of 1889, and on his return brought back to his people the first songs of the dance, these being probably some of the original Paiute songs of the messiah himself. The Ghost dance was at once inaugurated among the Shoshoni and northern Arapaho. In the summer of the same year the first rumors of the new redeemer reached the southern Arapaho and Cheyenne in Oklahoma, through the medium of letters written by returned pupils of eastern government schools.

Fresh reports of wonderful things beyond the mountains were constantly coming to the northern prairie tribes, and the excitement grew until the close of the year 1889, when a large delegation, including Sioux, northern Cheyenne, and northern Arapaho, crossed the mountains to the Paiute country to see and talk with the messiah. Among the Sioux delegates were Short Bull, Fire Thunder, and Kicking Bear, as already stated. Among the Cheyenne were Porcupine and several others, including one woman. The Arapaho representatives were Sitting Bull (Hänä′chä-thi′ăk) and Friday. The delegates from the different tribes met at Wind River reservation, in Wyoming, which they left about Christmas, and after stopping a short time among the Bannock and Shoshoni at Fort Hall, went on to Walker lake, in Nevada. They were gone some time and returned to Wyoming in March of 1890, the Sioux and Cheyenne continuing on to their homes farther east. According to the statement of Nakash they had a five days' conference with the messiah, who at one time went into a trance, but his visitors did not.

Before their return the southern Arapaho, in Oklahoma, had sent up Wa′tän-ga′a, "Black Coyote," an officer of the Indian police, and Washee, a scout at Fort Reno, to their relatives in Wyoming to learn definitely as to the truth or falsity of the rumors. Washee went on to Fort Hall, where his faith failed him, and he came back with the report that the messiah was only a half-blood. This was not correct, but Washee himself afterward acknowledged that he had based his report

Fig. 26.—Arapaho ghost shirt

on hearsay. Black Coyote remained until the other delegates returned from the Paiute country with the announcement that all that had been said of the messiah and the advent of a new earth was true. He listened eagerly to all they had to tell, took part with the rest in the dance, learned the songs, and returned in April, 1890, and inaugurated the first Ghost dance in the south among the Arapaho.

The Cheyenne, being skeptical by nature, were unwilling to trust entirely to the report of Black Coyote and so sent up two delegates of their own, Little Chief and Bark, to investigate the story in the north. Somewhat later White Shield, another Cheyenne, went up alone on the same errand. Their report being favorable, the Cheyenne also took up the Ghost dance in the summer of 1890. They never went into it with the same fervor, however, and although they had their separate dance with songs in their own language, they more commonly danced together with the Arapaho and sang with them the Arapaho songs. For several years the old Indian dances had been nearly obsolete with these tribes, but as the new religion meant a revival of the Indian idea they soon became common again, with the exception of the war dance and others of that kind which were strictly prohibited by the messiah.

From this time the Ghost dance grew in fervor and frequency among the Arapaho and Cheyenne. In almost every camp the dance would be held two or three times a week, beginning about sunset and often continuing until daylight. The excitement reached fever heat in September, 1890, when Sitting Bull came down from the northern Arapaho to instruct the southern tribes in the doctrine and ceremony.

At a great Ghost dance held on South Canadian river, about 2 miles below the agency at Darlington, Oklahoma, it was estimated that 3,000 Indians were present, including nearly all of the Arapaho and Cheyenne, with a number of Caddo, Wichita, Kiowa, and others. The first trances of the Ghost dance among the southern tribes occurred at this time through the medium of Sitting Bull. One informant states that a leader named Howling Bull had produced trances at a dance on the Washita some time before, but the statement lacks confirmation.

As Sitting Bull was the great apostle of the Ghost dance among the southern tribes, being regarded almost in the same light as the messiah himself, he merits special notice. He is now about 42 years of age and at the beginning of his apostleship in 1890 was but 36. He is a full-blood Arapaho, although rather light in complexion and color of eyes, and speaks only his native language, but converses with ease in the universal sign language of the plains. It was chiefly by means of this sign language that he instructed his disciples among the Caddo, Wichita, and Kiowa. He is about 5 feet 8 inches tall, dignified but plain in his bearing, and with a particularly winning smile. His power over those with whom he comes in contact is evident from the report of Lieutenant (now Captain) Scott, who had been ordered by the War Department to investigate the Ghost dance, and who for weeks had been denouncing him as a humbug, but who, on finally meeting him for the first time, declares that the opinion formed before seeing him began to change in his favor almost immediately. (*G. D., 53.*) In conversation with the author Sitting Bull stated that he was originally a southern Arapaho, but went up to live with the northern branch of the tribe, in Wyoming, about 1876. When a boy in the south he was known as Bítäye, "Captor," but on reaching manhood his name was changed, in conformity with a common Indian custom, to Hänä'chä-thi'ăk, "Sitting Bull." On returning to the south, after having visited the messiah, he found his brother known under the same name, and to avoid confusion the brother then adopted the name of Scabby Bull, by which he is now known. It should be mentioned that an Indian

Fig. 27.—Sitting Bull the Arapaho apostle

"brother" may be only a cousin, as no distinction is made in the Indian system. On removing to the south he fixed his abode near Cantonment, Oklahoma, where he now resides.

With regard to the reverence in which he was held by his disciples at this time, and of his own sincerity, Captain Scott says:

It was very difficult to get an opportunity to talk with him quietly on account of the persistent manner in which he was followed about. All sorts of people wanted to touch him, men and women would come in, rub their hands on him, and cry, which demonstration he received with a patient fortitude that was rather ludicrous at times. While he by no means told us everything he knew, it was easy to believe that he was not the rank impostor that I had before considered him. He makes no demands for presents while at these camps. This trip entailed a ride of 200 miles in

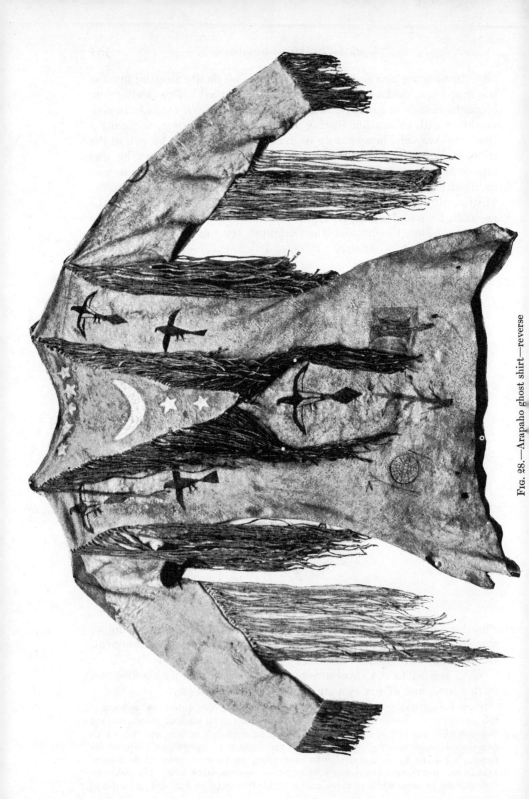

Fig. 28.—Arapaho ghost shirt—reverse

the winter season, at the request of the Wichitas, for which I understand they paid him $50 before starting, but everything that was given him while at this camp was a voluntary gift, prompted entirely by the good wishes of the giver. He took but little property away when he left, and I saw but one horse that I thought he had not brought down with him.

Upon being asked concerning his religion, he said that all I had heard must not be attributed to him, as some of it was false; that he does not believe that he saw the veritable "Jesus" alive in the north, but he did see a man there whom "Jesus" had helped or inspired. This person told him that if he persevered in the dance it would cause sickness and death to disappear. He avoided some of the questions about the coming of the buffalo, etc, and under the circumstances it was not possible to draw him out further, and the subject of religion was then dropped, with the intention of taking it up at a more favorable time, but this time never came. A great many of the doings seen at these dances are the afterthoughts of all kinds of people. I have seen some of them arise and have watched their growth. These are not the teachings of Sitting Bull, although he refrains from interfering with them through policy. He took no part in the humbuggery going on, but danced and sang like the humblest individual there. These things, taken in connection with Äpiatañ's letter, would make it seem that Sitting Bull has been a dupe himself partly, and there is a possibility that he is largely sincere in his teachings. There is this to be said in his favor, that he has given these people a better religion than they ever had before, taught them precepts which if faithfully carried out will bring them into better accord with their white neighbors, and has prepared the way for their final Christianization. For this he is entitled to no little credit. (*G. D., 54.*)

He made no claim to be a regular medicine-man, and so far as known never went into a trance himself. Since the failure of his predictions, especially with regard to the recovery of the ceded reservation, he has fallen from his high estate. Truth compels us also to state that, in spite of his apostolic character, he is about as uncertain in his movements as the average Indian.

After Sitting Bull, the principal leader of the Ghost dance among the southern Arapaho is Wa'tän-ga'a or Black Coyote, from whom the town of Watonga, in Canadian county, derives its name. Black Coyote is a man of considerable importance both in his tribe and in his own estimation, and aspires to be a leader in anything that concerns his people. With a natural predisposition to religious things, it is the dream of his life to be a great priest and medicine-man. At the same time he keeps a sharp lookout for his temporal affairs, and has managed to accumulate considerable property in wagons and livestock, including three wives. Although still a young man, being but little more than 40 years of age, he has had his share of the world's honors, being not only a leader in the Ghost dance and other Indian ceremonies, tribal delegate to Washington, and captain of the Indian police, but also, in his new character of an American citizen, deputy sheriff of Canadian county. He is a good-natured fellow, and vain of his possessions and titles, but at the same time thoroughly loyal and reliable in the discharge of his duties, and always ready to execute his orders at whatever personal risk. His priestly ambition led him to make the journey to the north, in which he brought back the first songs of the Ghost dance, and thus became a leader, and a year later he headed a delegation from Oklahoma to the messiah of Walker lake. He has repeatedly asked me to get for him a permanent license from the government to enable him to visit the various reservations at will as a general evangel of Indian medicine and ceremony. Black Coyote in full uniform, with official badge, a Harrison medal, and an immense police overcoat, which he procured in Washington, and riding with his three wives in his own double-seated coach, is a spectacle magnificent and impressive. Black Coyote in breechcloth, paint, and feathers, leading the Ghost dance, or sitting flat on the ground and beating the earth with his hand in excess of religious fervor, is equally impressive. It was this combination of vanity of leadership and sense of duty as a government officer that made him my first and most willing informant on the Ghost dance, and enabled me through him to do so much with the Arapaho.

In his portrait (Fig. 29) a number of scars will be noticed on his chest and arms. The full number of these scars is seventy, arranged in various patterns of lines, circles, crosses, etc, with a long figure of the sacred pipe on one arm. According to his own statement they were made in obedience to a dream as a sacrifice to save the lives of his children. Several of his children had died in rapid succession, and in accordance with Indian custom he undertook a fast of four days as an expiation to the overruling spirit. During this time, while lying on his bed, he heard a voice, somewhat resembling the cry of an owl or the subdued bark of a dog. The voice told him that if he wished to save his other children he must cut out seventy pieces of skin and offer them to the sun. He at once cut out seven pieces, held them out to the sun and prayed, and then buried them. But the sun was not satisfied, and soon after he was warned in a vision that the full number of seventy must be sacrificed if he would save his children. He then did as directed, cutting out the pieces of skin in the various patterns indicated, offering each in turn to the sun with a prayer for the health of his family, and then burying them. Since then there has been no death in his family. In cutting out the larger pieces, some of which were several inches long and nearly half an inch wide, the skin was first lifted up with an awl and then sliced away with a knife. This had to be done by an assistant, and Black Coyote was particular to show me by signs, sitting very erect and bracing himself firmly, that he had not flinched during the process.

As has been stated, the first trances in the southern Ghost dance occurred at the great dance held near the Cheyenne and Arapaho agency under the auspices of Sitting Bull in September, 1890. On this occasion Cheyenne and Arapaho, Caddo, Wichita, Kiowa, and Apache to the number of perhaps 3,000 assembled, and remained together for about two weeks, dancing every night until daylight. This was the largest Ghost dance ever held in the south. After dances had been held for two or three nights Sitting Bull announced that at the next one he would perform a great wonder in the sight of all the people, after

Fig. 29.—Black Coyote

which they would be able to make songs for themselves. He said no more, but dismissed them to their tipis, wondering what this miracle could be. On the next night he appeared wearing a wide-brim hat with a single eagle feather, the same hat in which he is generally seen. Nearly all of the two tribes of Cheyenne and Arapaho were present, and probably 600 or 800 were in the dance circle at one time. Nothing unusual occurred for several hours until the dancers had gradually worked themselves up to a high state of excitement, when Sitting Bull stepped into the circle, and going up close in front of a young Arapaho woman, he began to make hypnotic passes before her face with the eagle feather. In a few seconds she became rigid and then fell to the ground unconscious. Sitting Bull then turned his attention to another and another, and the same thing happened to each in turn until nearly a hundred were stretched out on the ground at once. As usual in the trances some lay thus for a long time, and others recovered sooner, but none were disturbed, as Sitting Bull told the dancers that these were now beholding happy visions of the spirit world. When next they came together those who had been in the trance related their experiences in the other world, how they had met and talked with their departed friends and joined in their oldtime amusements. Many of them embodied their visions in songs, which were sung that night and afterward in the dance, and from that time the Ghost dance was naturalized in the south and developed rapidly along new lines. Each succeeding dance resulted in other visions and new songs, and from time to time other hypnotists arose, until almost every camp had its own.

About this time a commission arrived to treat with the Cheyenne and Arapaho for the sale of their reservation. The Indians were much divided in opinion, the great majority opposing any sale whatsoever, even of their claim in the Cherokee strip, which they believed was all that the agreement was intended to cover. While the debate was in progress Left Hand, chief of the Arapaho, went to Sitting Bull and asked his opinion on the matter. Sitting Bull advised him to sell for what they could get, as they had need of the money, and in a short time the messiah would come and restore the land to them. On this advice Left Hand signed the agreement, in the face of threats from those opposed to it, and his example was followed by nearly all of his tribe. This incident shows how thoroughly Sitting Bull and the other Arapaho believed in the new doctrine. In view of the misery that has come on these tribes from the sale of their reservation, it is sad to think that they could have so deceived themselves by false hopes of divine interposition. A large party of the Cheyenne refused to have anything to do with the sale or to countenance the transaction by accepting their share of the purchase money, even after the whites had taken possession of the lands.

The troubles in the Sioux country now began to attract public attention, and there was suggestion of military interference. The newspaper liar has reached an abnormal development in Oklahoma, and dispatches from Guthrie, El Reno, and Oklahoma City were filled with vivid accounts of war dances, scalping parties, and imminent outbreaks, mingled with frantic appeals for troops. A specimen dispatch stated that a thousand Kickapoo were dancing, whereas in fact the whole tribe numbers only 325, very few of whom were in any way concerned with the Ghost dance. Indian Commissioner Morgan was at this time (November, 1890) on a tour of inspection among the western tribes of Oklahoma, and satisfied himself that all such sensational reports were false, and that there was no danger to be apprehended from the dance. (*G. D.*, *55.*) At the same time the War Department commissioned Lieutenant (now Captain) H. L. Scott, of the Seventh cavalry, then and now stationed at Fort Sill, Oklahoma, to investigate the meaning of the excitement and the possibility of an outbreak. Captain Scott was eminently fitted for the work by his intimate acquaintance with the Indians and his perfect knowledge of the sign language. In the course of December, 1890, and January and February, 1891, he visited the various camps of the western tribes of the territory, attended a number of dances, and talked with the leaders. His reports on the Ghost dance are most valuable, and confirmed the War Department in its previous opinion that no danger was to be apprehended, and that the true policy was one of noninterference.

The dance constantly gathered strength among the Arapaho and Cheyenne, in spite of the failure of the first prediction, and spread rapidly to the neighboring tribes, Sitting Bull himself being the high priest and chief propagandist. The adverse report brought back by Ä′piatañ, the Kiowa, in the spring of 1891 had no effect outside of his own tribe. In the early part of that year the Arapaho and Cheyenne sent a delegation, including one woman, to visit the messiah in Nevada and bring back the latest news from heaven. They were gone a considerable time and returned with some of the sacred medicine paint given them by Wovoka, after having taken part with the Paiute in a Ghost dance under his leadership at the regular dance ground near Mason valley. Tall Bull, captain of the Cheyenne police, was one of this party, and Arnold Woolworth, a Carlisle student, acted as interpreter.

In August, 1891, another delegation went out, consisting of Black Coyote, Little Raven, Red Wolf, Grant Left Hand, and Casper Edson (Arapaho), and Black Sharp Nose and Standing Bull (Cheyenne). Grant Left Hand and Casper Edson, Carlisle students, acted as interpreters, wrote down the words of the messiah, and delivered his message to their people on their return. This message, as written down at the time by Casper Edson, is given in the preceding chapter on the doctrine of the Ghost dance. In accord with the messiah's instructions the two tribes now changed their manner of dancing from frequent small dances at each camp at irregular intervals to larger dances participated in by several camps together at regular intervals of six weeks, each dance continuing for five consecutive days. The Caddo and Wichita also adopted the new rule in agreement with instructions brought back by a delegation sent out about the same time. The change was opposed by Sitting Bull and some others, but the delegates, having the authority of the messiah for the innovation, succeeded in carrying their point, and thereafter assumed a leadership on equal terms with Sitting Bull, who from that time lost much of his interest in the dance. They were gone about two weeks, and brought back with them a quantity of the sacred paint and a large number of magpie feathers, the kind commonly worn by the Paiute in the Ghost dance. This started a demand for magpie feathers, and the shrewd traders soon turned the fact to their own advantage by importing selected crow feathers, which they sold to the unsuspecting Indians for the genuine article at the rate of two feathers for a quarter. While in the land of the Paiute the delegates took part in the Ghost dance at Mason valley, and were thrown into a trance by Wovoka, as related in chapter i.

The Ghost dance practically superseded all other dances among the Cheyenne and Arapaho, and constantly developed new features, notably the auxiliary "crow dance," which was organized by Grant Left Hand. This was claimed as a dance seen in a trance vision of the spirit world, but is really only a modification of the "Omaha dance," common to the northern prairie tribes. The opening of the reservation and the influx of the whites served to intensify the religious fervor of the Indians, who were now more than ever made to feel their dependent and helpless condition. It was impossible, however, that the intense mental strain could endure forever, and after the failure of the predictions on the appointed dates the wild excitement gradually cooled and crystallized into a fixed but tranquil expectation of ultimate happiness under the old conditions in another world.

In October, 1892, another delegation, consisting of Sitting Bull and his wife, with Washee and two other Arapaho, and Edward Guerrier, a half-blood Cheyenne, visited the messiah. They brought back a very discouraging report, which was in substance that the messiah was tired of so many visitors and wanted them to go home and tell their tribes to stop dancing. Although the Indians generally refused to accept the message as genuine, the effect was naturally depressing. A year later, in October, 1893, Black Coyote and several others dictated through me a letter to Wovoka, asking him to send them some of the sacred paint or anything else that would make them think of him, with "some good words to help us and our children," and requesting to know whether he had been truthfully reported by the delegates of the preceding year. To one who knows these people their simple religious faith is too touching to be a subject of amusement.

The messiah doctrine never gained many converts among the Comanche, excepting those of the Penätĕ'ka division and a few others living on the Little Washita and other streams on the northern boundary of the reservation, adjoining the tribes most interested in the Ghost dance. These Comanche held a few Ghost dances and made a few songs, but the body of the tribe would have nothing to do with it. This lack of interest was due partly to the general skeptical temperament of the Comanche, evinced in their carelessness in regard to ceremonial forms, and partly to their tribal pride, which forbade their following after the strange gods of another people, as they considered their own mescal rite sufficient to all their needs. Quanah Parker, their head chief, a shrewd half-blood, opposed the new doctrine and prevented its spread among his tribe.

The Ghost dance was brought to the Pawnee, Ponca, Oto, Missouri, Kansa, Iowa, Osage, and other tribes in central Oklahoma by delegates from the Arapaho and Cheyenne in the west. The doctrine made slow progress for some time, but by February, 1892, the majority of the Pawnee were dancing in confident expectation of the speedy coming of the messiah and the buffalo. Of all these tribes the Pawnee took most interest in the new doctrine, becoming as much devoted to the Ghost dance as the Arapaho themselves. The leader among the Pawnee was Frank White, and among the Oto was Buffalo Black. The agent in charge took stringent measures against the dance, and had the Oto prophet arrested and confined in the Wichita jail, threatening at the same time to cut off supplies from the tribe. As the confederated Oto and Missouri number only 362 in all, they were easily brought into subjection, and the dance was abandoned. The same method was pursued with the Pawnee prophet and his people, but as they are stronger in number than the Oto, they were proportionately harder to deal with, but the final result was the same. (*Comr.*, *43.*) The Osage gave but little heed to the story, perhaps from the fact that, as they are the wealthiest tribe in the country, they feel no such urgent need of a redeemer as their less fortunate brethren. The Sauk, Fox, Kickapoo, and Potawatomi engaged in the dance only to a limited extent, for the reason that a number of the natives of these tribes, particularly the Potawatomi, are under Catholic influences, while most of the others adhere to the doctrine of Känakûk, the Potawatomi prophet.

The Ghost dance doctrine was communicated directly to the Caddo, Wichita, Kichai, Delaware, and Kiowa by the Arapaho and Cheyenne, their neighbors on the north. We shall speak now of the tribes first mentioned, leaving the Kiowa until the last. The Caddo, Wichita, Kichai, and several remnants of cognate tribes, with a small band of the Delaware, numbering in all about a thousand Indians, occupy a reservation between the Washita and the South Canadian in western Oklahoma, having the Arapaho and Cheyenne on the north and west, the Kiowa on the south, and the whites of Oklahoma and the Chickasaw nation on the east. The Caddo are the leading tribe, numbering more than half of the whole body. They were the first of these to take up the dance, and have manifested the greatest interest in it from the time it was introduced among them.

A number of Caddo first attended the great Ghost dance held by the Cheyenne and Arapaho on the South Canadian in the fall of 1890 on the occasion when Sitting Bull came down from the north and inaugurated the trances. On returning to their homes they started the Ghost dance, which they kept up, singing the Arapaho songs as they had heard them on the Canadian, until Sitting Bull came down about December, 1890, to give them further instruction in the doctrine and to "give the feather" to the seven persons selected to lead the ceremony. From this time the Caddo had songs and trances of their own, the chief priest and hypnotist of the dance being Nĭshkû'ntŭ, "Moon Head," or John Wilson. The Caddo and the Delaware usually danced together on Boggy creek. The Wichita and the Kichai, who took the doctrine from the Caddo, usually danced together on Sugar creek about 15 miles from the agency at Anadarko, but manifested less interest in the matter until Sitting Bull came down about the beginning of February, 1891, and "gave the feather" to the leaders. From this time all these tribes went into the dance heart and soul, on some occasions dancing for days and nights together from the middle of the afternoon until the sun was well up in the morning. The usual custom was to continue until about midnight. Cold weather had no deterrent effect, and they kept up the dance in the snow, the trance subjects sometimes lying unconscious in the snow for half an hour at a time. At this time it was confidently expected that the great change would occur in the spring, and as the time drew near the excitement became most intense. The return of the Kiowa delegate, Ä'piatañ, in the middle of February, 1891, with a report adverse to the messiah, produced no effect on the Caddo and their confederates, who refused to put any faith in his statements, claiming that he had not seen the real messiah or else had been bribed by the whites to make a false report.

About the time that Black Coyote and the others went out to see the messiah in the fall of 1891 the Caddo and their confederates sent out a delegation for the same purpose. The delegates were Billy Wilson and Squirrel (Caddo), Nashtowi and Lawrie Tatum (Wichita), and Jack Harry (Delaware). Tatum was a schoolboy and acted as interpreter for the party. Like the Arapaho they came back impressed with reverence for the messiah, and at once changed the time and method of the dancing, in accordance with his instructions, to periodical dances at intervals of six weeks, continuing for five consecutive days, the dance on the last night being kept up until daylight, when all the participants went down to bathe in the stream and then dispersed to their homes. They were dancing in this fashion when last visited in the fall of 1893.

The principal leader of the Ghost dance among the Caddo is Nĭsh-kû'ntŭ, "Moon Head," known to the whites as John Wilson. Although considered a Caddo, and speaking only that language, he is very much of a mixture, being half Delaware, one-fourth Caddo, and one-fourth French. One of his grandfathers was a Frenchman. As the Caddo lived originally in Louisiana, there is a considerable mixture of French blood among them, which manifests itself in his case in a fairly heavy beard. He is about 50 years of age, rather tall and well built, and wears his hair at full length flowing loosely over his shoulders. With a good head and strong, intelligent features, he presents the appearance of a natural leader. He is also prominent in the mescal rite, which has recently come to his tribe from the Kiowa and Comanche. He was one of the first Caddo to go into a trance, the occasion being the great Ghost dance held by the Arapaho and Cheyenne near Darlington agency, at which Sitting Bull presided, in the fall of 1890. On his return to consciousness he had wonderful things to tell of his experiences in the spirit world, composed a new song, and from that time became the high priest of the Caddo dance. Since then his trances have been frequent, both in and out of the Ghost dance, and in addition to his leadership in this connection he assumes the occult powers and authority of a great medicine-man, all the powers claimed by him being freely conceded by his people.

When Captain Scott was investigating the Ghost dance among the Caddo and other tribes of that section, at the period of greatest excitement, in the winter of 1890–91, he met Wilson, of whom he has this to say:

John Wilson, a Caddo man of much prominence, was especially affected, performing a series of gyrations that were most remarkable. At all hours of the day and night his cry could be heard all over camp, and when found he would be dancing in the ring, possibly upon one foot, with his eyes closed and the forefinger of his right hand pointed upward, or in some other ridiculous posture. Upon being asked his reasons for assuming these attitudes he replied that he could not help it; that it came over him just like cramps.

Somewhat later Captain Scott says:

John Wilson had progressed finely, and was now a full-fledged doctor, a healer of diseases, and a finder of stolen property through supernatural means. One day, while we were in his tent, a Wichita woman entered, led by the spirit. It was explained to us that she did not even know who lived there, but some force she could not account for brought her. Having stated her case to John, he went off into a fit of the jerks, in which his spirit went up and saw "his father" [i. e., God], who directed him how to cure this woman. When he came to, he explained the cure to her, and sent her away rejoicing. Soon afterwards a Keechei man came in, who was blind of one eye, and who desired to have the vision restored. John again consulted his father, who informed him that nothing could be done for that eye because that man held aloof from the dance.

While the author was visiting the Caddo on Sugar creek in the fall of 1893, John Wilson came down from his own camp to explain his part in the Ghost dance. He wore a wide-brim hat, with his hair flowing down to his shoulders, and on his breast, suspended from a cord about his neck, was a curious amulet consisting of the polished end of a buffalo horn, surrounded by a circlet of downy red feathers, within another circle of badger and owl claws. He explained that this was the source of his prophetic and clairvoyant inspiration. The buffalo horn was "God's heart," the red feathers contained his own heart, and the circle of claws represented the world. When he prayed for help, his heart communed with "God's heart," and he learned what he wished to know. He had much to say also of the moon. Sometimes in his trances he went to the moon and the moon taught him secrets. It must be remembered that sun, moon, stars, and almost every other thing in nature are considered by the Indians as endowed with life and spirit. He claimed an intimate acquaintance with the other world and asserted positively that he could tell me "just what heaven is like." Another man who accompanied him had a yellow sun with green rays painted on his forehead, with an elaborate rayed crescent in green, red, and yellow on his chin, and wore a necklace from which depended a crucifix and a brass clock-wheel, the latter, as he stated, representing the sun.

On entering the room where I sat awaiting him, Nĭshkû′ntŭ approached and performed mystic passes in front of my face with his hands, after the manner of the hypnotist priests in the Ghost dance, blowing upon me the while, as he afterward explained to blow evil things away from me before beginning to talk on religious subjects. He was good enough to state also that he had prayed for light before coming, and had found that my heart was good. Laying one hand on my head, and grasping my own hand with the other, he prayed silently for some time with bowed head, and then lifting his hand from my head, he passed it over my face, down my shoulder and arm to the hand, which he grasped and pressed slightly, and then released the fingers with a graceful upward sweep, as in the minuet. The first part of this—the laying of the hands upon the head, afterward drawing them down along the face and chest or arms—is the regular Indian form of blessing, reverential gratitude, or prayerful entreaty, and is of frequent occurrence in connection with the Ghost dance, when the believers ask help of the priests or beg the prayers of the older people. The next day about twenty or more Caddo came by on their way to the agency, all dressed and painted for a dance that was to be held that night. They stopped awhile to see us, and on entering the room where we were the whole company, men, women, and children, went through the same ceremony, with each one of the inmates in turn, beginning with Wilson and myself, and ending with the members of the family. The ceremony occupied a considerable time, and was at once beautiful and impressive. Not a word was said by either party during the while, excepting as someone in excess of devotion would utter prayerful exclamations aloud like the undertone of a litany. Every face wore a look of reverent solemnity, from the old men and women down to little children of 6 and 8 years. Several of them, the women especially, trembled while praying, as under the excitement of the Ghost dance. The religious greeting being over, the women of the family, with those of the party, went out to prepare the dinner, while the rest remained to listen to the doctrinal discussion.

The Kiowa were predisposed to accept the doctrine of the Ghost dance. No tribe had made more desperate resistance to the encroachments of the whites upon their hunting grounds, and even after the failure of the last effort of the confederated tribes in 1874–75, the Kiowa were slow to accept the verdict of defeat. The result of this unsuccessful struggle was to put an end to the boundless freedom of the prairie, where they had roamed unquestioned from Dakota almost to central Mexico, and henceforth the tribes were confined within the narrow limits of reservations. Within five years the great southern buffalo herd was extinct and the Indians found themselves at once prisoners and paupers. The change was so swift and terrible in its effects that they could not believe it real and final. It seemed to them like a dream of sorrow, a supernatural cloud of darkness to punish their derelictions, but which could be lifted from them by prayer and sacrifice. Their old men told of years when the buffalo was scarce or had gone a long way off, but never since the beginning of the world of a time when there was no buffalo. The buffalo still lived beyond their horizon or in caves under the earth, and with its return would come back prosperity and freedom. Before we wonder at their faith we must remember that the disappearance of these millions of buffalo in the space of a few years has no parallel in the annals of natural history.

In 1881 a young Kiowa named Da'tekañ, "Keeps-his-name-always," began to "make medicine" to bring back the buffalo. He set up a sacred tipi, in front of which he erected a pole with a buffalo skin at the top, and made for himself a priestly robe of red color, trimmed with rows of eagle feathers. Then standing in front of his tipi he called the people around him and told them that he had been commanded and empowered in a dream to bring back the buffalo, and if they observed strictly the prayers and ceremonies which he enjoined the great herds would once more cover the prairie. His hearers believed his words, promised strict obedience, and gave freely of their blankets and other property to reward his efforts in their behalf. Da'tekañ retired to his sacred tipi, where, in his feathered robe of office, he continued to prophesy and make buffalo medicine for a year, when he died without seeing the realization of his hopes. The excitement caused by his predictions came to the notice of the agent then in charge, who mentions it in his annual report, without understanding the cause. On a Kiowa calendar obtained by the author the event is recorded in a pictograph which represents the medicine-man in his tipi, with his scarlet robe over his shoulders and a buffalo beneath his feet (Fig. 30).

About six years later, in 1887, another prophet, named Pa'-iñgya, "In the Middle," revived the prophecy, claiming to be heir to all the supernatural powers of his late predecessor. He amplified the doctrine by asserting, logically enough, that as the whites were responsible for the disappearance of the buffalo, the whites themselves would be destroyed by the gods when the time was at hand for the return of

the buffalo. He preached also his own invulnerability and claimed
the power to kill with a look those who might offend him, as far as
his glance could reach. He fixed his headquarters on Elk creek, near
the western limit of the reservation, where he inaugurated a regular
series of ritual observances, under the management of ten chosen
assistants. Finally he announced that the time was at hand when the
whites would be removed and the buffalo would return. He ordered
all the tribe to assemble on Elk creek, where after four days he would
bring down fire from heaven which would destroy the agency, the
schools, and the white race, with the Indian unbelievers all together.
The faithful need not fear pursuit by the troops, for the soldiers who
might follow would
wither before his glance
and their bullets would
have no effect on the
Indians. On the same
Kiowa calendar this
prediction is recorded in
another pictograph in-
tended to represent fly-
ing bullets. The whole
Kiowa tribe caught the
infection of his words.
Every camp was aban-
doned, parents took
their children from the
schools, and all fled to
the rendezvous on Elk
creek. Here they waited
patiently for their de-
liverance till the pre-
dicted day came and
passed without event,
when they returned

Fig. 30.—Two Kiowa prophecies (from a Kiowa calendar)

with sadness to their camps and their government rations of white
man's beef. Pa'-iñgya still lives, but the halo of prophecy no longer
surrounds him. To account for the disappointment he claimed that his
people had violated some of the ordinances and thereby postponed the
destined happiness. In this way their minds were kept dwelling on
the subject, and when at last the rumor of a messiah came from the
north he hailed it as the fulfillment of the prediction.

Early in the summer of 1890 the news of the advent of the messiah
reached the Kiowa, and in June of that year they sent a delegation of
about twenty men under the leadership of Pa'tadal, "Poor Buffalo," to
Cheyenne and Arapaho agency at Darlington to learn more about the
matter. They brought back a favorable report and also a quantity of

the sacred red paint procured originally from the country of the messiah. Soon after there was a great gathering of the Kiowa and Apache at the agency at Anadarko to receive a payment of "grass money" due from the cattlemen for the lease of pasturage on the reservation. On this occasion the Ghost dance was formally inaugurated among the Kiowa, Poor Buffalo assuming direction of the ceremony, and painting the principal participants with the sacred red paint with his own hands. The dance was carried back to their various camps and became a part of the tribal life.

About this time a Sioux chief, High Wolf, came down from the north to visit the Cheyenne, Arapaho, Kiowa, and other tribes in that section. He remained some time among them, and on his return to the north invited a young Kiowa named Ä'piatañ, "Wooden Lance," whose grandmother had been a Sioux captive, to come up and visit his relatives at Pine Ridge. The invitation was accepted by Ä'piatañ, partly for the pleasure of seeing a new tribe and meeting his mother's kindred, but chiefly for the purpose of investigating for himself and for the Kiowa the truth of the messiah story. Äpiatañ,

Fig. 31.—Poor Buffalo   who speaks but little English, and who was then about 30 years of age, had recently lost a child to whom he had been very much attached. He brooded over his loss until the new doctrine came with its promise of a reunion with departed friends and its possibility of seeing and talking with them in visions of the trance. Moved by parental affection, which is the ruling passion with an Indian, he determined on this long journey in search of the messiah, who was vaguely reported to be somewhere in the north, to learn from his own lips the wonderful story, and to see if it were possible to talk again with his child. He discussed the matter with the chiefs, who decided to send him as a delegate to find the messiah and

Fig. 32.—Bi'äñki the Kiowa dreamer

learn the truth or falsity of the reports, in order that the Kiowa might be guided by the result on his return. A sufficient sum of money was raised for his expenses, and he left for the north in September, 1890. Almost the whole tribe had assembled at the agency to witness his departure, and each in turn of the principal men performed over him a ceremony of blessing, such as has already been described. His going and return are both recorded on the calendar previously mentioned.

In October, 1890, shortly after Ä'piataṅ's departure, Sitting Bull, the Arapaho prophet of the Ghost dance, came down from his tribe and gave new impetus to the excitement among the Kiowa. This event also is recorded on the same Kiowa calendar in a well-drawn picture representing a buffalo standing beside the figure of a man (Fig. 33). It is also indicated less definitely on another calendar obtained from the tribe. Sitting Bull confirmed, as by personal knowledge, all that had been told of the messiah, and predicted that the new earth would arrive in the following spring, 1891. The Kiowa assembled on the Washita, at the mouth of Rainy Mountain creek, and here, at the largest Ghost dance ever held by the tribe, Sitting Bull consecrated seven men

Fig. 33.—Sitting Bull comes down (from a Kiowa calendar)

and women as leaders of the dance and teachers of the doctrine by giving to each one a sacred feather to be worn in the dance as the badge of priesthood. Until the Ghost dance came to the prairie tribes their women had never before been raised to such dignity as to be allowed to wear feathers in their hair. After "giving the feather" to the leaders thus chosen, they were taught the songs and ritual of the dance. At first the songs were all in the Arapaho language, but after the trances, which now began to be frequent, the Kiowa composed songs of their own.

Among the dreamers and prophets who now came to the front was one who merits more than a passing notice. His original name was Bi'äṅk'i, "Eater," but on account of his frequent visits to the spirit world he is now known as Äsa'tito'la, which may be freely rendered "The Messenger." For a long time he had been in the habit of going alone upon the mountain, there to fast and pray until visions came to him, when he would return and give to his people the message of inspiration. Frequently these vigils were undertaken at the request of friends of sick people to obtain spiritual knowledge of the proper remedies to be applied, or at the request of surviving relatives who wished to hear from their departed friends in the other world. He is now about 55 years of age, quiet and dignified in manner, with a thoughtful cast of countenance which accords well with his character as a priest and seer. His intellectual bent is further shown by the fact that he has invented a system of ideographic writing which is nearly as distinct from the ordinary Indian pictograph system as it is from our own alphabet. It is based on the sign language of the plains tribes, the primary effort being to convey the idea by a pictured representation of the gesture sign; but, as in the evolution of the alphabet, a part is frequently put for the whole, and numerous arbitrary or auxiliary characters are added, until the result is a well-developed germ of an alphabetic system. He has taught the system to his sons, and by this means was able to keep up a correspondence with them while they were attending Carlisle school. It is unintelligible to the rest of the tribe. I have specimens of this curious graphic method, obtained from the father and his sons, which may be treated at length at some future time. In the picture of Äsa'ti-to'la (Fig. 32), he holds in one hand a paper on which is depicted one of his visions, while in the other is the pointer with which he explains its meaning.

Figure 34 herewith represents this vision. On this occasion, after reaching the spirit world he found himself on a vast prairie covered with herds of buffalo and ponies, represented respectively in the picture by short black and green lines at the top. He went on through the buffalo, the way being indicated by the dotted green lines, until he came to a large Kiowa camp, in which, according to their old custom, nearly every tipi had its distinctive style of painting or ornamentation to show to what family it belonged, all these families being still represented in the tribe. He went on to the point indicated by the first heavy blue mark, where he met four young women, whom he knew as having died years before, returning on horseback with their saddle-pouches filled with wild plums. After some conversation he asked them about two brothers, his relatives, who had died some time ago. He went in the direction pointed out by the young women and soon met the two young men coming into camp with a load of fresh buffalo meat hung at their saddles. Their names were Emanki'na, "Can't-hold-it," a policeman, and E''pea, "Afraid-of-him," who had died while held as a prisoner of war in Florida about fifteen years before. It will be noted that they are represented in the picture as armed only with bows and arrows, in agreement with the Ghost-dance doctrine of a return to aboriginal things. After proceeding some distance he retraced his steps and met two curious beings, represented in the picture by green figures with crosses instead of heads. These told him to go on, and on doing so he came to an immense circle of Kiowa danc-ing the Ghost dance around a cedar tree, indicated by the black circle with a green figure resembling a tree in the center. He stood for a while near the tree, shown by another blue mark, when he saw a woman, whom he knew, leave the dance. He hurried after her until she reached her own tipi and went into it—shown by the blue mark beside the red tipi with red flags on the ends of the tipi poles—when he turned around and came back. She belonged to the family of the great chief Set-t'aiñti, "White Bear," as indicated by the red tipi with red flags, no other warrior in the tribe having such a tipi. On inquiring for his own relatives he was directed to the other side of the camp, where he met a man—represented by the heavy black mark—who told him his own people were inside of the next tipi. On entering he found the whole family, consisting of his father, two brothers, two sisters, and several children, feasting on fresh buffalo beef from a kettle hung over the fire. They welcomed him and offered him some of the meat, which for some reason he was afraid to taste. To convince him that it was good they held it up for him to smell, when he awoke and found himself lying alone upon the mountain.

Ä'piatañ went on first to Pine Ridge, where he was well received by the Sioux, who had much to say of the new messiah in the west. He was urged to stop and join them in the Ghost dance, but refused and hurried on to Fort Washakie, where he met the northern Arapaho and the Shoshoni, whom he called the "northern Comanches." Here the new prophecy was the one topic of conversation, and after stopping only long enough to learn the proper route to the Paiute country, he went on over the Union Pacific railroad to Nevada. On arriving at the agency at Pyramid lake the Paiute furnished him a wagon and an Indian guide across the country to the home of Wovoka in the upper end of Mason valley. The next day he was admitted to his presence. The result was a complete disappointment. A single interview con-vinced him of the utter falsity of the pretensions of the messiah and the deceptive character of the hopes held out to the believers.

Saddened and disgusted, Ä'piatañ made no stay, but started at once on his return home. On his way back he stopped at Bannock agency at Fort Hall, Idaho, and from there sent a letter to his people, stating briefly that he had seen the messiah and that the messiah was a fraud. This was the first intimation the Kiowa had received from an Indian source that their hopes were not well grounded. The author was pres-ent when the letter was received at Anadarko and read to the assem-bled Indians by Ä'piatañ's sister, an educated woman named Laura Dunmoi, formerly of Carlisle school. The result was a division of opinion. Some of the Indians, feeling that the ground had been taken from under them, at once gave up all hope and accepted the inevitable of despair. Others were disposed to doubt the genuineness of the let-ter, as it had come through the medium of a white man, and decided

Fig. 34.—Bi'äñki's vision

to withhold their decision until they could hear directly from the delegate himself. Ä′piatañ returned in the middle of February, 1891. The agent sent notice to the various camps on the reservation for the Indians

Fig. 35.—Ä′piatañ

to assemble at the agency to hear his report, and also sent a request to Cheyenne and Arapaho agency to have Sitting Bull come down at the same time so that the Indians might hear both sides of the story.

The council was held at the agency at Anadarko, Oklahoma, on February 19, 1891, the author being among those present on the occasion. It was a great gathering, representing every tribe on the reservation, there being also in attendance a number of Arapaho who had accompanied Sitting Bull from the other agency. Everything said was interpreted in turn into English, Kiowa, Comanche, Caddo, Wichita, and Arapaho. This was a slow process, and necessitated frequent repetition, so that the talk occupied all day. Ä'piataň first made his report, which was interpreted into the various languages. Questions were asked by the agent, Mr Adams, and by leading Indians, and after the full details had been obtained in this manner Sitting Bull, the Arapaho, was called on to make his statement. The scene was dramatic in the highest degree. Although in a certain sense Sitting Bull himself was on trial, it meant more than that to the assembled tribe. Their power, prosperity, and happiness had gone down, their very race was withering away before the white man. The messiah doctrine promised a restoration of the old conditions through supernatural assistance. If this hope was without foundation, the Indian had no future and his day was forever past.

After some preliminaries Ä'piataň arose and told his story. He had gone on as related until he arrived at the home of Wovoka in Mason valley. Here he was told that the messiah could not be seen until the next day. On being finally admitted to his presence he found him lying down, his face covered with a blanket, and singing to himself. When he had finished the song the messiah uncovered his face and asked Ä'piataň, through an interpreter, what he wanted. As Ä'piataň had approached with great reverence under the full belief that the messiah was omniscient, able to read his secret thoughts and to speak all languages, this question was a great surprise to him, and his faith at once began to waver. However, he told who he was and why he had come, and then asked that he be permitted to see some of his dead relatives, particularly his little child. Wovoka replied that this was impossible, and that there were no spirits there to be seen. With their mixture of Christian and aboriginal ideas many of the Indians had claimed that this messiah was the veritable Christ and bore upon his hands and feet the scars of the crucifixion. Not seeing these scars, Ä'piataň expressed some doubt as to whether Wovoka was really the messiah he had come so far to see, to which Wovoka replied that he need go no farther for there was no other messiah, and went on to say that he had preached to Sitting Bull and the others and had given them a new dance, but that some of them, especially the Sioux, had twisted things and made trouble, and now Ä'piataň had better go home and tell his people to quit the whole business. Discouraged and sick at heart Ä'piataň went out from his presence, convinced that there was no longer a god in Israel.

After the story had been told and interpreted to each of the tribes, Sitting Bull was called on for his statement. He told how he had visited the messiah a year before and what the messiah had said to

Fig. 32.—Kinnoull's new children's holiday

him. The two versions were widely different, and there can be little question that Wovoka made claims and prophecies, supported by hypnotic performances, from which he afterward receded when he found that the excitement had gone beyond his control and resulted in an Indian outbreak. Sitting Bull insisted on the truth of his own representations, and when accused by Ä'piatañ of deceiving the Indians in order to obtain their property he replied that he had never asked them for the ponies which they had given him, and that if they did not believe what he had told them they could come and take their ponies again. Ä'piatañ replied that that was not the Kiowa road; what had once been given was not taken back. Sitting Bull spoke in a low musical voice, and the soft Arapaho syllables contrasted pleasantly with the choking sounds of the Kiowa and the boisterous loudness of the Wichita. I could not help a feeling of pity for him when at the close of the council he drew his blanket around him and went out from the gathering to cross the river to the Caddo camp, attended only by his faithful Arapahos. For his services in reporting against the dance Ä'piatañ received a medal from President Harrison.

This was for some time the end of the Ghost dance among the Kiowa, for while some few of the tribes were disposed to doubt the honesty or correctness of the report, the majority accepted it as final, and from that time the dance became a mere amusement for children. The other tribes, however—the Caddo, Wichita, and their allies—refused to accept the report, claiming that Ä'piatañ had been hired by white men to lie to the Indians, and that he had never really seen the messiah, as he claimed. Even the Apache, although in close tribal connection with the Kiowa, continued to hold to the doctrine and the dance.

NOTE.—Since the above was written and while awaiting publication there has been a revival of the Ghost dance among the Kiowa, brought about chiefly through the efforts of Bi'äñk'i, Pa'tadal, and others of its former priests. After several times dispersing the dancers and threatening them with severe penalties if they persisted, the agent was finally obliged to give permission, on the earnest request of a delegation of chiefs and head men of the tribe, with the result that in September, 1894, the Kiowa publicly revived the ceremony in a great dance on the Washita, which lasted four days and was attended by several thousand Indians from all the surrounding tribes.

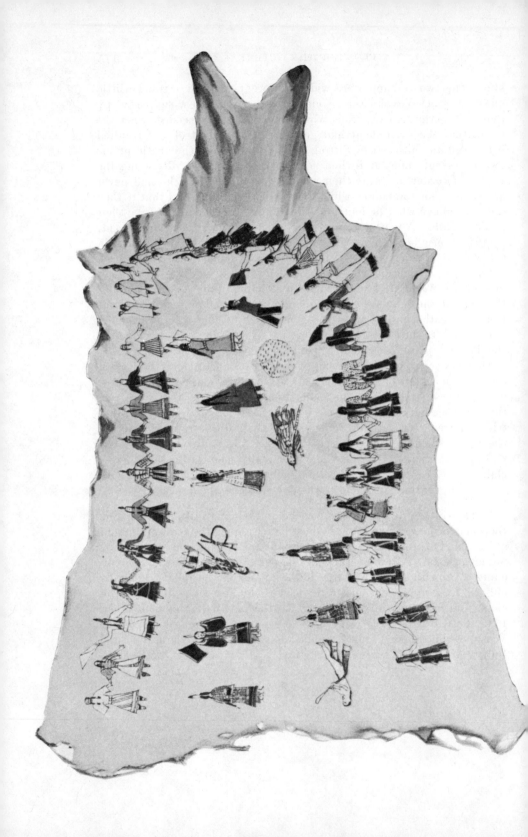

EXPLANATION OF FIGURE 37

The original of this picture was drawn in colored inks on buckskin by Yellow Nose, a Ute captive among the Cheyenne, in 1891. It was obtained from him by the author and is now deposited in the National Museum at Washington. Besides being a particularly fine specimen of Indian pictography, it gives an excellent idea of the ghost dance as it was at that time among the Cheyenne and Arapaho. The dancers are in full costume, with paint and feathers. The women of the two tribes are plainly distinguished by the arrangement of their hair, the Cheyenne women having the hair braided at the side, while the Arapaho women wear it hanging loosely. Two of the women carry children on their backs. One of the men carries the *bä'qati* wheel, another a shinny stick, and a woman holds out the sacred crow, while several wave handkerchiefs which aid in producing the hypnotic effect. In the center are several persons with arms outstretched and rigid, while at one side is seen the medicine-man hypnotizing a subject who stretches out toward him a blue handkerchief. The spotted object on the ground behind the medicine-man is a shawl which has fallen from the shoulders of the woman standing near.

CHAPTER VII

The Ceremony of the Ghost Dance

In chapter I we have spoken of the Ghost dance as it existed among the Paiute, Shoshoni, Walapai, and Cohonino, west of the mountains. We shall now give a more detailed account of the ceremony and connected ritual among the prairie tribes.

AMONG THE NORTHERN CHEYENNE

According to Dr Grinnell the Ghost dance among the northern Cheyenne had several features not found in the south. Four fires were built outside of the dance circle and about 20 yards back from it, toward each of the cardinal points. These fires were built of long poles set up on end, so as to form a rude cone, much as the poles of a tipi are erected. The fires were lighted at the bottom, and thus made high bonfires, which were kept up as long as the dance continued. (*J. F. L.*, 5.)

AMONG THE SIOUX

Perhaps the most important feature in connection with the dance among the Sioux was the "ghost shirt," already noticed and to be described more fully hereafter. On account of the scarcity of buckskin, these shirts were almost always made of white cloth cut and figured in the Indian fashion. The Sioux wore no metal of any kind in the dance, differing in this respect from the southern tribes, who wore on such occasions all their finery of German silver ornaments. The Sioux also began the dance sometimes in the morning, as well as in the afternoon or evening. Another important feature not found among the southern tribes, excepting the Kiowa, was the tree planted in the center of the circle and decorated with feathers, stuffed animals, and strips of cloth.

At a Ghost dance at No Water's camp, near Pine Ridge, as described by J. F. Asay, formerly a trader at the agency, the dancers first stood in line facing the sun, while the leader, standing facing them, made a prayer and waved over their heads the "ghost stick," a staff about 6 feet long, trimmed with red cloth and feathers of the same color. After thus waving the stick over them, he faced the sun and made another prayer, after which the line closed up to form a circle around the tree and the dance began. During the prayer a woman standing near the tree held out a pipe toward the sun, while another beside her held out several (four?) arrows from which the points had been removed. On another occasion, at a Ghost dance at the same camp, four arrows, headed with bone in the olden fashion, were shot up into the air from the center of the circle and afterward gathered up and hung upon the tree, together with the bow, a gaming wheel and sticks, and a staff of peculiar shape (ghost stick?).   See Figure 38. The ceremonies of fasting, painting, and the sweat-bath in connection with the Ghost dance among the Sioux have been already described.

The best account of the dance itself and of the ghost shirt is given by Mrs Z. A. Parker, at that time a teacher on the Pine Ridge reservation, writing of a Ghost dance observed by her on White Clay creek, on June 20, 1890. We quote at length from her description:

We drove to this spot about 10.30 oclock on a delightful October day. We came upon tents scattered here and there in low, sheltered places long before reaching the dance ground.   Presently we saw over three hundred tents placed in a circle, with a large pine tree in the center, which was covered with strips of cloth of various colors, eagle feathers, stuffed birds, claws, and horns—all offerings to the Great Spirit. The ceremonies had just begun.   In the center, around the tree, were gathered their medicine-men; also those who had been so fortunate as to have had visions and in them had seen and talked with friends who had died. A company of fifteen had started a chant and were marching abreast, others coming in behind as they marched. After marching around the circle of tents they turned to the center, where many had gathered and were seated on the ground.

I think they wore the ghost shirt or ghost dress for the first time that day. I noticed that these were all new and were worn by about seventy men and forty women. The wife of a man called Return-from-scout had seen in a vision that her friends all wore a similar robe, and on reviving from her trance she called the women together and they made a great number of the sacred garments. They were of white cotton cloth. The women's dress was cut like their ordinary dress, a loose robe with wide, flowing sleeves, painted blue in the neck, in the shape of a three-cornered handkerchief, with moon, stars, birds, etc, interspersed with real feathers, painted on the waist and sleeves. While dancing they wound their shawls about their waists, letting them fall to within 3 inches of the ground, the fringe at the bottom. In the hair, near the crown, a feather was tied. I noticed an absence of any manner of bead ornaments, and, as I knew their vanity and fondness for them, wondered why it was. Upon making inquiries I found they discarded everything they could which was made by white men.

The ghost shirt for the men was made of the same material—shirts and leggings painted in red. Some of the leggings were painted in stripes running up and down, others running around. The shirt was painted blue around the neck, and the whole garment was fantastically sprinkled with figures of birds, bows and arrows, sun, moon, and stars, and everything they saw in nature. Down the outside of the sleeve were rows of feathers tied by the quill ends and left to fly in the breeze, and also a row around the neck and up and down the outside of the leggings. I noticed that a number had stuffed birds, squirrel heads, etc, tied in their long hair. The faces of all were painted red with a black half-moon on the forehead or on one cheek.

As the crowd gathered about the tree the high priest, or master of ceremonies, began his address, giving them directions as to the chant and other matters. After he had spoken for about fifteen minutes they arose and formed in a circle. As nearly as I could count, there were between three and four hundred persons. One stood directly behind another, each with his hands on his neighbor's shoulders. After walking about a few times, chanting, "Father, I come," they stopped marching, but

FIG. 38.—Sacred objects from the Sioux Ghost dance

in the trance, he has seen worn by some departed relative. If he has not yet been in a trance, the design is suggested by a vision of one who does the painting. In making the request the dancer lays his hands upon the head of the leader and says, "My father, I have come to be painted, so that I may see my friends; have pity on me and paint me," the sacred paint being held to sharpen the spiritual vision as well as to be conducive to physical health. The painting consists of elaborate designs in red, yellow, green, and blue upon the face, with a red or yellow line along the parting of the hair. Suns, crescents, stars, crosses, and birds (crows) are the designs in most common use.

THE CEREMONY

The dance commonly begins about the middle of the afternoon or later, after sundown. When it begins in the afternoon, there is always an intermission of an hour or two for supper. The announcement is made by the criers, old men who assume this office apparently by tacit understanding, who go about the camp shouting in a loud voice to the people to prepare for the dance. The preliminary painting and dressing is usually a work of about two hours. When all is ready, the leaders walk out to the dance place, and facing inward, join hands so as to form a small circle. Then, without moving from their places they sing the opening song, according to previous agreement, in a soft undertone. Having sung it through once they raise their voices to their full strength and repeat it, this time slowly circling around in the dance. The step is different from that of most other Indian dances, but very simple, the dancers moving from right to left, following the course of the sun, advancing the left foot and following it with the right, hardly lifting the feet from the ground. For this reason it is called by the Shoshoni the "dragging dance." All the songs are adapted to the simple measure of the dance step. As the song rises and swells the people come singly and in groups from the several tipis, and one after another joins the circle until any number from fifty to five hundred men, women, and children are in the dance. When the circle is small, each song is repeated through a number of circuits. If large, it is repeated only through one circuit, measured by the return of the leaders to the starting point. Each song is started in the same manner, first in an undertone while the singers stand still in their places, and then with full voice as they begin to circle around. At intervals between the songs, more especially after the trances have begun, the dancers unclasp hands and sit down to smoke or talk for a few minutes. At such times the leaders sometimes deliver short addresses or sermons, or relate the recent trance experience of the dancer. In holding each other's hands the dancers usually intertwine the fingers instead of grasping the hand as with us. Only an Indian could keep the blanket in place as they do under such circumstances. Old people hobbling along with sticks, and little children hardly past the toddling period sometimes form a part of the circle, the more vigorous dancers accommodating the movement to their weakness. Frequently a woman will be seen to join the circle with an infant upon her back and dance with the others, but should she show the least sign of approaching excitement watchful friends lead her away that no harm may come to the child. Dogs are driven off from the neighborhood of the circle lest they should run against any of those who have fallen into a trance and thus awaken them. The dancers themselves are careful not to disturb the trance subjects while their souls are in the spirit world. Full Indian dress is worn, with buckskin, paint, and feathers, but among the Sioux the women discarded the belts ornamented with disks of German silver, because the metal had come from the white man. Among the southern tribes, on the contrary, hats were sometimes worn in the dance, although this was not considered in strict accordance with the doctrine.

No drum, rattle, or other musical instrument is used in the dance, excepting sometimes by an individual dancer in imitation of a trance vision. In this respect particularly the Ghost dance differs from every other Indian dance. Neither are any fires built within the circle, so far as known, with any tribe excepting the Walapai. The northern Cheyenne, however, built four fires in a peculiar fashion outside of the circle, as already described. With most tribes the dance was performed around a tree or pole planted in the center and variously decorated. In the southern plains, however, only the Kiowa seem ever to have followed this method, they sometimes dancing around a cedar tree. On breaking the circle at the end of the dance the performers shook their blankets or shawls in the air, with the idea of driving away all evil influences. On later instructions from the messiah all then went down to bathe in the stream, the men in one place and the women in another, before going to their tipis. The idea of washing away evil things, spiritual as well as earthly, by bathing in running water is too natural and universal to need comment.

The peculiar ceremonies of prayer and invocation, with the laying on of hands and the stroking of the face and body, have several times been described and need only be mentioned here. As trance visions became frequent the subjects strove to imitate what they had seen in the spirit world, especially where they had taken part with their departed friends in some of the old-time games. In this way gaming wheels, shinny sticks, hummers, and other toys or implements would be made and carried in future dances, accompanied with appropriate songs, until the dance sometimes took on the appearance of an exhibition of Indian curios on a small scale.

THE CROW DANCE

Within the last few years the southern Arapaho and Cheyenne have developed an auxiliary dance called the "crow dance," which is performed in the afternoon as a preliminary to the regular Ghost dance at night. As it is no part of the original Ghost dance and is confined to these two tribes, it deserves no extended notice in this connection. Although claimed by its inventors as a direct inspiration from the other world, where they saw it performed by "crows," or spirits of departed friends, it is really only a modification of the picturesque Omaha dance of the prairie tribes, with the addition of religious features borrowed from the new doctrine. The men participating are stripped to the breechcloth, with their whole bodies painted as in the Omaha dance, and wear elaborate pendants of varicolored feathers hanging down behind from the waist. An immense drum is an important feature. Men and women take part, and the songs refer to the general subject of the crow and the messiah, but are set to a variety of dance steps and evolutions performed by the dancers. As the leaders, who are chiefly young men, are constantly studying new features, the crow dance has become one of the most attractive ceremonies among the prairie tribes. Hypnotism and trances form an essential feature of this as of the Ghost dance proper. (See Fig. 47.)

THE HYPNOTIC PROCESS

The most important feature of the Ghost dance, and the secret of the trances, is hypnotism. It has been hastily assumed that hypnotic knowledge and ability belong only to an overripe civilization, such as that of India and ancient Egypt, or to the most modern period of scientific investigation. The fact is, however, that practical knowledge, if not understanding, of such things belongs to people who live near to nature, and many of the stories told by reliable travelers of the strange performances of savage shamans can be explained only on this theory. Numerous references in the works of the early Jesuit missionaries, of the Puritan writers of New England and of English explorers farther to the south, would indicate that hypnotic ability no less than sleight-of-hand dexterity formed part of the medicine-man's equipment from the Saint Lawrence to the Gulf. Enough has been said in the chapters on Smoholla and the Shakers to show that hypnotism exists among the tribes of the Columbia, and the author has had frequent opportunity to observe and study it in the Ghost dance on the plains. It can not be said that the Indian priests understand the phenomenon, for they ascribe it to a supernatural cause, but they know how to produce the effect, as I have witnessed hundreds of times. In treating of the subject in connection with the Ghost dance the author must be understood as speaking from the point of view of an observer and not as a psychologic expert.

Immediately on coming among the Arapaho and Cheyenne in 1890, I heard numerous stories of wonderful things that occurred in the Ghost dance—how people died, went to heaven and came back again, and how they talked with dead friends and brought back messages from the other world. Quite a number who had thus "died" were mentioned and their adventures in the spirit land were related with great particularity of detail, but as most of the testimony came from white men, none of whom had seen the dance for themselves, I preserved the scientific attitude of skepticism. So far as could be ascertained, none of the intelligent people of the agency had thought the subject sufficiently worthy of serious consideration to learn whether the reports were true or false. On talking with the Indians I found them unanimous in their statements as to the visions, until I began to think there might be something in it.

The first clew to the explanation came from the statement of his own experience in the trance, given by Paul Boynton, a particularly bright Carlisle student, who acted as my interpreter. His brother had died some time before, and as Paul was anxious to see and talk with him, which the new doctrine taught was possible, he attended the next Ghost dance, and putting his hands upon the head of Sitting Bull, according to the regular formula, asked him to help him see his dead brother. Paul is of an inquiring disposition, and, besides his natural longing to meet his brother again, was actuated, as he himself said, by a desire to try "every Indian trick." He then told how Sitting Bull had hypnotized him with the eagle feather and the motion of his hands, until he fell unconscious and did really see his brother, but awoke just as he was about to speak to him, probably because one of the dancers had accidentally brushed against him as he lay on the ground. He embodied his experience in a song which was afterward sung in the dance. From his account it seemed almost certain that the secret was hypnotism. The explanation might have occurred to me sooner but for the fact that my previous Indian informants, after the manner of some other witnesses, had told only about their trance visions, forgetting to state how the visions were brought about.

This was in winter and the ground was covered deeply with snow, which stopped the dancing for several weeks. In the meantime I improved the opportunity by visiting the tipis every night to learn the songs and talk about the new religion. When the snow melted, the dances were renewed, and as by this time I had gained the confidence of the Indians I was invited to be present and thereafter on numerous occasions was able to watch the whole process by which the trances were produced. From the outside hardly anything can be seen of what goes on within the circle, but being a part of the circle myself I was able to see all that occurred inside, and by fixing attention on one subject at a time I was able to note all the stages of the phenomenon from the time the subject first attracted the notice of the medicine-man, through the staggering, the rigidity, the unconsciousness, and back again to wakefulness. On two occasions my partner in the dance, each time a woman, came under the influence and I was thus enabled to note the very first nervous tremor of her hand and mark it as it increased in violence until she broke away and staggered toward the medicine-man within the circle.

Young women are usually the first to be affected, then older women, and lastly men. Sometimes, however, a man proves as sensitive as the average woman. In particular I have seen one young Arapaho become rigid in the trance night after night. He was a Carlisle student, speaking good English and employed as clerk in a store. He afterward took part in the sun dance, dancing three days and nights without food, drink, or sleep. He is of a quiet, religious disposition, and if of white parentage would perhaps have become a minister, but being an Indian, the same tendency leads him into the Ghost dance and the sun dance. The fact that he could endure the terrible ordeal of the sun dance would go to show that his physical organization is not frail, as is frequently the case with hypnotic or trance subjects. So far as personal observation goes, the hypnotic subjects are usually as strong and healthy as the average of their tribe. It seems to be a question more of temperament than of bodily condition or physique. After having observed the Ghost dance among the southern tribes at intervals during a period of about four years, it is apparent that the hypnotic tendency is growing, although the original religious excitement is dying out. The trances are now more numerous among the same number of dancers. Some begin to tremble and stagger almost at the beginning of the dance, without any effort on the part of the medicine-man, while formerly it was usually late in the night before the trances began, although the medicine-men were constantly at work to produce such result. In many if not in most cases the medicine-men themselves have been in trances produced in the same fashion, and must thus be considered sensitives as well as those hypnotized by them.

Not every leader in the Ghost dance is able to bring about the hypnotic sleep, but anyone may try who feels so inspired. Excepting the seven chosen ones who start the songs there is no priesthood in the dance, the authority of such men as Sitting Bull and Black Coyote being due to the voluntary recognition of their superior ability or interest in the matter. Any man or woman who has been in a trance, and has thus derived inspiration from the other world, is at liberty to go within the circle and endeavor to bring others to the trance. Even when the result is unsatisfactory there is no interference with the performer, it being held that he is but the passive instrument of a higher power and therefore in no way responsible. A marked instance of this is the case of Cedar Tree, an Arapaho policeman, who took much interest in the dance, attending nearly every performance in his neighborhood, consecrating the ground and working within the circle to hypnotize the dancers. He was in an advanced stage of consumption, nervous and excitable to an extreme degree, and perhaps it was for this reason that those who came under his influence in the trance constantly complained that he led them on the "devil's road" instead of the "straight road;" that he made them see monstrous and horrible shapes, but never the friends whom they wished to see. On this account they all dreaded to see him at work within the circle, but no one commanded him to desist as it was held that he was controlled by a stronger power and was to be pitied rather than blamed for his ill success. A similar idea

FIG. 40.—The Ghost dance—small circle

MARY IRVIN WRIGHT

Fig. 41.—The Ghost dance—larger circle

FIG. 42.—The Ghost dance—large circle

MARY IRVIN WRIGHT.

Fig. 43.—The Ghost dance—praying

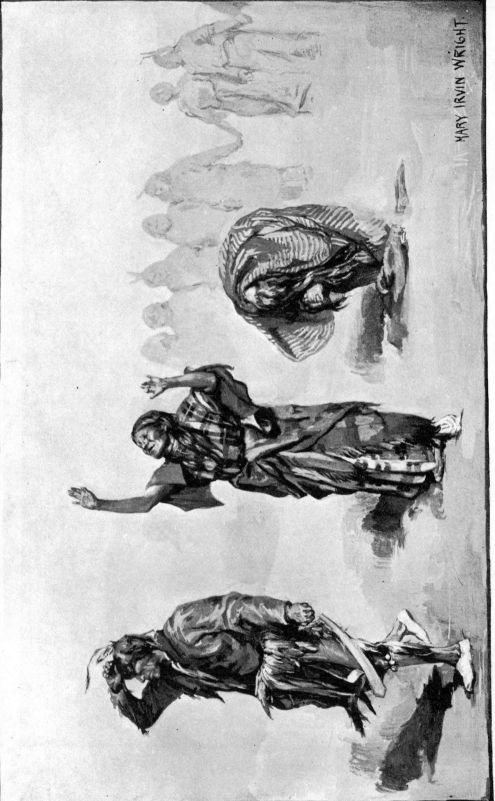

MARY IRVIN WRIGHT.

FIG. 44.—The Ghost-dance—inspiration.

FIG. 45.—The Ghost dance—rigid

FIG. 46.—The Ghost dance—unconscious

Fig. 47.—The crow dance

exists in Europe in connection with persons reputed to possess the evil eye. Cedar Tree himself deplored the result of his efforts and expressed the hope that by earnest prayer he might finally be able to overcome the evil influence.

We shall now describe the hypnotic process as used by the operators, with the various stages of the trance. The hypnotist, usually a man, stands within the ring, holding in his hand an eagle feather or a scarf or handkerchief, white, black, or of any other color. Sometimes he holds the feather in one hand and the scarf in the other. As the dancers circle around singing the songs in time with the dance step the excitement increases until the more sensitive ones are visibly affected. In order to hasten the result certain songs are sung to quicker time, notably the Arapaho song beginning *Nŭ'nanŭ'naatani'na Hu'hu.* We shall assume that the subject is a woman. The first indication that she is becoming affected is a slight muscular tremor, distinctly felt by her two partners who hold her hands on either side. The medicine-man is on the watch, and as soon as he notices the woman's condition he comes over and stands immediately in front of her, looking intently into her face and whirling the feather or the handkerchief, or both, rapidly in front of her eyes, moving slowly around with the dancers at the same time, but constantly facing the woman. All this time he keeps up a series of sharp exclamations, Hu! Hu! Hu! like the rapid breathing of an exhausted runner. From time to time he changes the motion of the feather or handkerchief from a whirling to a rapid up-and-down movement in front of her eyes. For a while the woman continues to move around with the circle of dancers, singing the song with the others, but usually before the circuit is completed she loses control of herself entirely, and, breaking away from the partners who have hold of her hands on either side, she staggers into the ring, while the circle at once closes up again behind her. She is now standing before the medicine-man, who gives his whole attention to her, whirling the feather swiftly in front of her eyes, waving his hands before her face as though fanning her, and drawing his hand slowly from the level of her eyes away to one side or upward into the air, while her gaze follows it with a fixed stare. All the time he keeps up the Hu! Hu! Hu! while the song and the dance go on around them without a pause. For a few minutes she continues to repeat the words of the song and keep time with the step, but in a staggering, drunken fashion. Then the words become unintelligible sounds, and her movements violently spasmodic, until at last she becomes rigid, with her eyes shut or fixed and staring, and stands thus uttering low pitiful moans (Fig. 45). If this is in the daytime, the operator tries to stand with his back to the sun, so that the full sunlight shines in the woman's face (Fig. 44). The subject may retain this fixed, immovable posture for an indefinite time, but at last falls heavily to the ground, unconscious and motionless (Fig. 46). The dance and the song never stop, but as soon as the woman falls the medicine-man gives his attention to another subject among the dancers. The first one may lie unconscious for ten or twenty minutes or sometimes for hours, but no one goes near to disturb her, as her soul is now communing with the spirit world. At last consciousness gradually returns. A violent tremor seizes her body as in the beginning of the fit. A low moan comes from her lips, and she sits up and looks about her like one awaking from sleep. Her whole form trembles violently, but at last she rises to her feet and staggers away from the dancers, who open the circle to let her pass. All the phenomena of recovery, except rigidity, occur in direct reverse of those which precede unconsciousness.

Sometimes before falling the hypnotized subject runs wildly around the circle or out over the prairie, or goes through various crazy evolutions like those of a lunatic. On one occasion—but only once—I have seen the medicine-man point his finger almost in the face of the hypnotized subject, and then withdrawing his finger describe with it a large circle about the tipis. The subject followed the direction indicated, sometimes being hidden from view by the crowd, and finally returned, with his eyes still fixed and staring, to the place where the medicine-man was standing. There is frequently a good deal of humbug mixed with these performances, some evidently pretending to be hypnotized in order to attract notice or to bring about such a condition from force of imitation, but the greater portion is unquestionably genuine and beyond the control of the subjects. In many instances the hypnotized person spins around for minutes at a time like a dervish, or whirls the arms with apparently impossible speed, or assumes and retains until the final fall most uncomfortable positions which it would be impossible to keep for any length of time under normal conditions. Frequently a number of persons are within the ring at once, in all the various stages of hypnotism. The proportion of women thus affected is about three times that of men.

THE AREA COVERED BY THE DANCE

It is impossible to give more than an approximate statement as to the area of the Ghost dance and the messiah doctrine and the number of Indians involved. According to the latest official report, there are about 146,000 Indians west of Missouri river, exclusive of the five civilized nations in Indian Territory. Probably all these tribes heard of the new doctrine, but only a part took any active interest in it. Generally speaking, it was never taken up by the great tribe of the Navaho, by any of the Pueblos except the Taos, or by any of the numerous tribes of the Columbia region. The thirty or thirty-five tribes more or less concerned with the dance have an aggregate population of about 60,000 souls. A number of these were practically unanimous in their acceptance of the new doctrine, notably the Paiute, Shoshoni, Arapaho, Cheyenne, Caddo, and Pawnee, while of others, as the Comanche, only a small minority ever engaged in it. Only about one-half of the 26,000 Sioux took an active part in it. It may safely be said, however, that the doctrine and ceremony of the Ghost dance found more adherents among our tribes than any similar Indian religious movement within the historic period, with the single possible exception of the crusade inaugurated by Tenskwatawa, the Shawano prophet, in 1805.

PRESENT CONDITION OF THE DANCE

Among most of these tribes the movement is already extinct, having died a natural death, excepting in the case of the Sioux. The Shoshoni and some others lost faith in it after the failure of the first predictions. The Sioux probably discontinued the dance before the final surrender, as the battle of Wounded Knee and the subsequent events convinced even the most fanatic believers that their expectations of invulnerability and supernatural assistance were deceptive. The Paiute were yet dancing a year ago, and as their dream has received no such rude awakening as among the Sioux, they are probably still patiently awaiting the great deliverance, in spite of repeated postponements, although the frenzied earnestness of the early period has long ago abated. The Kiowa, who discarded the doctrine on the adverse report of Ä'piatañ, have recently taken up the dance again and are now dancing as religiously as ever under the leadership of the old men, although the progressive element in the tribe is strongly opposed to it. Among the other tribes in Oklahoma—especially the Arapaho, Cheyenne, Caddo, Wichita, Pawnee, and Oto—the Ghost dance has become a part of the tribal life and is still performed at frequent intervals, although the feverish expectation of a few years ago has now settled down into something closely approaching the Christian hope of a reunion with departed friends in a happier world at some time in the unknown future.

As for the great messiah himself, when last heard from Wovoka was on exhibition as an attraction at the Midwinter fair in San Francisco. By this time he has doubtless retired into his original obscurity.

[Wovoka (Jack Wilson) died in October, 1932, about ten days before Cora Dubois began her field work among the Paviotso (Cora Dubois, *The 1870 Ghost Dance* ["University of California Anthropological Records," Vol. III, No. 1, 1939]).—EDITOR.]

CHAPTER VIII

The Songs

INTRODUCTORY

The Ghost-dance songs are of the utmost importance in connection with the study of the messiah religion, as we find embodied in them much of the doctrine itself, with more of the special tribal mythologies, together with such innumerable references to old-time customs, ceremonies, and modes of life long since obsolete as make up a regular symposium of aboriginal thought and practice. There is no limit to the number of these songs, as every trance at every dance produces a new one, the trance subject after regaining consciousness embodying his experience in the spirit world in the form of a song, which is sung at the next dance and succeeding performances until superseded by other songs originating in the same way. Thus, a single dance may easily result in twenty or thirty new songs. While songs are thus born and die, certain ones which appeal especially to the Indian heart, on account of their mythology, pathos, or peculiar sweetness, live and are perpetuated. There are also with each tribe certain songs which are a regular part of the ceremonial, as the opening song and the closing song, which are repeated at every dance. Of these the closing song is the most important and permanent. In some cases certain songs constitute a regular series, detailing the experiences of the same person in successive trance visions. First in importance, for number, richness of reference, beauty of sentiment, and rhythm of language, are the songs of the Arapaho.

THE ARAPAHO

TRIBAL SYNONYMY

Ähyä′to—Kiowa name; meaning unknown; the Kiowa call the wild plum by the same name.

Ano′s-anyotskano—Kichai name.

Ärä′păho—popular name; derivation uncertain; but, perhaps, as Dunbar suggests, from the Pawnee word *tirapihu* or *larapĭhu*, "he buys or trades," in allusion to the Arapaho having formerly been the trading medium between the Pawnee, Osage, and others on the north, and the Kiowa, Comanche, and others to the southwest (*Grinnell letter*).

Äräpăkata—Crow name, from word Arapaho.

Bĕtidĕĕ—Kiowa Apache name.

Detseka′yaa—Caddo name, "dog eaters."

Hitäniwo′ĭv—Cheyenne name, "cloud men."

Inúna-ina—proper tribal name, "our people," or "people of our kind."

Kaninahoic or *Kanină′vish*—Ojibwa name; meaning unknown.

Komse'ka-K'iñahyup—former Kiowa name; "men of the worn-out leggings;" from *komse'*, "smoky, soiled, worn out;" *kati*, "leggings;" *k'iñahyup*, "men."

Maqpi'áto—Sioux name, "blue cloud," i. e., clear sky; reason unknown.

Niä'rhari's-kûrikiwä's-hûski—Wichita name.

Sani'ti'ka—Pawnee name, from the Comanche name.

Särĕtika—Comanche and Shoshoni name, "dog eaters," in allusion to their special liking for dog flesh.

Sarĕtika—Wichita name, from the Comanche name.

TRIBAL SIGNS

Southern Arapaho, "*rub noses;*" northern Arapaho, "*mother people;*" Gros Ventres of the Prairie, "*belly people.*"

SKETCH OF THE TRIBE

The Arapaho, with their subtribe, the Gros Ventres, are one of the westernmost tribes of the wide-extending Algonquian stock. According to their oldest traditions they formerly lived in northeastern Minnesota and moved westward in company with the Cheyenne, who at that time lived on the Cheyenne fork of Red river. From the earliest period the two tribes have always been closely confederated, so that they have no recollection of a time when they were not allies. In the westward migration the Cheyenne took a more southerly direction toward the country of the Black hills, while the Arapaho continued more nearly westward up the Missouri. The Arapaho proper probably ascended on the southern side of the river, while the Gros Ventres went up the northern bank and finally drifted off toward the Blackfeet, with whom they have ever since been closely associated, although they have on several occasions made long visits, extending sometimes over several years, to their southern relatives, by whom they are still regarded as a part of the "Inûna-ina." The others continued on to the great divide between the waters of the Missouri and those of the Columbia, then turning southward along the mountains, separated finally into two main divisions, the northern Arapaho continuing to occupy the head streams of the Missouri and the Yellowstone, in Montana and Wyoming, while the southern Arapaho made their camps on the head of the Platte, the Arkansas, and the Canadian, in Colorado and the adjacent states, frequently joining the Comanche and Kiowa in their raids far down into Mexico. From their earliest recollection, until put on reservations, they have been at war with the Shoshoni, Ute, Pawnee, and Navaho, but have generally been friendly with their other neighbors. The southern Arapaho and Cheyenne have usually acted in concert with the Comanche, Kiowa, and Kiowa Apache.

They recognize among themselves five original divisions, each having a different dialect. They are here given in the order of their importance:

1. *Na'kasinĕ'na, Ba'achinĕna* or *Northern Arapaho*. Nakasinĕna, "sagebrush men," is the original name of this portion of the tribe and the divisional name used by themselves. The name Baachinĕna, by which they are commonly known to the rest of the tribe, is more

modern and may mean "red willow (i. e., kinikinik) men," or possibly "blood-pudding men," the latter meaning said to have been an allusion to a kind of sausage formerly made by this band. They are commonly known as northern Arapaho, to distinguish them from the other large division living now in Oklahoma. The Kiowa distinguished them as Tägyä'ko, "sagebrush people," a translation of their proper name, Baachinĕna. Although not the largest division, the Baachinĕna claim to be the "mother people" of the Arapaho, and have in their keeping the grand medicine of the tribe, the sĕicha or sacred pipe.

2. Na'wunĕna, "southern men," or Southern Arapaho, called Nawa-thi'nĕha, "southerners," by the northern Arapaho. This latter is said to be the archaic form. The southern Arapaho, living now in Oklahoma, constitute by far the larger division, although subordinate in the tribal sociology to the northern Arapaho. In addition to their every-day dialect, they are said to have an archaic dialect, some words of which approximate closely to Cheyenne.

3. Aä'ninĕna, Hitu'nĕna, or Gros Ventres of the Prairie. The first name, said to mean "white clay people" (from aäti, "white clay"), is that by which they call themselves. Hitunĕna or Hitunĕnina, "begging men," "beggars," or, more exactly, "spongers," is the name by which they are called by the other Arapaho, on account, as these latter claim, of their propensity for filling their stomachs at the expense of someone else. The same idea is intended to be conveyed by the tribal sign, which signifies "belly people," not "big bellies" (Gros Ventres), as rendered by the French Canadian trappers. The Kiowa call them Bot-k'iñ'ago, "belly men." By the Shoshoni, also, they are known as Sä'pani, "bellies," while the Blackfeet call them Atsina, "gut people." The Ojibwa call them Bahwetegow-ēninnewug, "fall people," according to Tanner, whence they have sometimes been called Fall Indians or Rapid Indians, from their former residence about the rapids of the Saskatchewan. To the Sioux they are known as Sku'tani. Lewis and Clark improperly call them "Minnetarees of Fort de Prairie." The Hidatsa or Minitari are sometimes known as Gros Ventres of the Missouri.

4. Bä'sawunĕ'na, "wood lodge men," or, according to another authority, "big lodge people." These were formerly a distinct tribe and at war with the other Arapaho. They are represented as having been a very foolish people in the old times, and many absurd stories are told of them, in agreement with the general Indian practice of belittling conquered or subordinate tribes. They have been incorporated with the northern Arapaho for at least a hundred and fifty years, according to the statements of the oldest men of that band. Their dialect is said to have differed very considerably from the other Arapaho dialects. There are still about one hundred of this lineage among the northern Arapaho, and perhaps a few others with the two other main divisions. Weasel Bear, the present keeper of the sacred pipe, is of the Bäsaw-unĕna.

5. *Ha'nahawunĕna* or *Aanŭ'hawă* (meaning unknown). These, like the Bäsawunĕna, lived with the northern Arapaho, but are now practically extinct.

There seems to be no possible trace of a clan or gentile system among the Arapaho, and the same remark holds good of the Cheyenne, Kiowa, and Comanche. It was once assumed that all Indian tribes had the clan system, but later research shows that it is lacking over wide areas in the western territory. It is very doubtful if it exists at all among the prairie tribes generally. Mr Ben Clark, who has known and studied the Cheyenne for half a lifetime, states positively that they have no clans, as the term is usually understood. This agrees with the result of personal investigations and the testimony of George Bent, a Cheyenne half-blood, and the best living authority on all that relates to his tribe. With the eastern tribes, however, and those who have removed from the east or the timbered country, as the Caddo, the gentile system is so much a part of their daily life that it is one of the first things to attract the attention of the observer.

In regard to the tribal camping circle, common to most of the prairie tribes, the Arapaho state that on account of their living in three main divisions they have had no common camping circle within their recollection, but that each of these three divisions constituted a single circle when encamped in one place.

Among the northern Arapaho, on the occasion of every grand gathering, the sacred pipe occupied a special large tipi in the center of the circle, and the taking down of this tipi by the medicine keeper was the signal to the rest of the camp to prepare to move. On the occasion of a visit of several hundred Cheyenne and Arapaho to the Kiowa and Comanche at Anadarko, in the summer of 1892, each of the visiting tribes camped in a separate circle adjacent to the other. The opening of the circle, like the door of each tipi, always faces the east.

Under the name of Kanenävish the Arapaho proper are mentioned by Lewis and Clark in 1805, as living southwest of the Black hills. As a tribe they have not been at war with the whites since 1868, and took no part in the outbreak of the Cheyenne, Kiowa, and Comanche in 1874. At present they are in three main divisions. First come the Gros Ventres, numbering 718 in 1892, associated with the Asiniboin on Fort Belknap reservation in Montana. There are probably others of this band with the Blackfeet on the British side of the line. Next come the northern Arapaho, numbering 829, associated with the Shoshoni on Wind River reservation in Wyoming. They were placed on this reservation in 1876, after having made peace with the Shoshoni, their hereditary enemy, in 1869. They are divided into three bands, the "Forks of the River Men" under Black Coal, the head chief of the whole division; the "Bad Pipes" under Short Nose, and the "Greasy Faces" under Spotted Horse. The third division, the southern Arapaho, associated with the Cheyenne in Oklahoma, constitute the main body

of the tribe and numbered 1,091 in 1892.   They have five bands:
1, Wa'quithi, "bad faces," the principal band and the one to which the
head chief, Left Hand, belongs; 2, Aqa'thinĕ'na, "pleasant men;"
3, Gawunĕ'na or Ga'wunĕhäna (Kawinahan, "black people"—*Hayden*),
"Blackfeet," so called because said to be of part Blackfoot blood, the
same name being applied to the Blackfoot tribe; 4, Ha'qihana, "wolves,"
because they had a wolf (not coyote) for medicine; 5, Säsa'bä-ithi,
"looking up," or according to another authority, "looking around, i. e.,
watchers or lookouts."   Under the treaty of Medicine Lodge in 1867,
they and the southern Cheyenne were placed on the reservation which
they sold in 1890 to take allotments and become citizens.   Their present

Fɪɢ. 48.—Arapaho tipi and windbreak

chief is Left Hand (Nawat), who succeeded the celebrated Little Raven
(Hosa) a few years ago.   The whole number of the Arapaho and Gros
Ventres, including a few in eastern schools, is about 2,700.
   Until very recently the Arapaho have been a typical prairie tribe,
living in skin tipis and following the buffalo in its migrations, yet they
retain a tradition of a time when they were agricultural.   They are
of a friendly, accommodating disposition, religious and contemplative,
without the truculent, pugnacious character that belongs to their confederates, the Cheyenne, although they have always proven themselves
brave warriors.   They are also less mercenary and more tractable than
the prairie Indians generally, and having now recognized the inevitable
of civilization have gone to work in good faith to make the best of it.

Their religious nature has led them to take a more active interest in the Ghost dance, which, together with the rhythmic character of their language, has made the Arapaho songs the favorite among all the tribes of Oklahoma. The chief study of the Ghost dance was made among the Arapaho, whom the author visited six times for this purpose. One visit was made to those in Wyoming, the rest of the time being spent with the southern branch of the tribe.

SONGS OF THE ARAPAHO

1. OPENING SONG—EYEHE′! NÄ′NISA′NA

E-ye-he′! A - nä′-ni-sa′ - na,   E-ye-he′! A - nä′-ni-sa′ - na,   Hi′ - nä chä′-säq

ä-ti-cha′ nĭ-na He′-e - ye′! Hi′-nä chä′-säq   ä-ti-cha′ nĭ′-na   He′-e - ye′! Na′-hă̆ - ni nä′-ni-

thä′-tu-hŭ′-na   He′-e-ye′!   Na′-hă-ni nä′-ni-thä′-tu-hŭ′-na   He′-e-ye′!   Bi′-ta-a′-wu′

da′ - na - a′ - bä-na′-wa He′-e - ye′!   Bi′-ta - a′-wu′   da′ - na - a′ - bä - na′-wa He′-e - ye′!

Eyehe′! nä′nisa′na,
Eyehe′! nä′nisa′na,
Hi′nä chä′sä′ äticha′nĭ′na He′eye′!
Hi′nä chä′sä′ äticha′nĭ′na He′eye′!
Na′hăni nä′nithä′tuhŭ′na He′eye′!
Na′hăni nä′nithä′tuhŭ′na He′eye′!
Bi′taa′wu′ da′naa′bäna′wa He′eye′!
Bi′taa′wu′ da′naa′bäna′wa He′eye′!

Translation

O, my children! O, my children!
Here is another of your pipes—*He′eye′!*
Here is another of your pipes—*He′eye′!*
Look! thus I shouted—*He′eye′!*
Look! thus I shouted—*He′eye′!*
When I moved the earth—*He′eye′!*
When I moved the earth—*He′eye′!*

This opening song of the Arapaho Ghost dance originated among the northern Arapaho in Wyoming and was brought down to the southern branch of the tribe by the first apostles of the new religion. By "another pipe" is probably meant the newer revelation of the messiah, the pipe being an important feature of all sacred ceremonies, and all their previous religious tradition having centered about the sĕicha or flat pipe, to be described hereafter. The pipe, however, was not commonly carried in the dance, as was the case among the Sioux. In this song, as in many others of the Ghost dance, the father or messiah, *Hesúna'nin,* is supposed to be addressing "my children," *nänisa'na.* The tune is particularly soft and pleasing, and the song remains a standard favorite. The second reference is to the new earth which is supposed to be already moving rapidly forward to slide over and take the place of this old and worn-out creation.

2. SĔ'ICHA HEI'TA'WUNI'NA

Sĕ'icha' hei'ta'wuni'na — E'yahe'eye,
Sĕ'icha hei'ta'wuni'na — E'yahe'eye.
He'sûna'nini — Yahe'eye',
He'sûna'nini — Yahe'eye'.
Ûtnitha'wuchä'wahănänina — E'yahe'eye',
Ûtnitha'wuchä'wahănänina — E'yahe'eye'.
He'sana'nini — E'yahe'eye,
He'sana'nini — E'yahe'eye.

Translation

The sacred pipe tells me — *E'yahe'eye!*
The sacred pipe tells me — *E'yahe'eye!*
Our father — *Yahe'eye'!*
Our father — *Yahe'eye'!*
We shall surely be put again (with our friends) — *E'yahe'eye!*
We shall surely be put again (with our friends) — *E'yahe'eye!*
Our father — *E'yahe'eye!*
Our father — *E'yahe'eye!*

The sĕicha or flat pipe is the sacred tribal medicine of the Arapaho. According to the myth it was given to their ancestors at the beginning of the world after the Turtle had brought the earth up from under the water. It was delivered to them by the Duck, which was discovered swimming about on the top of the water after the emergence of the land. At the same time they were given an ear of corn, from which comes all the corn of the world. The Arapaho lost the art of agriculture when they came out upon the buffalo plains, but the sacred pipe the Turtle long since changed to stone, and the first ear of corn, also transformed to stone, they have cherished to this day as their great medicine. The pipe, turtle, and ear of corn are preserved among the northern Arapaho in Wyoming, who claim to be the "mother people" of the tribe. They are handed down in the keeping of a particular family from generation to generation, the present priestly guardian being Se'hiwûq, "Weasel Bear" (from *sea,* weasel, and *wúq,* bear; the name has also been rendered "Gray Bear," from *se,* gray, and *wúq,* bear), of the Bäsawunĕ'na division.

The three sacred things are preserved carefully wrapped in deerskins, and are exposed only on rare occasions, always within the sacred tipi and in the presence of but a small number of witnesses, who take this opportunity to smoke the sacred pipe and pray for the things which they most desire. The pipe itself is of stone, and is described as apparently made in double, one part being laid over the other like the bark of a tree, the outer part of both bowl and stem being of the regular red pipestone, while the inner part of both is of white stone. The stem is only about 10 inches long, while the bowl is large and heavy, with the characteristic projection for resting the end upon the ground. Both bowl and stem are rounded, but with a flange of perhaps an inch in width along each side of the stem and up along the bowl. From this comes its name of sĕicha, or "flat pipe." When exposed on such occasions, the devotees sit around the fire in a circle, when the bundle is opened upon the ground so that all may see the sacred objects. The medicine keeper then lights the pipe and after taking one or two whiffs passes it to the one next him, who takes a single whiff and passes it on to the next. It thus goes sunwise (?) around the circle. In taking the sĕicha the devotees do not grasp the stem, as when smoking on other occasions, but receive it upon the outstretched palm of the right hand, smoke, and pass it on around the circle. The flanges along the side of the pipe allow it to rest flat upon the hand. After all have smoked, the priest recites the genesis myth of the origin of the land, and the manner in which the pipe and the corn were given to their ancestors. The corresponding myth of the Cheyenne occupies "four smokes" (i. e., four consecutive nights) in the delivery, but I am unable to state whether or not this is the case with the Arapaho. So sacred is this tradition held that no one but the priest of the pipe dares to recite it, for fear of divine punishment should the slightest error be made in the narration. At the close of the recital the devotees send up their prayers for the blessings of which they stand most in need, after which the priest again carefully wraps up the sacred objects in the skins. Before leaving the lodge the worshipers cover the bundle with their offerings of blankets or other valuables, which are taken by the medicine keeper as his fee.

When encamped in the tribal circle, the sacred pipe and its keeper occupied a large tipi, reserved especially for this purpose, which was set up within the circle and near its western line, directly opposite the doorway on the east. In the center of the circle, between the doorway and the sacred tipi, was erected the sweat-house of the Chi'nachichinĕ'na or old men of the highest degree of the warrior order. The taking down of the sacred tipi by the attendants of the pipe keeper was the signal for moving camp, and no other tipi was allowed to be taken down before it. When on the march, the pipe keeper proceeded on foot—never on horse—carrying the sacred bundle upon his back and attended by a retinue of guards. As a matter of course, the sacred pipe was not carried by war parties or on other expeditions requiring celerity of movement. Of late years the rules have

so far relaxed that its present guardian sometimes rides on horseback
while carrying the pipe, but even then he carries the bundle upon
his own back instead of upon the saddle. He never rides in a wagon
with it. Since the tribe is permanently divided under the modern
reservation system, individuals or small parties of the southern Arapaho
frequently make the long journey by railroad and stage to the reservation in Wyoming in order to see and pray over the sĕicha, as it is
impossible, on account of the ceremonial regulations, for the keeper to
bring it down to them in the south.

So far as known, only one white man, Mr J. Roberts, formerly superintendent of the Arapaho school in Wyoming, has ever seen the sacred
pipe, which was shown to him on one occasion by Weasel Bear as a
special mark of gratitude in return for some kindness. After having
spent several months among the southern Arapaho, from whom I
learned the songs of the pipe with much as to its sacred history, I
visited the messiah in Nevada and then went to the northern Arapaho
in Wyoming, with great hope of seeing the sĕicha and hearing the tradition in full. On the strength of my intimate acquaintance with their
relatives in the south and with their great messiah in the west, the
chiefs and head-men were favorable to my purpose and encouraged me
to hope, but on going out to the camp in the mountains, where nearly
the whole tribe was then assembled cutting wood, my hopes were dashed
to the ground the first night by hearing the old priest, Weasel Bear,
making the public announcement in a loud voice throughout the camp
that a white man was among them to learn about their sacred things,
but that these belonged to the religion of the Indian and a white man
had no business to ask about them. The chief and those who had
been delegates to the messiah came in soon after to the tipi where I
was stopping, to express their deep regret, but they were unable to
change the resolution of Weasel Bear, and none of themselves would
venture to repeat the tradition.

3. Ate′bĕ tiăwu′nănu′

Ate′bĕ tiăwu′nănu′, nä′nisa′nă,
Ate′bĕ tiăwu′nănu′, nä′nisa′nă,
Ni′athu′ă′, Ni′athu′ă′,
Ni′binu′ ga′awa′ti′na,
Ni′binu′ ga′awa′ti′na.

Translation

My children, when at first I liked the whites,
My children, when at first I liked the whites,
I gave them fruits,
I gave them fruits.

This song referring to the whites was composed by Nawat or Left
Hand, chief of the southern Arapaho, and can hardly be considered
dangerous or treasonable in character. According to his statement, in

his trance vision of the other world the father showed him extensive
orchards, telling him that in the beginning all these things had been
given to the whites, but that hereafter they would be given to his children, the Indians. *Nia'tha*, plural *Nia'thuă*, the Arapaho name for the
whites, signifies literally, expert, skillful, or wise.

4. A'BÄ'NI'HI'

A'bä'ni'hi',
A'bä'ni'hi',
Ätichä'bi'näsänä,
Ätichä'bi'näsänä,
Chi'chita'ně,
Chi'chita'ně.

Translation

My partner, my partner,
Let us go out gambling,
Let us go out gambling,
At *chi'chita'ně*, at *chi'chita'ně*.

Chi'chita'ně is a favorite game of contest with the boys, in which the
player, while holding in his hands a bow and an arrow ready to shoot,
keeps in the hand which grasps the string a small wisp of grass bound
with sinew. He lets this drop and tries to shoot it with the arrow before it touches the ground. The wisp is about the size of a man's finger.
The song came from the north, and was suggested by a trance vision
in which the dreamer saw his former boy friends playing this game in
the spirit world.

5. A'-NISÛNA'A'HU ÄCHĬSHINĬ'QAHI'NA

A'-nisûna'a'hu',
A'-nisûna'a'hu',
Ä'chĭshinĭ'qahi'na,
Ä'chĭshinĭ'qahi'na,
E'hihä'sina'kăwu'hu'nĭt,
E'hihä'sina'kăwu'hu'nĭt.

Translation

My father, my father,
While he was taking me around,
While he was taking me around,
He turned into a moose,
He turned into a moose.

This song relates the trance experience of Waqui'si or "Ugly Face
Woman." In his vision of the spirit world he went into a large Arapaho
camp, where he met his dead father, who took him around to the various tipis to meet others of his departed friends. While they were thus
going about, a change came o'er the spirit of his dream, as so often

Fig. 49.—Arapaho bed

happens in this fevered mental condition, and instead of his father he found a moose standing by his side. Such transformations are frequently noted in the Ghost-dance songs.

6. E'YEHE'! WÛ'NAYU'UHU'

E'yehe' ! Wû'nayu'uhu' —
E'yehe' ! Wû'nayu'uhu' —
A'ga'nă',
A'ga'nă'.

Translation

E'yehe' ! they are new —
E'yehe' ! they are new —
The bed coverings,
The bed coverings.

The composer of this song is a woman who, in her trance, was taken to a large camp where all the tipis were of clean new buffalo skins, and the beds and interior furniture were all in the same condition.

Fig. 50.—Bed of the prairie tribes

The bed of the prairie tribes is composed of slender willow rods, peeled, straightened with the teeth, laid side by side and fastened together into a sort of mat by means of buckskin or rawhide strings passed through holes at the ends of the rods. The bed is stretched upon a platform raised about a foot above the ground, and one end of the mat is raised up in hammock fashion by means of a tripod and buckskin hanger. The rods laid across the platform, forming the bed proper, are usually about 3½ or 4 feet long (the width of the bed), while those forming the upright part suspended from the tripod are shorter as they approach the top, where they are only about half that length. The bed is bordered with buckskin binding fringed and beaded, and the exposed rods are painted in bright colors. The hanging portion is distinct from the part resting upon the platform, and in some cases there is a hanger at each end of the bed. Over the platform portion are spread the buckskins and blankets, which form a couch by day and a bed by night. A pillow of buckskin, stuffed with buffalo hair and elaborately ornamented with beads or porcupine quills, is sometimes added. The bed is placed close up under the tipi. In the largest tipis there are usually three beds, one being opposite the doorway and the others on each side, the fire being built in a hole scooped out in the ground in the center of the lodge. They are used as seats during waking hours, while the ground, with a rawhide spread upon it, constitutes the only table at mealtime (Figs. 49, 50). In going to bed there is no undressing, each person as he becomes sleepy simply stretching out and drawing a blanket over himself, head and all, while the other occupants of the tipi continue their talking, singing, or other business until they too lie down to pleasant dreams.

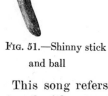

FIG. 51.—Shinny stick and ball

7. Hi′sähi′hi

Hi′sähi′hi, Hi′sähi′hi,
Ha′nä ta′wŭnä ga′awä′ha,
Ha′nä ta′wŭnä ga′awä′ha.
A′tanä′tähinä′na,
A′tanä′tähinä′na.

Translation

My partner! My partner!
Strike the ball hard—
Strike the ball hard.
I want to win,
I want to win.

½

FIG. 52.—Wakuna or head-feathers

This song refers to the woman's game of *gŭ′gä′hawa′t* or "shinny," played with curved sticks and a ball like a baseball, called *gaawä′ha,*

made of (buffalo) hair and covered with buckskin (Fig. 51).   Two
stakes are set up as goals at either end of the ground, and the object
of each party is to drive the ball through the goals of the other.   Each
inning is a game.   The song was composed by a woman, who met her
former girl comrade in the spirit world and played this game with her
against an opposing party.

8. Ä′-NANI′NI′BI′NÄ′SI WAKU′NA

Nä′nisa′na, Nä′nisa′na,
Ä′-nani′ni′bi′nä′si waku′na,
Ä′-nani′ni′bi′nä′si waku′na.
Nä′nisa′na, Nä′nisa′na.

Translation

My children, my children.
The wind makes the head-feathers sing—
The wind makes the head-feathers sing.
My children, my children.

By the *wakuna* or head-feathers (Fig. 52) is meant the two crow
feathers mounted on a short stick and worn on the head by the leaders
of the dance, as already described.

9. HE′! NÄNÉ′TH BI′SHIQA′WĂ

He′! Nä-ne′th bi′-shi-qa′-wä,   He′! Nä-ne′th bi′-shi-qa′-wä,   Nä′ - ni - sa′ - na,

nä′ - ni - sa′-na,   Nä′ - i - na′ - ha′t - dä′-bä′-naq, Nä′ - i - na′ - ha′t - dä′ - bä′-naq.

He′! näne′th bi′shiqa′wä,
He′! näne′th bi′shiqa′wä,
Nä′nisa′na, nä′nisa′na,
Nä′ina′ha′tdä′bä′naq,
Nä′ina′ha′tdä′bä′naq.

Translation

He! When I met him approaching—
He! When I met him approaching—
My children, my children—
I then saw the multitude plainly,
I then saw the multitude plainly.

This song was brought from the north to the southern Arapaho by
Sitting Bull.   It refers to the trance vision of a dancer, who saw the

messiah advancing at the head of all the spirit army. It is an old favorite, and is sung with vigor and animation.

10. Häna'na'wunănu ni'tawu'na'na'

Nä'nisa'na, nä'nisa'na,
Häna'na'wunănu ni'tawu'na'na',
Häna'na'wunănu ni'tawu'na'na',
Di'chin niănita'wa'thi,
Di'chin niănita'wa'thi.
Nithi'na hesûna'nĭn,
Nithi'na hesûna'nĭn.

Translation

My children, my children,
I take pity on those who have been taught,
I take pity on those who have been taught,
Because they push on hard,
Because they push on hard.
Says our father,
Says our father.

This is a message from the messiah to persevere in the dance. In the expressive idiom of the prairie tribes, as also in the sign language, the term for persevering signifies to "push hard."

11. A-ni'qu wa'wanä'nibä'tia'

A-ni'qu wa'wanä'nibä'tia' — Hi'ni'ni'!
A-ni'qu wa'wanä'nibä'tia' — Hi'ni'ni'!
Hi'niqa'agayetu'sa,
Hi'niqa'agayetu'sa,
Hi'ni ni'nitu'sa nibä'tia—Hi'ni'ni'!
Hi'ni ni'nitu'sa nibä'tia—Hi'ni'ni'!

Translation

Father, now I am singing it — *Hi'ni'ni!*
Father, now I am singing it — *Hi'ni'ni!*
That loudest song of all,
That loudest song of all—
That resounding song — *Hi'ni'ni!*
That resounding song — *Hi'ni'ni!*

This is another of the old favorites. The rolling effect of the vocalic Arapaho syllables renders it particularly sonorous when sung by a full chorus. *Ni'qa* or *a-ni'qu,* "father," is a term of reverential affection, about equivalent to "our father" in the Lord's prayer. The ordinary word is *hesûna'nin,* from *nisû'na,* "my father."

12. Ha'yana'-usi'ya'

Ha'yana'-usi'ya'!
Ha'yana'-usi'ya'!
Bi'ga ta'cha'wagu'na,
Bi'ga ta'cha'wagu'na.

Translation

How bright is the moonlight!
How bright is the moonlight!
Tonight as I ride with my load of buffalo beef,
Tonight as I ride with my load of buffalo beef.

The author of this song, on meeting his friends in the spirit world, found them preparing to go on a great buffalo hunt, the prairies of the new earth being covered with the countless thousands of buffalo that have been swept from the plains since the advent of the white man. They returned to camp at night, under the full moonlight, with their ponies loaded down with fresh beef. There is something peculiarly touching in this dream of the old life—this Indian heaven where—

> "In meadows wet with moistening dews,
> In garments for the chase arrayed,
> The hunter still the deer pursues—
> The hunter and the deer a shade."

13. HA′TI NI′BÄT—E′HE′EYE′

Ha′ti ni′bät — E′he′eye′!
Ha′ti ni′bät — E′he′eye′!
Nä′nibä′tawa′,
Nä′nibä′tawa′,
He′yäya′ahe′ye!
He′yäya′ahe′ye!

Translation

The cottonwood song — *E′he′eye′!*
The cottonwood song — *E′he′eye′!*
I am singing it,
I am singing it,
He′yäya′ahe′ye!
He′yäya′ahe′ye!

The cottonwood (*Populus monilifera*) is the most characteristic tree of the plains and of the arid region between the Rockies and the Sierras. It is a species of poplar and takes its name from the white downy blossom fronds, resembling cotton, which come out upon it in the spring. The cottonwood and a species of stunted oak, with the mesquite in the south, are almost the only trees to be found upon the great plains extending from the Saskatchewan southward into Texas. As it never grows out upon the open, but always close along the borders of the few streams, it is an unfailing indication of water either on or near the surface, in a region well-nigh waterless. Between the bark and the wood there is a sweet milky juice of which the Indians are very fond—as one who had been educated in the east said, "It is their ice cream"—and they frequently strip off the bark and scrape the trunk in order to procure it. Horses also are fond of this sweet juice, and in seasons when the grass has been burned off or is otherwise scarce, the

Indian ponies sometimes resort to the small twigs and bark of the cottonwood to sustain life. In extreme cases their owners have sometimes been driven to the same shift. In winter the camps of the prairie tribes are removed from the open prairie to the shelter of the cottonwood timber along the streams. The tree is held almost sacred, and the sun-dance lodge is usually or always constructed of cottonwood saplings.

14. EYEHE′! A′NIE′SA′NA

Eyehe′! A′nie′sa′na′,
Eyehe′! A′nie′sa′na′,
He′ee′ä′ehe′yuhe′yu!
He′ee′ä′ehe′yuhe′yu!
A′-baha′ ni′esa′na′,
A′-baha′ ni′esa′na′.

Translation

Eyehe′! The young birds,
Eyehe′! The young birds,
He′ee′ä′ehe′yuhe′yu!
He′ee′ä′ehe′yuhe′yu!
The young Thunderbirds,
The young Thunderbirds.

Among the Algonquian tribes of the east, the Sioux, Cheyenne, Arapaho, Kiowa, Comanche, and prairie tribes generally, as well as among those of the northwest coast and some parts of Mexico, thunder and lightning are produced by a great bird, whose shadow is the thunder cloud, whose flapping wings make the sound of thunder, and whose flashing eyes rapidly opening or closing send forth the lightning. Among some tribes of the northwest this being is not a bird, but a giant who puts on a dress of bird skin with head, wings, and all complete, by means of which he flies through the air when in search of his prey. The myth is not found among the Iroquois or the Cherokee, or, perhaps, among the Muskhogean tribes.

The Thunderbird usually has his dwelling on some high mountain or rocky elevation of difficult access. Within the territory of the myth several places are thus designated as the Thunder's Nest. Thunder bay of Lake Huron, in lower Michigan, derives its name in this way. Such a place, known to the Sioux as *Waqkiñ′a-oye′*, "The Thunder's Nest," is within the old territory of the Sisseton Sioux in eastern South Dakota in the neighborhood of Big Stone lake. At another place, near the summit of the Coteau des Prairies, in eastern South Dakota, a number of large round bowlders are pointed out as the eggs of the Thunderbird. According to the Comanche there is a place on upper Red river where the Thunderbird once alighted on the ground, the spot being still identified by the fact that the grass remains burned off over a space having the outline of a large bird with outstretched wings. The same people tell how a hunter once shot and wounded a large bird which fell to the ground. Being afraid to attack it alone on account of its size, he returned to camp for help, but on again approaching the spot the hunters heard the thunder rolling and saw flashes of lightning shooting out from the ravine where the bird lay wounded. On coming nearer, the lightning blinded them so that they could not see the bird, and one flash struck and killed a hunter. His frightened companions then fled back to camp, for they knew it was the Thunderbird.

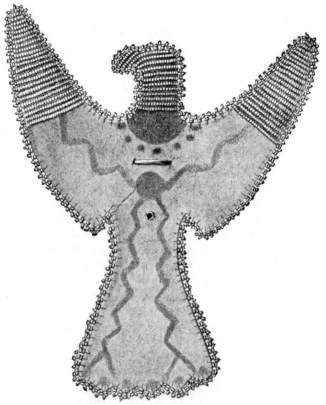

Fig. 53.—The Thunderbird

With both Cheyenne and Arapaho the thunder (*ba'a'*) is a large bird, with a brood of smaller ones, and carries in its talons a number of arrows with which it strikes the victim of lightning. For this reason they call the eagle on our coins *baa*. When it thunders, they say *ba'a' nänitŭ'-hut,* "the thunder calls." In Indian pictography the Thunderbird is figured with zigzag lines running out from its heart to represent the lightning. A small figure of it (represented in Fig. 53), cut from rawhide and ornamented with beads. is frequently worn on the heads of the dancers.

15. A′HE′SÛNA′NINI NĂYA′QÛTI′HI

A′he′sûna′nini năya′qûti′hi,
A′he′sûna′nini năya′qûti′hi,
Hä′ni′nihiga′hŭna′,
Hä′ni′nihiga′hŭna′,
He′sûna′nin hä′ni na′ha′waŭ′.
He′sûna′nin hä′ni na′ha′waŭ′.

Translation

Our father, the Whirlwind,
Our father, the Whirlwind—
By its aid I am running swiftly,
By its aid I am running swiftly,
By which means I saw our father,
By which means I saw our father.

The idea expressed in this song is that the dreamer "rides the whirlwind" in order sooner to meet the messiah and the spirit hosts. Father or grandfather are terms of reverence and affection, applied to anything held sacred or awful.

16. A′HE′SÛNA′NINI NĂYA′QÛTI′

A′he′sûna′nini năya′qûti′,
A′he′sûna′nini năya′qûti′,
Wa′wă chä′niĭ′nagu′nĭti hu′na,
Wa′wă chä′niĭ′nagu′nĭti hu′na.

Translation

Our father, the Whirlwind,
Our father, the Whirlwind,
Now wears the headdress of crow feathers,
Now wears the headdress of crow feathers.

In this song the Whirlwind, personified, wears on his head the two crow feathers, by which the dancers are to be borne upward to the new spirit world.

17. NINAÄ′NIAHU′NA

Ninaä′niahu′na,
Ninaä′niahu′na
Bi′taa′wu hä′näi′säĭ,
Bi′taa′wu hä′näi′säĭ,
Hi′nää′thi nä′niwu′hŭnă,
Hi′nää′thi nä′niwu′hŭnă.

Translation

I circle around—
I circle around
The boundaries of the earth,
The boundaries of the earth—
Wearing the long wing feathers as I fly,
Wearing the long wing feathers as I fly.

This song probably refers to the Thunderbird. There is an energetic swing to the tune that makes it a favorite. In Indian belief the earth is a circular disk, usually surrounded on all sides by water, and the sky is a solid concave hemisphere coming down at the horizon to the level of the earth. In Cherokee and other Indian myth the sky is continually lifting up and coming down again to the earth, like the upper blade of the scissors. The sun, which lives upon the outside of this hemisphere, comes through from the east in the morning while there is a momentary opening between the earth and the edge of the sky, climbs along upon the underside of the sky from east to west, and goes out at the western horizon in the evening, to return during the night to its starting point in the east.

18. Ha'nahawu'nĕn bĕni'ni'na

Ha'nahawu'nĕn bĕni'ni'na,
Ha'nahawu'nĕn bĕni'ni'na,
Hina'wûn ga'na'ni'na,
Hina'wûn ga'na'ni'na.

Translation

The *Hanahawunĕn* gave to me,
The *Hanahawunĕn* gave to me,
His paint—He made me clean,
His paint—He made me clean.

The author of this song met in the spirit world a man of the now extinct Arapaho band of the *Hanahawunĕna*, who washed the face of the visitor and then painted him afresh with some of the old-time mineral paint of the Indians. In accord with the Indian belief, all the extinct and forgotten tribes have now their home in the world of shades.

19. Ate'be'tana'-ise'ti he'sûna'nini'

Ate'be'tana'-ise'ti he'sûna'nini'—Ahe'eye'!
Ate'be'tana'-ise'ti he'sûna'nini'—Ahe'eye'!
Na'waa'tănû', Na'waa'tănû,
Danatinĕnawaŭ,
Nita-isa, nita-isa,
He'yahe'eȳe'!

Translation

When first our father came—*Ahe'eye'!*
When first our father came—*Ahe'eye'!*
I prayed to him, I prayed to him—
My relative, my relative—
He'yahe'eȳe'!

This song was composed by Paul Boynton (Bääku'ni, "Red Feather"), a Carlisle student, after having been in a trance. His brother had died some time before, and being told by the Indians that he might be able to see and talk with him by joining the dance, Paul went to Sitting Bull, the leader of the dance, at the next gathering, and asked him to help him to see his dead brother. The result was that he was hypnotized by Sitting Bull, fell to the ground in a trance, and saw his brother. While talking with him, however, he suddenly awoke, much to his regret, probably from some one of the dancers having touched against him as he lay upon the ground. According to his statement, the words were spoken by him in his sleep after coming from the dance and were overheard by some companions who questioned him about it in the morning, when he told his experience and put the words into a song. The "father" here referred to is Sitting Bull, the great apostle of the Arapaho Ghost dance. It was from Paul's statement, intelligently told in good English before I had yet seen the dance, that I was first led to suspect that hypnotism was the secret of the trances.

20. A-NI′ÄNĔ′THĂHI′NANI′NA NISA′NA

A-ni′änĕ′thăhi′nani′na nisa′na,
A-ni′änĕ′thăhi′nani′na nisa′na.
He′chä′ na′hăbi′na,
He′chä′ na′hăbi′na,
Hewa-u′sa häthi′na,
Hewa-u′sa häthi′na.

Translation

My father did not recognize me (at first),
My father did not recognize me (at first).
When again he saw me,
When again he saw me,
He said, "You are the offspring of a crow,"
He said, "You are the offspring of a crow."

This song was composed by Sitting Bull, the Arapaho apostle of the dance, and relates his own experience in the trance, in which he met his father, who had died years before. The expression, "You are the child of a crow," may refer to his own sacred character as an apostle, the crow being regarded as the messenger from the spirit world.

21. NI′-ATHU′-A-U′ A′HAKÄ′NITH′II

I′yehe′! anä′nisa′nă′ — Uhi′yeye′heye′!
I′yehe′! anä′nisa′nă′ — Uhi′yeye′heye′!
I′yehe′! ha′dawu′hana′ — Eye′äe′yuhe′yu!
I′yehe′! ha′dawu′hana′ — Eye′äe′yuhe′yu!
Ni′athu′-a-u′ a′hakä′nith′iI — Ahe′yuhe′yu!

Translation

I′yehe′! my children — Uhi′yeye′heye′!
I′yehe′! my children — Uhi′yeye′heye′!
I′yehe′! we have rendered them desolate — Eye′äe′yuhe′yu!
I′yehe′! we have rendered them desolate — Eye′äe′yuhe′yu!
The whites are crazy — Ahe′yuhe′yu!

In this song the father tells his children of the desolation, in consequence of their folly and injustice, that would come upon the whites when they will be left alone upon the old world, while the Indians will be taken up to the new earth to live in happiness forever.

22. NA′HA′TA BITAA′WU

Nä′nisa′nă, nä′nisa′nă,
Na′ha′ta bi′taa′wu hätnaa′waa′-u′hu′,
Na′ha′ta bi′taa′wu hätnaa′waa′-u′hu′.
Häthi′na hi′nisû′na-hu′,
Häthi′na hi′nisû′na-hu′.

Translation

My children, my children,
Look! the earth is about to move,
Look! the earth is about to move.
My father tells me so,
My father tells me so.

In this song the dreamer tells his friends, on the authority of the messiah, that the predicted spiritual new earth is about to start to come over and cover up this old world. It was also taught, as appears from the messiah's letter, that at the moment of contact this world would tremble as in an earthquake.

23. AHE′SÛNA′NINI ÄCHIQA′HĂ′WA-Ŭ′

Ahe′sûna′nini, ahe′sûna′nini,
Ächiqa′hă′wa-ŭ′, Ächiqa′hă′wa-ŭ′,
E′hihä′sĭni′ĕhi′nĭt,
E′hihä′sĭni′ĕhi′nĭt.

Translation

My father, my father—
I am looking at him,
I am looking at him.
He is beginning to turn into a bird,
He is beginning to turn into a bird.

In this, as in the fifth Arapaho song, we have a transformation. According to the story of the author, his father is transformed into a bird even while he looks at him. The song is sung in quick time to hasten the trance.

24. HA′ÄNAKE′I

Ha′änake′i, ha′änake′i,
Dä′nasa′ku′tăwa′,
Dä′nasa′ku′tăwa′,
He′sûna′nin hä′ni na′ha′waŭ′,
He′sûna′nin hä′ni na′ha′waŭ′.

The rock, the rock,
I am standing upon it,
I am standing upon it.
By its means I saw our father,
By its means I saw our father.

This is one of the old songs now obsolete, and its meaning is not clear. It may mean simply that the author of it climbed a rock in order to be able to see farther, but it is more likely that it contains some mythic reference.

25. WaʹWaʹNaʹDanäʹDiă̆ʹ

Näʹnisaʹnaăñʹ, näʹnisaʹnaăñʹ,
Waʹwaʹnaʹdanäʹdiăʹ,
Waʹwaʹnaʹdanäʹdiăʹ,
Nänisaʹna, nänisaʹna.

Translation

My children, my children,
I am about to hum.
I am about to hum.
My children, my children.

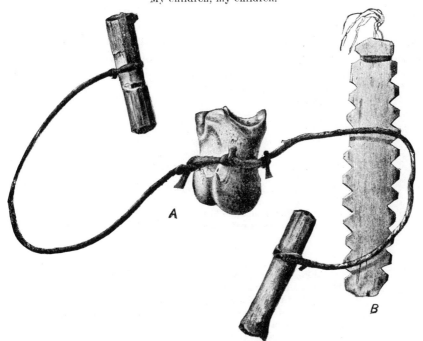

Fig. 54.—Hummer and bullroarer

The author of this song saw her children in the other world playing with the *hätikuʹtha*, or hummer. On going home after awaking from her trance, she made the toy and carried it with her to the next dance and twirled it in the air while singing the song. The *hätiku'tha*, or hummer, is used by the boys of the prairie tribes as our boys use the "cut-water," a circular tin disk, suspended on two strings passed through holes in the middle, and set in rapid revolution, so as to produce a humming sound, by alternately twisting the strings upon each other and allowing them to untwist again. One of these which I examined consists of a bone from a buffalo hoof, painted in different colors, with four buckskin strings tied around the middle and running out on each side and fastened at each end to a small peg, so as to be more firmly grasped by the fingers. It was carried in the dance in 1890 by an old Arapaho named Tall Bear, who had had it in his possession for twenty years. Another specimen, shown in Figure 54, *a*, now in possession of the National Museum, is similar in construction, but with only one string on each side.

A kindred toy—it can hardly be considered a musical instrument—is that known among the whites as the "bull-roarer." It is found among most of the western tribes, as well as among our own children and primitive peoples all over the world. It is usually a simple flat piece of wood, about 6 inches long, sometimes notched on the edges and fancifully painted, attached to a sinew or buckskin string of convenient length. It is held in one hand, and when twirled rapidly in the air produces a sound not unlike the roaring of a bull or of distant thunder. With most tribes it is simply a child's toy, but among the Hopi, according to Fewkes, and the Apache, according to Bourke, it has a sacred use to assist the prayers of the medicine-man in bringing on the storm clouds and the rain.

26. A-TE'BĔ' DII'NĔTITA'NIĔG

A-te'bĕ' dii'nĕtita'niĕg — I'yehe'eye'!
A-te'bĕ' dii'nĕtita'niĕg — I'yehe'eye'!
Nii'te'gu be'na nĕ'chäi'hit — I' yehe'eye'!
Bi'taa'wuu — I'yahe'eye'!
Nii'te'gu be'na nĕ'chäi'hit — I'yehe'eye'!
Bi'taa'wuu — I'yahe'eye'!
De'tawu'ni'na ni'sa'na — Ahe'eye'-he'eye'!
De'tawu'ni'na ni'sa'na' — Ahe'eye'-he'eye'!

Translation

At the beginning of human existence—*I'yehe'eye'!*
At the beginning of human existence—*I'yehe'eye'!*
It was the turtle who gave this grateful gift to me—
The earth—*I'yahe'eye'!*
It was the turtle who gave this grateful gift to me—
The earth—*I'yahe'eye'!*
(Thus) my father told me—*Ahe'eye'-he'eye'!*
(Thus) my father told me—*Ahe'eye'-he'eye'!*

In the mythology of many primitive nations, from the ancient Hindu to our own Indian tribes, the turtle or tortoise is the supporter of the earth, the Atlas on whose back rests the burden of the whole living universe. A reason for this is found in the amphibious character of the turtle, which renders it equally at home on land and in the water, and in its peculiar shape, which was held to be typical of the world, the world itself being conceived as a huge turtle swimming in a limitless ocean, the dome of the sky being its upper shell, and the flat surface of the earth being the bony breastplate of the animal, while inclosed between them was the living body, the human, animal, and vegetal creation. In Hindu mythology, when the gods are ready to destroy mankind, the turtle will grow weary and sink under his load and then the waters will rise and a deluge will overwhelm the earth. (*Fiske.*)

The belief in the turtle as the upholder of the earth was common to all the Algonquian tribes, to which belong the Arapaho and Cheyenne, and to the northern Iroquoian tribes. Earthquakes were caused by his shifting his position from time to time. In their pictographs the turtle was frequently the symbol of the earth, and in their prayers it was sometimes addressed as mother. The most honored clan was the Turtle clan; the most sacred spot in the Algonquian territory was Mackinaw, the "Island of the Great Turtle;" the favorite medicine bowl of their doctors is the shell of a turtle; the turtle is pictured on the ghost shirts of the Arapaho, and farther south in Oklahoma it is the recognized stock brand by which it is known that a horse or cow belongs to one of the historic Delaware tribe.

27. Tahu′na′änä′nia′huna

Nä′nisa′na, nä′nisa′na,
Nä′näni′na ta′hu′na′änä′nia hunä′,
Tahu′na′änä′nia′huna,
Nä′nisa′na, nä′nisa′na,
Nä′näni′na ta′hĕti′nia′hunä′,
Ta′hĕti′nia′hunä′.

Translation

My children, my children,
It is I who make the thunder as I circle about—
The thunder as I circle about.
My children, my children,
It is I who make the loud thunder as I circle about—
The loud thunder as I circle about.

This song evidently refers to the Thunderbird. It is one of the old favorites from the north, and is sung to a sprightly tune in quick time. It differs from the others in having only a part instead of all of the line repeated.

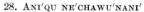

28. Ani'qu ne'chawu'nani'

A - ni'-qu ne'-cha - wu' - na - ni', a - ni'-qu ne'-cha - wu' - na - ni';

a - wa' - wa bi'-qă - na' - ka - ye' - na, a - wa' - wa bi'-qă - na' - ka - ye' - na;

i - ya - hu'h ni' - bi - thi' - ti, i - ya - hu'h ni' - bi - thi' - ti.

Ani'qu ne'chawu'nani',
Ani'qu ne'chawu'nani';
Awa'wa biqăna'kaye'na,
Awa'wa biqăna'kaye'na;
Iyahu'h ni'bithi'ti,
Iyahu'h ni'bithi'ti.

Translation

Father, have pity on me,
Father, have pity on me;
I am crying for thirst,
I am crying for thirst;
All is gone—I have nothing to eat,
All is gone—I have nothing to eat.

This is the most pathetic of the Ghost-dance songs. It is sung to a plaintive tune, sometimes with tears rolling down the cheeks of the dancers as the words would bring up thoughts of their present miserable and dependent condition. It may be considered the Indian paraphrase of the Lord's prayer.

29. A-ni'niha'niahu'na

A-ni'niha'niahu'na,
A-ni'niha'niahu'na,
Yeni's-iti'na ku'niahu'na,
Yeni's-iti'na ku'niahu'na,
Hi'chäbä'i—He'e'e'!
Hi'chäbä'i—He'e'e'!

Translation

I fly around yellow,
I fly around yellow,
I fly with the wild rose on my head,
I fly with the wild rose on my head,
On high—*He'e'e'*!
On high—*He'e'e'*!

The meaning of this song is not clear. It may refer to the Thunderbird or to the Crow, the sacred bird of the Ghost dance. The *ye'nis* or wild rose is much esteemed among the prairie tribes for its red seed berries, which are pounded into a paste and dried for food. It is frequently mentioned in the ghost songs, and is sometimes pictured on the ghost shirts. Although rather insipid, the berries possess nutritive qualities. They are gathered in winter, and are sometimes eaten raw, but more generally are first boiled and strained to get rid of the seeds. This dough-like substance is sometimes mixed with marrow from broken bones and pasted around sticks and thus roasted before the fire. It is never packed away for future use. The Cherokee call the same plant by a name which means "rabbit food," on account of this animal's fondness for the berries.

30. NIHA'NATA'YECHE'TI

He'yoho'ho'! He'yoho'ho'!
Niha'nata'yeche'ti, na'naga'qanĕ'tihi,
Wa'waga'thänŭhu,
Wa'waga'thänŭhu,
Wa'wa ne'hawa'wŭna'nahu',
Wa'wa ne'hawa'wŭna'nahu'.
He'yoho'ho'! He'yoho'ho'!

Translation

He'yoho'ho'! He'yoho'ho'!
The yellow-hide, the white-skin (man).
I have now put him aside—
I have now put him aside—
I have no more sympathy with him,
I have no more sympathy with him.
He'yoho'ho'! He'yoho'ho'!

This is another song about the whites, who are spoken of as "yellow hides" or "white skins." The proper Arapaho name for a white man is *Nia'tha,* "skillful." A great many names are applied to the whites by the different Indian tribes. By the Comanche, Shoshoni, and Paiute they are called *Tai'vo,* "easterners;" by the Hopi, of the same stock as the three tribes mentioned, they are known as *Paha'na,* "eastern water people;" by the Kiowa they are called *Be'dălpago,* "hairy mouths," or *Ta'ka'-i,* "standing ears." It is very doubtful if the "pale face" of romance ever existed in the Indian mind.

31. A-BÄÄ'THINA'HU

A-bää'thina'hu, a-bää'thina'hu,
Ha'tnithi'aku'ta'na,
Ha'tnithi'aku'ta'na,
Ha'-bätä'nani'hi,
Ha'-bätä'nani'hi.
Ha'tnithi'aku'ta'na,
Ha'tnithi'aku'ta'na.

Translation

The cedar tree, the cedar tree,
We have it in the center,
We have it in the center
When we dance,
When we dance.
We have it in the center,
We have it in the center.

The Kiowa, the Sioux, and perhaps some other tribes performed the Ghost dance around a tree set up in the center of the circle. With the Kiowa this tree was a cedar, and such was probably the case with the other tribes, whenever a cedar could be obtained, as it is always a sacred tree in Indian belief and ceremonial. The southern Arapaho and Cheyenne never had a tree in connection with the Ghost dance, so that this song could not have originated among them. The cedar is held sacred for its evergreen foliage, its fragrant smell, its red heart wood, and the durable character of its timber. On account of its fine grain and enduring qualities the prairie tribes make their tipi poles of its wood, which will not warp through heat or moisture. Their flageolets or flutes are also made of cedar, and in the mescal and other ceremonies its dried and crumbled foliage is thrown upon the fire as incense. In Cherokee and Yuchi myth the red color of the wood comes from the blood of a wizard who was killed and decapitated by a hero, and whose head was hung in the top of several trees in succession, but continued to live until, by the advice of a medicine-man, the people hung it in the topmost branches of a cedar tree, where it finally died. The blood of the severed head trickled down the trunk of the tree and thus the wood was stained.

32. WA′WA NŮ′NANŮ′NAKU′TI

Nä′nisa′na, nä′nisa′na,
Wa′wa nŭ′nanŭ′naku′ti waku′hu,
Wa′wa nŭ′nanŭ′naku′ti waku′hu.
Hi′yu nä′nii′bä′-i,
Hi′yu nä′nii′bä′-i.
Hä′tä-i′naku′ni häthi′na nisŭ′nahu,
Hä′tä-i′naku′ni häthi′na nisŭ′nahu.

Translation

My children, my children,
Now I am waving an eagle feather,
Now I am waving an eagle feather.
Here is a spotted feather for you,
Here is a spotted feather for you.
You may have it, said my father,
You may have it, said my father.

While singing this song the author of it waved in his right hand an eagle feather prepared for wearing in the hair, while he carried a spotted hawk feather in the other hand. In his trance vision he had received such a spotted feather from the messiah.

33. A-NI'QANA'GA

A-ni'qana'ga,
A-ni'qana'ga,
Ha'tăni'i'na'danĕ'na,
Ha'tăni'i'na'danĕ'na.

Translation

There is a solitary bull,
There is a solitary bull —
I am going to use him to "make medicine,"
I am going to use him to "make medicine."

From the buffalo they had food, fuel, dress, shelter, and domestic furniture, shields for defense, points for their arrows, and strings for their bows. As the old Spanish chronicles of Coronado put it: "To be short, they make so many things of them as they have need of, or as many as suffice them in the use of this life."

Among Indians the professions of medicine and religion are inseparable. The doctor is always a priest, and the priest is always a doctor. Hence, to the whites in the Indian country the Indian priest-doctor has come to be known as the "medicine-man," and anything sacred, mysterious, or of wonderful power or efficacy in Indian life or belief is designated as "medicine," this term being the nearest equivalent of the aboriginal expression in the various languages. To "make medicine" is to perform some sacred ceremony, from the curing of a sick child to the consecration of the sun-dance lodge. Among the prairie tribes the great annual tribal ceremony was commonly known as the "medicine dance," and the special guardian deity of every warrior was spoken of as his "medicine."

The buffalo was to the nomad hunters of the plains what corn was to the more sedentary tribes of the east and south—the living, visible symbol of their support and existence; the greatest gift of a higher being to his children. Something of the buffalo entered into every important ceremony. In the medicine dance—or sun dance, as it is frequently called—the head and skin of a buffalo hung from the center pole of the lodge, and in the fearful torture that accompanied this dance among some tribes, the dancers dragged around the circle buffalo skulls tied to ropes which were fastened to skewers driven through holes cut in their bodies and limbs. A buffalo skull is placed in front of the sacred sweat-lodge, and on the battlefield of Wounded Knee I have seen buffalo skulls and plates of dried meat placed at the head of the graves. The buffalo was the sign of the Creator on earth as the sun was his glorious manifestation in the heavens. The hair of the buffalo was an important element in the preparation of "medicine," whether for war, hunting, love, or medicine proper, and for such

Fig. 55.—The sweat-lodge: Kiowa camp on the Washita

purpose the Indian generally selected a tuft taken from the breast close under the shoulder of the animal. When the Kiowa, Comanche, and Apache delegates visited Washington in the spring of 1894, they made an earnest and successful request for some buffalo hair from the animals in the Zoological Park, together with some branches from the cedars in the grounds of the Agricultural Department, to take home with them for use in their sacred ceremonies.

34. A-NĔÄ'THIBIWĂ'HANĂ

A'-nĕä'thibiwă'hană,
A'-nĕä'thibiwă'hană—
Thi'äya'nĕ,
Thi'äya'nĕ.

Translation

The place where crying begins,
The place where crying begins—
The *thi'äya*,
The *thi'äya*.

This song refers to the sweat-lodge already described in treating of the Ghost dance among the Sioux. In preparing the sweat-lodge a small hole, perhaps a foot deep, is dug out in the center of the floor space, to serve as a receptacle for the heated stones over which the water is poured to produce the steam. The earth thus dug out is piled in a small hillock a few feet in front of the entrance to the sweat-lodge, which always faces the east. This small mound is called *thi'äya* in the Arapaho language, the same name being also applied to a memorial stone heap or to a stone monument. It is always surmounted by a buffalo skull, or in these days by the skull of a steer, placed so as to face the doorway of the lodge. The *thi'äya* is mentioned in several of the Ghost-dance songs, and usually, as here, in connection with crying or lamentation, as though the sight of these things in the trance vision brings up sad recollections.

35. THI'ÄYA HE'NĂĂ'AWĂ'

Thi'äya' he'năă'awă'—
Thi'äya' he'năă'awă',
Nä'hibiwa'huna',
Nä'hibiwa'huna'.

Translation

When I see the *thi'äya*—
When I see the *thi'äya*,
Then I begin to lament,
Then I begin to lament.

This song refers to a trance vision in which the dreamer saw a sweat-lodge, with the *thi'äya*, or mound, as described in the preceding song.

36. A-HU'HU HA'GENI'STI'TI BA'HU

A-hu'hu ha'geni'sti'ti ba'hu,
Ha'geni'sti'ti ba'hu.
Hä'nisti'ti,
Hä'nisti'ti.
Hi'nisa'nă,
Hi'nisa'nă —
Ne'a-i'qaha'ti,
Ne'a-i'qaha'ti.

Translation

The crow is making a road,
He is making a road;
He has finished it,
He has finished it.
His children,
His children —
Then he collected them,
Then he collected them (i. e., on the farther side).

The crow (*ho*) is the sacred bird of the Ghost dance, being revered as the messenger from the spirit world because its color is symbolic of death and the shadow land. The raven, which is practically a larger crow, and which lives in the mountains, but occasionally comes down into the plains, is also held sacred and regarded as a bringer of omens by the prairie tribes, as well as by the Tlinkit and others of the northwest coast and by the Cherokee in the east. The crow is depicted on the shirts, leggings, and moccasins of the Ghost dancers, and its feathers are worn on their heads, and whenever it is possible to kill one, the skin is stuffed as in life and carried in the dance, as shown in the picture of Black Coyote (Fig. 29). At one time the dancers in Left Hand's camp had a crow which it was claimed had the power of speech and prophetic utterance, and its hoarse inarticulate cries were interpreted as inspired messages from the spirit world. Unfortunately the bird did not thrive in confinement, and soon took its departure for the land of spirits, leaving the Arapaho once more dependent on the guidance of the trance revelations. The eagle, the magpie, and the sagehen are also sacred in the Ghost dance, the first being held in veneration by Indians, as well as by other peoples throughout the world, while the magpie and the sage-hen are revered for their connection with the country of the messiah and the mythology of his tribe.

The crow was probably held sacred by all the tribes of the Algonquian race. Roger Williams, speaking of the New England tribes, says that although the crows sometimes did damage to the corn, yet hardly one Indian in a hundred would kill one, because it was their tradition that this bird had brought them their first grain and vegetables, carrying a grain of corn in one ear and a bean in the other, from the field of their great god Cautantouwit in Sowwani'u, the southwest, the happy spirit world where dwelt the gods and the souls of the great and good. The souls of the wicked were not permitted to enter this elysium after death, but were doomed to wander without rest or home. (*Williams, Key into the Language of America, 1643.*)

In Arapaho belief, the spirit world is in the west, not on the same level with this earth of ours, but higher up, and separated also from it by a body of water. In their statement of the Ghost-dance mythology referred to in this song, the crow, as the messenger and leader of the spirits who had gone before, collected their armies on the other side and advanced at their head to the hither limit of the shadow land. Then, looking over, they saw far below them a sea, and far out beyond it toward the east was the boundary of the earth, where lived the friends they were marching to rejoin. Taking up a pebble in his beak, the crow then dropped it into the water and it became a mountain towering up to the land of the dead. Down its rocky slope he brought his army until they halted at the edge of the water. Then, taking some dust in his bill, the crow flew out and dropped it into the water as he flew, and it became a solid arm of land stretching from the spirit world to the earth. He returned and flew out again, this time with some blades of grass, which he dropped upon the land thus made, and at once it was covered with a green sod. Again he returned, and again flew out, this time with some twigs in his bill, and dropping these also upon the new land, at once it was covered with a forest of trees. Again he flew back to the base of the mountain, and is now, for the fourth time, coming on at the head of all the countless spirit host which has already passed over the sea and is marshaling on the western boundary of the earth.

37. Bi'taa'wu hu'hu'

Bi'taa'wu hu'hu',
Bi'taa'wu hu'hu'—
Nû'nagûna'-ua'ti hu'hu',
Nû'nagûna'-ua'ti hu'hu'—
A'hene'heni'ä'ä'! A'he'yene'hene'!

Translation

The earth—the crow,
The earth—the crow—
The crow brought it with him,
The crow brought it with him—
A'hene'heni'ä'ä'! A'he'yene'hene'!

The reference in this song is explained under the song immediately preceding.

38. Ni'nini'tubi'na hu'hu'—I

Ni'nini'tubi'na hu'hu',
Ni'nini'tubi'na hu'hu'.
Nana'thina'ni hu'hu,
Nana'thina'ni hu'hu.
Ni'nita'naû,
Ni'nita'naû.

Translation

The crow has called me,
The crow has called me.
When the crow came for me,
When the crow came for me,
I heard him,
I heard him.

The reference in this song is explained under number 36. The song is somewhat like the former closing song, number 52.

39. Nŭ'nanŭ'naa'tăni'na hu'hu'—I

Nŭ'nanŭ'naa'tăni'na hu'hu',
Nŭ'nanŭ'naa'tăni'na hu'hu'.
Da'chi'nathi'na hu'hu',
Da'chi'nathi'na hu'hu'.

Translation

The crow is circling above me,
The crow is circling above me,
The crow having come for me,
The crow having come for me.

The author of this song, in his trance vision, saw circling above his head a crow, the messenger from the spirit world, to conduct him to his friends who had gone before. The song is a favorite one, and is sung with a quick forcible tune when the excitement begins to grow more intense, in order to hasten the trances, the idea conveyed to the dancers being that their spirit friends are close at hand.

40. I'yu hä'thäbĕ'nawa'

Ä'näni'sa'na—E'e'ye'!
Ä'näni'sa'na—E'e'ye'!
I'yu hä'thäbĕ'nawa'.
Bi'taa'wu—E'e'ye'!
Bi'taa'wu—E'e'ye'!

Translation

My children—*E'e'ye'!*
My children—*E'e'ye'!*
Here it is, I hand it to you.
The earth—*E'e'ye'!*
The earth—*E'e'ye'!*

In this song the father speaks to his children and gives them the new earth.

41. Ha'naĕ'hi ya'ga'ahi'na

Ha'naĕ'hi ya'ga'ahi'na—
Ha'naĕ'hi ya'ga'ahi'na—
Să'niya'gu'nawa'—Ahe'e'ye'!
Să'niya'gu'nawa'—Ahe'e'ye'!
Nä'yu hä'nina'ta i'tha'q,
Nä'yu hä'nina'ta i'tha'q.

Little boy, the coyote gun—
Little boy, the coyote gun—
I have uncovered it—*Ahe′e′ye′* !
I have uncovered it—*Ahe′e′ye′* !
There is the sheath lying there,
There is the sheath lying there.

This song was composed by Nakash, or "Sage," one of the northern Arapaho delegates to the messiah. It evidently refers to one of his trance experiences in the other world, and has to do with an interesting feature in the sociology of the Arapaho and other prairie tribes. The *ga′ahinĕ′na* or *gaahi′na*, "coyote men," were an order of men of middle age who acted as pickets or lookouts for the camp. When the band encamped in some convenient situation for hunting or other business, it was the duty of these men, usually four or six in a band, to take their stations on the nearest hills to keep watch and give timely warning in case of the approach of an enemy. It was an office of danger and responsibility, but was held in corresponding respect. When on duty, the *gaahi′nĕn* wore a white buffalo robe and had his face painted with white clay and carried in his hand the *ya′haga′ahi′na* or "coyote gun," a club decorated with feathers and other ornaments and usually covered with a sheath of bear gut (*i′tha′q*). He must be unmarried and remain so while in office, finally choosing his own successor and delivering to him the "coyote gun" as a staff of authority. They were never all off duty at the same time, but at least half were always on guard, one or more coming down at a time to the village to eat or sleep. They built no shelter on the hills, but slept there in their buffalo robes, or sometimes came down in turn and slept in their own tipis. They usually, however, preferred to sleep alone upon the hills in order to receive inspiration in dreams. If attacked or surprised by the enemy, they were expected to fight. The watcher was sometimes called *higa′ahi′na-ĭt*, "the man with the coyote gun." The corresponding officer among the Cheyenne carried a bow and arrows instead of a club.

42. He′sûna′ na′nahatha′hi

He′sûna′ na′nahatha′hi,
He′sûna′ na′nahatha′hi.
Ni′itu′qawigû′niĕ′,
Ni′itu′qawigû′niĕ′.

Translation

The father showed me,
The father showed me,
Where they were coming down,
Where they were coming down.

In his trance vision the author of this song saw the spirit hosts descending from the upper shadow land to the earth, along the mountain raised up by the crow, as already described in song number 36. The song comes from the northern Arapaho.

43. Nänisa'täqu'thi Chïnachi'chibä'iha'

Nänisa'täqu'thi Chïnachi'chibä'iha',
Nänisa'täqu'thi Chïnachi'chibä'iha'—
Ni'nahawa'na,
Ni'nahawa'na.
Nibäi'naku'nithi—
Nibäi'naku'nithi—
Ä-bäna'änahu'u',
Ä-bäna'änahu'u'.
Nä'hibi'wahuna'na,
Nä'hibi'wahuna'na.

Translation

The seven venerable *Chǐ'nachichi'bät* priests,
The seven venerable *Chǐ'nachichi'bät* priests—
We see them,
We see them.
They all wear it on their heads—
They all wear it on their heads—
The Thunderbird,
The Thunderbird.
Then I wept,
Then I wept.

In his trance vision the author of this song saw a large camp of Arapaho, and in the midst of the camp circle, as in the old days, were sitting the seven priests of the *Chǐ'nachichi'bät*, each wearing on his head the Thunderbird headdress, already described and figured under song number 14. This vision of the old life of the tribe brought up sorrowful memories and caused him to weep. In the similar song next given the singer laments for the *Chǐ'nachichi'bät* and the *bä'qati* gaming wheel. The priests here referred to were seven in number, and constituted the highest order of the military and social organization which existed among the Blackfeet, Sioux, Cheyenne, Kiowa, and probably all the prairie tribes excepting the Comanche in the south, among whom it seems to have been unknown. The society, so far as it has come under the notice of white men, has commonly been designated by them as the "Dog Soldier" society—a misapprehension of a name belonging probably to only one of the six or eight orders of the organization. The corresponding Blackfoot organization, the *Ikunuhkatsi* or "All Comrades," is described by Grinnell in his "Blackfoot Lodge Tales." The Kiowa organization will be noted later.

Among the Arapaho the organization was called *Běni'něna,* "Warriors," and consisted of eight degrees or orders, including nearly all the men of the tribe above the age of about seventeen. Those who were not enrolled in some one of the eight orders were held in but little respect, and were not allowed to take part in public ceremonies or to accompany war expeditions. Each of the first six orders had its own peculiar dance, and the members of the principal warrior orders had also their peculiar staff or badge of rank.

First and lowest in rank were the *Nuhinĕ'na* or Fox men, consisting of young men up to the age of about 25 years. They had no special duties or privileges, but had a dance called the *Nuha'wŭ* or fox dance.

Next came the *Hă'thahu'ha* or Star men, consisting of young warriors about 30 years of age. Their dance was called the *Ha'thahŭ*.

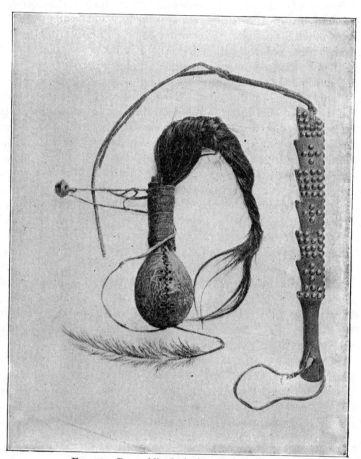

Fig. 56.—Dog-soldier insignia—rattle and quirt

The third order was that of the *Hichăä'quthi* or Club men. Their dance was called *Hichăä'qawŭ*. They were an important part of the warrior organization, and were all men in the prime of life. The four leaders carried wooden clubs, bearing a general resemblance in shape to a gun, notched along the edges and variously ornamented. In an attack on the enemy it was the duty of these leaders to dash on ahead and strike the enemy with these clubs, then to ride back again and take their places in the front of the charge. It hardly need be said that the position of leader of the *Hǐchǎ́ä'quthi* was a dangerous honor, but the honor was in proportion to the very danger, and there were always candidates for a vacancy. It was one of those offices where the holder sometimes died but never resigned. The other members of the order carried sticks carved at one end in the rude semblance of a horse head and pointed at the other. In desperate encounters they were expected to plant these sticks in the ground in line in front of the body of warriors and to fight beside them to the death unless a retreat should be ordered by the chief in command.

The fourth order was called *Bǐtahi'nĕna* or Spear men, and their dance was called *Bitaha'wŭ*. This order came originally from the Cheyenne. Their duties and peculiar insignia of office were about the same among all the tribes. They performed police duty in camp, when traveling, and on the hunt, and were expected to see that the orders of the chief were obeyed by the tribe. For instance, if any person violated the tribal code or failed to attend a general dance or council, a party of *Bitahi'nĕna* was sent to kill his dogs, destroy his tipi, or in extreme cases to shoot his ponies. On hunting expeditions it was their business to keep the party together and see that no one killed a buffalo until the proper ceremonies had been performed and the order was given by the chief. They were regarded as the representatives of the law and were never resisted in performing their duty or inflicting punishments. In war they were desperate warriors, equaling or surpassing even the *Hǐchǎ́ä'quthi*. Of the leaders of the order, two carried a sort of shepherd's crook called *nu'sa-icha'tha*, having a lance point at its lower end; two others carried lances wrapped around with otter skin; four carried lances painted black; one carried a club shaped like a baseball bat, and one carried a rattle made of the scrotum of a buffalo and ornamented with its hair. In battle, if the enemy took shelter behind defenses, it was this man's duty to lead the charge, throw his rattle among the enemy, and then follow it himself.

The fifth order was called *Aha'känĕ'na* or Crazy men. They were men more than 50 years of age, and were not expected to go to war, but must have graduated from all the lower orders. Their duties were religious and ceremonial, and their insignia consisted of a bow and a bundle of blunt arrows. Their dance was the *Ahaka'wŭ* or crazy dance, which well deserved the name. It will be described in another place.

The sixth was the order of the *Hĕthĕ'hinĕ'na* or Dog men. Their dance was called *Hĕthĕwa'wŭ'*. They had four principal leaders and two lesser leaders. The four principal leaders were the generals and directors of the battle. Each carried a rattle and wore about his neck a buckskin strap (two being yellow, the other two black) which hung down to his feet. On approaching the enemy, they were obliged to go forward, shaking their rattles and chanting the war song, until some other warriors of the party took the rattles out of their hands. When forming for the attack, they dismounted, and, driving their lances into

Fig. 57.—Dog-soldier insignia—lance and sash

the ground, tied themselves to them by means of the straps, thus anchoring themselves in front of the battle. Here they remained until, if the battle seemed lost, they themselves gave the order to retreat. Even then they waited until some of their own society released them by pulling the lances out of the ground and whipping them away from the place with a peculiar quirt carried only by the private members of this division. No one was allowed to retreat without their permission, on penalty of disgrace, nor were they themselves allowed to retire until thus released. Should their followers forget to release them in the confusion of retreat, they were expected to die at their posts. They could not be released excepting by one of their own division, and anyone else attempting to pull up the lances from the ground was resisted as an enemy. When pursued on the retreat, they must give up their horses to the women, if necessary, and either find other horses or turn and face the enemy alone on foot. They seldom accompanied any but large war parties, and, although they did but little actual fighting, their very presence inspired the warriors with desperate courage, and the driving of their lances into the ground was always understood as the signal for an encounter to the death.

The seventh order was that of the *Nûnaha'wŭ*, a word of which the meaning is now unknown. This was a secret order. They had no dance and their ceremonies were witnessed only by themselves. They did not fight, but accompanied the war parties, and every night in secret performed ceremonies and prayers for their success.

The eighth and highest order was that of the *Chĭ'nachinĕ'na* or Water-pouring men, the "seven venerable priests" to whom the song refers. They were the high priests and instructors of all the other orders, and were seven in number, from among the oldest warriors of the tribe. Their name refers to their pouring the water over the heated stones in the sweat-house to produce steam. They had no dance, and were not expected to go to war, although one of the seven was allowed to accompany the war party, should he so elect. Their ceremonies were performed in a large sweat-lodge, called *chĭnachichi'bät*, which, when the whole tribe was camped together, occupied the center of the circle, between the entrance and the lodge in which was kept the sacred medicine pipe. Unlike the ordinary sweat-lodge, this one had no mound and buffalo skull in front of the entrance.

The warrior organization of the Kiowa is called *Yä'păhe*, "Soldiers," and consisted of six orders, each with its own dance, songs, and ceremonial dress. 1. *Poläñyup* or *Tsän'yui*, "Rabbits." These were boys and young men from 8 to 15 years of age. Their dance, in which they were drilled by certain old men, has a peculiar step, in imitation of the jumping movement of a rabbit; 2. *Ädalto'yui*, or *Te'ñbiyu'i*, "Young Mountain Sheep," literally "Herders or Corralers;" 3. *Tsentä'nmo*, "Horse Head-dress (?) people;" 4. "*Toñkoñ'ko* (?) "Black-leg people;" 5. *T'äñpe'ko*, "Skunkberry (?) people;" 6. *Ká'itseñ'ko*, "Principal Dogs or Real Dogs." These last were the highest warrior order, and also the camp police, combining the functions of the *Bita-hi'nĕna* and the *Hĕthĕ'binĕ'na* of the Arapaho organization. Their two leaders carried an arrow-shape lance, with which they anchored themselves in the front of the battle by means of buckskin straps brought over the shoulders. The *Toñkoñ'ko* captains carried in a similar way a crook-shape lance, called *pabo'n*, similar to that of the *Bitahi'nĕna* of the Arapaho.

44. Nänisa'tăqi Chi'năchi'chibä'iha'

Nä'-ni-sa'-tă-qi   Chi'-nă-chi' - chi-bä'-i-ha',   nä'-ni-sa'-tă-qi

Chi'-nă-chi' - chi-bä'-i-ha',   bä'-hi-bi' - wă'-hĭ-nă,   bä-hi-bi' - wă-hĭ-nă'.

Bä'-qă-ti'   hä'-ni-bi' - wă'-hĭ-nă',   bä'-qă-ti'   hä'-ni-bi - wă'hĭ-nă'.

Nä'nisa'tăqi Chĭ'năchi'chibä'iha' —
Nä'nisa'tăqi Chĭ'năchi'chibä'iha' —
Bä'hibi'wă'hĭnă',
Bä'hibi'wă'hĭnă'.
Bä'qăti hä'nibi'wă'hĭnă',
Bä'qăti hä'nibi'wă'hĭnă'.

Translation

The seven venerable *Chĭnachichi'băt* priests—
The seven venerable *Chĭnachichi'băt* priests—
For them I am weeping,
For them I am weeping.
For the gaming wheel I am weeping,
For the gaming wheel I am weeping.

The first reference in this song is explained under number 43. The *bä'qati* or gaming wheel will be described later.

45. Nû'nanû'naatani'na hu'hu'—II

Nû'-na-nû'-naa'-ta - ni'-na   hu'-hu',   nû'-na-nû'-naa'-ta - ni' - na   hu'-hu'.

Da'-chi'-bi - ni'-na hä-thi'-na,   da'-chi'-bi - ni'-na hä-thi'-na.

Nû'nanû'naatani'na hu'hu',
Nû'nanû'naatani'na hu'hu'.
Da'chi'bini'na häthi'na,
Da'chi'bini'na häthi'na.

Translation

The crow is circling above me,
The crow is circling above me.
He says he will give me a hawk feather,
He says he will give me a hawk feather.

This song is very similar to number 39, and requires no further explanation. It is sung to the same quick time.

46. NA'TĂNU'YA CHĔ'BI'NH

Na'tănu'ya chĕ'bi'nh —
Na'tănu'ya chĕ'bi'nh,
Na'chicha'ba'n,
Na'chicha'ba'n.

Translation

The pemmican that I am using —
The pemmican that I am using,
They are still making it,
They are still making it.

This song refers to the pemmican or preparation of dried and pounded meat, which formerly formed a favorite food of the prairie tribes, and which the author of the song evidently tasted as it was being prepared by the women in the spirit world. (See Sioux song 7.) One must be an Indian to know the thrill of joy that would come to the heart of the dancers when told that some dreamer had seen their former friends in the spirit world still making and feasting on pemmican. During the first year or two of the excitement, it several times occurred at Ghost dances in the north and south, among Sioux as well as among Arapaho and others, that meat was exhibited and tasted as genuine buffalo beef or pemmican brought back from the spirit world by one of the dancers. It is not necessary to explain how this deception was accomplished or made successful. It is sufficient to know that it was done, and that the dancers were then in a condition to believe anything.

47. HĂÏ'NAWA' HĂ'NI'TA'QUNA'NI

Hăï'nawa' hä'ni'ta'quna'ni —
Hăï'nawa' hä'ni'ta'quna'ni —
Ninĕ'n nänä' hänita'quna'ni,
Ninĕ'n nänä' hänita'quna'ni.

Translation

I know, in the pitfall —
I know, in the pitfall —
It is tallow they use in the pitfall,
It is tallow they use in the pitfall.

This song refers to the vision of a northern Arapaho, who found one of his friends in the spirit world preparing a pitfall trap to catch eagles.

Wherever found, the eagle was regarded as sacred among the Indian tribes both east and west, and its feathers were highly prized for ornamental and "medicine" purposes, and an elaborately detailed ritual of prayer and ceremony was the necessary accompaniment to its capture. Among all the tribes the chief purpose of this ritual was to obtain the help of the gods in inducing the eagle to approach the hunter, and to turn aside the anger of the eagle spirits at the necessary sacrilege. The feathers most valued were those of the tail and wings. These were used to ornament lances and shields, to wear upon the head, and to decorate the magnificent war bonnets, the finest of which have a pendant or trail of eagle-tail feathers reaching from the warrior's head to the ground when he stands erect. The whistle used in the sun dance and other great ceremonies is made of a bone from the leg or wing of the eagle, and the fans carried by the warriors on parade and used also to sprinkle the holy water in the mescal ceremony of the southern prairie tribes is commonly made of the entire tail or wing of that bird. Hawk feathers are sometimes used for these various purposes, but are always considered far inferior to those of the eagle. The smaller feathers are used upon arrows. Eagle feathers and ponies were formerly the standard of value and the medium of exchange among the prairie tribes, as wampum was with those of the Atlantic coast. The standard varied according to place and season, but in a general way from two to four eagles were rated as equal to a horse. In these days the eagle-feather war bonnets and eagle-tail fans are the most valuable parts of an Indian's outfit and the most difficult to purchase from him. Among the pueblo tribes eagles are sometimes taken from the nest when young and kept in cages and regularly stripped of their best feathers. Among the Caddo, Cherokee, and other tribes of the timbered country in the east they were shot with bow and arrow or with the gun, but always according to certain ritual ceremonies. Among the prairie tribes along the whole extent of the plains they were never shot, but must be captured alive in pitfalls and then strangled or crushed to death, if possible without the shedding of blood. A description of the Arapaho method will answer with slight modifications for all the prairie tribes.

The hunter withdrew with his family away from the main camp to some rough hilly country where the eagles were abundant. After some preliminary prayers he went alone to the top of the highest hill and there dug a pit large enough to sit or lie down in, being careful to carry the earth taken out of the hole so far away from the place that it would not attract the notice of the eagle. The pit was roofed over with a covering of light willow twigs, above which were placed earth and grass to give it a natural appearance. The bait was a piece of fresh meat, or, as appears from this song, a piece of tallow stripped from the ribs of the buffalo. This was tied to a rawhide string and laid upon the top of the pit, while the rope was passed down through the roof into the cavity below. A coyote skin, stuffed and set up erect as in life, was sometimes placed near the bait to add to the realistic effect. Having sat up all night, singing the eagle songs and purifying himself for the ceremony, the hunter started before daylight, without eating any breakfast or drinking water, and went up the hill to the pit, which he entered, and, having again closed the opening, he seated himself inside holding the end of the string in his hands, to prevent a coyote or other animal from taking the bait, and waiting for the eagles to come.

Should other birds come, he drove them away or paid no attention to them. When at last the eagle came the other birds at once flew away. The eagle swooped down, alighting always at one side and then walking over upon the roof of the trap to get at the bait, when the hunter, putting up his hand through the framework, seized the eagle by the legs, pulled it down and quickly strangled it or broke its neck. He then rearranged the bait and the roof and sat down to wait for another eagle. He might be so lucky as to capture several during the day, or so unfortunate as to take none at all. At night, but not before, he repaired to his own tipi to eat, drink, and sleep, and was at the pit again before daylight. While in the pit he did not eat, drink, or sleep. The eagle hunt, if it may be so called, lasted four days, and must end then, whatever might have been the good or bad fortune of the hunter.

At the expiration of four days he returned to his home with the dead bodies of the eagles thus caught. A small lodge was set up outside his tipi and in this the eagles were hung up by the neck upon a pole laid across two forked sticks driven into the ground. After some further prayers and purifications the feathers were stripped from the bodies as they hung.

The Blackfoot method, as described by Grinnell, in his Blackfoot Lodge Tales, was the same in all essentials as that of the Arapaho. He adds several details, which were probably common to both tribes and to others, but which my Arapaho informants failed to mention. While the hunter was away in the pit his wife or daughters at home must not use an awl for sewing or for other purposes, as, should they do so, the eagle might scratch the hunter. He took a human skull with him into the pit, in order that he might be as invisible to the eagle as the spirit of the former owner of the skull. He must not eat the berries of the wild rose during this period, or the eagle would not attack the bait, and he must put a morsel of pemmican into the mouth of the dead eagle in order to gain the good will of its fellows and induce them to come in and be caught.

The eagle-catching ceremony of the Caddo, Cherokee, and other eastern tribes will be noticed in treating of the Caddo songs.

48. BÄ′HINÄ′NINA′TÄ NI′TABÄ′NA

Bä′hinä′nina′tä ni′tabä′na,
Bä′hinä′nina′tä ni′tabä′na.
Nänä′nina hu′hu,
Nänä′nina hu′hu.

Translation

I hear everything,
I hear everything.
I am the crow,
I am the crow.

This is another song expressive of the omniscience of the crow, which, as their messenger from the spirit world, hears and knows everything, both on this earth and in the shadow land. The tune is one of the prettiest of all the ghost songs.

49. A-BÄ′QATI′ HÄ′NICHÄ′BI′HINÄ′NA

A-bä′qati′ hä′nichä′bi′hinä′na,
A-bä′qati′ hä′nichä′bi′hinä′na.
A-wa′täna′ni ani′ä′tähï′näna,
A-wa′täna′ni ani′ä′tähï′näna.

Translation

With the *bä′qati* wheel I am gambling,
With the *bä′qati* wheel I am gambling.
With the black mark I win the game,
With the black mark I win the game.

This song is from the northern Arapaho. The author of it, in his visit to the spirit world, found his former friends playing the old game of the *bä′qati* wheel, which was practically obsolete among the prairie tribes, but which is being revived since the advent of the Ghost dance. As it was a favorite game with the men in the olden times, a great many of the songs founded on these trance visions refer to it, and the wheel and sticks are made by the dreamer and carried in the dance as they sing.

The game is played with a wheel (*bä′qati*, "large wheel") and two pairs of throwing sticks (*qa′qa-u′nûtha*). The Cheyenne call the wheel *ä′ko′yo* or *äkwi′u*, and the sticks *hoo′isi′yonots*. It is a man's game, and there are three players, one rolling the wheel, while the other two, each armed with a pair of throwing sticks, run after it and throw the sticks so as to cross the wheel in a certain position. The two throwers are the contestants, the one who rolls the wheel being merely an assistant. Like most Indian games, it is a means of gambling, and high stakes are sometimes wagered on the result. It is common to the Arapaho, Cheyenne, Sioux, and probably to all the northern prairie tribes, but is not found among the Kiowa or Comanche in the south.

The wheel is about 18 inches in diameter, and consists of a flexible young tree branch, stripped of its bark and painted, with the two ends fastened together with sinew or buckskin string. At equal distances around the circumference of the wheel are cut four figures, the two opposite each other constituting a pair, but being distinguished by different colors, usually blue or black and red, and by lines or notches on the face. These figures are designated simply by their colors. Figures of birds, crescents, etc, are sometimes also cut or painted upon the wheel, but have nothing to do with the game. (See Fig. 39.)

The sticks are light rods, about 30 inches long, tied in pairs by a peculiar arrangement of buckskin strings, and distinguished from one another by pieces of cloth of different colors fastened to the strings. There is also a pile of tally sticks, usually a hundred in number, about the size of lead pencils and painted green, for keeping count of the game. The sticks are held near the center in a peculiar manner between the fingers of the closed hand. When the wheel is rolled, each player runs from the same side, and endeavors to throw the sticks so as to strike the wheel in such a way that when it falls both sticks of his pair shall be either over or under a certain figure. It requires dexterity to do this, as the string has a tendency to strike the wheel in such a way as to make one stick fall under and the other over, in which case the throw counts for nothing. The players assign their own value to each figure, the usual value being five points for one and ten for the other figure, with double that number for a throw which crosses the two corresponding figures, and one hundred tallies to the game.

The wheel-and-stick game, in some form or another, was almost universal among our Indian tribes. Another game among the prairie tribes is played with a netted wheel and a single stick or arrow, the effort being to send the arrow through the netting as nearly as possible to the center or bull's-eye. This game is called *ana'wati'n-hati*, " playing wheel," by the Arapaho.

50. Ani'äsa'kua'na dä'chäbi'hati'tani

Ani'äsa'kua'na dä'chäbi'hati'tani bä'qati'bä,
Ani'äsa'kua'na dä'chäbi'hati'tani bä'qati'bä.
Ni'ati'biku'thahu' bä'qatihi,
Ni'ati'biku'thahu' bä'qatihi.
Di'chäbi'häti'ta'ni',
Di'chäbi'häti'ta'ni'.

Translation

I am watching where they are gambling with the *bä'qati* wheel,
I am watching where they are gambling with the *bä'qati* wheel.
They are rolling the *bä'qati*,
They are rolling the *bä'qati*.
While they gamble with it,
While they gamble with it.

In this song the dancer tells how he watched a group of his friends in the spirit world playing the game of the *bä'qati*, as has been explained in the song last treated.

51. Ni'chi'a i'theti'hi

Ni'chi'ă i'theti'hi,
Ni'chi'ă i'theti'hi,
Chana'ha'ti i'nĭt,—
Chana'ha'ti i'nĭt—
Gu'n baa'-ni'bină thi'aku'-u,
Gu'n baa'-ni'bină thi'aku'-u.

Translation

(There) is a good river,
(There) is a good river,
Where there is no timber—
Where there is no timber—
But thunder-berries are there,
But thunder-berries are there.

This song refers to a trance vision in which the dreamer found his people camped by a good, i. e., perennial, river, fringed with abundant bushes or small trees of the *baa-ni'bin* or "thunder-berry," which appears to be the black haw, being described as a sort of wild cherry, in size between the chokecherry and the wild plum. It was eaten raw, or dried and boiled, the seeds having first been taken out. It is very scarce, if found at all, in the southern plains.

52. NI'NINI'TUBI'NA HU'HU' (former closing song)

Ni'nini'tubi'na hu'hu',
Ni'nini'tubi'na hu'hu'.
Bäta'hina'ni hu'hu',
Bäta'hina'ni hu'hu',
Nă'hinä'ni hithi'na,
Nă'hinä'ni hithi'na.

Translation

The crow has given me the signal,
The crow has given me the signal.
When the crow makes me dance,
When the crow makes me dance,
He tells me (when) to stop,
He tells me (when) to stop.

This was formerly the closing song of the dance, but is now super-seded as such by number 73, beginning *Ahu'yu häthi'na*. It was also the last song sung when a small party gathered in the tipi at night for a private rehearsal, and was therefore always held in reserve until the singers were about ready to separate. The tune is one of the best.

The special office of the crow as the messenger from the spirit world and representative of the messiah has been already explained. He is supposed to direct the dance and to give the signal for its close.

53. Anihä'ya atani'tă'nu'nawa'

Anihä'ya atani'tă'nu'nawa',
Anihä'ya atani'tă'nu'nawa',
Häthi'na hesûna'nĭn,
Häthi'na hesûna'nĭn,
Da'chä'-ihi'na he'sûna'nĭn,
Da'chä'-ihi'na he'sûna'nĭn—Ih! Ih!

Translation

I use the yellow (paint),
I use the yellow (paint),
Says the father,
Says the father,
In order to please me, the father,
In order to please me, the father—*Ih! Ih!*

The meaning of this song is somewhat obscure. It seems to be a message from the messiah to the effect that he paints himself with yellow paint, because it pleases him, the inference being that it would please him to have his children do the same. Those who take part in the sun dance are usually painted yellow, that being the color of the sun. This song is peculiar in having at the end two sharp yelps, in the style of the ordinary songs of the warrior dances.

54. Ni'naä'niahu'tawa bi'taa'wu

A'-näni'sa'na, a'-näni'sa'na,
Ni'naä'niahu'tawa bi'taa'wu,
Ni'naä'niahu'tawa bi'taa'wu,
A'-tini'ehi'ni'na nä'nisa'na,
A'-tini'ehi'ni'na nä'nisa'na,
Häthi'na hesûna'nĭn,
Häthi'na hesûna'nĭn.

Translation

My children, my children,
I am flying about the earth,
I am flying about the earth.
I am a bird, my children,
I am a bird, my children,
Says the father,
Says the father.

In this song the messiah, addressing his children, is represented as a bird (crow?) flying about the whole earth, symbolic of his omniscience. The song has one or two variants.

55. I'NITA'TA'–USÄ'NA

I'nita'ta'-usä'na,
I'nita'ta'-usä'na.
Hä'tini'tubibä' hu'hu',
Hä'tini'tubibä' hu'hu.
Hä'tina'ha'wa'bä hu'hu,
Hä'tina'ha'wa'bä hu'hu.

Translation

Stand ready,
Stand ready.
(So that when) the crow calls you,
(So that when) the crow calls you.
You will see him,
You will see him.

This song was composed by Little Raven, one of the delegation of seven from the southern Arapaho and Cheyenne which visited the messiah in Nevada in August, 1891. It is a message to the believers to be ready for the near coming of the new earth. The first line is sometimes sung *I'nita'ta-u'sä-hu'na.*

56. WA'WÄTHÄ'BI

Nä'nisa'na-ŭ', nä'nisa'na-ŭ',
Wa'wäthä'bicḫä'chinï'nabä'nagu'wa-u'i'naga'thi—He'e'ye'!
Häthi'na ne'nahu',
Häthi'na ne'nahu'.

Translation

My children, my children,
I have given you magpie feathers again to wear on your heads—*He'e'ye'!*
Thus says our mother,
Thus says our mother.

This song affords a good specimen of the possibilities of Indian word building. The second word might serve as a companion piece to Mark Twain's picture of a complete word in German. It consists of seventeen syllables, all so interwoven to complete the sense of the word sentence that no part can be separated from the rest without destroying the whole. The verbal part proper indicates that "I have given you (plural) a headdress again." The final syllables, *wa-u'i-naga'thi*, show that the headdress consists of the tail feathers (*wagathi*) of the magpie (*wa-u-i*). The syllable *cha* implies repetition or return of action, this being probably not the first time that the messiah had given magpie feathers to his visitors.

The magpie (*Pica hudsonica* or *mittalii*) of the Rocky mountains and Sierra Nevada and the intermediate region of Nevada and Utah is perhaps the most conspicuous bird in the Paiute country. It bears a general resemblance to a crow or blackbird, being about the size of the latter, and jet black, with the exception of the breast, which is white, and a white spot on each wing. In its tail are two long feathers with beautiful changeable metallic luster. It is a home bird, frequenting the neighborhood of the Paiute camps in small flocks. It is held sacred among the Paiute, by whom the long tail feathers are as highly prized for decorative purposes as eagle feathers are among the tribes of the plains. The standard price for such feathers in 1891 was 25 cents a pair. The delegates who crossed the mountains to visit the messiah brought back with them quantities of these feathers, which thenceforth filled an important place in the ceremonial of the Ghost dance. In fact they were so eagerly sought after that the traders undertook to meet the demand, at first by importing genuine magpie feathers from the mountains, but later by fraudulently substituting selected crow feathers from the east at the same price.

The song is also peculiar in referring to the messiah as "my mother" (*nena*) instead of "our father" (*hesûnanin*), as usual.

57. ANI'QA HĔ'TABI'NUHU'NI'NA

Ani'qa hĕ'tabi'nuhu'ni'na,
Ani'qa hĕ'tabi'nuhu'ni'na.
Hatăna'wunăni'na hesûna'nĭn,
Hatăna'wunăni'na hesûna'nĭn.
Ha'tăni'ni'ahu'hi'na he'sûna'nĭn,
Ha'tăni'ni·ahu'hi'na he'sûna'nĭn.

Translation

My father, I am poor,
My father, I am poor.
Our father is about to take pity on me,
Our father is about to take pity on me.
Our father is about to make me fly around.
Our father is about to make me fly around.

This song refers to the present impoverished condition of the Indians, and to their hope that he is now about to take pity on them and remove them from this dying world to the new earth above; the feathers worn on their heads in the dance being expected to act as wings, as already explained, to enable them to fly to the upper regions.

58. NÄ'NISA'TAQU'THI HU'NA

Nä'nisa'taqu'thi hu'na — Hi'ă hi'ni'ni'!
Nä'nisa'taqu'thi hu'na — Hi'ă hi'ni'ni'!
Hi'bithi'ni'na gasi'tu — Hi'ă hi'ni'ni'!
Hi'bithi'ni'na gasi'tu — Hi'ă hi'ni'ni'!

Translation

The seven crows — *Hi'ă hi'ni'ni'!*
The seven crows — *Hi'ă hi'ni'ni'!*
They are flying about the carrion — *Hi'ă hi'ni'ni'!*
They are flying about the carrion — *Hi'ă hi'ni'ni'!*

In this song the dreamer tells of his trance visit to the spirit world, where he found his friends busily engaged cutting up the meat after a successful buffalo hunt, while the crows were hovering about the carrion. Four and seven are the constant sacred numbers of the Ghost dance, as of Indian ritual and story generally.

59. Ahu′nä he′sûna′nĭn

Ahu′nä he′sûna′nĭn —
Ahu′nä he′sûna′nĭn —
Ni′tabä′tani′ bäta′hina′ni,
Ni′tabä′tani′ bäta′hina′ni,
Ha kă hä′sabini′na he′sûna′nĭn,
Ha′kă hä′sabini′na he′sûna′nĭn.

Translation

There is our father —
There is our father —
We are dancing as he wishes (makes) us to dance,
We are dancing as he wishes (makes) us to dance,
Because our father has so commanded us,
Because our father has so commanded us.

The literal meaning of the last line is "because our father has given it to us," the prairie idiom for directing or commanding being to "give a road" or to "make a road" for the one thus commanded. To disobey is to "break the road" and to depart from the former custom is to "make a new road." The idea is expressed in the same way both in the various spoken languages and in the sign language.

60. Ga′awa′hu

Ga′awa′hu, ga′awa′hu,
Ni′hii′nä gu′shi′nä,
Ni′hii′nä gu′shi′nä.
A′tanä′tähinä′na,
A′tanä′tähinä′na.

Translation

The ball, the ball—
You must throw it swiftly,
You must throw it swiftly.
I want to win,
I want to win.

The author of this song was a woman who in her trance vision saw her girl friends in the other world playing the ball game, as described in song number 7. In this case, however, her partner is urged to *throw* the ball, instead of to strike it.

61. Ahu′ ni′higa′hu

Ahu′ ni′higa′hu,
Ahu′ ni′higa′hu.
Ha′tani′ni′tani′na,
Ha′tani′ni′tani′na.

Translation

The Crow is running,
The Crow is running.
He will hear me.
He will hear me.

This song implies that the Crow (messiah) is quick to hear the prayer of the dancer and comes swiftly to listen to his petition.

62. YA′THÄ-YÛ′NA TA′NA-U′QAHE′NA

Ne′sûna′ — He′e′ye′!
Ne′sûna′ — He′e′ye′!
Ya′thä-yûna ta′na-u′qahe′na — He′e′ye′!
Ya′thä-yûna ta′na-u′qahe′na — He′e′ye′!
Ta′bini′na hi′ticha′ni — He′e′ye′!
Ta′bini′na hi′ticha′ni — He′e′ye′!
Bi′taa′wu ta′thi′aku′tawa′ — He′e′ye′!
Bi′taa′wu ta′thi′aku′tawa′ — He′e′ye′!

Translation

My father — *He′e′ye′!*
My father — *He′e′ye′!*
He put me in five places — *He′e′ye′!*
He put me in five places — *He′e′ye′!*
I stood upon the earth — *He′e′ye′!*
I stood upon the earth — *He′e′ye′!*

The author of this song tells how in his trance he went up to the other world, where he stood upon the new earth and saw the messiah, who took him around to five different places and gave him a pipe. The number five may here have some deeper mythic meaning besides that indicated in the bare narrative.

63. NI′NAÄQA′WA CHIBÄ′TI

Ni′naäqa′wa chibä′ti,
Ni′naäqa′wa chibä′ti.
Ha′-ina′tä be′yi thi′äya′na,
Ha′-ina′tä be′yi thi′äya′na.

Translation

I am going around the sweat-house,
I am going around the sweat-house.
The shell lies upon the mound,
The shell lies upon the mound.

The maker of this song saw in his vision a sweat-house with a white shell lying upon the mound in front, where a buffalo skull is usually placed. The song evidently refers to some interesting religious ceremony, but was heard only once, and from a young man who could give no fuller explanation. I have never seen a shell used in this connection. It may be, as suggested by Reverend H. R. Voth, that the word shell is really a figurative expression for skull. In the old days the whole buffalo head was used, instead of the mere skull

64. HISE'HI, HISE'HI

Hise'hi, hise'hi,
Hä'tine'bäku'tha'na,
Hä'tine'bäku'tha'na,
Häti'ta-u'seta'na,
Häti'ta-u'seta'na.

Translation

My comrade, my comrade,
Let us play the awl game,
Let us play the awl game,
Let us play the dice game,
Let us play the dice game.

The woman who composed this song tells how, on waking up in the spirit world, she met there a party of her former girl companions and sat down with them to play the two games universally popular with the women of all the prairie tribes.

The first is called *në'bäku'thana* by the Arapaho and *tsoñä* or "awl game" (from *tsoñ*, an awl) by the Kiowa, on account of an awl, the Indian woman's substitute for a needle, being used to keep record of the score.

FIG. 58.—Diagram of awl game

The game is becoming obsolete in the north, but is the everyday summer amusement of the women among the Kiowa, Comanche, and Apache in the southern plains. It is very amusing on account of the unforeseen "rivers" and "whips" that are constantly turning up to disappoint the expectant winner, and a party of women will frequently sit around the blanket for half a day at a time, with a constant ripple of laughter and good-humored jokes as they follow the chances of the play. It would make a very pretty picnic game, or could readily be adapted to the parlor of civilization.

The players sit upon the ground around a blanket marked in charcoal with lines and dots, and quadrants in the corners, as shown in Figure 58. In the center is a stone upon which the sticks are thrown. Each dot, excepting those between the parallels, counts a point, making twenty-four points for dots. Each of the parallel lines, and each end of the curved lines in the corners, also counts a point, making sixteen points for the lines or forty points in all. The players start from the bottom, opposing players moving in opposite directions, and with each throw of the sticks the thrower moves her awl forward and sticks it into the blanket at the dot or line to which her throw carries her. The parallels on each of the four sides are called "rivers," and the dots within these parallels do not count in the game. The rivers at the top and bottom are "dangerous" and can not be crossed, and when the player is so unlucky as to score a throw which brings her upon the edge of the river (i. e., upon the first line of either of these pairs of parallels), she "falls into the river" and must lose all she has hitherto gained, and begin again at the start. In the same way, when a player moving around in one direction makes a throw which brings her awl to the place occupied by the awl of her opponent coming around from the other side, the said opponent is "whipped back" to the starting point and must begin all over again. Thus there is a constant succession of unforeseen accidents which furnish endless amusement to the players.

The game is played with four sticks, each from 6 to 10 inches long,

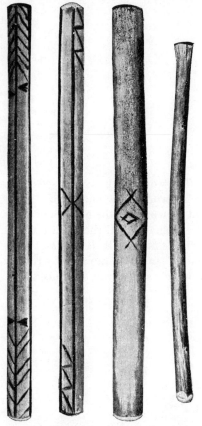

Fig. 59.—Sticks used in awl game

flat on one side and round on the other (Fig. 59). One of these is the trump stick and is marked in a distinctive manner in the center on both sides, and is also distinguished by having a green line along the

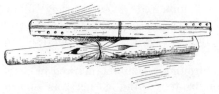

Fig. 60.—Trump sticks used in awl game

flat side (Fig. 60), while the others have each a red line. The Kiowa call this trump stick *sahe*, "green," on account of the green stripe, while the others are called *guadal*, "red." There are also a number of small green sticks, about the size of lead pencils, for keeping tally. Each player in turn takes up the four sticks together in her hand and throws them down on end upon the stone in the center. The number of points depends on the number of flat or round sides which turn up. A lucky throw with the green or trump stick generally gives the thrower another trial in addition. The formula is:

One flat side up counts 1
One flat side (if *sahe*) counts .... 1 and another throw.
Two flat sides up, with or without *sahe*, count................ 2
Three flat sides up count 3
Three flat sides up, including *sahe*, count..................... 3 and another throw.
All four flat sides up count...................................... 6 and another throw.
All four round sides up count.................................... 10 and another throw.

Only the flat sides count except when all the sticks turn round side up. This is the best throw of all, as it counts ten points and another throw. On completing one round of forty points the player takes one of the small green tally sticks from the pile and she who first gets the number of tally sticks previously agreed on wins the game. Two, four, or any even number of persons may play the game, half on each side. When two or more play on a side, all the partners move up the same number of points at each throw, but only the lucky thrower gets a second trial in case of a trump throw.

Fig. 61.—Baskets used in dice game

The other woman's game mentioned, the dice game, is called *ta-u'sïta'tina* (literally, "striking," or "throwing against" something) by the Arapaho, and *mo'nshimûnh* by the Cheyenne, the same name being now given to the modern card games. It was practically universal among all the tribes east and west, and under the name of "hubbub" is described by a New England writer as far back as 1634, almost precisely as it exists today among the prairie tribes. The only difference seems to have been that in the east it was played also by the men, and to the accompaniment of a song such as is used in the hand games of the western tribes.

The requisites are a small wicker bowl or basket (*hatĕchi′na*), five dice made of bone or of plum stones, and a pile of tally sticks such as are used in the awl game. The bowl is 6 or 8 inches in diameter and about 2 inches deep, and is woven in basket fashion of the tough fibers of the yucca (Fig. 61). The dice may be round, elliptical, or diamond-shape and are variously marked on one side with lines and figures, the turtle being a favorite design among the Arapaho (Fig. 62). Two of the five must be alike in shape and marking. The other three are marked with another design and may also be of another shape. Any number of women or girls may play, each throwing in turn, and sometimes one set of partners playing against another. The players toss up the dice from the basket, letting them drop again into it, and score points according to the way the dice turn up in the basket. The first throw by each player is made from the hand instead of from the basket. One hundred points usually count a game, and stakes are wagered on the result as in almost every other Indian contest of skill or chance. For the purpose of explanation, we shall designate two of the five as "rounds" and the other three as "diamonds," it being understood that only the marked side counts in the game, excepting when the throw happens to turn up the three diamonds blank while the other two show the marked side, or, as sometimes happens, when all five dice turn up blank. In

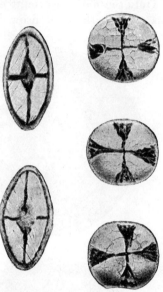

FIG. 62.—Dice used in dice game

every case all of one kind at least must turn up to score a point. A successful throw entitles the player to another throw, while a failure obliges her to pass the basket to some one else. The formula is:

1 only of either kind... 0
2 rounds.. 3
3 diamonds (both rounds with blank side up)................................. 3
3 diamonds blank (both rounds with marked side up)...................... 3
4 marked sides up 1
5 (all) blank sides up.. 1
5 (all) marked sides up 8

A game similar in principle, but played with six dice instead of five, is also played by the Arapaho women, as well as by those of the Comanche and probably also of other tribes.

65. NA′TU′WANI′SA

Nänisa′na, nänisa′na,
Na′tu′wani′sa, na′tu′wani′sa—
Hä′nätä′hĭ′näti′,
Hä′nätä′hĭ′näti′.

Translation

My children, my children,
My top, my top—
It will win the game,
It will win the game.

The man who made this song when he entered the spirit world in his vision met there one of his boy friends who had died long years before, and once more spun tops with him as in childhood.

Tops are used by all Indian boys, and are made of wood or bone. They are not thrown or spun with a string, but are kept in motion by whipping with a small quirt or whip of buckskin. In winter they are spun upon the ice. The younger children make tops to twirl with the fingers by running a stick through a small seed berry.

66. HE'NA'GA'NAWA'NEN

He'na'ga'nawa'nen näa'wu'nani'nä bi'gushi'shi He'sûna'nini' — Ahe'e'ye'!
He'na'ga'nawa'nen näa'wu'nani'nä bi'gushi'shi He'sûna'nini' — Ahe'e'ye'!
Nithi'na hesûna'nini' — Ahe'e'ye'!
Nithi'na hesûna'nini' — Ahe'e'ye'!

Translation

When we dance until daylight our father, the Moon, takes pity on us—*Ahe'e'ye'!*
When we dance until daylight our father, the Moon, takes pity on us—*Ahe'e'ye'!*
The father says so — *Ahe'e'ye'!*
The father says so — *Ahe'e'ye'!*

With the Arapaho, as with many other tribes, the moon is masculine, and the sun is feminine. In mythology the two are brother and sister. There are various myths to account for the spots on the moon's surface, some discerning in them a large frog, while to others they bear a likeness to a kettle hung over the fire. The Arapaho name for the moon, *bi'gushish*, means literally "night sun," the sun itself being called *hishinishish*, "day sun." A similar nomenclature exists among most other tribes.

67. NI'NÄ'NINA'TI'NAKU'NI'NA NA'GA'QU'

A'-nä - ni'-sa'-na, a'-nä - ni'-sa'-na,   ni'-nä'-ni-na' - ti'-na-ku' - ni' - na na' - ga'-qu',

ni' - nä'-ni-na' - ti' - na-ku' - ni' - na na' - ga'-qu';   ti'-na-ha'-thi-hu' nä'-ni - sa'-na,

ti'-na-ha'-thi-hu' nä' - ni - sa'- na,   hä-thi'-na He'-sû-na'-nĭn, hä - thi' -na He'-sû-na'-nin.

A'näni'sa'na, a'näni'sa'na,
Ni'nä'nina'ti'naku'ni'na na'ga'qu',
Ni'nä'nina'ti'naku'ni'na na'ga'qu';
Ti'naha'thihu' nä'nisa'na,
Ti'naha'thihu' nä'nisa'na,
Häthi'na He'sûna'nĭn,
Häthi'na He'sûna'nĭn.

Translation

My children, my children,
It is I who wear the morning star on my head,
It is I who wear the morning star on my head;
I show it to my children,
I show it to my children,
Says the father,
Says the father.

This beautiful song originated among the northern Arapaho, and is a favorite north and south. In it the messiah is supposed to be addressing his children. There is a rhythmic swing to the vocalic syllables that makes the tune particularly pleasing, and the imagery of thought expressed is poetry itself. The same idea occurs in European ballad and legend, and has a parallel in the angel of the evangelist, "clothed with a cloud, and a rainbow upon his head."

68. A'-NENA' TABI'NI'NA

A'-nena' tabi'ni'na nĕ'tĭqta'wa'hu',
A'-nena' tabi'ni'na nĕ'tĭqta'wa'hu'.
Ä'nii'nahu'gahu'nahu,
Ä'nii'nahu'gahu'nahu.
Tahu'naha'thihi'na nä'nisa'na,
Tahu'naha'thihi'na nä'nisa'na.

Translation

My mother gave me my *tĭ'qtawa* stick,
My mother gave me my *tĭ'qtawa* stick.
I fly around with it,
I fly around with it,
To make me see my children,
To make me see my children.

This song was composed by a woman of the southern Arapaho. The reference is not entirely clear, but it is probable that in her trance vision she saw her children in the other world playing the game mentioned, and that afterward she made the game sticks and carried them in the dance, hoping by this means to obtain another vision of the spirit world, where she could again talk with her children who had gone before her to the shadow land. In one Ghost dance seven different women carried these game sticks.

The *băti'qtûba* (abbreviated *ti'qtúp*) game of the Arapaho and other prairie tribes somewhat resembles the Iroquois game of the "snow snake," and is played by children or grown persons of both sexes. It

is a very simple game, the contestants merely throwing or sliding the
sticks along the ground to see who can send them farthest. Two persons or two parties play against each other, boys sometimes playing
against girls or men against women. It is, however, more especially a
girl's game. The game sticks (*bătĭqta'wa*) are slender willow rods about
4 feet long, peeled and painted and tipped with a point of buffalo horn
to enable them to slide more easily along the ground. In throwing, the
player holds the stick at the upper end with the thumb and fingers,
and, swinging it like a pendulum, throws it out with a sweeping motion.
Young men throw arrows about in the same way, and small boys sometimes throw ordinary reeds or weed stalks. Among the Omaha, according to Dorsey, bows, unstrung, are made to slide along the ground or
ice in the same manner.

69. YĬ'HÄ'Ä'Ä'HĬ'HĬ'

Yĭ'hä'ä'ä'hi'hĭ', Yĭ'hä'ä'ä'hi'hĭ,
Hä'nänä'hi'gutha'-u ga'qaä'-hu'hu',
Hä'nänä'hi'gutha'-u ga'qaä -hu'hu'.

Translation

Yĭ'hä'ä'ä'hi'hĭ', Yĭ'hä'ä'ä'hi'hĭ',
I throw the "button,"
I throw the "button."

In his trance vision the author of this song entered a tipi and found
it filled with a circle of his old friends playing the *ga'qutit*, or "hunt the
button" game. This is a favorite winter game with the prairie tribes,
and was probably more or less general throughout the country. It is
played both by men and women, but never by the two sexes together.
It is the regular game in the long winter nights after the scattered
families have abandoned their exposed summer positions on the open
prairie, and moved down near one another in the shelter of the timber along the streams. When hundreds of Indians are thus camped
together, the sound of the drum, the rattle, and the gaming song resound
nightly through the air. To the stranger there is a fascination about
such a camp at night, with the conical tipis scattered about under
the trees, the firelight from within shining through the white canvas and
distinctly outlining upon the cloth the figures of the occupants making
merry inside with jest and story, while from half a dozen different directions comes the measured tap of the Indian drum or the weird chorus
of the gaming songs. Frequently there will be a party of twenty to
thirty men gaming in one tipi, and singing so that their voices can be
heard far out from the camp, while from another tipi a few rods away
comes a shrill chorus from a group of women engaged in another game
of the same kind.

The players sit in a circle around the tipi fire, those on one side of the
fire playing against those on the other. The only requisites are the
"button" or *ga'qaä*, usually a small bit of wood, around which is
tied a piece of string or otter skin, with a pile of tally sticks, as has

been already described. Each party has a "button," that of one side being painted black, the other being red. The leader of one party takes the button and endeavors to move it from one hand to the other, or to pass it on to a partner, while those of the opposing side keep a sharp lookout, and try to guess in which hand it is. Those having the button try to deceive their opponents as to its whereabouts by putting one hand over the other, by folding their arms, and by putting their hands behind them, so as to pass the *ga'qaä* on to a partner, all the while keeping time to the rhythm of a gaming chorus sung by the whole party at the top of their voices. The song is very peculiar, and well-nigh indescribable. It is usually, but not always or entirely, unmeaning, and jumps, halts, and staggers in a most surprising fashion, but always in perfect time with the movements of the hands and arms of the singers. The greatest of good-natured excitement prevails, and every few minutes some more excitable player claps his hands over his mouth or beats the ground with his flat palms, and gives out a regular war-whoop. All this time the opposing players are watching the hands of the other, or looking straight into their faces to observe every tell-tale movement of their features, and when one thinks he has discovered in which hand the button is, he throws out his thumb toward that hand with a loud *"that!"* Should he guess aright, his side scores a certain number of tallies, and in turn takes the button and begins another song. Should the guess be wrong, the losing side must give up an equivalent number of tally sticks. So the play goes on until the small hours of the night. It is always a gambling game, and the stakes are sometimes very large.

The first line of the song here given is an imitation of one of these gambling songs. Among the prairie tribes each song has one or perhaps two words with meaning bearing on the game, the rest of the song being a succession of unmeaning syllables. Among some other tribes, particularly among the Navaho, as described by Dr Washington Matthews, the songs have meaning, being prayers to different animal or elemental gods to assist the player.

As specimens of another variety of gambling songs, we give here two heard among the Paiute of Nevada when visiting the messiah in the winter of 1891–92. They have pretty tunes, very distinct from those of the prairie tribes, and were borrowed by the Paiute from the Mohave, in whose language they may have a meaning, although unintelligible to the Paiute.

Paiute gambling song

Yo'- ho' ma- ho'- yo o-wa'-na, ha'-yä-mä ha'-yä-mä kă- ni'- yo-wï'. Yo'- ho' ma-ho'-

yo o-wa'-na, ha'yä-mä ha'-yä-mä kă-ni-yo- wï'. Ho'- tsĭ-ni'-ă- ni tsai'- o- wi'-a-ni',

i - ha' - ha' tsi-ma'-ni-mi - na, ha - tsi-ma'-ni-mi - na'. Ho' - tsä - ni'-ä - ni

tsai' - o - wi' - a - ni', i - ha' - ha tsi-ma'-ni-mi - na'. ha - tsi-ma'-ni-mi - na'.

1. Yo'ho' maho'yo owa'na,
   Ha'yämä ha'yämä käni'yowĭ'. (*Repeat.*)
2. Ho'tsäni'äni tsai'-owi'ani',
   Iha'ha' tsima'nimina' ha' tsima'nimina'. (*Repeat.*)

70. Nɪ'QA-HU'HU'

Ni'qa-hu'hu', ni'qa-hu'hu',
Hu'wĭ'säna', hu'wĭ'säna' —
Ga'qa'ä-hu'hu', ga'qa'ä-hu'hu'.

Translation

My father, my father,
I go straight to it, I go straight to it—
The *ga'qaä*, the *ga'qaä*.

This song also refers to the game of *ga'qutit*, just described. The *ga'qaä* is the "button."

71. A'HU'NAWU'HU'

A'hu'nawu'hu'-u'-u', a'hu'nawu'hu'-u'-u',   Ga'qu'tina'ni,
Hä'tani'i'bii'na—He'e'ye'!   Ga'qu'tina'ni,
Hä'tani'i'bii'na—He'e'ye'!   Hi'nä'ähä'k ga'qa'ä—He'e'ye'!
                                              Hi'nä'ähä'k ga'qa'ä—He'e'ye'!

Translation

With red paint, with red paint,   When I play *ga'qutit*,
I want to paint myself—*He'e'ye'!*   When I play *ga'qutit*.
I want to paint myself—*He'e'ye'!*   It is the "button"—*He'e'ye*
                                          It is the "button"—*He'e'ye'!*

This song refers to the same game described under songs 69 and 70, and like them is based on the trance experience of the composer.

72. Anɪ'qa naga'qu

Ani'qa naga'qu !   Ina'habi'ä nina'gänawa'ni.
Ani'qa naga'qu !   Awu'näni'ä—Hi'i'i'!
Ina'habi'ä nina'gänawa'ni,   Awu'näni'ä—Hi'i'i'!

Translation

Father, the Morning Star !
Father, the Morning Star !
Look on us, we have danced until daylight,
Look on us, we have danced until daylight.
Take pity on us—*Hi'i'i'!*
Take pity on us—*Hi'i'i'!*

This song is sung about daylight, just before the closing song, after the dancers have danced all night and are now ready to quit and go home. When the new doctrine came among the prairie tribes, the Ghost dance was held at irregular and frequent intervals, almost every other night, in fact—lasting sometimes until about midnight, sometimes until daylight, without any rule. As the ceremonial became crystallized, however, the messiah gave instructions that the dance should be held only at intervals of six weeks, and should then continue four consecutive nights, lasting the first three nights until about midnight, but on the fourth night to continue all night until daylight of the next morning. The original letter containing these directions is given in chapter II. For a long time these directions were implicitly followed, but the tendency now is to the original fashion of one-night dances, at short intervals. This song to the morning star was sung just before daylight on the final morning of the dance.

With all the prairie tribes the morning star is held in great reverence and is the subject of much mythological belief and ceremony. It is universally represented in their pictographs as a cross, usually of the Maltese pattern. In this form it is frequently pictured on the ghost shirts. The Arapaho name, *nagaq'*, means literally "a cross." The Kiowa know it as *t'aiñso*, "the cross," or sometimes, as *dä-e'dal*, "the great star."

73. AHU'YU HÄTHI'NA (closing song)

A - hu' - yu hä - thi' - na he - sû - na' - ni - ni hu' - hu, a - hu' - yu hä -
thi' - na he - sû - na' - ni - ni hu' - hu, ya - thû'n ä - ta' - u - sä' - bä, ya - thû'n ä-
ta' - u - sä' - bä, ni - thi' - na he - sû - na' - nĭn, ni - thi' - na he - sû - na' - nĭn.

Ahu'yu häthi'na hesûna'nini hu'hu,
Ahu'yu häthi'na hesûna'nini hu'hu,
Yathû'n äta'-usä'bä—

Yathû'n äta'-usä'bä—
Nithi'na hesûna'nĭn,
Nithi'na hesûna'nĭn.

Translation

Thus says our father, the Crow,
Thus says our father, the Crow.
Go around five times more—
Go around five times more—
Says the father,
Says the father.

This is the closing song of the dance since the return of the great delegation of southern Arapaho and Cheyenne who visited the messiah in August, 1891. Before that time the closing song had been number 52, beginning *Ni'nini'tubi'na hu'hu'*. The literal rendering of the second part is "stop five times," the meaning and practice being that they must make five circuits singing this song and then stop. As already stated, in accordance with the instructions of the messiah, the Ghost dance is now held (theoretically) at intervals of six weeks and continues for four consecutive nights, closing about midnight, excepting on the last night, when the believers dance until daylight. As daylight begins to appear in the east, they sing the song to the morning star, as just given (number 72), and then, after a short rest, the leaders start this, the closing song, which is sung while the dancers make five circuits, resting a few moments between circuits. Then they unclasp hands, wave their blankets in the air to fan away all evil influences, and go down to the river to bathe, the men in one place and the women in another. After bathing, they resume their clothing and disperse to their various camps, and the Ghost dance is over.

THE CHEYENNE

TRIBAL SYNONYMY

Ba'hakosïn—Caddo name; "striped arrows," *bäh*, arrow. The Caddo sometimes also call them Siä'näbo, from their Comanche name.

Cheyenne—popular name, a French spelling of their Sioux name. It has no connection with the French word *chien*, "dog."

Dzïtsï'stäs—proper tribal name; nearly equivalent to "our people."

Gatsa'lghi—Kiowa Apache name.

Hïtäsi'na (singular *Hï'täsi*)—Arapaho name, signifying "scarred people," from *hïtäshi'ni*, "scarred or cut." According to the Arapaho statement the Cheyenne were so called because they were more addicted than the other tribes to the practice of gashing themselves in religious ceremonies. The name may have more special reference to the tribal custom of cutting off the fingers and hands of their slain enemies. (See tribal sign, page 264.)

Itäsupuzi—Hidatsa name, "spotted arrow quills" (Matthews).

Ka'naheäwastsïk—Cree name, "people with a language somewhat like Cree" (Grinnell).

Niere'rikwats-kúni'ki—Wichita name.

Nanonï'ks-kare'nïki—Kichai name.

Pägänävo—Shoshoni and Comanche name; "striped arrows," from *päga*, "arrow," and *nävo*, "striped."

Säk̲'o'ta—Kiowa name; seems to refer to "biting."

Sa-sis-e-tas—proper tribal name according to Clark (Indian Sign Language, 99, 1885). The form should be *Dzïtsï'stäs* as given above.

Shaiela or *Shaiena*—Sioux name; "red," or decorated with red paint. According to Riggs, as quoted by Clark, the Sioux call an alien language a "red" language, while they designate one of their own stock as "white," so that the name would be equivalent to "aliens." The Sioux apply the same name also to the Cree.

Shiä'navo—another Comanche name, probably a derivative from the word *Cheyenne*.

Shiě'da—another Wichita name, derived from the word *Cheyenne*.

Staitan—unidentified tribal name, given by Lewis and Clark. Identical with the Cheyenne, from their own word *Hïstä'itän*, "I am a Cheyenne."

TRIBAL SIGN

The Cheyenne tribal sign, made by drawing the right index finger several times across the left forefinger, is commonly interpreted "cut fingers" or "cut wrists," and is said to be derived from their custom of cutting off the fingers and hands of slain enemies. Although the same practice was found among other tribes, the Cheyenne were particularly distinguished in this regard. In Mackenzie's great fight with the Cheyenne in Wyoming, in 1876, two necklaces made of human fingers were found in the captured Indian camp, together with a small bag filled with hands cut from the bodies of children of the Shoshoni tribe, their enemies. One of these necklaces was afterward deposited in the National Museum at Washington. (See *Bourke* in *Ninth Annual Report of the Bureau of Ethnology*.) Some competent Indian authorities say, however, that the sign is intended to indicate "stripe people," or "striped-arrow people," referring to the fact that the Cheyenne usually feathered their arrows with the striped feathers of the wild turkey. This agrees with the interpretation of the name for the Cheyenne in several different languages.

SKETCH OF THE TRIBE

The Cheyenne are one of the westernmost tribes of the great Algonquian stock. In one of their ghost songs they sing of the "turtle river," on which they say they once lived. (*Cheyenne song 3.*) From several evidences this seems to be identical with the Saint Croix, which forms the boundary between Wisconsin and Minnesota. This statement agrees with the opinion of Clark (*Indian Sign Language*), who locates their earliest tradition in the neighborhood of Saint Anthony falls. They were driven out by the Sioux and forced toward the northwest, where they came in contact with the Asiniboin (called by them Hohe'), with whom they were never afterward at peace. At a later period, according to Lewis and Clark, they lived on the Cheyenne branch of Red river, in northern Minnesota, whence they were again driven by the Sioux into the prairie.

In 1805 they wandered about the head of Cheyenne river of Dakota and in the Black hills, and were at war with the Sioux, though at peace with most other tribes. Since then they have pushed on to the west and south, always in close confederation with the Arapaho. These two tribes say they have never known a time when they were not associated. About forty years ago, in Wyoming, the band since known as the northern Cheyenne separated from the others (Clark), and have since lived chiefly in Montana or with the Sioux, with whom the Cheyenne made peace about sixty years ago. The other and larger portion of the tribe continued to range chiefly on the lands of the Arkansas and Canadian in Colorado and the western part of

Kansas and Oklahoma. They and the Arapaho made peace with the Kiowa and Comanche in 1840, and raided in connection with these tribes into Texas and Mexico until assigned in 1869 to a reservation in what is now western Oklahoma. In 1874 they, as well as the Kiowa, Comanche, and Kiowa Apache, again went on the warpath in consequence of the depredations of the buffalo hunters, but the outbreak was speedily suppressed. In 1890 they sold their reservation and took allotments in severalty. The northern Cheyenne joined the Sioux in the "Custer war" of 1876–77. At the surrender of the hostiles they were removed to Oklahoma and placed with the southern Cheyenne, but were much dissatisfied with their location, the dissatisfaction culminating in the attempt of a large party, under Dull Knife, to escape to the north, in September, 1878. They were pursued, and a part of them captured and confined at Fort Robinson, Nebraska, whence they made a desperate attempt to escape on the night of January 9, 1879, resulting in the killing of nearly all of the prisoners. They were finally assigned a reservation in Montana, where they now are, with the exception of a few among the Sioux. According to the official report for 1892, the southern Cheyenne in Oklahoma numbered 2,119, the northern Cheyenne in Montana, 1,200, and those with the Sioux at Pine Ridge, South Dakota, 120, a total of 3,439.

The Cheyenne have eleven tribal divisions. They have at least two dialects, but probably more. The tribal divisions in their order in the camping circle are—

1. *Evĭ′sts-unĭ′pahĭs* ("smoky lodges"—Grinnell, *fide* Clark).

2. *Sŭta′ya* or *Sŭ′tasi′na*. This is one of the most important divisions and formerly constituted a distinct tribe, but was afterward incorporated with the Cheyenne. According to concurrent Cheyenne and Blackfoot tradition, as given by Grinnell, they seem originally to have been a part of the Blackfeet, who became separated from the main body of their tribe by the sudden breaking up of the ice while crossing a large river. They drifted to the southward and finally met and joined the Cheyenne in the Black hills. Their name, spelled *Suti* by Grinnell, is said to mean "strange talkers." They live now on the upper Washita in Oklahoma and speak a dialect differing considerably from that of the rest of the tribe.

3. *Ĭ′sium-itä′niuw′*, ("ridge-people;" singular, *Ĭ′siumi-tän*—Grinnell, *fide* Clark).

4. *Hĕwă-tä′niuw′*, "hairy men." The name is also sometimes used collectively to designate all of the southern Cheyenne as distinguished from the northern Cheyenne, called collectively *Hmĭ′sĭs*. The southern Cheyenne are also designated collectively as *So′wănĭă*, "southerners."

5. *Ŏ′ivimă′na*, "scabby." This name is said to have been given them originally on account of an epidemic which once broke out among their horses and rendered them mangy.

6. *Wĭ′tapi′u* ("haters"—Grinnell, *fide* Clark).

7. *Hotă'mi-tä'niuw'*, "dog men," or *Mĭ'stăviĭ'nŭt*, "heavy eyebrows." This is also the name of one of the divisions of their warrior organization.

8. *O'tu'gŭnŭ*.

9. *Hmĭ'sĭs*, "eaters." This is the most important division of the northern Cheyenne, and the name is also used by those of the south to designate all the northern Cheyenne collectively.

10. *Anskowĭ'nĭs*.

11. *Pĭnû'tgû'*.

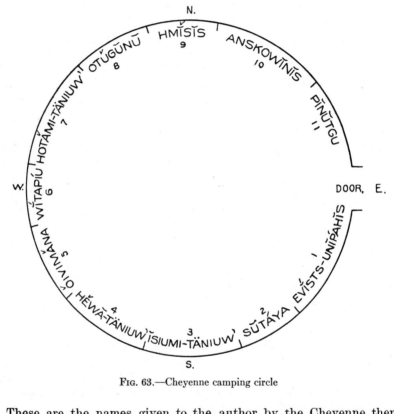

Fig. 63.—Cheyenne camping circle

These are the names given to the author by the Cheyenne themselves as the complete list of their tribal divisions. Grinnell, on the authority of the Clark manuscript, names six of these with two others, *Matsĭ'shkota*, "corpse from a scaffold," and *Miayŭma*, "red lodges," which may be identical with some of the others named above, or may perhaps be degrees of their military organization instead of tribal divisions.

In the great ceremony of the "medicine arrow," last enacted on the Washita in 1890, the camping circle opened to the south. At all other gatherings of the tribe the circle opened to the east, agreeable to the general Indian custom, the several divisions encamping in the order shown in Figure 63.

The Cheyenne, like the prairie tribes generally, are, or were until within a few years past, a nation of nomads, living in skin tipis, and depending almost entirely on the buffalo for food. Yet they have a dim memory of a time when they lived in permanent villages and planted corn, and in their genesis tradition, which occupies four " smokes" or nights in the telling, they relate how they "lost" the corn a long time ago before they became wanderers on the plains. They deposit their dead on scaffolds in trees, unlike their confederates, the Arapaho, who bury in the ground. Their most sacred possession is the bundle of "medicine arrows," now in possession of the southern division of the tribe. They have a military organization similar to that existing among the Arapaho and other prairie tribes, as described under number 43 of the Arapaho songs. Above all the tribes of the plains they are distinguished for their desperate courage and pride of bearing, and are preeminently warriors among people whose trade is war. They are strongly conservative and have steadily resisted every advance of civilization, here again differing from the Arapaho, who have always shown a disposition to meet the white man half-way. In fact, no two peoples could well exhibit more marked differences of characteristics on almost every point than these two confederated tribes. The Cheyenne have quick and strong intelligence, but their fighting temper sometimes renders them rather unmanageable subjects with whom to deal. Their conservatism and tribal pride tend to restrain them from following after strange gods, so that in regard to the new messiah they assume a rather skeptical position, while they conform to all the requirements of the dance code in order to be on the safe side.

Clark, in his *Indian Sign Language*, thus sums up the characteristics of the Cheyenne:

As a tribe they have been broken and scattered, but in their wild and savage way they fought well for their country, and their history during the past few years has been written in blood. The men of the Cheyenne Indians rank as high in the scale of honesty, energy, and tenacity of purpose as those of any other tribe I have ever met, and in physique and intellect they are superior to those of most tribes and the equal of any. Under the most demoralizing and trying circumstances they have preserved in a remarkable degree that part of their moral code which relates to chastity, and public sentiment has been so strong in them in regard to this matter that they have been, and are still, noted among all the tribes which surround them for the virtue of their women.

The Cheyenne language lacks the liquids *l* and *r*. It is full of hissing sounds and difficult combinations of consonants, so that it does not lend itself readily to song composition, for which reason, among others, the Cheyenne in the south usually join the Arapaho in the Ghost dance and sing the Arapaho songs.

SONGS OF THE CHEYENNE

1. O'TÄ NÄ'NISĬ'NÄSĬSTS

O'tä nä'nisĭ'näsĭsts — Ehe'e'ye'!
O'tä nä'nisĭ'näsĭsts,— Ehe'e'ye'!
Mä'tesemä'moestä'nowe't — Ähe'e'ye'!
Mä'tesemä'moestä'nowe't — Ähe'e'ye'!
Ho'ivitu'simo'moĭ'ts — E'ähe'e'ye'!
Ho'ivitu'simo'moĭ'ts — E'ähe'e'ye'!
Nu'ka'eshe'väo'e'tse'
Nitu'si'mitä'nun,
Nitu'si'mitä'nun.

Translation

Well, my children — *Ehe'e'ye'!*
Well, my children — *Ehe'e'ye'!*
When you meet your friends again — *Ähe'e'ye'!*
When you meet your friends again — *Ähe'e'ye'!*
The earth will tremble — *E'ähe'e'ye'!*
The earth will tremble — *E'ähe'e'ye'!*
The summer cloud (?)
It will give it to us,
It will give it to us.

The interpretation of this song is imperfect and the meaning is not clear. It evidently refers to the earthquake which it is supposed will occur at the moment of contact of the spirit world with the old earth. The literal meaning of the second line, rendered " when you meet your friends again," is " when you are living together again."

2. EHÄ'N ESHO'INI'

Ehä'n esho'ini',
Ehä'n esho'ini',
Hoi'v esho'ini',
Hoi'v esho'ini',
I'yohä' — Eye'ye'!
I'yohä' — Eye'ye'!
I'nisto'niwo'ni — Ahe'e'ye'!
I'nisto'niwo'ni — Ahe'e'ye'!

Translation

Our father has come,
Our father has come,
The earth has come,
The earth has come,
It is rising — *Eye'ye'!*
It is rising — *Eye'ye'!*
It is humming — *Ahe'e'ye'!*
It is humming — *Ahe'e'ye'!*

This is the song composed by Porcupine, the great leader of the Ghost dance among the northern Cheyenne. It refers to the coming of the new earth which is to come over this old world and which is represented as making a humming or rolling noise as it swiftly approaches.

3. NÄ'NISO'NÄSĬ'STSIHI'

Nä'niso'näsĭ'stsihi',
Nä'niso'näsĭ'stsihi',
Hi'tää'ni mä'noyu'hii',
Hi'tää'ni mä'noyu'hii',
Owa'ni tsi'nitai'-wosi'hi',
Owa'ni tsi'nitai'-wosi'hi',
Tsĭ'nitai'-womai'-wosihi',
Tsĭ'nitai'-womai'-wosihi'.
I'häni' i'hiwo'uhi',
I'häni' i'hiwo'uhi'.

Translation

My children, my children,
Here is the river of turtles,
Here is the river of turtles,
Where the various living things,
Where the various living things,
Are painted their different colors,
Are painted their different colors.
Our father says so,
Our father says so.

This song has a very pretty tune. The Cheyenne claim to have lived originally in the north on a stream known to them as the "River of Turtles." Reverend H. R. Voth, former missionary among the Cheyenne and Arapaho, states that the Indians say that along the banks of this stream were clays of different colors which they used for paint. In a letter of October 1, 1891, he says: "I have now in my possession some red and some gray or drab paint that Black Coyote brought with him from the north, which he claims came from that ancient Turtle river, and which the Indians are now using to paint themselves. They say there are more than two kinds of color at that river, or at least used to be." According to Clark (*Indian Sign Language*, page 99) the oldest traditions of the Cheyenne locate their former home on the headwaters of the Mississippi in Minnesota, about where Saint Paul now is. Other facts corroborate this testimony, and the traditional "Turtle river" would seem to be identical with the Saint Croix, which is thus described by Coxe in 1741:

A little higher up is the river Chabadeda, above which the Meschacebe makes a fine lake twenty miles long and eight or ten broad. Nine or ten miles above that lake, on the east side, is a large fair river, called the river of Tortoises, after you have entered a little way, which leads far into the country to the northeast, and is navigable by the greatest boats forty miles. About the same distance farther up, the Meschacebe is precipitated from the rocks about fifty feet, but is so far navigable by considerable ships, as also beyond; excepting another fall, eighty or ninety miles higher, by large vessels, unto its sources, which are in the country of the Sieux, not at a very great distance from Hudson's bay. There are many other smaller rivers which fall into the Meschacebe, on both sides of it, but being of little note, and the description of them of small consequence, I have passed over them in silence. (Coxe, Carolana, 1741, in French's Hist. Coll. of La., part 2, 233, 1850.)

4. NÄ'SEE'NEHE' EHE'YOWO'MI

Nä'see'nehe' ehe'yowo'mi,
Nä'see'nehe' ehe'yowo'mi,
E'nää'ne mä'noyo'h ehe'yowo'mi,
E'nää'ne mä'noyo'h ehe'yowo'mi.

Translation

I waded into the yellow river,
I waded into the yellow river,
This was the Turtle river into which I waded,
This was the Turtle river into which I waded.

This song is probably explained by the one immediately preceding.

5. WOSI'VÄ-Ă'Ă'

Wosi'vä-ă'ă',
Wosi'vä-ă'ă',
Nänima-iyä,
Nänima-iyä,
Ä'hiya'e'yee'heye'!
Ä'hiya'e'yee'heye'!

Translation

The mountain,
The mountain,
It is circling around,
It is circling around,
Ä'hiya'e'yee'heye' !
Ä'hiya'e'yee'heye' !

The interpretation of this song is not satisfactory. It was explained that by the mountain was meant the new earth, which was represented as approaching rapidly with a circular motion.

6. NI'HA-I'HI'HI'

Ni'ha-i'hi'hi',
Ni'ha-i'hi'hi',
Na'eso'yutu'hi',
Na'eso'yutu'hi',
U'guchi'hi'hi',
U'guchi'hi'hi',
Na'nisto'hewu'hi',
Na'nisto'hewu'hi',
Ga'! Na'hewu'hi,
Ga'! Na'hewu'hi.

Translation

My father,
My father,
I come to him,
I come to him,
The crow,
The crow,
I cry like it,
I cry like it,
Caw! I say,
Caw! I say.

The connection of the crow with the doctrine of the Ghost dance has already been explained. See Arapaho song 36.

7. Hi'awu'hi — Hi'hi'hai'-yai'

Hi'awu'hi — Hi'hi'hai'-yai'!
Hi'awu'hi — Hi'hi'hai'-yai'!
Ni'äsĭ'tano'ni — Hi'hi'hai'-yai'!
Ni'äsĭ'tano'ni — Hi'hi'hai'-yai'!
Hi'äma' wihu'i — Hi'hi'hai'-yai'!
Hi'äma' wihu'i — Hi'hi'hai'-yai'!
Ni'hihi'no'ni — Hi'hi'hai'-yai'!
Ni'hihi'no'ni — Hi'hi'hai'-yai'!
Nĭ'shibä'tämo'ni — Hi'hi'hai'-yai'!
Nĭ'shibä'tämo'ni — Hi'hi'hai'-yai'!

Translation

The devil — *Hi'hi'hai'-yai'!*
The devil — *Hi'hi'hai'-yai'!*
We have put him aside — *Hi'hi'hai'-yai'!*
We have put him aside — *Hi'hi'hai'-yai'!*
The White Man Above — *Hi'hi'hai'-yai'!*
The White Man Above — *Hi'hi'hai'-yai'!*
He is our father — *Hi'hi'hai'-yai'!*
He is our father — *Hi'hi'hai'-yai'!*
He has blest us — *Hi'hi'hai'-yai'!*
He has blest us — *Hi'hi'hai'-yai'!*

It is hardly necessary to state that the idea of a devil is not aboriginal, although now embodied in the Indian mythology and language from contact with the whites. The "White Man Above" is understood to mean the ruler whose precursor the messiah is, equivalent to our idea of God.

8. Ni'ha — E'yehe'! E'he'eye

Ni'ha — E'yehe'! E'he'eye'!
Ni'ha — E'yehe'! E'he'eye'!
Tsĭ'stamo'nohyo't — Ehe'eye'!
Tsĭ'stamo'nohyo't — Ehe'eye'!
O'täta'wome'mäpe'wä — He'eye'!
O'täta'wome'mäpe'wä — He'eye'!
Ni'mistä'tuhä'mi — He'eye'!
Ni'mistä'tuhä'mi — He'eye'!
E'hiwou', E'hiwou' — He'!

Translation

My father—*E'yehe'! E'he'eye'!*
My father—*E'yehe'! E'he'eye'!*
When I first met him—*Ehe'eye'!*
When I first met him—*Ehe'eye'!*
"In the blue-green water—*He'eye'!*
"In the blue-green water—*He'eye'!*
You must take a bath"—*He'eye'!*
You must take a bath"—*He'eye'!*
Thus he told me, thus he told me—*He'!*

Quite a number of the Cheyenne ghost songs refer to rivers seen in the spirit world, these being frequently designated by colors, as yellow, blue, etc. It may be that certain rivers play a prominent part in their mythology, and as has been said they locate their earliest traditional home on the "Turtle river." The word here rendered "blue-green" might mean either blue or green, as in Cheyenne and in many other Indian languages the two colors are not differentiated. Compare Cheyenne song number 16.

9. Ä′minû′qi

Ä′minû′qi—I′yahe′yahe′e′!
Ä′minû′qi—I′yahe′yahe′e′!
Nĭ′stsishi′hiyo′honi′mäni—Ahe′e′ye′!
Nĭ′stsishi′hiyo′honi′mäni—Ahe′e′ye′!
Nĭ′shka′nĭ nĭ′stsishĭ′nutsi′mani—Ahe′e′ye′!
Nĭ′shka′nĭ nĭ′stsishĭ′nutsi′mani—Ahe′e′ye′!
Ehä′ni ni′nĭni′etä′ni—Ahe′e′ye′!
Ehä′ni ni′nĭni′etä′ni—Ahe′e′ye′!

Translation

My comrade—*I'yahe'yahe'e'!*
My comrade—*I'yahe'yahe'e'!*
Let us go and play shinny—*Ahe'e'ye'!*
Let us go and play shinny—*Ahe'e'ye'!*
Let us look for our mother—*Ahe'e'ye'!*
Let us look for our mother—*Ahe'e'ye'!*
Our father tells us to do it—*Ahe'e'ye'!*
Our father tells us to do it—*Ahe'e'ye'!*

This song was composed by Mo ki, "Little Woman," the Cheyenne wife of Grant Left-hand. Although a young woman, she is regarded as a leader in the Cheyenne Ghost dance, having been in frequent trances and composed numerous songs. In this she relates her experience in one trance, during which she and her girl comrade played together the woman's game of shinny, already described, and then went to look for their mothers, who had gone to the spirit world years before.

10. He′stutu′ai

He′stutu′ai—Yä′hä′yä′!
He′sutu′äi—
[*Ad libitum*].

Translation

The buffalo head — *Yä'hä'yä'!*
The half buffalo —
[*Ad libitum*].

This song refers to the crazy dance, which the author of the song saw the former warriors of his tribe performing in the spirit world. The crazy dance, called *Psam* by the Cheyenne and *Ahaka'wŭ* by the Arapaho, belonged to one order of the military organization already described in treating of the Arapaho songs. (See Arapaho song 43.) The name in both languages is derived from the word for "crazy." Men, women, and children took part in the ceremony, dressed in skins or other costume to represent various animals, as buffalos, panthers, deer, and birds, with one bear, two foxes, and seven wolves, besides two "medicine wolves." Each strove to imitate the animal personated in action as well as in appearance. It was the business of the two foxes to be continually running and stumbling over the others in their efforts to escape from the crowd. The dance, whose essential feature was the doing of everything by contraries, had its parallel among many eastern tribes, particularly among the old Huron and Iroquois. It was considered the most picturesque and amusing dance among the prairie tribes. The "half buffalo" of the song refers to the robe worn by certain of the dancers, which consisted of the upper half of a buffalo skin, the head portion, with the horns attached, coming over the head of the dancers. The dance was an exhibition of deliberate craziness in which the performers strove to outdo one another in nonsensical and frenzied actions, particularly in constantly doing the exact opposite of what they were told to do. It was performed only in obedience to a vow made by some person for the recovery of a sick child, for a successful war expedition, or for some other Indian blessing. It lasted four days, the performers dancing naked the first three days and in full dance costume on the fourth. The leaders in the absurdities were two performers whose bodies and cheeks were painted with white clay, and whose ears were filled with hair shed by the buffalo, which was believed to confer strong "medicine" powers. They carried whistles, and shot at the spectators with blunt arrows. Almost every license was permitted to these two, who in consequence were really held in dread by the others. Among other things the crazy dancers were accustomed to dance through a fire until they extinguished it by their tramping. This was done in imitation of the fire-moth, called *aha'kăa'*, "crazy," by the Arapaho, which hovers about a flame or fire and finally flies into it. They also handled poisonous snakes, and sometimes, it is said, would even surround and kill a buffalo by their unaided physical strength. The Cheyenne dance differed somewhat from that of the Arapaho. It was last performed in the south about ten years ago.

11. NÄ′MIO′TS

Nä′mio′ts — Ehe′ee′ye′!
Nä′mio′ts — Ehe′ee′ye′!
Nĭ′tosĭ′noe′yotsĭ′nots he′wowi′täs — E′yahe′eye′!
Nĭ′tosĭ′noe′yotsĭ′nots he′wowi′täs — E′yahe′eye′!
Nĭ′tsävĭ′sĭwo′mätsĭ′nowa′ —
Nĭ′tsävĭ′sĭwo′mätsĭ′nowa′.

Translation

I am coming in sight — *Ehe′ee′ye′!*
I am coming in sight — *Ehe′ee′ye′!*
I bring the whirlwind with me — *E′yahe′eye′!*
I bring the whirlwind with me — *E′yahe′eye′!*
That you may see each other —
That you may see each other.

The whirlwind is regarded with reverence by all the prairie tribes. In the mythology of the Ghost dance it seems to be an important factor in assisting the onward progress of the new world and the spirit army. It is mentioned also in several Arapaho ghost songs.

12. A′GACHI′HI

A′gachi′hi,
A′gachi′hi,
I′nimä′iha′,
I′nimä′iha′.
Hi′tsina′yo,
Hi′tsina′yo —
Na′vishi′nima′ yu′suwu′nutu′,
Na′vishi′nima′ yu′suwu′nutu′.

Translation

The crow, the crow,
He is circling around,
He is circling around,
His wing, his wing —
I am dancing with it,
I am dancing with it.

This song refers to the sacred crow feathers, which certain of the dancers wear upon their heads in the Ghost dance, as explained in the Arapaho songs.

13. NÄ′NISE′NÄSĔ′STSE

Nä′nise′näsĕ′stse nä′shi′nisto′ni′va — He′eye′!
Nä′nise′näsĕ′stse nä′shi′nisto′ni′va — He′eye′!
Nä′niso′niwo′, nä′niso′niwo′,
I′votä′omo′mĕstä′o — He′eye′!
I′votä′omo′mĕstä′o — He′eye′!
Nä′visi′vämä′, nä′vi′sivämä′.

Translation

My children, I am now humming — *He'eye'!*
My children, I am now humming — *He'eye'!*
Your children, your children,
They are crying — *He'eye'!*
They are crying — *He'eye'!*
They are hurrying me along,
They are hurrying me along.

This song is supposed to be addressed by the father or messiah to his disciples. He tells them that their children in the spirit world are crying to be reunited with their friends here, and thus are hastening their coming. The expression, "I am humming," may possibly refer to his rapid approach.

14. Ogo'ch—Ehe'eye'

Ogo'ch — Ehe'eye'!
Ogo'ch — Ehe'eye'!
Tseä'nehä'sĭ nä'viho'm,
Tseä'nehä'sĭ nä'viho'm.
A'ae'vä, A'ae'vä,
Nĭ'stsistä'nä' e'wova'shimä'nĭsts,
Nĭ'stsistä'nä' e'wova'shimä'nĭsts.
Ni'shivä'tämä'ni,
Ni'shivä'tämä'ni.

Translation

The crow — *Ehe'eye'!*
The crow — *Ehe'eye'!*
I saw him when he flew down,
I saw him when he flew down.
To the earth, to the earth.
He has renewed our life,
He has renewed our life.
He has taken pity on us,
He has taken pity on us.

This song was composed by Grant Left-hand's wife. The Crow is here considered as the lord of the new spirit world.

15. Tsĭso'soyo'tsĭto'ho

Tsĭso'soyo'tsĭto'ho,
Tsĭso'soyo'tsĭto'ho,
He'stänowä'hehe',
He'stänowä'hehe',
Näviho'säni'hi,
Näviho'säni'hi,
Tse'novi'tätse'stovi,
Tse'novi'tätse'stovi,
Ä'koyoni'vähe',
Ä'koyoni'vähe'.

Translation

While I was going about,
While I was going about,
Among the people, at my home,
Among the people, at my home,
I saw them,
I saw them,
Where they gambled,
Where they gambled,
With the *ä′ko′yo* wheel,
With the *ä′ko′yo* wheel.

This song was also composed by Mo′ki, the wife of Grant Left-hand. The expression here rendered "my home" is literally "where I belonged," as, since the death of her children, she speaks of the spirit world as her own proper home. In this song she tells how she found her departed friends playing the game of the *ä′ko′yo* or *bä′qăti* wheel, as described in Arapaho song 49.

16. Nɪ′ʜᴀ—E′ʏᴇʜᴇ′ᴇ′ʏᴇʏᴇ′

Ni′ha—E′yehe′e′yeye′!
Ni′ha—E′yehe′e′yeye′!
Hi′niso′nihu′—Hi′yeye′!
Hi′niso′nihu′—Hi′yeye′!
O′tätä′womi′ mä′piva′—He′e′ye′!
O′tätä′womi′ mä′piva′—He′e′ye′!
E′tätu′hamo′tu—He′eye′!
E′tätu′hamo′tu—He′eye′!
Nä′hisi′maqa′niwo′m—Ähe′eye′!
Nä′hisi′maqa′niwo′m—Ähe′eye′!
E′ta′wu′hotä′nu—He′eye′!
E′tä′wu′hotä′nu—He′eye′!

Translation

My father—*E′yehe′e′yeye′!*
My father—*E′yehe′e′yeye′!*
His children—*Hi′yeye′!*
His children—*Hi′yeye′!*
In the greenish water—*He′e′ye′!*
In the greenish water—*He′e′ye′!*
He makes them swim—*He′eye′!*
He makes them swim—*He′eye′!*
We are all crying—*Ähe′eye′!*
We are all crying—*Ähe′eye′!*

This song conveys nearly the same idea as that of number 8. The expression "We are all crying" might be rendered "We are all pleading, or praying" to the father, to hasten his coming.

17. A'GA'CH—EHE'E'YE'

A'ga'ch — Ehe'e'ye'!
A'ga'ch — Ehe'e'ye'!
Ve'ta chi — He'e'ye'!
Ve'ta'chi — He'e'ye'!
E'hoi'otsĭ'stu,
E'hoi'otsĭ'stu.
Ma'e'tumu'nu' — He'e'ye'!
Ma'e'tumu'nu' — He'e'ye'!
E'ho'i'o'tso',
E'ho'i'o'tso'.
Nä'vi'sivû'qewo'nĭt,
Nä'vi'sivû'qewo'nĭt.
Nĭstä'kona'oe'vo,
Nĭstä'kona'oe'vo.
E'he'vo'o', E'he'vo'o'.

Translation

The crow — *Ehe'e'ye'!*
The crow — *Ehe'e'ye'!*
The grease paint — *He'e'ye'!*
The grease paint — *He'e'ye'!*
He brings it to me,
He brings it to me.
The red paint — *He'e'ye'!*
The red paint — *He'e'ye'!*
He brings it,
He brings it.
I prepare myself with it,
I prepare myself with it.
It will make you strong,
It will make you strong.
He tells me, He tells me.

Red is a sacred color with all Indians, and is usually symbolic of strength and success, and for this reason is a favorite color in painting the face and body for the dance or warpath, and for painting the war pony, the lance, etc. On all important occasions, when painting the face or body, the skin is first anointed with grease to make the paint adhere better, so as not to obscure the sharp lines of the design.

18. NÄ'NISO'NÄSĬ'STSI—HE'E'YE'

Nä'niso'näsĭ'stsi — He'e'ye'!
Nä'niso'näsĭ'stsi — He'e'ye'!
Vi'nänä'tuu'wa o'gochi' — Ahe'e'ye'!
Vi'nänä'tuu'wa o'gochi' — Ahe'e'ye'!
Nĭ'stsivĭ'shiwo'mätsĭ'no,
Nĭ'stsivĭ'shiwo'mätsĭ'no.

Translation

My children — *He'e'ye'!*
My children — *He'e'ye'!*

Kill a buffalo (or beef) for the Crow — *Ahe′e′ye′!*
Kill a buffalo (or beef) for the Crow — *Ahe′e′ye′!*
By that means I shall see you,
By that means I shall see you.

This song refers to the feast which accompanies every dance. The implied meaning is that the people must get ready for a dance in order that they may see the Crow, their father.

19. A′GUGA′-IHI

A′guga′-ihi,
A′guga′-ihi.
Tsi′shistä′hi′sihi′,
Tsi′shistä′hi′sihi′.
I′hoo′ᶜtsihi′,
I′hoo′ᶜtsihi′.
Tsïtäwo′ᶜtähi′,
Tsïtäwo′ᶜtähi′.
Hi′nisa′nûhi′,
Hi′nisa′nûhi′.
Tsïtäwo′mohu′,
Tsïtäwo′mohu′.

Translation

The crow woman —
The crow woman —
To her home,
To her home,
She is going,
She is going.
She will see it,
She will see it.
Her children,
Her children.
She will see them,
She will see them.

This song was also composed by Mo′ki, "Little Woman," the wife of Grant Left-hand. On account of her frequent trances and consequent leadership in the Cheyenne Ghost dance, she assumes the title of the Crow Woman, i. e., the woman messenger from the spirit world. The story of her own and her husband's connection with the Ghost dance is of interest for the light it throws on the working of the Indian mind, especially with regard to religion.

Mo′ki is a young Cheyenne woman married to a young Arapaho, Grant Left-hand, about 30 years of age, a former Carlisle student, and the son of Nawat, or Left-hand, the principal chief of the southern Arapaho. Notwithstanding several years of English education, Grant is a firm believer in the doctrine and the dance, and the principal organizer and leader of the auxiliary "crow dance" in his own tribe, while his wife is as prominent in the Ghost dance among the Cheyenne, and has composed a series of a dozen or more songs descriptive of her various trance experiences in the other world.

Her first child died soon after birth, and the young mother was keenly affected by the bereavement. Afterward a boy was born to them, and became the idol of his parents, especially of the father. He grew up into a bright and active little fellow, but when about 4 years of age was suddenly seized with a spasm in the night and died in a few minutes, almost before his father could reach his bed. This second loss brought deep sorrow to them both, and the mother brooded over it so that there was serious fear for her own life. Then came the Ghost dance and the new doctrine of a reunion with departed friends. The mother went to the dance, fell into a trance, met her children as in life, and played with her little boy. On awaking and returning home she told her husband. He could hardly believe it at first, but it required but little persuasion to induce him to attend the next Ghost dance with her, because, as he said, "I want to see my little boy." He himself fell into a trance, saw his children, and rode with his little boy on the horse behind him over the green prairies of the spirit land. From that time both became devoted adherents and leaders of the Ghost dance; their trances have been frequent, and every dance is welcomed as another opportunity of reunion with departed friends. The young man was deeply affected as he spoke of his love for his children, the sudden death of the little boy, and their second meeting in the other world, and as his wife sat by his side looking up into our faces and listening intently to every word, although she understood but little English, it could not be doubted that their faith in the reality of the vision was real and earnest. Every Indian parent who has lost a child, every child who has lost a parent, and every young man and woman who has lost a brother, sister, or friend affirms a similar reason for belief in the Ghost dance.

THE COMANCHE

TRIBAL SYNONYMY

Bo'dălk''iñago — common Kiowa name, signifying "reptile people" or "snake men," from *bo'dal*, reptile, insect, and *k'iñago*, people.

Cha'tha — (singular *Cha'*) Arapaho name, signifying "enemies."

Comanche — popular name; of Mexican-Spanish origin and unknown meaning. It occurs as early as 1757, and in the form *Cumanche* as early as 1720.

Gyai'-ko — the common name given by the Kiowa to the Comanche, signifying "enemies."

Iatan — the French spelling of the name applied by several of the plains tribes to the Ute Indians, and by extension to the cognate Comanche and Shoshoni. It is a derivative from the name Yuta or Ute, the final *n* representing a nasalized vowel sound. The nearest approximation is perhaps *Iätä-go*, the Kiowa (plural) name for the Ute. Variants are *L'Iatan, Aliatan, Halitane, Ayutan, Tetau* (for *Ietau* or *Ietan*), *Jetan, Yutan*, etc. The form *Läitanes* occurs as early as 1740 (Margry, VII, 457).

Idahi — Kiowa Apache name; meaning unknown.

Ietan — a name applied by some of the prairie tribes to several Shoshonean tribes, particularly the Shoshoni and the *Comanche*. It occurs in a number of forms and appears as *Läitanes* as early as 1740 (Margry, VII, 457).

La Playe — former French trader's name, perhaps a corruption of *Tête Pele'e*.

Na''lani — Navaho name, signifying "many aliens" or "many enemies," applied collectively to the southern plains tribes, but more especially to the Comanche.

Na'nita — Kichai name.

Na'tăa' — Wichita name, variously rendered "snakes," i. e., "enemies" or "dandies."

Nŭma — proper tribal name used by themselves, and signifying "people." The Shoshoni and Paiute designate themselves by the same name.

Pa'douca — the name given to the Comanche by the Osage, Quapaw, Kansa, Oto, and other Siouan tribes. It has several dialectic forms and is used in this form by Pénicaut as early as 1719. It may perhaps be a contraction of *Pe'nä-tĕka*, the name of the principal eastern division of the Comanche.

Sänko — obsolete Kiowa name; it may signify "snakes," from *säne*, snake.

Sau'hto — Caddo name.

Shĭshino'wĭts-Itäniuw' — Cheyenne name, signifying "snake people."

Tête Pele'e — a name said to have been applied to the Comanche by the French traders, signifying "bald heads." The identification seems doubtful, as the Comanche cut their hair only when mourning.

Yä'mpai-ni or *Yä'mpai-Rĭ'kani* — Shoshoni name, signifying "yampa people," or "yampa eaters." It is properly the name of only one division, but is used collectively for the whole tribe. The yampa plant is the *Carum gairdneri*.

TRIBAL SIGN

The tribal sign for the Comanche is "snakes," the same as that for the Shoshoni, but with the finger drawn toward the rear instead of thrust forward.

SKETCH OF THE TRIBE

The Comanche are one of the southern tribes of the great Shoshonean stock, and the only one of that group living entirely on the plains. Their language and traditions show that they are a comparatively recent offshoot from the Shoshoni of Wyoming, both tribes speaking practically the same dialect and until very recently keeping up constant and friendly communication. Within the traditionary period the two tribes lived adjacent to each other in southern Wyoming, since which time the Shoshoni have been beaten back into the mountains by the Sioux and other prairie tribes, while the Comanche have been driven steadily southward by the same pressure. In this southern migration the Pe'näteka seem to have preceded the rest of the tribe. The Kiowa say that when they themselves moved southward from the Black-hills region, the Arkansas was the northern boundary of the Comanche.

In 1719 the Comanche are mentioned under their Siouan name of Pa'douca as living in what now is western Kansas. It must be remembered that from 500 to 800 miles was an ordinary range for a prairie tribe, and that the Comanche were equally at home on the Platte and in the Bolson de Mapimi of Chihuahua. As late as 1805 the North Platte was still known as Padouca fork. At that time they roamed over the country about the heads of the Arkansas, Red, Trinity, and Brazos rivers, in Colorado, Kansas, Oklahoma, and Texas. For nearly two hundred years they were at war with the Spaniards of Mexico and extended their raids far down into Durango. They were friendly to the Americans generally, but became bitter enemies of the Texans, by whom they were dispossessed of their best hunting grounds, and carried on a relentless war against them for nearly forty years. They have been close confederates of the Kiowa for perhaps one hundred and fifty years. In 1835 they made their first treaty with the government, and by the treaty of Medicine Lodge in 1867 agreed to go on their present reservation, situated between Washita and Red rivers, in the southwestern part of Oklahoma; but it was not until after the last outbreak of the southern prairie tribes in 1874–75 that they and their allies, the Kiowa and Apache, finally settled on it. They were probably never a large tribe, although supposed to be populous on account of their wide range. Within the last fifty years they have been terribly wasted by war and disease. They numbered 1,512 in 1893.

The gentile system seems to be unknown among the Comanche. They have, or still remember, thirteen recognized divisions or bands, and may have had others in former times. Of these all but five are practically extinct. The Kwă'hări and Pe'näteka are the most important. Following in alphabetic order is the complete list as given by their leading chiefs:

1. *Detsăna'yuka* or *No'koni*. This band, to which the present head chief Quanah Parker belongs, was formerly called *No'koni*, "wanderers," but on the death of Quanah's father, whose name was also No'koni, the name was tabued, according to Comanche custom, and the division took the name of *Detsăna'yuka*, "bad campers," intended to convey the same idea of wandering.

2. *Ditsä'kăna*, *Wĭ'dyu*, *Yäpä*, or *Yä'mpäri'ka*. This division was formerly known as *Wĭ'dyu*, "awl," but for a reason similar to that just

mentioned the name was changed to *Ditsä'kăna,* "sewers," which conveys the same idea, an awl being the substitute for a needle. They are equally well known as *Yäpä,* the Comanche name of the root of the *Carum gairdneri,* known to the Shoshoni and Bannock as *yampa,* or sometimes as *Yämpä-ri'ka,* a dialectic form signifying "yampa eaters." The whole Comanche tribe is known to the Shoshoni under the name of *Yä'mpaini* or *Yämpai-ri'kani,* "yampa people" or "yampa eaters." The Yäpä are sometimes known also as *Etsitü'biwat,* "northerners," or "people of the cold country," from having usually ranged along the northern frontier of the tribal territory; a fact which may account for the Shoshoni having designated the whole tribe by their name.

3. *Kewa'tsăna.* "No ribs;" extinct.

4. *Kotsa'i.* Extinct.

5. *Ko'tso-tĕ'ka.* "Buffalo eaters," from *ko'tso,* buffalo, and *tĕ'ka,* the root of the verb "to eat."

6. *Kwa'hări* or *Kwa'hădi.* "Antelopes." This division was one of the most important of the tribe, and was so called because its members frequented the prairie country and the staked plains, while the Pe'nätĕka and others ranged farther east on the edge of the timber region. They were the last to come in after the surrender in 1874. The Kwa'hări, Ditsä'kana, and Detsăna'yuka were sometimes designated together by the whites as northern Comanche as distinguished from the Pe'nätĕka, who were known as eastern or southern Comanche.

7. *Motsai'.* Perhaps from *pä-motsan,* "a loop in a stream." These and the Tĕna'wa were practically exterminated in a battle with the Mexicans about 1845.

8. *Pä'gatsú.* "Head of the stream" (*pä,* a stream); extinct.

9. *Pe'nätĕka,* or *Penä'nde.* "Honey eaters." These and the Kwa'hări were the two most important divisions in the tribe. They lived on the edge of the timber country in eastern Texas, and hence were frequently known to the whites as eastern or southern Comanche. They had but a loose alliance with their western kinsmen, and sometimes joined the Texans against them. Other Comanche names for them are *Te'yuwĭt,* "hospitable;" *Tĕ''kăpwai* "no meat," and *Ku'baratpat,* "steep climbers."

10. *Po'hoi.* "Wild-sage people," i. e., Shoshoni. This is not properly the name of a Comanche division, but of some immigrant Shoshoni from the north incorporated with the Comanche.

11. *Täni'ma.* "Liver eaters," from *nĭm* or *nüm,* liver. This band is extinct, only one old man being known to survive.

12. *Tĕna'wa* or *Te'nähwĭt.* From *tĕ'näw',* "down stream." Extinct. See *Motsai'* above.

13. *Wa-ai'h.* "Maggot." Extinct.

The Comanche were nomad buffalo hunters, constantly on the move, cultivating nothing from the ground, and living in skin tipis. Excepting that they are now confined to a reservation and forced to depend on government rations, they are but little changed from their original condition. They are still for the most part living in tipis of canvas, and are dressed in buckskin. They were long noted as the finest horsemen of the plains, and bore a reputation for dash and courage. They have a high sense of honor, and hold themselves superior to the other tribes with which they are associated. In person they are well built and rather corpulent. Their language is the trade language of the region, and is more or less understood by all the neighboring tribes. It is sonorous and flowing, its chief characteristic being a rolling *r*. It has no *l*. The language has several dialects, and is practically the same as that of the Shoshoni in the north. Their present head chief is Quanah Parker, an able man, whose mother was an American captive. His name, *Kwäna* or *Kwaiʻna*, signifies a sweet smell.

Having taken but little part in the Ghost dance, the Comanche have but few songs in their own language, but these are particularly pleasing for their martial ring or soothing softness. They call the dance *Aʻp-Anĕʻkaʻra*, "the father's dance" (from *aʻpă*, father; *nĕʻkaʻra*, a dance), or by another name which signifies the "dance with joined hands."

SONGS OF THE COMANCHE

1. HEYOʻHÄNÄ HÄEʻYO

He'e'yo'!
Heyo'hänä' Häe'yo!
Heyo'hänä' Häe'yo!
Te'äyä' torä'bi ai''-gi'na—He'e'yo'!
Te'äyä' torä'bi ai''-gi'na—He'e'yo'!
Te'äyä' toa'hä tä'bi wo'n'gin—Ähi'ni'yo'!
Te'äyä' toa'hä tä'bi wo'n'gin—Ähi'ni'yo'!

Translation

He'e'yo'!
Heyo'hänä' Häe'yo!
Heyo'hänä' Häe'yo!
The sun's beams are running out—*He'e'yo'!*
The sun's beams are running out—*He'e'yo'!*
The sun's yellow rays are running out—*Ähi'ni'yo'!*
The sun's yellow rays are running out—*Ähi'ni'yo'!*

This song was probably sung at daylight, when the first rays of the sun shone in the east, after the dancers had been dancing all night. The introductory part is a suggestion from the songs of the mescal rite, to which the Comanche are so much attached. Although the words convey but little meaning, the tune is unique and one of the best of all the ghost songs on account of its sprightly measure.

Te'äyä refers to the sun's rays or beams; *torä'bi*, a possessive form of *tä'bi*, sun; (*mú'ä*, moon); *toa'hä*, from *a'häp*, yellow; *ai'ʳ-gi'na* and *wo'n'gin* or *wa'n'gin*, running out, streaming out.

2. YA'HI'YÛ'NIVA'HU

Ya'hi'yû'niva'hu
Hi'yû'niva'hi'yû'niva'hu
Ya'hi'yû'niva'hi'na'he'ne'na'
Hi'ya'hi'nahi'ni'na'
Hi'yû'niva'hu
Hi'yû'niva'hi'yû'niva'hu
Ya'hi'yû'niva'hi'ya'he'ne'na'.

This song has no meaning, but is of the lullaby order, with a sweet, soothing effect.

3. YANI'TSINI'HAWA'NA

Yani'tsini'hawa'na!
Yani'tsini'hawa'na!
Hi'niswa'vita'ki'nĭ,
Hi'niswa'vita'ki'nĭ.

Translation

Yani'tsini'hawa'na!
Yani'tsini'hawa'na!
We shall live again,
We shall live again.

The term *hi'niswa'vita'ki'nĭ* signifies "we are coming to life again," or "we shall live again;" from *nüswa'vitaki'nĭ*, "I am beginning to be alive again."

4. NI'NINI'TUWI'NA

Ni'nini'tuwi'na hu'hu
Ni'nini'tuwi'na hu'hu
Wäta'tsina'na hu'hu
Wäta'tsina'na hu'hu
Ni'hima'tsi asi'si
Ni'hima'tsi asi'si.

This is the Arapaho closing song (Arapaho song 52), as adopted by the Comanche, to whom, of course, it has no real meaning. It is given here as an example of the change which comes to an Indian song when adopted by an alien tribe.

THE PAIUTE, WASHO, AND PIT RIVER TRIBES

PAIUTE TRIBAL SYNONYMY

Hogăpä'goni—Shoshoni name, "rush arrow people" (*hogăp*, a small water reed; *pägă*, "arrow").

Nüma—proper tribal name, signifying "people" or "Indians;" the same name is also used for themselves by the Shoshoni and Comanche.

Pai-yu'chimŭ—Hopi name.

Pai-yu'tsĭ—Navaho name.

Palŭ—Washo name.

Paiute or *Piute*—popular name, variously rendered "true (*pai*) Ute" or "water (*pä*) Ute"—pronounced among themselves *Paiuti*.

NOTE.—The northern bands of the Paiute are frequently included with Shoshoni and others under the name of Snakes, while the others are often included with various Californian tribes under the collective name of Diggers

SKETCH OF THE PAIUTE

CHARACTERISTICS

The Paiute belong to the great Shoshonean stock and occupy most of Nevada, together with adjacent portions of southwestern Utah, northwestern Arizona, and northwestern and southeastern California. The Pahvant and Gosiute on their eastern border are frequently, but improperly, classed as Paiute, while the Chemehuevi, associated with the Walapai in Arizona, are but a southern offshoot of the Paiute and speak the same language. With regard to the Indians of Walker River and Pyramid Lake reservations, who constitute the main body of those commonly known as Paiute, Powell claims that they are not Paiute at all, but another tribe which he calls Paviotso. He says: "The names by which the tribes are known to white men and the department give no clue to the relationship of the Indians. For example, the Indians in the vicinity of the reservation on the Muddy and the Indians on the Walker River and Pyramid Lake reservations are called Pai or Pah Utes, but the Indians know only those on the Muddy by that name, while those on the other two reservations are known as Paviotsoes, and speak a very different language, but closely allied to, if not identical with, that of the Bannocks." (*Comr.*, 45.) The Ghost dance originated among these Indians in the neighborhood of Walker river, from whom the songs here given were obtained, and for convenience of reference we shall speak of them under their popular title of Paiute, without asserting its correctness.

The different small bands have little political coherence and there is no recognized head chief. The most influential chiefs among them in modern times have been Winnemucca, who died a few years ago, and Natchez. Wovoka's leadership is spiritual, not political. The Indians of Walker river and Pyramid lake claim the Bannock as their cousins, and say that they speak the same language. As a rule they have been peaceable and friendly toward the whites, although in the early sixties they several times came into collision with miners and emigrants, hostility being frequently provoked by the whites themselves. The

FIG. 64.—Paiute wikiup

northern Paiute are more warlike than those of the south, and a considerable number of them took part with the Bannock in the war of 1878. Owing to the fact that the great majority of the Paiute are not on reservations, many of them being attached to the ranches of white men, it is impossible to get any correct statement of their population, but they may be safely estimated at from 7,000 to 8,000 and are thought to be increasing. In 1893 those on reservations, all in Nevada, were reported to number, at Walker River, 563; at Pyramid Lake, 494; at Duck Valley (Western Shoshone agency, in connection with the Shoshoni), 209. Nevada Indians off reservation were estimated to number 6,815, nearly all of whom were Paiute.

As a people the Paiute are peaceable, moral, and industrious, and are highly commended for their good qualities by those who have had the best opportunities for judging. While apparently not as bright in intellect as the prairie tribes, they appear to possess more solidity of character. By their willingness and efficiency as workers, they have made themselves necessary to the white farmers and have been enabled to supply themselves with good clothing and many of the comforts of life, while on the other hand they have steadily resisted the vices of civilization, so that they are spoken of by one agent as presenting the "singular anomaly" of improvement by contact with the whites. Another authority says: "To these habits and excellence of character may be attributed the fact that they are annually increasing in numbers, and that they are strong, healthy, active people. Many of them are employed as laborers on the farms of white men in all seasons, but they are especially serviceable during the time of harvesting and haymaking." (*Comr., 46.*) They would be the last Indians in the world to preach a crusade of extermination against the whites, such as the messiah religion has been represented to be. Aside from their earnings among the whites, they derive their subsistence from the fish of the lakes, jack rabbits and small game of the sage plains and mountains, and from piñon nuts and other seeds which they grind into flour for bread. Their ordinary dwelling is the wikiup or small rounded hut of tulé rushes over a framework of poles, with the ground for a floor and the fire in the center and almost entirely open at the top. Strangely enough, although appreciating the advantages of civilization so far as relates to good clothing and such food as they can buy at the stores, they manifest no desire to live in permanent houses or to procure the furniture of civilization, and their wikiups are almost bare of everything excepting a few wicker or grass baskets of their own weaving.

The Paiute ghost songs have a monotonous, halting movement that renders them displeasing to the ear of a white man, and are inferior in expression to those of the Arapaho and the Sioux. A number of words consisting only of unmeaning syllables are inserted merely to fill in the meter. Like the cognate Shoshoni and Comanche, the language has a strong rolling *r*.

GENESIS MYTH

At first the world was all water, and remained so a long time. Then the water began to go down and at last Kura'ngwa (Mount Grant) emerged from the water, near the southwest end of Walker lake. There was fire on its top (it may have been a volcano), and when the wind blew hard the water dashed over the fire and would have extinguished it, but that the sage-hen (*hutsi—Centrocercus urophasianus*) nestled down over it and fanned away the water with her wings. The heat scorched the feathers on the breast of the sage-hen and they remain black to this day. Afterward the Paiute got their first fire from the mountain through the help of the rabbit, who is a great wonder-worker, "same as a god." As the water subsided other mountains appeared, until at last the earth was left as it is now.

Then the great ancestor of the Paiute, whom they call *Nümi'naă'*, "Our Father," came from the south in the direction of Mount Grant, upon which his footprints can still be seen, and journeyed across to the mountains east of Carson sink and made his home there. A woman, *Ibidsii*, "Our Mother," followed him from the same direction, and they met and she became his wife. They dressed themselves in skins, and lived on the meat of deer and mountain sheep, for there was plenty of game in those days. They had children—two boys and two girls. Their father made bows and arrows for the boys, and the mother fashioned sticks for the girls with which to dig roots. When the children grew up, each boy married his sister, but the two families quarreled until their father told them to separate. So one family went to Walker lake and became *Aga'ih-tĭka'ra*, "fish eaters" (the Paiute of Walker lake), while the other family went farther north into Idaho and became *Kotso'-tĭkăra*, "buffalo eaters" (the Bannock), but both are one people and have the same language. After their children had left them, the parents went on to the mountains farther east, and there *Nüminaă'* went up into the sky and his wife followed him.

THE WASHO

Associated with the Paiute are the Washo, or *Wâ'siu*, as they call themselves, a small tribe of about 400 souls, and having no affinity, so far as known, with any other Indians. They occupy the mountain region in the extreme western portion of Nevada, about Washo and Tahoe lakes and the towns of Carson and Virginia City. They formerly extended farther east and south, but have been driven back by the Paiute, who conquered them, reducing them to complete subjection and forbidding them the use of horses, a prohibition which was rigidly enforced until within a few years. Thus broken in spirit, they became mere hangers-on of the white settlements on the opening up of the mines, and are now terribly demoralized. They have been utterly neglected by the government, have never been included in any treaty, and have now no home that they can call their own. They are devoted adherents of the messiah, but usually join in the dance with the nearest camp of Paiute, whose songs they sing, and have probably no Ghost songs in their own language. We quote a gloomy account of their condition in 1866. The description will apply equally well today, excepting that their numbers have diminished:

This is a small tribe of about 500 Indians, living in the extreme western part of the state. They are usually a harmless people, with much less physical and mental development than the Piutes, and more degraded morally. They are indolent improvident, and much addicted to the vices and evil practices common in savage life. They manifest an almost uncontrollable appetite for intoxicating drinks. They are sensual and filthy, and are annually diminishing in numbers from the diseases contracted through their indulgences. A few have learned the English language and will do light work for a reasonable compensation. They spend the winter months about the villages and habitations of white men, from whom they obtain tolerable supplies of food and clothing. The spring, summer, and autumn months are spent in fishing about Washo and Tahoe lakes and the streams which flow through their country. They also gather grass seed and pine nuts, hunt rabbits, hares, and ducks. There is no suitable place for a reservation in the bounds of their territory, and, in view of their rapidly diminishing numbers and the diseases to which they are subjected, none is required. (*Comr., 47.*)

THE PIT RIVER INDIANS

Another group of Indians closely associated with the Paiute on the northwest consists of a number of small tribes, known collectively to the whites as Pit River or Hot Springs Indians, holding the basin of Pit river in northeastern California from Goose lake to the junction with the Sacramento. Among their tribes or bands are the Achoma'wi, Huma'whi, Estakéwach, Hantéwa, Chumâ'wa, Atua'mih or Hamefku'ttelli, Ilma'wi, and Pa'kamalli. (*Powers, Tribes of California.*) They are at present supposed to constitute a distinct linguistic group, but it is probable that better information will show their affinity with some of the neighboring Californian stocks. With the exception of a few at Round Valley reservation, California, none of them are on reservations or have any official recognition by the government. They probably number 1,000 to 1,500 souls. The northern bands have suffered much from Modoc slave raids in former days, and are much inferior in physique and intellect to those lower down the river, who were the terror of northern California thirty years ago, and who are described by recent observers as good workers, intelligent, brave, and warlike. (*A. G. O., 9.*)

SONGS OF THE PAIUTE

1. Nüvä' ka ro'răni'

Nüvä' ka ro'răni'!
Nüvä' ka ro'răni'!
Nüvä' ka ro'răni'!
Nüvä' ka ro'răni'!
Gosi'pa' hävi'gĭnû',
Gosi'pa' hävi'gĭnû'.

Translation

The snow lies there—*ro'răni'!*
The snow lies there—*ro'răni'!*
The snow lies there—*ro'răni'!*
The snow lies there—*ro'răni'!*
The Milky Way lies there,
The Milky Way lies there.

This is one of the favorite songs of the Paiute Ghost dance. The tune has a plaintive but rather pleasing effect, although inferior to the tunes of most of the ghost songs of the prairie tribes. The words as they stand are very simple, but convey a good deal of meaning to the Indian. It must be remembered that the dance is held in the open air at night, with the stars shining down on the wide-extending plain walled in by the giant sierras, fringed at the base with dark pines, and with their peaks white with eternal snows. Under such circumstances this song of the snow lying white upon the mountains, and the Milky Way stretching across the clear sky, brings up to the Paiute the same patriotic home love that comes from lyrics of singing birds and leafy trees and still waters to the people of more favored regions. In the mythology of the Paiute, as of many other tribes, the Milky Way is the road of the dead to the spirit world. *Ro'răni'* serves merely to fill in the meter.

2. Děna' gayo'n

Děna' gayo'n, Dě'na ga'yoni',
Děna' gayo'n, Dě'na ga'yoni',
Bawă' doro'n, Ba'wă do'roni',
Bawă' doro'n, Ba'wă do'roni'.

Translation

A slender antelope, a slender antelope,
A slender antelope, a slender antelope,
He is wallowing upon the ground,
He is wallowing upon the ground,
He is wallowing upon the ground,
He is wallowing upon the ground.

This song evidently refers to a trance vision in which the sleeper saw an antelope rolling in the dust, after the manner of horses, buffalo, and other animals.

3. Do' tĭ'mbi

Do' tĭ'mbi, Do' tĭ'mbi-nä'n,
Do' tĭ'mbi, Do' tĭ'mbi-nä'n,
Tĭ'mbi bai'-yo, Tĭ'mbi ba'i-yo-ä'n,
Tĭ'mbi bai'-yo, Tĭ'mbi ba'i-yo-ä'n.

Translation

The black rock, the black rock,
The black rock, the black rock,
The rock is broken, the rock is broken,
The rock is broken, the rock is broken.

This song may refer to something in Paiute mythology. *Nä'n* and *ä'n* are unmeaning syllables added to fill out the measure.

4. Päsü' wĭ'noghän

Päsü' wĭ'noghän,
Päsü' wĭ'noghän,
Päsü' wĭ'noghän,

Wai'-va wĭ'nogʻhän,
Wai'-va wĭ'noghän,
Wai'-va wĭ'noghän.

Translation

The wind stirs the willows,
The wind stirs the willows,
The wind stirs the willows,
The wind stirs the grasses,
The wind stirs the grasses,
The wind stirs the grasses.

Wai'-va (or *wai* in composition) is the sand grass or wild millet of Nevada (*Oryzopsis membranacea*), the seeds of which are ground by the Paiute and boiled into mush for food.

5. Pägü'nävä'

Pägü'nävä'! Pägü'nävä'!
Tûngwü'kwiji'! Tûngwü'kwiji'!
Wûmbe'doma'! Wûmbe'doma'!

Translation

Fog! Fog!
Lightning! Lightning!
Whirlwind! Whirlwind!

This song is an invocation of the elemental forces. It was composed by an old woman, who left the circle of dancers and stood in the center of the ring while singing it.

6. Wûmbĭ'ndomä'n

Wûmbĭ'ndomä'n, Wûmbĭ'ndomä'n,
Wûmbĭ'ndomä'n, Wûmbĭ'ndomä'n.
Nuvä'rĭ'p noyo'wană', Nuvä'rĭ'p noyo'wană',
Nuvä'rĭ'p noyo'wană', Nuvä'rĭ'p noyo'wană'.

Translation

The whirlwind! The whirlwind!
The whirlwind! The whirlwind!
The snowy earth comes gliding, the snowy earth comes gliding;
The snowy earth comes gliding, the snowy earth comes gliding.

This song may possibly refer to the doctrine of the new earth, here represented as white with snow, advancing swiftly, driven by a whirl-wind. Such an idea occurs several times in the Arapaho songs.

7. Kosi' wûmbi'ndomä'

Kosi' wûmbi'ndomä',
Kosi' wûmbi'ndomä',
Kosi' wûmbi'ndomä'.

Kai'-va wûmbi'ndomä',
Kai'-va wûmbi'ndomä',
Kai'-va wûmbi'ndomä'.

Translation

There is dust from the whirlwind,
There is dust from the whirlwind,
There is dust from the whirlwind.
The whirlwind on the mountain,
The whirlwind on the mountain,
The whirlwind on the mountain.

8. DOMBI'NA SO'WINA'

Dombi'na so'wina',
Dombi'na so'wina',
Dombi'na so'wina'.
Kai'-va so'wina',
Kai'-va so'wina',
Kai'-va so'wina'

Translation

The rocks are ringing,
The rocks are ringing,
The rocks are ringing.
They are ringing in the mountains,
They are ringing in the mountains,
They are ringing in the mountains.

This song was explained to refer to the roaring of a storm among the rocks in the mountains.

9. SÛ'NG-Ä RO'YONJI'

Sû'ng-ä ro'yonji', Sû'ng-a ro'yon,
Sû'ng-ä ro'yonji', Sû'ng-a ro'yon,
Sû'ng-ä ro'yonji', Sû'ng-a ro'yon.
Pu'i do'yonji', Pu'i do'yon,
Pu'i do'yonji', Pu'i do'yon,
Pu'i do'yonji', Pu'i do'yon.

Translation

The cottonwoods are growing tall,
The cottonwoods are growing tall,
The cottonwoods are growing tall.
They are growing tall and verdant.
They are growing tall and verdant,
They are growing tall and verdant.

This song seems to refer to the return to spring. Throughout the arid region of the west the cottonwood skirting the borders of the streams is one of the most conspicuous features of the landscape. See Arapaho song 13.

THE SIOUX

TRIBAL SYNONYMY

Chahrarat — Pawnee name (Grinnell).

Dakota, Nakota, or *Lakota* — proper tribal name, according to dialect, "allies, friends;" sometimes also they speak of themselves as *Oceti Sakowin,* the "seven council fires," in allusion to their seven great divisions.

Itahatski — Hidatsa name, "long arrows" (Matthews).

K'odalpä-K'iñago — Kiowa name, "necklace people," perhaps a misconception of neck-cutting people, i. e., beheaders.

Maranshobishgo — Cheyenne name, "cut-throats" (Long). The name is plainly incorrect, as the Cheyenne language has no *r.*

Nadowesi or *Nadowesiu* — "little snakes" or "little enemies," *Nadowe,* "snake" and figuratively "enemy," being the common Algonquian term for all tribes of alien lineage. The Ojibwa and others designated the Iroquois, living east of them, as *Nadowe,* while the Sioux, living to the west, were distinguished as *Nadowesi* or *Nadowesiu,* whence come Nadouessioux and Sioux.

Natnihina or *Natni* — Arapaho name; Hayden gives the form as *Natenehina,* which he renders "cut-throats or beheaders," but it may be derived from *Nadowe,* as explained above.

Niake'tsikûtk — Kichai name.

Pambizimina — Shoshoni name, "beheaders."

Papitsinima — Comanche name, "beheaders," from *papitsi,* signifying to behead, and *nĭma* or *nüma,* people.

Shahañ — Osage, Kansa, Oto, etc, name (Dorsey).

Sioux — popular name, abbreviated from Nadouessioux, the French form of their Ojibwa name.

Tsaba'kosh — Caddo name, "cut-throats."

TRIBAL SIGN

A sweeping pass of the right hand in front of the neck, commonly rendered "cut-throats" or "beheaders," but claimed by the Kiowa to refer to a kind of shell necklace formerly peculiar to the Sioux.

SKETCH OF THE TRIBE

The Sioux constitute the largest tribe in the United States, and are too well known to need an extended description here. Although now thought of chiefly as a prairie tribe, their emergence upon the plains is comparatively recent, and within the historic period their range extended as far eastward as central Wisconsin, from which, and most of Minnesota, they have been driven out by the westward advance of the Ojibwa. There is ground for believing that the true home of the whole Siouan stock is not in the west, or even in the central region, but along the south Atlantic slope. (See the author's *Siouan Tribes of the East.*)

The Sioux language has three well-marked dialects — the eastern or Santee, the middle or Yankton (including the Asiniboin in the north), and the western or Teton. The tribe consists of seven great divisions, each of which again has or had subdivisions. Dorsey enumerates over one hundred in all. Each grand division had its own camping circle, and when two or more such divisions camped together they usually camped in concentric circles. (*Dorsey.*) The seven great divisions are: 1. *Mde-wakaṅ-toṅwaṅ* (Medewacanton), "village of the Spirit lake;" 2. *Waqpekute* (Wahpacoota), "leaf shooters;" 3. *Waqpetoṅwaṅ* (Wahpeton), "leaf village;" 4. *Sisitoṅwaṅ* (Sisseton), variously rendered "slimy village" or "swamp village;" 5. *Ihanktoṅwaṅ* (Yankton), "end village;" 6. *Ihanktoṅwaṅna* (Yanktonais), "upper end village;" 7. *Titoṅwaṅ* (Teton), "prairie village."

The first four divisions collectively are known as Isañati or Santee Sioux. The name is supposed to be derived from *isañ*, the dialectic word for "knife." They formerly held Mississippi, Minnesota, and upper Red rivers in Minnesota and were afterward gathered on reservations at Devils lake, North Dakota; Lake Traverse (Sisseton agency) and Flandreau, South Dakota; and Santee agency, Nebraska. Those at Lake Traverse and Flandreau have now taken allotments as citizens.

The Yankton and Yanktonais, together speaking the middle dialect, occupied chiefly the country of James river, east of the Missouri, in North Dakota and South Dakota and extending into Iowa. They are now on Yankton and Crow Creek reservations in South Dakota, and Fort Peck reservation, Montana.

The Teton constitute more than two-thirds of the whole Sioux tribe, and held nearly the whole country southwest of the Missouri from Cannonball river to the South Platte, extending westward beyond the Black hills. They are all now on reservations in South and North Dakota. They are again subdivided into seven principal divisions: 1. *Sichaṅgu*, "burnt thighs" (Brulés), now on Rosebud reservation; 2. *Ogalala*, referring to "scattering" of dust in the face (Clark), now on Pine Ridge reservation, under the celebrated chief Red Cloud (*Maqpe-Luta*); 3. *Hunkpapa*, "those who camp at the end (or opening) of the camping circle" (Clark), on Standing Rock reservation; 4. *Minikaṅzu*, "those who plant by the water," on Cheyenne River reservation; 5. *Itazipko*, "without bows" (Sans Arcs), on Cheyenne River reservation; 6. *Sihasapa*, "black feet" (not to be confounded with the Blackfoot tribe), on Cheyenne River and Standing Rock reservations; 7. *Ohenoñpa*, "two kettles," on Cheyenne River and Rosebud reservations. According to the official report for 1893, the Sioux within the United States number about 23,410, which, with 600 permanently settled in Manitoba, make the whole population about 24,000 souls.

The Sioux, under the name of Nadouessi, are mentioned by the Jesuit missionaries as early as 1632. They made their first treaties with our government in 1815. The most prominent events in their history since that date have been the treaty of Prairie du Chien in 1825, which defined their eastern boundary and stopped the westward advance of the Ojibwa; the Minnesota massacre of 1862, which resulted in the expulsion of the Sioux from Minnesota; the Sioux war of 1876–77, largely consequent on the unauthorized invasion of the Black hills by miners, and the chief incident of which was the defeat and massacre of an entire detachment under General Custer; the treaty by which the great reservation was broken up in 1889, and the outbreak of 1890, with the massacre of Wounded Knee.

By reason of their superior numbers the Sioux have always assumed, if not exercised, the lordship over all the neighboring tribes with the exception of the Ojibwa, who, having acquired firearms before the Sioux, were enabled to drive the latter from the headwaters of the Mississippi, and were steadily pressing them westward when stopped by the intervention of the United States government. The Sioux in

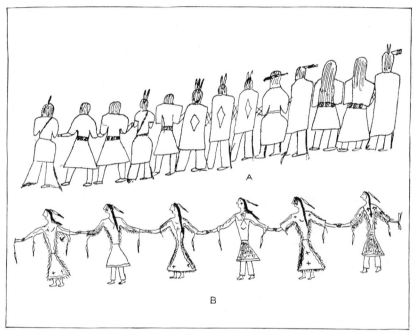

Fig. 65.—Native drawings of Ghost dance—*A*, Comanche; *B*, Sioux

turn drove the Cheyenne, Crow, Kiowa, and others before them and forced them into the mountains or down into the southern prairies. The eastern bands were sedentary and largely agricultural, but the Teton were solely and preeminently wandering buffalo hunters. All dwelt in *tipis*—the word is from the Sioux language—which were of bark in the timber country and of buffalo skins on the plains. In warlike character they are probably second only to the Cheyenne, and have an air of proud superiority rather unusual with Indians. Clark says of them, "In mental, moral, and physical qualities I consider the Sioux a little lower but still nearly equal to the Cheyenne, and the Teton are the superior branch of the family." (*Indian Sign Language*, 345.)

The eastern Sioux are now far advanced toward civilization through the efforts of teachers and missionaries for over a generation, and the same is true in a less degree of the Yankton, while the majority of the Teton are still nearly in their original condition.

I found the Sioux very difficult to approach on the subject of the Ghost dance. This was natural, in view of the trouble that had resulted to them in consequence of it. When I was first at Pine Ridge, the troops still camped there served as a reminder of the conflict, while in the little cemetery at the agency were the fresh graves of the slain soldiers, and only a few miles away was the Wounded Knee battlefield and the trench where the bodies of nearly three hundred of their people had been thrown. To my questions the answer almost invariably was, "The dance was our religion, but the government sent soldiers to kill us on account of it. We will not talk any more about it." Another reason for their unwillingness was the fact that most of the interpreters were from the eastern or Santee portion of the tribe, and looked with contempt on the beliefs and customs of their more primitive western brethren, between whom and themselves there was in consequence but little friendly feeling. On one occasion, while endeavoring to break the ice with one of the initiates of the dance, I told him how willingly the Arapaho had given me information and even invited me to join in the dance. "Then," said he, "don't you find that the religion of the Ghost dance is better than the religion of the churches?" I could not well say yes, and hesitated a moment to frame an answer. He noticed it at once and said very deliberately, "Well, then, if you have not learned that you have not learned anything about it," and refused to continue the conversation.

The Sioux ghost songs are all in the dialect of the Teton, who took the most active interest in the dance, which was hardly known among the bands east of the Missouri. The vocalic character of the language, and the frequent liquid *l* of this dialect, renders these songs peculiarly musical, while for beauty of idea and expression they are second only to those of the Arapaho.

SONGS OF THE SIOUX

1. A′TE HE′YE E′YAYO

Opening song

A′te he′ye e′yayo!
A′te he′ye e′yayo!
A′te he′ye lo,
A′te he′ye lo.
Nitu′ñkañshi′la wa′ñyegala′ke—kta′ e′yayo′!
Nitu′ñkañshi′la wa′ñyegala′ke—kta′ e′yayo′!
A′te he′ye lo,
A′te he′ye lo.
Ni′takuye wañye′găla′ke—kta e′yayo′!

Ni'takuye wañye'gǎla'ke—kta e'yayo'!
A'te he'ye lo,
A'te he'ye lo.

Translation

The father says so—*E'yayo!*
The father says so—*E'yayo!*
The father says so,
The father says so.
You shall see your grandfather—*E'yayo'!*
You shall see your grandfather—*E'yayo'!*
The father says so,
The father says so.
You shall see your kindred—*E'yayo'!*
You shall see your kindred—*E'yayo'!*
The father says so,
The father says so.

This is the opening song of the dance. While singing it, all the dancers stand motionless with hands stretched out toward the west, the country of the messiah and the quarter whence the new spirit world is to come. When it is ended, all cry together, after which they join hands and begin to circle around to the left. "Grandfather," as well as "father," is a reverential term applied to the messiah.

2. MI'CHĬ'NKSHI NAÑPE

Michĭ'nkshi nañpe ma'yuzaye,
Michĭ'nkshi nañpe ma'yuzaye,
A'te he'ye lo,
A'te he'ye lo.
Ini'chaghe-kte,
Ini'chaghe-kte,
A'te he'ye lo,
A'te he'ye lo.

Chǎno'ñpa wa'ñ chi'cha-u'pi,
Chǎno'ñpa wa'ñ chi'cha-u'pi,
A'te he'ye lo',
A'te he'he lo'.
Cha'-yani'pi-kta',
Cha'-yani'pi-kta',
A'te he'ye lo',
A'te he'ye lo'.

Translation

My son, let me grasp your hand,
My son, let me grasp your hand,
Says the father,
Says the father.
You shall live,
You shall live,
Says the father,
Says the father.

I bring you a pipe,
I bring you a pipe,
Says the father,
Says the father.
By means of it you shall live,
By means of it you shall live,
Says the father,
Says the father.

This song refers to the sacred pipe which, according to the Sioux tradition, was brought to them by a mysterious young woman from the spirit world. The story, as outlined by Captain J. M. Lee, is as follows: In the old times the Sioux were always at war, not only with other tribes, but also among themselves. On one occasion two young men were out hunting when they saw a young woman approaching them with folded arms. Seeing that she was not of their own tribe, one proposed to the other that they kill her, but he refused and urged that they wait until they learned what she wanted. The first speaker, however, was about to kill her as she drew near, when she suddenly stooped down and took from around her ankle something resembling an anklet, which she waved about her head. The motion was so rapid that it seemed as though a cloud encircled her for a few moments, when she ceased, and the snake which she had taken from off her ankle glided away through the grass. But the young warrior who had thought to kill her had disappeared, swept from the face of the earth.

Turning now to his companion, she said, "To you I come as a friend and helper. Your people have been killing each other. I bring you a pipe, which is a token of peace," and she held out a pipe as she spoke. "When you smoke it your thoughts will be of peace, and no murderer (i. e., no one who kills a member of his own tribe) must be allowed to smoke it." She returned with him to his village, where the women prepared for her reception a large tipi, to which the chiefs of the tribe came to listen to her instructions. She taught them to be at peace with one another, if they would be happy, and when they listened to her words and accepted her teachings, she gave them the sacred medicine pipe to smoke thenceforth in their councils as a perpetual reminder of the peace covenant of the Lakota. Her mission now ended, she said she must leave them, and although they begged her earnestly to stay with them, she could not tarry longer, but disappeared as suddenly and mysteriously as she had come.

A variant of this legend is given by Colonel Mallery in his paper in the Tenth Annual Report of the Bureau of Ethnology, where it is illustrated by a colored plate from a picture by the Indian story teller. According to this version, the pipe maiden was the mysterious white Buffalo Cow, and brought, with the pipe, a package of four grains of maize of different colors. This corn sprang from the milk which dropped from her udder, and was thus, with the flesh of the buffalo itself, appointed from the beginning to be the food of all the red tribes. The seeming snakes about her waist and ankles were really blades of grass (corn?). She taught the people to call her "grandmother," a reverential title among Indians, and after leading them to her relatives, the buffalo, she faded from their sight as they stood gazing at her.

The pipe holds an important part in the mythology and ritual of almost all our tribes, east and west, and no great ceremony is complete and no treaty was ever ratified without it. It is generally symbolic of peace and truth. As a peace emblem, it was formerly carried by every bearer of a friendly message from one tribe to another and was smoked in solemn ratification of treaties, the act of smoking being itself in the nature of an oath. Among the prairie tribes an individual accused of crime is offered the sacred pipe, and if he accepts it and smokes he is declared innocent, as no Indian would dare to smoke it if guilty. The ordinary ceremonial pipe of the prairie tribes is made of the red stone, known as catlinite, from the famous pipestone quarry in Minnesota in the old country of the Sioux. The peace pipe of the Cherokee was made of a white stone, somewhat resembling talc, from a quarry near Knoxville, Tennessee. It is said to have had seven stem holes, emblematic of the seven clans of the Cherokee, and was smoked by seven counselors at the same time. In every case the tribe has a legend to account for the origin of the pipe. A flat pipe is the tribal "medicine" of the Arapaho, and is still preserved with the northern band in Wyoming. (See Arapaho songs 1 and 2.) Besides the stone pipe, there are also in use pipes of clay or bone, as well as cigarettes, but as a rule no ceremonial character attaches to these. In ceremonial smoking the pipe is passed around the circle of councilors, each of whom takes only a few whiffs and then hands it to his neighbor. Each one as he receives the pipe offers it first to the sun, holding the bowl up toward the sky and saying, "Grandfather, smoke;" then to the earth, the fire, and perhaps also to each of the four cardinal points and to one or another of their mythologic heroes. Among the Kiowa I have seen a man hold up the pipe to the sky, saying, "Smoke, Sinti" (Sinti being their great mythologic trickster), and then in the same way, "Smoke, Jesus."

In the Ghost dance at Rosebud and Pine Ridge, as usually performed, a young woman stood in the center of the circle holding out a pipe toward the messiah in the west, and remained thus throughout the dance. Another young woman usually stood beside her holding out a *bäqati* wheel (see Arapaho song 49) in the same way. This feature of the dance is said to have been introduced by Short Bull.

3. He tuwe′cha he   *Translation*

He tuwe′cha he u echa′ni hwo?	Who think you comes there?
He tuwe′cha he u echa′ni hwo?	Who think you comes there?
Huñku oki′le chaya he u hwo?	Is it someone looking for his mother?
Huñku oki′le chaya he u hwo?	Is it someone looking for his mother?
A′te-ye he′ye lo,	Says the father,
A′te-ye he′ye lo.	Says the father.

In this the singer tells how he was greeted by his former friend upon entering the spirit world, to which he had gone in search of his mother.

4. Wana′yañ ma′niye   *Translation*

Wana′yañ ma′niye,	Now he is walking,
Wana′yañ ma′niye.	Now he is walking.
Tata′ñka wañ ma′niye,	There is a buffalo bull walking,
Tata′ñka wañ ma′niye,	There is a buffalo bull walking,
A′te he′ye lo,	Says the father,
A′te he′ye lo.	Says the father.

The maker of this song, in her vision of the spirit world, evidently saw a herd of buffalo, with a bull walking about near them. The form of the verb shows that a woman is supposed to be talking.

5. Lechel miyo′qañ-kte

Lechel miyo′qañ-kte lo — Yo′yoyo′!
Lechel miyo′qañ-kte lo — Yo′yoyo′!
Taku maka′ a-icha′gha hena mita′wa-ye lo — Yo′yoyo′!
Taku maka′ a-icha′gha hena mita′wa-ye lo — Yo′yoyo′!
A′te he′ye lo — Yo′yoyo′!
A′te he′ye lo — Yo′yoyo′!
E′ya Yo′yoyo′!
E′ya Yo′yoyo′!

Translation

This is to be my work — *Yo′yoyo′!*
This is to be my work — *Yo′yoyo′!*
All that grows upon the earth is mine — *Yo′yoyo′!*
All that grows upon the earth is mine — *Yo′yoyo′!*
Says the father — *Yo′yoyo′!*
Says the father — *Yo′yoyo′!*
E′ya Yo′yoyo′!
E′ya Yo′yoyo′!

6. Michinkshi′yi tewa′qila che

Michinkshi′yi tewa′qila che — Ye′ye′!
Michinkshi′yi tewa′qila che — Ye′ye′!
Oya′te-ye i′nichagha′pi-kta che — Ye′ye′!
Oya′te-ye i′nichagha′pi-kta che — Ye′ye′!
A′teye he′ye lo,
A′teye he′ye lo.
Haye′ye′ E′yayo′yo′!
Haye′ye′ E′yayo′yo′!

Translation

I love my children — *Ye′ye′!*
I love my children — *Ye′ye′!*
You shall grow to be a nation — *Ye′ye′!*
You shall grow to be a nation — *Ye′ye′!*
Says the father, says the father.
Haye′ye′ Eyayo′yo′! Haye′ye′ E′yayo′yo′!

7. Mila kiñ hiyu′michi′chiyana

Mila kiñ hiyu′michi′chiyana,
Mila kiñ hiyu′michi′chiyana.
Wa′waka′bla-kte — Ye′ye′!
Wa′waka′bla-kte — Ye′ye′!
Oñchi he′ye lo — Yo′yo′!

Oñchi he′ye lo — Yo′yo′!
Puye chiñyi wa′sna wakaghiñyiñ-kte,
Puye chiñyi wa′sna wakaghiñyiñ-kte,
Oñchi heye lo — Yo′yo !
Oñchi heye lo — Yo′yo!

Translation

Give me my knife,
Give me my knife,
I shall hang up the meat to dry — *Ye'ye'!*
I shall hang up the meat to dry — *Ye'ye'!*
Says grandmother — *Yo'yo'!*
Says grandmother — *Yo'yo'!*
When it is dry I shall make pemmican,
When it is dry I shall make pemmican,
Says grandmother — *Yo'yo!*
Says grandmother — *Yo'yo!*

This song brings up a vivid picture of the old Indian life. In her trance vision the old grandmother whose experience it relates came upon her friends in the spirit world just as all the women of the camp were engaged in cutting up the meat for drying after a successful buffalo hunt. In her joy she calls for her knife to assist in the work, and says that as soon as the meat is dry she will make some pemmican.

FIG. 66.—Jerking beef

In the old days an Indian camp during the cutting up of the meat after a buffalo hunt was a scene of the most joyous activity, some faint recollection of which still lingers about ration day at the agency. Thirty years ago, when a grand hunt was contemplated, preparations were made for days and weeks ahead. Couriers were sent out to collect the neighboring bands at a common rendezvous, medicine-men began their prayers and ceremonies to attract the herd, the buffalo songs were sung, and finally when all was ready the confederated bands or sometimes the whole tribe—men, women, children, horses, dogs, and travois—moved out into the buffalo grounds. Here the immense camp of hundreds of tipis was set up, more ceremonies were performed, and the mounted warriors rode out in a body to surround and slaughter the herd. The women followed close after them to strip the hides from the fresh carcasses and cut out the choice portion of the meat and tallow and bring it into camp. Here the meat was cut into thin strips and hung upon frames of horizontal poles to dry, while the tallow was stripped off in flakes. In the dry prairie atmosphere one day is usually sufficient to cure the meat, without the aid of salt or smoke. When thus dried it is known as "jerked beef." While the meat is fresh, for the first day or two the camp is a scene of constant feasting, the juicy steaks or the sweet ribs being kept broiling over the coals in one tipi or another until far into the night. It is the harvest home of the prairie tribes. As soon as the meat is dry, the tipis are taken down and packed into the wagons along with the meat, and one family after another starts for home until in a short time the great camp is a thing of the past.

The jerked beef or venison is commonly prepared for eating by being boiled until reasonably tender. In eating, the Indian takes a strip thus cooked, dips one end into a soup made by dissolving some salt in warm water, takes the portion thus salted between his teeth, and saws off enough for a mouthful with a knife held in his other hand. Between mouthfuls he takes bites from a strip of dried tallow placed in the dish with the meat.

For pemmican the jerked beef or other meat is toasted over a fire until crisp and is then pounded into a hash with a stone hammer. In the old times a hole was dug in the ground and a buffalo hide was staked over so as to form a skin dish, into which the meat was thrown to be pounded. The hide was that from the neck of the buffalo, the toughest part of the skin, the same used for shields, and the only part which would stand the wear and tear of the hammers. In the meantime the marrow bones are split up and boiled in water until all the grease and oil come to the top, when it is skimmed off and poured over the pounded beef. As soon as the mixture cools, it is sewed up into skin bags (not the ordinary painted parfléche cases) and laid away until needed. It was sometimes buried or otherwise cached. Pemmican thus prepared will keep indefinitely. When prepared for immediate use, it is usually sweetened with sugar, mesquite pods, or some wild fruit mixed and beaten up with it in the pounding. It is extremely nourishing, and has a very agreeable taste to one accustomed to it. On the march it was to the prairie Indian what parched corn was to the hunter of the timber tribes, and has been found so valuable as a condensed nutriment that it is extensively used by arctic travelers and explorers. A similar preparation is in use upon the pampas of South America and in the desert region of South Africa, while the canned beef of commerce is an adaptation from the Indian idea. The name comes from the Cree language, and indicates something mixed with grease or fat. (*Lacombe.*)

8. LE HE′YAHE′

Le he′yahe′—Ye′ye!
Le he′yahe′—Ye′ye!
Kañghi-ye oya′te-ye cha-ya waoñ we lo,
Kañghi-ye oya′te-ye cha-ya waoñ we lo.

Translation

This one says—*Ye′ye!*
This one says—*Ye′ye!*
I belong indeed to the nation of Crows,
I belong indeed to the nation of Crows.

This song may better be rendered, "I am a Crow nation," i. e., I represent the nation of Crows, the Crow nation probably typifying the spirits of the dead in the other world, as explained in Arapaho song 36. In several of the ghost songs there occur such expressions as "I am a Crow," "the Crow woman is going home," etc. Compare Sioux song 18.

9. NIYA′TE-YE′ HE′UW′E

Niya′te-ye′ he′uw′e, niya′te-ye′ he′uw′e,
Wa′ñbăli gălĕ′shka wa′ñ-yañ nihi′youwe,
Wa′ñbăli gălĕ′shka wa′ñ-yañ nihi′youwe.

Translation

It is your father coming, it is your father coming,
A spotted eagle is coming for you,
A spotted eagle is coming for you.

This song probably refers to a transformation trance vision, such as is frequently referred to in the ghost songs, where the spirit friend suddenly assumes the form of a bird, a moose, or some other animal.

10. MIYO′QAÑ KIÑ WAÑLA′KI

Miyo′qañ kiñ wañla′ki—Ye′yeye′!
Miyo′qañ kiñ wañla′ki—Ye′yeye′!
Hena wa′ñlake,
Hena wa′ñlake,
Ha′eye′ya he′yeye′,
Ha′eye′ya he′yeye′.

Translation

You see what I can do—*Ye′yeye′!*
You see what I can do—*Ye′yeye′!*
You see them, you see them,
Ha′eye′ya he′yeye′! Ha′eye′ya he′yeye′!

In this song the Father is probably represented as calling his children to witness that he has shown them visions of the spirit world and their departed friends.

11. Michǐ'nkshi mita'waye

E'yaye'ye'! E'yaye'ye'!
Michǐ'nkshi mita'waye,
Michǐ'nkshi mita'waye.

Translation

E'yaye'ye'! E'yaye'ye'!
It is my own child,
It is my own child.

The form of the verb indicates that this song was composed by a woman, who had evidently met her dead child in the spirit world.

12. A'te he' u-we

A'te he' u-we, A'te he' u-we,
A'te eya'ya he' u-we' lo,
A'te eya'ya he' u-we' lo,
Ya'nipi-kta' e'ya u'-we lo,
Ya'nipi-kta' e'ya u'-we lo.

Translation

There is the father coming,
There is the father coming.
The father says this as he comes,
The father says this as he comes,
"You shall live," he says as he comes,
"You shall live," he says as he comes.

This is a reiteration of the messiah's promise of eternal life in the new spirit world.

13. Wa'sna wa'tiñ-kta'

Wa'sna wa'tiñ-kta' — E'yeye'yeye'!
Wa'sna wa'tiñ-kta — E'yeye'yeye'!
Le'chiya'-ya eya'pi-lo — E'yeye'yeye'!
Le'chiya'-ya eya'pi-lo — E'yeye'yeye'!
E'ya he'-ye lo, E'ya he'-ye lo,
A'te-ye he'ye lo, A'te-ye he'ye lo.

Translation

I shall eat pemmican — *E'yeye'yeye'!*
I shall eat pemmican — *E'yeye'yeye'!*
They say so, they say so,
The father says so, the father says so.

For the explanation of this song reference, see song number 7.

14. A'te lena ma'qu-we

A'te lena ma'qu-we — Ye'ye'ye'!
A'te lena ma'qu-we — Ye'ye'ye'!
Peta wañ — yañyañ ma'qu-we — Ye'ye'ye'!
Peta wañ — yañyañ ma'qu-we — Ye'ye'ye'!
A'te ma'qu-we — Ye'ye'ye'!
A'te ma'qu-we — Ye'ye'ye'!

Translation

It was the father who gave us these things — *Ye'ye'ye'!*
It was the father who gave us these things — *Ye'ye'ye'!*
It was the father who gave us fire — *Ye'ye'ye'!*
It was the father who gave us fire — *Ye'ye'ye'!*
The father gave it to us — *Ye'ye'ye'!*
The father gave it to us — *Ye'ye'ye'!*

This was frequently used as the opening song of the Sioux Ghost dance. Fire is held in reverence among all Indian tribes as one of the greatest gifts of the Author of Life, and every tribe has a myth telling how it originated and how it was obtained by the people. In most of these myths the fire is represented as being at first in the possession of some giant or malevolent monster, from whom it is finally stolen by a hero, after a series of trials and difficulties worthy of the heroes of the Golden Fleece.

15. Ina' he'kuwo'

Ina' he'kuwo'; ina' he'kuwo'.
Misu'nkala che'yaya oma'ni-ye,
Misu'nkala che'yaya oma'ni-ye.
I'na he'kuwo'; i'na he'kuwo'.

Translation

Mother, come home; mother, come home.
My little brother goes about always crying,
My little brother goes about always crying.
Mother, come home; mother, come home.

This touching song was a favorite among the Sioux. It was composed by a young woman who saw her dead mother in the other world, and on waking out of her trance vision implores the mother to come back to them again, as her little brother is forever crying after her.

16. Wa'na wanasa'pi-kta

Wa'na wanasa'pi-kta,
Wa'na wanasa'pi-kta.
Ŭñchi' ita'zipa michu'-ye,
Ŭñchi' ita'zipa michu'-ye,
A'te he'ye lo, a'te he'ye lo.

Translation

Now they are about to chase the buffalo,
Now they are about to chase the buffalo,
Grandmother, give me back my bow,
Grandmother, give me back my bow,
The father says so, the father says so.

The author of this song, in his trance vision of the spirit world, sees his old-time friends about to start on a buffalo hunt, and calls to his grandmother to give him back his bow, so that he may join them. The form, "give it back to me," is intended to show how far remote is the old life of the Indians, before they used the guns and other things of the white man. The last line has no particular connection with the rest, except as a common refrain of the ghost songs.

17. HE′! KII′ÑYAÑKA A′GALI′-YE

He′! kii′ñyañka a′gali′-ye,
He′! kii′ñyañka a′gali′-ye,
Wañ! le′chiya wanasa′pi-kta′ keya′pi lo,
Wañ! le′chiya wanasa′pi-kta′ keya′pi lo,
Wañhi′nkpe ka′gha-yo!
Wañhi′nkpe ka′gha-yo!
A′te he′ye lo, A′te he′ye lo.

Translation

He! They have come back racing,
He! They have come back racing,
Why, they say there is to be a buffalo hunt over here,
Why, they say there is to be a buffalo hunt over here,
Make arrows! Make arrows!
Says the father, says the father.

This song may be considered supplementary to the last. In the old times, when going on a buffalo hunt, it was customary among the Sioux to send out a small advance party to locate the herd. On finding it, these men at once returned at full gallop to the main body of hunters, but instead of stopping on reaching them they dashed past and then turned and fell in behind. It is to this custom that the first line refers. The author of the song, on waking up in the spirit world, sees the scouting party just dashing in with the news of the presence of the buffalo. Everyone at once prepares to join the hunt and "the father" commands him to make (or get ready) his arrows and go with them.

18. MI′YE WAÑMA′YAÑKA-YO

Mi′ye wañma′yañka-yo!
Mi′ye wañma′yañka-yo!
Ka′ñghi oya′te wañ chañku′ waka′ghe lo,
Ka′ñghi oya′te wañ chañku′ waka′ghe lo,
Yani′pi-kta′-cha, yani′pi-kta′-cha.
Kola he′ye lo, kola he′ye lo.

Translation

Look at me! Look at me!
I make a road for one of the Crow nation (?),
I make a road for one of the Crow nation (?).
You shall live indeed, you shall live indeed.
Our friend says so, our friend says so.

The idea of this song is somewhat similar to that of number 8. It has no reference to the Crow Indians. As has been already explained, the crow is symbolic of the spirit world, and when the "friend"—the father or messiah—declares that he makes a road for one of the Crow nation he means that he has prepared the way for the return of their friends who are gone before.

19. MAKA′ SITO′MANIYAŇ

Maka′ sito′maniyañ ukiye,
Oya′te uki′ye, oya′te uki′ye,
Wa′ñbali oya′te wañ hoshi′hi-ye lo,
Ate heye lo, ate heye lo,
Maka o′wañcha′ya uki′ye.
Pte kiñ ukiye, pte kiñ ukiye,
Kañghi oya′te wañ hoshi′hi-ye lo,
A′te he′ye lo, a′te he′ye lo.

Translation

The whole world is coming,
A nation is coming, a nation is coming,
The Eagle has brought the message to the tribe.
The father says so, the father says so.
Over the whole earth they are coming.
The buffalo are coming, the buffalo are coming,
The Crow has brought the message to the tribe,
The father says so, the father says so.

This fine song summarizes the whole hope of the Ghost dance—the return of the buffalo and the departed dead, the message being brought to the people by the sacred birds, the Eagle and the Crow. The eagle known as *wañ′bali* is the war eagle, from which feathers are procured for war bonnets.

20. LE′NA WA′KAŇ

Le′na wa′kañ waka′gha-che,
A′te he′ye lo, a′te he′ye lo,
O′gäle kiñhañ wakañ waka′gha-che,
A′te he′ye lo, a′te he′ye lo,
Chănoñ′pa kiñ waka′gha-che,
A′te he′ye lo, a′te he′ye lo.

Translation

It is I who make these sacred things,
Says the father, says the father.
It is I who make the sacred shirt,
Says the father, says the father.
It is I who made the pipe,
Says the father, says the father.

This song refers to the sacred pipe (see Sioux song 2 and Arapaho song 2) and the ghost shirt.

21. MIYO′QAŇ KIŇ CHICHU′-CHE

Miyo′qañ kiñ chichu′-che,
A′te he′ye lo′, a′te he′ye lo′,
O′gäle kiñ ni′niye′-kta,
A′te he′ye lo′, a′te he′ye lo′.

Translation

Verily, I have given you my strength,
Says the father, says the father.
The shirt will cause you to live,
Says the father, says the father.

This song also refers to the ghost shirt, which was supposed to make the wearer invulnerable.

22. Michĭ'nkshi tahe'na

Michĭ'nkshi tahe'na ku'piye,
Michĭ'nkshi tahe'na ku'piye,
Mako'che wañ washte aya'găli'pi-kte,
A'te he'ye lo', a'te he'ye lo'.

Translation

My child, come this way,
My child, come this way.
You will take home with you a good country,
Says the father, says the father.

This song may refer to the vision of the new earth, which the messiah showed to the Sioux delegates when they visited him. (See page 41.) The first line means literally "return in this direction," the imperative form used being between a command and an entreaty.

23. Wana wichĕ'shka

Wana wichĕ'shka a'ti-ye,
Wana wichĕ'shka a'ti-ye.
Wihu'ta oho'măni, wihu'ta oho'măni,
Oka'tañna, oka'tañna,
Koyañ wowa'hiñ-kte,
Koyañ wowa'hiñ-kte.

Translation

Now set up the tipi,
Now set up the tipi.
Around the bottom,
Around the bottom,
Drive in the pegs,
Drive in the pegs.
In the meantime I shall cook,
In the meantime I shall cook.

The form of the verb *oka'tañna* shows that it is a woman speaking, even if we did not learn this from the context. To those who know the Indian life it brings up a vivid picture of a prairie band on the march, halting at noon or in the evening. As soon as the halt is called by some convenient stream, the women jump down and release the horses from the wagons (or the travois in the old times), and hobble them to prevent them wandering away. Then, while some of the women set up the tipi poles, draw the canvas over them, and drive in the pegs around the bottom and the wooden pins up the side, other women take axes and buckets and go down to the creek for wood and water. When they return, they find the tipis set up and the blankets spread out upon the grass, and in a few minutes fires are built and the meal is in preparation. The woman who composed the song evidently in her vision accompanied her former friends on such a march.

24. A'TE MI'CHUYE

A'te mi'chuye,
A'te mi'chuye,
Wañhi'nkpe mi'chuye,
Wañhi'nkpe mi'chuye,

A'hiye, a'hiye.
Wa'sna wa'tiñkte,
Wa'sna wa'tiñkte.

Translation

Father, give them to me,
Father, give them to me,
Give me my arrows,
Give me my arrows.

They have come, they have come.
I shall eat pemmican,
I shall eat pemmican.

The maker of this song, while in the spirit world, asks and receives from the Father some of the old-time arrows with which to kill buffalo, so that he may once more feast upon pemmican.

25. HAÑPA WECHA'GHE

Hañpa wecha'ghe,
Hañpa wecha'ghe,
Tewa'qila-la he,
Tewa'qila-la he.
Wa'ñbleni'chala he kaye lo,

Wa'ñbleni'chala he kaye lo,
Toke'cha wa'ñwegalaki'ñ-kte,
Toke'cha wa'ñwegalaki'ñ-kte,
Nihu'ñ koñ he he'ye lo,
Nihu'ñ koñ he he'ye lo.

Translation

I made moccasins for him,
I made moccasins for him,
For I love him,
For I love him.
To take to the orphan,

To take to the orphan.
Soon I shall see my child,
Soon I shall see my child,
Says your mother,
Says your mother.

This song evidently relates the trance vision of a mother who saw her child in the spirit world, and expresses the hope that she may soon be united with him. In accordance with the custom of the Ghost dance, it is probable that she made a pair of moccasins to give him when next they met, and that she carried them in the dance as she sang.

26. WAKA'ÑYAÑ IÑYA'ÑKIÑ-KTE

Waka'ñyañ iñya'nkiñ-kte,
Waka'ñyañ iñya'nkiñ-kte,
Chañgăle'shka wañ luza'hañ iñya'ñkiñ-kte,

Chañgăle'shka wañ luza'hañ iñya'ñkiñ-kte,
Wañwa'yag upo, wañwa'yag upo,
A'te he'ye lo, a'te he'ye lo.

Translation

The holy (hoop) shall run,	Come and see it,
The holy (hoop) shall run,	Come and see it,
The swift hoop shall run,	Says the father,
The swift hoop shall run.	Says the father.

This song refers to the game wheel and sticks (*bä'qati*, Arapaho) already described in the Arapaho songs. It is said that the medicine-man of Big Foot's band carried such a hoop with him in their flight from the north, and displayed it in every dance held by the band until the fatal day of Wounded Knee. A similar hoop was carried and hung upon the center tree at the dance at No Water's camp near Pine Ridge. To the Indian it symbolizes the revival of the old-time games.

THE KIOWA AND KIOWA APACHE

KIOWA TRIBAL SYNONYMY

Be'shĭltchă—Kiowa Apache name, meaning unknown.
Caygua—Spanish form, from their proper name, *Kaijwu.*
Gahe'wa—Wichita and Kichai name; another form of Kiowa.
Kă'igwŭ—"real or principal people," proper tribal name.
Kai-wă—Comanche and Caddo name; from their proper name, *Kaigwu.*
Kiowa—popular name, a corruption of the name used by themselves.
Kwŭ'da—"going out;" old name formerly used by the Kiowa for themselves.
Nŭ'chihinĕ'na—"river men," Arapaho name; so called because they formerly lived on upper Arkansas river, from which the Arapaho claim to have driven them.
Tepda—"coming out," "issuing;" another old name formerly used by the Kiowa for themselves.
Witapä'hat or *Witapä'tu*—Cheyenne name, from their Sioux name, *Witapähä'tu.*
Wĭ'tapähä'tu—"island butte people" (?), Sioux name.

KIOWA TRIBAL SIGN

The Kiowa tribal sign indicates "hair cut off at right ear," in allusion to a former custom of the warriors. From a careless habit in making this sign it has sometimes been wrongly interpreted to mean "foolish," or "rattle-brain."

SKETCH OF THE KIOWA

So far as present knowledge goes, the Kiowa constitute a distinct linguistic stock; but it is probable that more material will enable us to prove their connection with some tribes farther north, from which direction they came. They are noticed in the Spanish records as early at least as 1732. Their oldest tradition, which agrees with the concurrent testimony of the Shoshoni and Arapaho, locates them about the junction of Jefferson, Madison, and Gallatin forks, at the extreme head of Missouri river, in the neighborhood of the present Virginia

City, Montana. They afterward moved down from the mountains and formed an alliance with the Crow, with whom they have since continued on friendly terms. From here they drifted southward along the base of the mountains, driven by the Cheyenne and Arapaho. About 1840 they made peace with the latter tribes, with which they have since commonly acted in concert. The Sioux claim to have driven them out of the Black hills, and in 1805 they were reported as living upon the North Platte. According to the Kiowa account, when they first reached Arkansas river they found their passage opposed by the Comanche, who claimed all the country to the south. A war followed, but peace was finally concluded, when the Kiowa crossed over to the south side of the Arkansas and formed a confederation with the Comanche, which continues to the present day. In connection with the Comanche they carried on a constant war upon the frontier settlements of Mexico and Texas, extending their incursions as far south at least as Durango. Among all the prairie tribes they were noted as the most predatory and bloodthirsty, and have probably killed more white men in proportion to their numbers than any of the others. They made their first treaty with the government in 1837, and were put upon their present reservation jointly with the Comanche and Apache in 1868. Their last outbreak was in 1874–75, in connection with the Comanche, Apache, and Cheyenne. While probably never very numerous, they have been greatly reduced by war and disease. Their last terrible blow came in the spring of 1892, when the measles destroyed over 300 of the three confederated tribes. Their present chief is *Gu'i-pä'go*, Lone Wolf. They occupy the same reservation with the Comanche and Apache, between Washita and Red rivers, in southwestern Oklahoma, and numbered 1,017 in 1893.

The Kiowa do not have the gentile system, and there is no restriction as to intermarriage among the divisions. They have six tribal divisions, including the Apache associated with them, who form a component part of the Kiowa camping circle. A seventh division, the *K uăto*, is now extinct. The tribal divisions in the order of the camping circle are:

1. *K a't'a*—"biters," i. e., Arikara or Ree; so called, not because of Arikara origin, but because they were more intimate with that tribe in trade and otherwise when the Kiowa lived in the north.

2. *Ko' gu'i*—"elks."

3. *Kâ'igwŭ*—"Kiowa proper." This is the oldest division, to which belongs the keeping of the medicine tipi, in which is the grand medicine of the tribe.

4. *Kiñep*—"big shields." This is the largest division in the tribe and of corresponding importance.

5. *Semät*—"thieves," the Apache.

6. *Koñtä'lyui*—"black boys." Sometimes also called *Si'ndiyu'i*, "Sindi's children." Said to be of darker color than the rest of the

tribe, which, if true, might indicate a foreign origin. Sindi is the great mythic hero of the Kiowa.

7. *K̇'u'ato*—"pulling up from the ground or a hole." An extinct division, speaking a slightly different dialect, and exterminated by the Sioux in one battle about the year 1780. On this occasion, according to tradition, the Kiowa were attacked by an overwhelming force of Sioux and prepared to retreat, but the chief of the K̇ uato exhorted his people not to run, "because, if they did, their relatives in the other

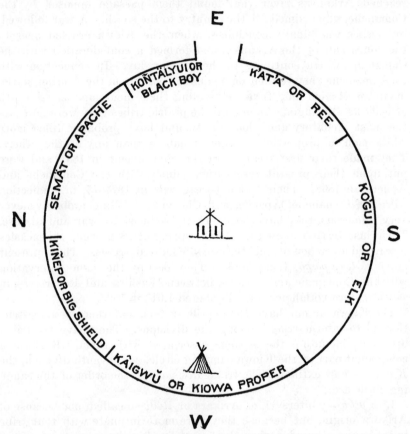

Fig. 67.—Kiowa camping circle

world would not receive them." So they stood their ground and were killed, while the others escaped. Their place in the tribal camp circle is not known.

In the annual sun dance and in other great tribal gatherings the several divisions camped in the order shown in Figure 67.

Although brave and warlike, the Kiowa are considered inferior in most respects to the Comanche. In person they are dark and heavily built, forming a marked contrast to the more slender and brighter-complexioned prairie tribes farther north. Their language is full of

choking and nasal sounds, and is not well adapted to rhythmic composition, for which reason they frequently used the Arapaho songs in the
Ghost dance, without any clear idea of the meaning or correct pronun-
ciation, although they have quite a number of songs of their own.

THE KIOWA APACHE

A small tribe of Athapascan stock, calling themselves *Na'-isha* or
Na-di'isha-de'na, and popularly known as Apache or Kiowa Apache,
has been associated with the Kiowa as far back as the traditions of
either tribe go. While retaining their distinct language, they nearly
all speak and understand Kiowa and form a component part of the
Kiowa camping circle. In dress and general habits of life they are in
no way distinguishable. They have come from the north with the
Kiowa, and are mentioned under the name of Cataka as living in the
Black-hills country in 1805. La Salle speaks of them under the name
of Gattacka as early as 1681. There is no reason to suppose that they
ever formed a part of the Apache proper of Arizona and New Mexico,
but are probably, like the Sarsi, a distinct Athapascan people who have
always lived east of the mountains, and who, having been obliged by
weakness of numbers to unite themselves with a stronger tribe, have
since shared their migratory fortunes southward along the plains. The
Na-isha are called *Ga'taqka* by the Pawnee and sometimes by the
Wichita; *Cataka* by Lewis and Clark, in 1805; *Kataka* in their first
treaty with the government, made jointly with the Kiowa in 1837;
Ta'shĭn by the Comanche; *Gĭnä's* by the Wichita; *Ka'ntsi*, "deceivers,"
by the Caddo; *Kĭri'năhĭs* by the Kichais; *Tha'kahinĕ'na*, "knife-whet-
ting men (?)" by the Arapaho, and *Mûtsiănätä'niuw'*, "whetstone
people," by the Cheyenne. They have several names among the Kiowa,
but are commonly known by them as *Semät*, "thieves." Other Kiowa
names for them are *Tagu'i*, of unknown meaning, and *Sa'dälso'mte-k'iñago*, "weasel people." The tribal sign for them, as for the Apache,
Lipan, and Navaho, conveys the idea of "knife whetters." In 1891 they
numbered 325. In 1893 they had been reduced, chiefly by an epidemic
of measles, to 224.

More extended information in regard to the Kiowa and Kiowa
Apache will be given in the author's memoir, "Calendar History of the
Kiowa Indians," now in preparation for the Bureau of Ethnology.

SONGS OF THE KIOWA

1. DA'TA-I SO'DA'TE

Da'ta i so'da'te,
Da'ta-i so'da'te.
Do'm ezä'nteda'te,
Do'm ezä'nteda'te.
De'ĭmhä'date,
De'ĭmhä'date.
Be'a'ma'nhäyi',
Be'a'ma'nhäyi'.

Translation

The father will descend,
The father will descend.
The earth will tremble,
The earth will tremble.
Everybody will arise,
Everybody will arise.
Stretch out your hands,
Stretch out your hands.

This is a summary of the Ghost dance doctrine, closing with an invocation to all present to stretch out their hands toward the west and pray to the Father to hasten his coming.

2. DA'K'I'ÑAGO (ÍM) ZÄ'NTEÄHE'DAL

Da'k·i'ñago (ĭm) zä'nteähe'dal,
Da'k·i'ñago (ĭm) zä'nteähe'dal,
De'dom ezä'nteähe'dal,
De'dom ezä'nteähe'dal.
De'ĭmgo (ä-)dä'tode'yo',
De'ĭmgo (ä-)dä'tode'yo'.
De'beko'datsä',
De'beko'datsä'.

Translation

The spirit army is approaching,
The spirit army is approaching,
The whole world is moving onward,
The whole world is moving onward.
See! Everybody is standing watching,
See! Everybody is standing watching.
Let us all pray,
Let us all pray.

In this song the verb *ĭmzä'nteähe'dal* implies that the spirits are coming on like an army or like a great herd of animals. The termination *he'dal* implies that it is a matter of report or common belief and not of personal knowledge.

3. GU'ATO ÄDÂ'GA

Gu'ato ädâ'ga nyä'ongu'm,
Gu'ato ädâ'ga nyä'ongu'm,
Go'mtäyä' ätso'dalsâ'dal,
Go'mtäyä' ätso'dalsâ'dal.
Ä'nyä'gâlo'nte,
Ä'nyä'gâlo'nte.
Tä'lyi ĭmhä'go,
Tä'lyi ĭmhä'go.

Translation

I scream because I am a bird,
I scream because I am a bird,
I bellow like a buffalo,
I bellow like a buffalo.
The boy will rise up,
The boy will rise up.

This song was composed by Pa-guadal, "Red Buffalo," at a Ghost dance held on Walnut creek in the summer of 1893, under the direction of the prophet Pa-iñgya (see page 164), for the purpose of resurrecting Red Buffalo's son, who had recently died. Pa-iñgya assured the people that if they held the dance as he directed, the dead boy would rise up alive from the ground before their eyes. In the dance Red Buffalo became "crazy" and composed this song. In his trance he evidently imagined himself a bird. His father was one of the "buffalo doctors," or surgeons of the tribe, who are under the special protection of the buffalo and whose war cry is an imitation of the bellowing of a buffalo bull. Red Buffalo claims to have inherited his father's knowledge; hence his assertion that he bellows like a bull. The boy was not resurrected.

4. Da'ta-i nyä'hoănga'mo

Ä'häyä' Ehä'eho'! Ä'häyä' Ehä'eho'!
E'häyä' Ehä'eho'! E'häyä' Ehä'eho'!
Da'ta-i nyä'hoănga'mo,
Da'ta-i nyä'hoănga'mo.
Äde'tepo'nbä,
Äde'tepo'nbä,
Ä'guänpo'nbä,
Ä'guänpo'nbä.

Translation

Ä'häyä' Ehä'eho'! Ä'häyä' Ehä'eho'!
E'häyä' Ehä'eho! E'häyä' Ehä'eho'!
The father shows me the road,
The father shows me the road.
I went to see my friends,
I went to see my friends,
I went to see the dances,
I went to see the dances.

The composer of this song went, in her trance, to the other world, led by the Father, who pointed out the way, and saw there her former friends and joined them in the dance.

5. Dak'iñ'a bate'yä

Dak'iñ'a bate'yä,
Dak'iñ'a bate'yä.
Guăto ton nyäämo,

Guăto ton nyää′mo.
Ähiñ′äih nyää′mo,
Ähiñ′äih nyää′mo.

Translation

The spirit (God) is approaching,
The spirit (God) is approaching.
He is going to give me a bird tail,
He is going to give me a bird tail.
He will give it to me in the tops of the cottonwoods,
He will give it to me in the tops of the cottonwoods.

The "bird tail" refers to the feathers (*wakuna*, Arapaho) worn on the heads of the dancers (Fig. 52). The song is peculiar in implying that the recipient must climb up into the tree tops to obtain it.

6. Na′da′g äka′na

Heyĕ′heyĕ′heyĕ′heye′ Äho′ho′!
Heyĕ′heyĕ′heyĕ′heye′ Äho′ho′!
Na′da′g äka′na,
Na′da′g äka′na,
De′gyägo′mga da′tsä′to,
De′gyägo′mga da′tsä′to.
Äo′ñyo, Äo′ñyo.

Translation

Heyĕ′heyĕ′heyĕ′heye′ Äho′ho′!
Heyĕ′heyĕ′heyĕ′heye′ Äho′ho′!
Because I am poor,
Because I am poor,
I pray for every living creature,
I pray for every living creature.
Äo′ñyo! Äo′ñyo!

Although the words of this song do not contain much meaning, the tune is one of the best among the Kiowa ghost songs. The introductory line gives somewhat the effect of Comanche song 1. The last line is supposed to be a prayer or entreaty to the messiah, and is an imitation of the Kiowa funeral wail.

7. Ze′bät-gâ′ga igu′änpa′-ima′

Ze′bät-gâ′ga igu′änpa′-ima′,
Ze′bät-gâ′ga igu′änpa′-ima′.
Bälä′gâ na′ta′dălgo′ma,
Bälä′gâ na′ta′dălgo′ma.
Tä′lyiă be′′pe′te,
Tä′lyiă be′′pe′te.

Translation

He makes me dance with arrows,
He makes me dance with arrows.
He calls the bow my father,

He calls the bow my father.
Grandmother, persevere,
Grandmother, persevere.

This song embodies the Ghost-dance idea of a return to the old Indian things. The expression, "He calls the bow my father," is worthy of an oriental poet. The last line is a general exhortation to the women to persevere or "push hard" in the dance.

8. BE′TA! TO′NGYÄ-GU′ADĂL

Be′ta! To′ngyä-gu′adăl äto′tl-e′dal,
Be′ta! To′ngyä-gu′adăl äto′tl-e′dal.
Bä′ate′ñyi, Bä′ate′ñyi.
Da′te gyäko′m ä′omhe′dăl,
Da′te gyäko′m ä′omhe′dăl.

Translation

Now I understand! Red Tail has been sent,
Now I understand! Red Tail has been sent.
We cry and hold fast to him,
We cry and hold fast to him.
He was made to live a long time,
He was made to live a long time.

This song was made by Mary Zoñtom, a woman who speaks very fair English, and refers to a young man named *To′ngyä-gu′adal*, Red Tail, who used to go into frequent trances. The expression "he was sent" implies that he is a recognized messenger to the spirit world, while "we hold fast to him" is equivalent to "we have faith in him."

9. DA′TA′-I ÄNKA′ÑGO′NA

Da′ta′-i änka′ñgo′na,
Da′ta′-i änka′ñgo′na.
Da′mânhä′go, Da′mânhä′go.
Ka′ante damânhä′go,
Ka′ante damânhä′go.

Translation

My father has much pity for us,
My father has much pity for us.
I hold out my hands toward him and cry,
I hold out my hands toward him and cry.
In my poverty I hold out my hands toward him and cry,
In my poverty I hold out my hands toward him and cry.

10. DA′TA-I IÑKA′ÑTÄHE′DAL

Ähä′yä Ehä′eho′,
Ähä′yä Ehä′eho′.
Da′ta-i iñka′ñtähe′dal.

A'da'ta'-i dä'sa,
Ä'da'ta'-i mâ'nsâ'dal,
Ä'da'ta'-i to'ñsâ'dal,
Ä'da'ta'-i o'mda.

Translation

Ähä'yä Ehä'eho',
Ähä'yä Ehä'eho'.
My father has had pity on me.
I have eyes like my father's,
I have hands like my father's,
I have legs like my father's,
I have a form like my father's,

"So God created man in his own image."

11. Dak'iñ'ago äho'ähe'dal

Dak'iñ'ago äho'ähe'dal,
Dak'iñ'ago äho'ähe'dal.
Gâ'dal-gâ'ga äho'ähe'dal,
Gâ'dal-gâ'ga äho'ähe'dal.
Do'm-gâ'ga äho'ähe'dal,
Do'm-gâ'ga äho'ähe'dal.

Translation

The spirit host is advancing, they say,
The spirit host is advancing, they say.
They are coming with the buffalo, they say,
They are coming with the buffalo, they say.
They are coming with the (new) earth, they say,
They are coming with the (new) earth, they say.

12. E'hyu'ñi degi'äta

E'hyuñ'i degi'äta,
E'hyuñ'i degi'äta.
Tsä'hop ä'ä'he'dal,
Tsä'hop ä'ä'he'dal.
Na de'gu'änta, de'gu'änta; Na de'gu'änta, de'gu'änta;
Gâ'dal-guñ t'añ'gya deo'ta,
Gâ'dal-guñ t'añ'gya deo'ta.
Go' dehi'äta, dehi'äta,
Go' dehi'äta, dehi'äta.

Translation

I am mashing the berries,
I am mashing the berries.
They say travelers are coming on the march,
They say travelers are coming on the march.
I stir (the berries) around, I stir them around;
I take them up with a spoon of buffalo horn,
I take them up with a spoon of buffalo horn,
And I carry them, I carry them (to the strangers),
And I carry them, I carry them (to the strangers).

This song gives a pretty picture of the old Indian home life and hospitality. In her dream the woman who composed it imagines herself cooking fruit, when the word comes that travelers are approaching, the verb implying that they are on the march with their children, dogs, and household property. She stirs the berries around a few times more, lifts them out with a spoon of buffalo horn, and goes to offer them to the strangers. The translation is an exact paraphrase of the rhythmic repetition of the original. The berry called *ehyuñ'i*, "principal or best fruit," is not found in the present country of the Kiowa, but is remembered among the pleasant things of their old home in the north. It is described as a species of cherry.

13. Go′mgyä-da′ga

Go′mgyä-da′ga,
Go′mgyä-da′ga,
Do′ nyä′zä′ngo,
Do′ nyä′zä′ngo,
Go′ da′gya iñhä′po,
Go′ da′gya iñhä′po.

Translation

That wind, that wind
Shakes my tipi, shakes my tipi,
And sings a song for me,
And sings a song for me.

To the familiar this little song brings up pleasant memories of the prairie camp when the wind is whistling through the tipi poles and blowing the flaps about, while inside the fire burns bright and the song and the game go round.

14. Dak′iñ′a daka′ñtähe′dal

Dak′iñ′a daka′ñtähe′dal,
Dak′iñ′a daka′ñtähe′dal.
Tsi′sûs-ä daka′ñtähe′dal,
Tsi′sûs-ä daka′ñtähe′dal.
Da′gya nyäpa′de,
Da′gya nyäpa′de.
Da′gya iñatä′gyi,
Da′gya iñatä′gyi.

Translation

God has had pity on us,
God has had pity on us.
Jesus has taken pity on us,
Jesus has taken pity on us.
He teaches me a song,
He teaches me a song.
My song is a good one,
My song is a good one.

In their confounding of aboriginal and Christian ideas the Kiowa frequently call the Indian messiah " Jesus," having learned the latter as a sacred name through the whites.

15. Anso′ gyätä′to

Anso′ gyätä′to,
Anso′ gyätä′to;
Â′dalte′m ga′tä′dalto′-o′,
Â′dalte′m ga′tä′dalto′-o′;
Änĭmhä′go, Änĭmhä′go.

Translation

I shall cut off his feet,
I shall cut off his feet;
I shall cut off his head,
I shall cut off his head;
He gets up again, he gets up again.

This is one of the favorite Kiowa ghost songs and refers to the miraculous resurrection of the dismembered buffalo, according to the promise of the messiah, as related in Sword's narrative. See page 41.

THE CADDO AND ASSOCIATED TRIBES

CADDO TRIBAL SYNONYMY

Asinais—an old French name, from *Hasinai*.

Caddo—popular name, from *Kä'dohadä'cho*.

Cadodaquio—Joutel (1687), another form of *Kä'dohadä'cho*.

Cenis—old French name used by Joutel in 1687; from *Hasinai*.

Dä'sha-i—Wichita name.

Dĕ'sa—another form of *Dä'sha-i*.

Hasi'nai or *Hasi'ni*—the proper generic term for at least the principal Caddo divisions, and perhaps for all of them. It is also used by them as synonymous with "Indians."

Kä'dohädä'cho—the name of the Caddo proper, as used by themselves.

Ma'se'p—Kiowa name; "pierced nose," from *mak'on*, nose, and *sep*, the root of a verb signifying to pierce or sew with an awl.

Na'shonĭt or *Na'shoni*—Comanche name, frequently used also by the neighboring tribes to designate the Caddo; the Nassonite of the early French writers on Texas.

Nez Percé—French traders' name; "pierced nose."

Ni'ris-häri's-ki'riki—another Wichita name.

Otä's-itä'niuw'—Cheyenne name; "pierced nose people."

Tani'bänĕn, Tani'bänĕnina, Tani'bätha—Arapaho name; "pierced nose people," *tani*, nose.

CADDO TRIBAL SIGN

"Pierced nose," in allusion to their former custom of boring the nose for the insertion of a ring.

SKETCH OF THE CADDO

The Caddo are the principal southern representatives of the Caddoan stock, which includes also the Wichita, Kichai, Pawnee, and Arikara. Their confederacy consisted of about a dozen tribes or divisions, claiming as their original territory the whole of lower Red river and adjacent country in Louisana, eastern Texas, and southern Arkansas. The names of these twelve divisions, including two of foreign origin, have been preserved as follows:

Kä'dohadä'cho (Caddo proper).

Nädä'ko (Anadarko).

Hai'-nai (Ioni).

Nä'bai-dä'cho (Nabedache).

Nä'kohodo'tsi (Nacogdoches).

Näshi'tosh (Natchitoches).

Nä'ka'na'wan.

Hädai'-i (Adai, Adaize).

Hai'-ĭsh (Eyeish, Aliche, Aes).

Yä'täsi.

I'mäha—a band of Omaha, or perhaps more probably Kwâpâ, who lived with the Kä'dohadä'cho, but retained their own distinct language.

There are still a few living with the Caddo, but they retain only the name. It will be remembered that when the Caddo lived in eastern Louisiana the Arkansas or Kwâpâ were their nearest neighbors on the north, and these Imaha may have been a part of the Kwâpâ who lived "up stream" (*U'mañhañ*) on the Arkansas. The Caddo call the Omaha tribe by the same name.

Yowa'ni—originally a band of the Heyowani division of the Choctaw. They joined the Caddo a long time ago, probably about the time the Choctaw began to retire across the Mississippi before the whites. Some few are still living with the Caddo and retain their distinct language. There is evidence that some Koasati (Cooshatties) were mixed with them.

The Kä'dohadä'cho seem to be recognized as the principal Caddo division, and the generic term *Hasi'nai* by which the confederates designate themselves is sometimes regarded as belonging more properly to the three divisions first named. According to their own statements some of the dialects spoken by the several divisions were mutually unintelligible. At present the Kädohadächo and Nädäko are the ruling dialects, while the Näbaidächo, Näkohodotsi, Hädai'-i, and Hai'-ïsh are practically extinct. The Kichai, Bidai, and Akokisa, who formerly lived near the Caddo on the eastern border of Texas, did not belong to the confederacy, although at least one of these tribes, the Kichai, is of the same stock and is now on the same reservation.

The Caddo have ten gentes: *Na'wotsi*, Bear; *Tasha*, Wolf; *Ta'năhă*, Buffalo; *Ta'o*, Beaver; *Iwi*, Eagle; *Oăt*, Raccoon; *Ka'g'aih*, Crow; *Ka'găhănĭn*, Thunder; *Kĭshi*, Panther; *Sûko*, Sun. The Bear gens is the most numerous. The Buffalo gens is sometimes called also *Koho'* or Alligator, because both animals bellow in the same way. These of a particular gens will not kill the animal from which the gens takes its name, and no Caddo in the old times would kill either an eagle or a panther, although they were not afraid to kill the bear, as are so many of the western tribes. The eagle might be killed, however, for its feathers by a hunter regularly initiated and consecrated for that purpose.

The original home of the Caddo was on lower Red river in Louisiana. According to their own tradition, which has parallels among several other tribes, they came up from under the ground through the mouth of a cave in a hill which they call *Cha'·kanĭ'nă*, "The place of crying," on a lake close to the south bank of Red river, just at its junction with the Mississippi. In those days men and animals were all brothers and all lived together under the ground. But at last they discovered the entrance to the cave leading up to the surface of the earth, and so they decided to ascend and come out. First an old man climbed up, carrying in one hand fire and a pipe and in the other a drum. After him came his wife, with corn and pumpkin seeds. Then followed the rest of the people and the animals. All intended to come out, but as soon as the wolf had climbed up he closed the hole, and shut up the rest of the people and animals under the ground, where they still remain. Those who had come out sat down and cried a long time for their friends below, hence the name of the place. Because the Caddo came out of the ground they call it *ină′*, mother, and go back to it when they die. Because they have had the pipe and the drum and the corn and pumpkins since they have been a people, they hold fast to these things and have never thrown them away.

From this place they spread out toward the west, following up the course of Red river, along which they made their principal settlements. For a long time they lived on Caddo lake, on the boundary between Louisiana and Texas, their principal village on the lake being called Sha′chidĭ′ni, "Timber hill." Their acquaintance with the whites began at a very early period. One of their tribes, the Nädäko, is mentioned under the name of Nandacao in the narrative of De Soto's expedition as early as 1540. The Kädohadächo were known to the French as early as 1687. The relations of the Caddo with the French and Spaniards were intimate and friendly. Catholic missions were established among them about the year 1700 and continued to exist until 1812, when the missions were suppressed by the Spanish government and the Indians were scattered. In the meantime Louisiana had been purchased by the United States, and the Caddo soon began to be pushed away from their ancient villages into the western territory, where they were exposed to the constant inroads of the prairie tribes. From this time their decline was rapid, and the events of the Texan and Mexican wars aided still further in their demoralization. They made their first treaty with the United States in 1835, at which time they were chiefly in Louisiana, southwest of Red river and adjoining Texas. They afterward removed to Brazos river in Texas, and to Washita river in Indian Territory in 1859. When the rebellion broke out, the Caddo, not wishing to take up arms against the government, fled north into Kansas and remained there until the close of the war, when they returned to the Washita. Their present reservation, which they hold only by executive order and jointly with the Wichita, lies between Washita and Canadian rivers in western Oklahoma, having the Cheyenne and Arapaho on the north and west and the Kiowa, Comanche, and Apache on the south. In 1893 they numbered 507.

In person the Caddo are rather smaller and darker than the neighboring prairie tribes, and from their long residence in Louisiana, they have a considerable admixture of French blood. They are an agricultural tribe, raising large crops of corn, pumpkins, and melons, and still retaining industrious habits in spite of their many vicissitudes of fortune. They were never buffalo hunters until they came out on the plains. They formerly lived in conical grass houses like the Wichita, but are now in log houses and generally wear citizen's dress excepting in the dance. The old custom which gave rise to the name and tribal sign of "Pierced Nose" is now obsolete. In 1806 Sibley said of them, "They are brave, despise danger or death, and boast that they have never shed white man's blood." Their former enemies, the prairie tribes, bear witness to their bravery, and their friendship toward the whites is a part of their history, but has resulted in no great advantage to themselves, as they have been dispossessed from their own country and are recognized only as tenants at will in their present location.

They and the Wichita received the new doctrine from the Arapaho, and were soon among its most earnest adherents, notwithstanding the fact that they were regarded as the most advanced of all the tribes in that part of the country. It may be that their history had led them to feel a special need of a messiah. They have been hard and constant dancers, at one time even dancing in winter when there was nearly a foot of snow upon the ground. Their first songs were those which they had heard from the Arapaho, and sang in corrupted form, with only a general idea of their meaning, but they now have a number of songs in their own language, some of which are singularly pleasing in melody and sentiment.

THE WICHITA, KICHAI, AND DELAWARE

Closely associated with the Caddo on the same reservation are the Wichita, with their subtribes, the Tawakoni and Waco, numbering together 316 in 1893; the Delaware, numbering 94, and the Kichai (Keechies), numbering only 52. Of these, all but the Delaware, who are Algonquian, belong to the Caddoan stock. The Wichita and their subtribes, although retaining in indistinct form the common Caddoan tradition, claim as their proper home the Wichita mountains, near which they still remain. Sixty years ago their principal village was on the north side of the north fork of Red river, a short distance below the mouth of Elm creek, in Oklahoma. They live in conical grass houses and, like the other tribes of the stock, are agricultural. They call themselves *Kï'tikïti'sh*—they are called *Tawe'hash* by the Caddo and Kichai—and are known to most of their other neighbors and in the sign language as the "Tattooed People" (*Do' kănă*, Coman-che; *Do'gu'at*, Kiowa), from an old custom now nearly obsolete. For the same reason and from their resemblance to the Pawnee, with whose language their own has a close connection, the French called them *Pani Pique's*.

The Kichai or Keechie, or *Kï'tsäsh*, as they call themselves, are a small tribe of the same stock, and claim to have moved up Red river in company with the Caddo. Their language is different from that of any of their neighbors, but approaches the Pawnee.

The Delaware are a small band of the celebrated tribe of that name. They removed from the east and settled with the main body in Kansas, but drifted south into Texas while it was still Spanish territory. After a long series of conflicts with the American settlers of Texas, before and after the Mexican war, they were finally taken under the protection of the United States government and assigned to their present reservation along with other emigrant tribes from that state.

SONGS OF THE CADDO

1. HA′YO TĂ′IA′ Ă′Ă′

Nä′nisa′na, Nä′nisa′na,
Ha′yo tă′ia′ ă′ă′,
Ha′yo tă′ia′ ă′ă′,
Na′wi hă′iă′ i′nă′,
Na′wi hă′iă′ i′nă′.

Translation

Nä′nisa′na, Nä′nisa′na,
Our father dwells above,
Our father dwells above,
Our mother dwells below,
Our mother dwells below.

" Our mother" here refers to the earth.

2. WÛ′NTI HA′YANO′ DI′WITI′A

Nä′nisa′na, nä′nisa′na,
Wû′nti ha′yano′ di′witi′a ha′yo′,
Wû′nti ha′yano′ di′witi′a ha′yo′,
A′ă ko′ia′ ha′yo′,
A′ă ko′ia′ ha′yo′,
Wû′nti ha′ya′no ta′-ia′ ha′yo′,
Wû′nti ha′ya′no ta′-ia′ ha′yo′.

Translation

Nä′nisa′na, nä′nisa′na,
All our people are going up,
All our people are going up,
Above to where the father dwells,
Above to where the father dwells,
Above to where our people live,
Above to where our people live.

3. Nû'na Ï'tsiya'

He'yawe'ya! He'yawe'ya!
Nû'na Ï'tsiya' si'bocha'ha',
Nû'na Ï'tsiya' si'bocha'ha',
Wû'nti ha'yano' ha'nĭn gû'kwû'ts-a',
Wû'nti ha'yano' ha'nĭn gû'kwû'ts-a',
He'yahe'eye'! He'yahe'eye'!

Translation

He'yawe'ya! He'yawe'ya!
I have come because I want to see them,
I have come because I want to see them,
The people, all my children,
The people, all my children.
He'yahe'eye! He'yahe'eye!

This song was composed by a woman named Nyu'taa. According to her story, she saw in her trance a large company approaching, led by a man who told her he was the Father and that he was coming because he wished to see all his children.

4. Na'tsiwa'ya

Na'tsiwa'ya, na'tsiwa'ya,
Na' ika'—Wi'ahe'e'ye',
Na' ika'—Wi'ahe'e'ye',
Wi'ahe'e'ye'ye'yeahe'ye',
Wi'ahe'e'ye'ye'yeahe'ye'.

Translation

I am coming, I am coming,
The grandmother from on high, *Wi'ahe'e'ye'*,
The grandmother from on high, *Wi'ahe'e'ye'*,
Wi'ahe'e'ye'ye'yeahe'ye',
Wi'ahe'e'ye'ye'yeahe'ye'!

This song also was composed by the woman Nyu'taa. In her trance vision she fell asleep and seemed (still in the vision) to be awakened by the noise of a storm, when she looked and saw approaching her the Storm Spirit, who said to her, "I come, the grandmother from on high." The Caddo call thunder the "grandmother above" and the sun the "uncle above."

5. Na'-iye' ino' ga'nio'sĭt

Wa'hiya'ne, wa'hiya'ne,
Na'-iye' ino' ga'nio'sĭt,
Na'-iye' ino' ga'nio'sĭt.
Wa'hiya'ne, wa'hiya'ne.

Translation

Wa'hiya'ne, wa'hiya'ne,
My sister above, she is painted,
My sister above, she is painted.
Wa'hiya'ne, wa'hiya'ne.

This is another song composed by Nyu'taa, who herself explained it. In this trance vision she saw a spirit woman painted with blue stripes on her forehead and a crow on her chin, who told her that she was "her sister, the Evening Star." While singing this song Nyu'taa was sitting near me, when she suddenly cried out and went into a spasm of trembling and crying lasting some minutes, lifting up her right hand toward the west at the same time. Such attacks were so common among the women at song rehearsals as frequently to interfere with the work, although the bystanders regarded them as a matter of course and took only a passing notice of these incidents.

6. NA'A HA'YO HA'WANO

Nä'nisa'na, nä'nisa'na,
Na'a ha'yo ha'wano,
Na'a ha'yo ha'wano.

Translation

Nä'nisa'na, nä'nisa'na,
Our father above (has) paint,
Our father above (has) paint.

This refers to the sacred paint used by the participants in the Ghost dance, and which is believed to confer health and the power to see visions.

7. WÛ'NTI HA'YANO KA'KA'NA'

Nänisa'na, nänisa'na,
Wû'nti ha'yano ka'ka'na' ni"tsiho',
Wû'nti ha'yano ka'ka'na' ni"tsiho',
Aa' ko'ia' ta'-ia' ha'yo',
Aa' ko'ia' ta'-ia' ha'yo',

Translation

Nä'nisa'na, nänisa'na,
All the people cried when I returned,
All the people cried when I returned,
Where the father dwells above,
Where the father dwells above.

This song was composed by a girl who went up to the spirit world and saw there all her friends, who cried when she started to leave them again.

8. NA'WI I'NA

Nä'nisa'na, nä'nisa'na,
E'yahe'ya, e'yahe'ya, he'e'ye'!
E'yahe'ya, e'yahe'ya, he'e'ye'!
Na'wi i'na ha'yo ä'ä—He'yoi'ya, he'e'ye'!
Na'wi i'na ha'yo ä'ä—He'yoi'ya, he'e'ye'!

Translation

Nä'nisa'na, nä'nisa'na,
E'yahe'ya, e'yahe'ya, he'e'ye'!
E'yahe'ya, e'yahe'ya, he'e'ye'!
We have our mother below; we have our father above—*He'yoi'ya, he'e'ye'!*
We have our mother below; we have our father above—*He'yoi'ya, he'e'ye'!*

This song was composed by a woman named Niaha'no', who used to have frequent trances in which she would talk with departed Caddo and bring back messages from them to their friends. "Our mother below" is the earth. (See page 325.)

9. NI' IKA' NA'A

Ni' ika' na'a ha'na',
Ni' ika' na'a ha'na';
Na'a-a' ha'na',
Na'a-a' ha'na'.

Translation

There are our grandmother and our father above,
There are our grandmother and our father above;
There is our father above,
There is our father above.

By "grandmother" is meant the storm spirit or thunder. (See Caddo song 4.)

10. HI'NA HA'NATOBI'NA

Hi'na ha'natobi'na i'wi-na',
Hi'na ha'natobi'na i'wi-na',
Na' iwi' i'wi-na',
Na' iwi' i'wi-na';
Na'nana' ha'taha',
Na'nana' ha'taha'.

Translation

The eagle feather headdress from above,
The eagle feather headdress from above,
From the eagle above, from the eagle above;
It is that feather we wear,
It is that feather we wear.

This refers to the eagle feather worn on the heads of the dancers. (See song number 12.) This song is in the Hai-nai dialect.

11. NA' ĂĂ' O'WI'TA'

Na' ăă' o'wi'ta',
Na' ăă' o'wi'ta',
Na' kiwa't Hai'-nai',
Na' kiwa't Hai'-nai'.

Translation

The father comes from above,
The father comes from above,
From the home of the Hai-nai above,
From the home of the Hai-nai above.

This song, like the last, was composed by one of the Hai-nai tribe, and refers to the silent majority of the band in the spirit world.

12. Na′ iwi′ o′wi′ta′

Na′ i - wi′   o′ - wi′ - ta′,   na′ i - wi′ - o′ - wi′ - ta′;   do′-hya di′-wa - bo′n na′ na′ i-wi′ o′ - wi′-ta′,

do′-hya di′-wa - bo′n na′   na′ i-wi′ o′ - wi′-ta′;   na′-ha′ na′-da-ka′-a′, na′-ha′ na′-da-ka′-a′.

Na′ iwi′ o′wi′ta′,
Na′ iwi′ o′wi′ta′;
Do′hya di′wabo′n na′ na′ iwi′ o′wi′ta′,
Do′hya di′wabo′n na′ na′ iwi′ o′wi′ta′;
Na′ha′ na′daka′a′, Na′ha′ na′daka′a′.

Translation

See! the eagle comes,
See! the eagle comes;
Now at last we see him — look! look! the eagle comes,
Now at last we see him — look! look! the eagle comes;
Now we see him with the people,
Now we see him with the people.

This refers to what the Caddo call the "return of the eagle feathers" in the Ghost dance. With the Caddo, as with other tribes, the eagle is a sacred bird, and in the old times only the few medicine-men who knew the sacred formula would dare to kill one for the feathers. Should any-one else kill an eagle, his family would die or some other great misfor-tune would come upon him. The formula consisted of certain secret prayers and ritual performances. Among the Cherokee the eagle killer's prayer was a petition to the eagle not to be revenged upon the tribe, because it was not an Indian, but a Spaniard, who had killed him — an indication of the vivid remembrance in which the cruelty of the early Spaniards was held among the southern tribes. To further guard against the anger of the eagles, the Cherokee eagle killer, on his return to the village, announced that he had killed, not an eagle, but a snowbird, the latter being too small and insignificant to be dreaded. The eagle-killing ceremony among the northern prairie tribes has been already described under Arapaho song 47. The Caddo eagle killer always took with him a robe or some other valuable offering, and after shooting the eagle, making the prayer, and pulling out the tail and wing feathers he covered the body with the robe and left it there as a peace offering to the spirit of the eagle. The dead eagle was never brought home, as among the Cherokee. The last man of the Caddo who knew the eagle-killing ritual died some years ago, and since then they have had to go without eagle feathers or buy them from the Kiowa and other tribes. Since Sitting Bull came down and "gave the feather" to the leaders of the dance the prohibition is removed, and men and women alike are now at liberty to get and wear eagle feathers as they will.

13. A′NANA′ HANA′NITO′

A′nana′ hana′nito′ ni′ahu′na — *He′e′ye′!*
A′nana′ hana′nito′ ni′ahu′na — *He′e′ye′!*
A′nana′sa′na′? A′nana′sa′na′?
Ha′yo ha′nitu′ ni′ahu′na — *He′e′ye′!*
Ha′yo ha′nitu′ ni′ahu′na — *He′e′ye′!*
A′nana′sa′na′? A′ana′sa′na′?

Translation

The feather has come back from above — *He′e′ye′!*
The feather has come back from above — *He′e′ye′!*
Is he doing it? Is he doing it?
The feather has returned from on high — *He′e′ye′!*
The feather has returned from on high — *He′e′ye′!*
Is he doing it? Is he doing it?

This refers to the return of the eagle feathers, as noted in the preceding song. The question "Is he doing it?" is equivalent to asking, "Is this the work of the father?"—an affirmative answer being understood.

14. NA′ IWI′ HA′NAA′

Na′ iwi′ ha′naa′,
Na′ iwi′ ha′naa′;
Wû′nti ha′yano′ na′nia′sana′,
Wû′nti ha′yano′ na′nia′sana′.
Na′ha na′ni′asa′,
Na′ha na′ni′asa·.

Translation

There is an eagle above,
There is an eagle above;
All the people are using it,
All the people are using it.
See! They use it,
See! They use it.

This song also refers to the use of eagle feathers in the dance.

15. WI′TŬ′ HA′SINI′

E′-ye - he′! Nä′-ni-sa′ - na,   E′-ye - he′! Nä′-ni-sa′ - na.   Wi′ - tŭ′ Ha′ - si - ni′

di′ - wi-ti′ - a′ - a′,   wi′ - tŭ′ Ha′ - si - ni′ di′ - wi-ti′ - a′ - a′   ki′-wat ha′ - i - me′ He′-

e′-ye′! Ki-wat ha′-i-me′ He′-e′-ye′! Na′-ha-yo′ na′, Na′-ha-yo′ na′ - ă′ - ă′ ko′-i-ă′,

He′ - e′-ye′! I′ - na ko′-iă′,   He′ - e′ ye′! I′ - na ko′-iă′,   He′ - e′-ye′!

E′yehe′! Nä′nisa′na,
E′yehe′! Nä′nisa′na.
Wi′tŭ′ Ha′sini′ di′witi′a′a′.
Wi′tŭ′ Ha′sini′ di′witi′a′a′
Ki′wat ha′-ime′ — He′e′ye′!
Ki′wat ha′-ime′ — He′e′ye′!
Na′hayo′ na′,
Na′hayo′ na′ă′ă′ ko′iă′ — He′e′ye′!
I′na ko′iă′ — He′e′ye′!
I′na ko′iă — He′e′ye′!

Translation

E′yehe′! Nä′nisa′na,
E′yehe′! Nä′nisa′na.
Come on, Caddo, we are all going up,
Come on, Caddo, we are all going up
To the great village — *He′e′ye′!*
To the great village — *He′e′ye′!*
With our father above,
With our father above where he dwells on high — *He′e′ye′!*
Where our mother dwells — *He′e′ye′!*
Where our mother dwells — *He′e′ye′!*

The sentiment and swinging tune of this spirited song make it one of the favorites. It encourages the dancers in the hope of a speedy reunion of the whole Caddo nation, living and dead, in the "great village" of their father above, and needs no further explanation.

Authorities Cited

Adjutant-General's Office [*A. G. O.*].—
(Documents on file in the office of the
Adjutant-General, in the War Department
ment at Washington, where each is
officially designated by its number,
followed by the initials A. G. O. In
response to specific inquiries additional
information was received in letters from
the same office and incorporated into
the narrative.)

 1—Report of Captain J. M. Lee, on the aban-
donment of Fort Bidwell, California (1890),
Doc. 16633-1, 1890; 2—Documents relating to the
Apache outbreak, 1881; 3—Documents relating
to Sword-bearer and the Crow outbreak, 1887;
4—Captain J. M. Lee, abandonment of Fort
Bidwell, Doc. 16633-1, 1890; 5—Report on the
Ghost dance, by Lieutenant H. L. Scott, February 10, 1891, Doc. ——; 6—Report on the
abandonment of Fort Bidwell, by Captain J.
M. Lee, Doc. 16633-1, 1890; 7—Statement of
Judge H. L. Spargur in Lee's report on Fort
Bidwell, Doc. 16633-1, 1890; 8—Letters of As-
sistant Adjutant-General Corbin and Quarter-
master-General Batchelder; 9—Affidavits with
Lee's report on the abandonment of Fort Bidwell, Doc. 16633-1, 1890.

Albany Institute. *See* MacMurray.

Allis, *Rev.* Samuel. Forty Years Among
the Indians and on the Eastern Borders
of Nebraska. (Transactions and Reports of the Nebraska State Historical
Society, II. Lincoln, Nebraska, 1887.
8°. 133–166.)

 1—135.

American Anthropologist. *See* Phister.

American Ethnology and Archæology,
Journal of. *See* Bandelier.

Archæological Institute of America,
Report of. *See* Bandelier.

Bancroft, G. History of the United States
of America, from the discovery of the
continent. The author's last edition.
New York, 1884. 8°.

 1—II, 371; 2—II, 378; 3—II, 463.

Bandelier, A. F. Documentary history of
the Zuñi tribe. (Journal of American
Ethnology and Archæology, III. Boston
and New York, 1892. 4°.)

 1 a —103-115.

Bandelier, A. F.—Continued.
—— Final report of investigations among
the Indians of the southwestern United
States, Part II. (Papers of the
Archæological Institute of America,
American Series, IV. Cambridge, 1892.
8°.)

 1 b—62.

Barclay, Robert. The inner life of the
religious societies of the common-
wealth; considered principally with
reference to the influence of church
organization on the spread of Christianity. London, 1876. 8°.

Bartlett, C. H. Letter to the Bureau of
Ethnology, dated October 29, 1895.

Bible. The Holy Bible, containing the
Old and New Testaments; translated
out of the original tongues, etc. New
York (American Bible Society), 1870.
12°.

Bourke, *Capt.* J. G. The medicine-men
of the Apache. (Ninth Annual Report
of the Bureau of Ethnology. Washington, 1892. 4°. The description of
the dance of the medicine-man, Nakai-
doklini, is taken from the account in
this paper, supplemented by a personal
letter from the author.)

 1—505.

Brinton, *Dr* D. G. Myths of the New
World: A treatise on the symbolism
and mythology of the Red race of
America. New York, Leypoldt and
Holt, 1868. 12°.

 1—168, passim.

Brown, John P. The Dervishes; or oriental spiritualism. By John P. Brown,
secretary and dragoman of the legation
of the United States of America at
Constantinople, etc. London, 1868.
12°.

Bureau of Ethnology, Reports of. *See*
Bourke and Mallery.

Catlin, G. Letters and notes on the manners, customs, and condition of the
North American Indians. Written dur-

Catlin, G.—Continued.

ing eight years' travel (1832–1839) among the wildest tribes of Indians in North America, etc. Two volumes. 4th edition. London, 1844. 8°.

1—II, 117; 2—II, 118; 3—II, 98; 4—II, 99.

Century Magazine. *See* **Roosevelt.**

Clark, Benjamin. The Cheyenne Indians. (A manuscript history and ethnography of the Cheyenne Indians, written at the request of General Philip Sheridan by Benjamin Clark, interpreter at Fort Reno, Oklahoma.)

Now in possession of Dr George Bird Grinnell of New York city.

Clark, W. P. The Indian sign language, with brief explanatory notes, etc, and a description of some of the peculiar laws, customs, myths, superstitions, ways of living, code of peace and war signals of our aborigines. Philadelphia, 1885. 8°.

Colby, *Gen.* L. W. The Sioux Indian war of 1890–91. By Brigadier-General L. W. Colby, commanding the Nebraska National Guard. (Transactions and reports of the Nebraska State Historical Society, III, 144–190; Fremont, Nebraska, 1892. 8°.)

1—153; 2—150; 3—155; 4—157; 5—159–170; 6—159; 7—164; 8—165–170; 9—(McGillycuddy) 180; 10—165.

Commissioner [*Comr.*]. Annual report of the Commissioner of Indian Affairs to the Secretary of the Interior. (Sixty-first annual report, Washington, 1892. 8°.)

1—Report of Agent W. P. Richardson, 1852, 71, and report of Agent W. P. Badger, 1859, 144; 2—Agent Danilson, 1875, 258; 3—Agent Tiffany, 1881, 10; 4—Commissioner Price, 1881, viii–ix; Agent Tiffany, 1881, 10–11; 5—Agent Linn, 1884, 102; 6—Agent Patrick, 1885, 111; 7—Agent Scott, 1891, vol. I, 258; 8—Agent Smith, 1873, 319; 9—Agent Boyle, 1870, 58; 10—Superintendent Meacham, 1870, 50; 11—Agent Cornoyer, 1873, 317–18; 12—Commissioner Brunot, 1871, 98; 13—Umatilla council, 1891, 95–7; 14—Superintendent Colonel Ross, 1870, 30; 15—Superintendent Meacham, 1870, 50–54; 16—Report, 1871, 95; 17—Superintendent Odeneal, 1872, 362; 18—Subagent White, 1843, 451; 19—ibid, 453; 20—Commissioner Hayt, 1877, 10; 21—ibid, 10; 22—ibid, 12; 23—ibid, 11; 24—ibid, 12; 25—ibid, 12–13; 26—Commissioner Hayt, 1878, xxxiv; 27a—ibid, xxxv; 27b—Agent Rust, 1891, I, 223; 28—Commissioner Morgan, 1891, I, 132–3; 29—Agent Wright,

Commissioner—Continued.

ibid, 411–2; 30—Dorchester report, ibid, 529; 31—Commissioner Morgan, ibid, 124; 32—Agent Wright, ibid, 411–12; 33—ibid, 128, 130; 34—ibid, 130; 35—ibid, 130; 36—ibid, 130; 37—ibid, 130; 38—ibid, 131; 39—ibid, 132; 40—ibid, 132; 41—Commissioner Morgan, 1892, 128; 42—Dorchester, 1891, vol. I, 532; 43—Agent Wood, 1892, 396, 399; 44—Mrs Z. A. Parker, in report of Superintendent Dorchester, vol. I, 1891, 529–531; also published in the New York Evening Post of April 18, 1891, and in Journal of American Folk-lore, April–June, 1891; 45—Report on the Utes, Pai-Utes, etc, by J. W. Powell and G. W. Ingalls, 1873, 45; 46—Superintendent Parker, 1866, 115; 47—ibid, 115.

Dorsey, *Rev.* J. O. *See* **Journal of American Folk-lore.**

Drake, B. Life of Tecumseh and of his brother the Prophet; with a historical sketch of the Shawanoe Indians. Cincinnati, 1852. 12°.

1—87, passim; 2—88; 3—93; 4—130; 5—142; 6—151; 7—153; 8—158; 9—193.

Drake, S. G. The aboriginal races of North America, comprising biographical sketches of eminent individuals and an historical account of the different tribes, from the first discovery of the continent to the present period, etc, 15th edition, revised with valuable additions, by Professor H. L. Williams. New York, 1880 (?). 8°.

1—625.

Dutton, *Major* C. E. The submerged trees of the Columbia river. (Science, New York, February 18, 1887, page 156.)

Eells, *Rev.* Myron. (Letter in regard to the Shakers of Puget sound, quoted at length in the chapter on that subject. Works by the same author, referred to in the same chapter and in the tribal synopsis accompanying the chapter on the Nez Percé war, are "History of Indian Missions on the Pacific Coast," and "Ten Years of Missionary Work among the Indians at Skokomish, Washington Territory, 1874–1884."— Congregational House, Boston, 1886. 12°.)

Mr Eells was born in the state of Washington, has been for many years engaged in mission work in that section, and is the author of valuable works relating to the tribes and languages of the state.

Eells, Myron—Continued.

—— History of Indian missions on the Pacific coast—Oregon, Washington, and Idaho. By Reverend Myron Eells, missionary of the association. Philadelphia and New York, American Sunday School Union, 1882 (?). 12°.

Evans, F. W. Shakers: Compendium of the origin, history, principles, rules and regulations, government, and doctrines of the United Society of Believers in Christ's second appearing, with biographies of Ann Lee, etc. New York, 1859. 12°.

Fletcher, J. E. *See* Schoolcraft, Indian Tribes.

Ghost Dance [*G. D.* **].** (Documents relating to the Ghost dance and the Sioux outbreak of 1890, on file in the Indian Office in special case 188, labeled "Ghost Dance and Sioux Trouble.")

1—Fisher, Document 37097-1890; 2—Campbell, Document 36274-1890; 3—Campbell, Document 26274-1890; 4—Report of Lieutenant H. L. Scott (copy from A. G. O.), Document 9234-1891; 5—Statement of Porcupine, the Cheyenne, Document 24075-1890; 6—Blakely, September 30, 1890, Document 32876-1890; 7—Agent McLaughlin, October 17, 1890, Document 32670-1890; 8—Document 17236-1891; 9—Statement of Porcupine, Document 24075-1890; 10—Agent Bartholomew, December 15, 1890, Document 39419-1890; 11—Clipping from Santa Fé (New Mexico) News, December 11, 1890, Document 39419-1890; 12—Agent Plumb, Document 35519-1890; 13—ibid, Document 38743-1890; 14—ibid, Document 2178-1891; 15—Agent Fisher, Document 37097-1890; 16—Clipping from Omaha (Nebraska) Bee, February 10, 1891, Document 6155-1891; 17—Blakely and Captain Bowman, Document 32876-1890; 18—Agent Simons, Document 37359-1890; 19—Agent Warner, Document 37260-1890; 20—Agent McChesney, Document 18807-1890; Document 17024-1890; 21—Gallagher, Document 18482-1890; McChesney, 18807-1890; Wright, 18823-1830; McLaughlin, 19200-1890; 22—Cook letter, September 11, Document 30628-1890; 23—Special Agent Reynolds, September 25, 30046-1890; 24—Wright, December 5, 38608-1890; 25—McLaughlin, October 17, 32607-1890; 26—Royer, October 12, 32120-1890; 27—Palmer, October 29 and November 4, 34061-1890, 34656-1890; 28—Letters and telegrams, October 30 to November 21, from Royer, Palmer, Dixon, Belt, et al., 34060-1890; 34807-1890; 34904-1890; 34906-1890; 34910-1890; 35104-1890; 35105-1890; 35349-1890; 35412-1890; 35413-1890; 35831-1890; 36021-1890; 29—McLaughlin, November 19, 36346-1890; 30—President Harrison, November 13, 35104-1890; 31—Secretary Noble, December 1, 37003-1890; 32—

Ghost Dance—Continued.

Palmer, 35956-1890; Reynolds, 36011-1890; McLaughlin, 36022-1890; Royer, 36560-1890; 33—Noble, 37003-1890; Wright, 37174-1890; Palmer, 38688-1890; 34—McLaughlin, 36868-1830; 37465-1890; Cody order, 37559-1890; Belt, 39602-1890; 35—McLaughlin, December 24, 1890-26; 36—McLaughlin, 38860-1890; 39602-1890; December 24, 1890-26; Miles, 39535-1890; 37—General Miles, December 11, 39216-1890; 38—Miles, December 28, 1890-415; 39—Miles, December 30, 1890-504; 40—Royer, December 29, 40415-1890; Miles, December 29, 1890-414; 41—Miles, December 29, 1890-414; 42—Cooper, 40415-1890; 43—Royer, December 31, 1890-529; 44—Royer, January 2, 1891-145; 45—Miles order, January 12, 6040-1891; 46—Corbin, 7724-1891; military letters, etc, 10937-1891; Welsh, etc, 12772-1891; Burns, 12561-1891; 47—Documents 3512-1891; 7720-1891; 7976-1891; 10937-1891; 11944-1891; including statements of Acting Agent Captain Pierce, of army officers, Dr McGillycuddy, Indian survivors, and Deadwood Pioneer; 48—Kingsbury, 8217-1891; 49—Viroqua, 38445-1890; 50—Texas Ben, 36087-1890; Johnson, November 27, 1890; 51—Herrick, 37440-1890; 52—Belt, 8699-1893; Hopkins, 9979-1893; 11305-1893; 13243-1893; Browne, 14459-1893; 53—Scott, February 10, 9234-1891; 54—ibid; 55—Commissioner Morgan, November 24, 36342-1890; 36467-1890.

Grinnell, Dr G. B. *See* Journal of American Folk-lore; also article on Early Blackfoot History (American Anthropologist, Washington, April, 1892), and personal letters.

Dr Grinnell, editor of Forest and Stream, in New York city, and author of Pawnee Hero Stories and Blackfoot Lodge Tales, is one of our best authorities on the prairie tribes.

Hamilton, *Rev.* William. Autobiography. (Transactions and Reports of the Nebraska State Historical Society, I, 60-73. Lincoln, Nebraska, 1885. 8°.)

1-72.

Hayden, F. V. Contributions to the ethnography and philology of the Indian tribes of the Missouri valley, etc. Prepared under the direction of Captain William F. Reynolds, T. E., U. S. A., and published by permission of the War Department. Philadelphia, 1862. 4°.

Heckewelder, J. History, manners, and customs of the Indian nations who once inhabited Pennsylvania and the neighboring states. New and revised edition, with introduction and notes by Reverend William C. Reichel. Philadelphia, 1876. 8°. Originally

Heckewelder, J.—Continued.

published in the Transactions of the American Philosophical Society, Vol. I.

1—291-293.

Howard, *Gen.* O. O. Nez Percé Joseph; an account of his ancestors, his lands, his confederates, his enemies, his murders, his war, his pursuit, and capture. By O. O. Howard, brigadier-general, U. S. A. New York, 1881. 12°.

1—52; 2—64-72; 3—83.

Huggins, E. L. Smohalla, the prophet of Priest rapids. (Overland Monthly, February, 1891; vol. XVII, No. 98; second series, pages 208-215.)

Captain Huggins, now of the staff of General Miles, visited Smohalla in an official capacity about the same time as Major MacMurray. Some additional details were furnished by him in personal conversation with the author.

1—209; 2—209-215.

Humboldt, A. Political essay on the kingdom of New Spain, etc. Translated from the original French by John Black. London, 1811; 4 volumes, 8°.

1—I, 200-203; IV, 262.

Indian Informants. (Among the Paiute in Nevada information and songs were obtained directly from Wovoka, the messiah, from his uncle, Charley Sheep, and others; among the Shoshoni and northern Arapaho in Wyoming, from Norcok, Shoshoni interpreter, Henry Reid, half-blood Cheyenne interpreter, Nakash, Sharp Nose, and others; at Pine Ridge, among the Sioux, from Fire-thunder, American Horse, Edgar Fire-thunder of Carlisle, Louis Menard and Philip Wells, mixed-blood interpreters, and others; among the Arapaho and Cheyenne in Oklahoma, from Black Coyote, Left-hand, Sitting Bull, Black Short Nose, and numerous others, and from the Carlisle students, Paul Boynton, Robert Burns, Clever Warden, Grant Left-hand, Jesse Bent, and others; among the Comanche, from Quanah, William Tivis (Carlisle) and his brother, Mo'tumi; among the Kiowa, from Biäñk'i; Gunaoi, Tama (a woman), Igiagyähona (a woman), Mary Zoñtam, and others, with the Carlisle or Hampton students, Paul Setk'opti, Belo Cozad, and Virginia Stumbling Bear,

Indian Informants—Continued.

and from Andres Martinez, a Mexican captive and interpreter; among the Caddo, from George Parton and his daughter Eliza, John Wilson, and Robert Dunlap, half-blood interpreter; among the Wichita, from the chief Towakoni Jim. Detailed information in regard to the Smohalla and Shaker beliefs and rituals among the Columbia river tribes was obtained in Washington from Charles Ike, half-blood Yakima interpreter, and chief Wolf Necklace of the Pälus.)

Indian Office [*Ind. Off.*]. (Documents on file in the Indian office, exclusive of those relating directly to the Ghost dance and Sioux outbreak of 1890, those being filed in separate cases labeled "Ghost Dance." *See* **Commissioner** and Ghost Dance.)

1—Letter of Agent Graham to General Clark, dated February 22, 1827; 2—Document indorsed "The Kickapoo Prophet's Speech," dated St Louis, February 10, 1827.

Jackson, Helen ("H. H."). A century of dishonor. A sketch of the United States government's dealings with some of the Indian tribes, etc. New edition, etc. Boston, 1885. 12°.

Janney, S. M. The life of George Fox; with dissertations on his views concerning the doctrine, testimonies, and discipline of the Christian church, etc. Philadelphia, 1853. 8°.

Journal of American Folk-lore [*J. F. L.*]. (An octavo quarterly magazine published at Boston.)

1—"The Ghost Dance in Arizona," an article originally published in the Mohave Miner, and reprinted from the Chicago Inter-Ocean of June 25, 1891, in V, No. 16, January-March, 1892, pages 65-67; 2—ibid; 3—ibid; 4—Mrs Z. A. Parker, "The Ghost Dance at Pine Ridge," from an article in the New York Evening Post of April 18, 1891, quoted in IV, No. 13, April-June, 1891, pages 160-162. The same number of the journal contains other notices of the messiah and the Ghost dance; 5—G. B. Grinnell, "Account of the Northern Cheyennes Concerning the Messiah Superstition," in IV, No. 12, January-March, 1891, pages 61-69; 6—"Messianic Excitements among the White Americans," from an article in the New York Times of November 30, 1890, in IV, No. 13, April-June, 1891; Rev. J. O. Dorsey, The Social Organization of the Siouan Tribes, in IV, No. 14, July-September, 1891.

Keam, Thomas V. Letters and oral information.

Mr Keam, of Keams Cañon, Arizona, has been for a number of years a trader among the Navaho and Hopi (Moki), speaks the Navaho language fluently, and takes an intelligent interest in everything relating to these tribes. He has furnished valuable information orally and by letter, together with much kind assist- ance while the author was in that country.

Kendall, E. A. Travels through the northern parts of the United States in the years 1807 and 1808. In three volumes. New York, 1809. 8°.

1—II, 290; 2—II, 292 and 296; 3—II, 287; 4— II. 292.

Lee, *Captain* **J. M.** *See* **Adjutant-General's Office.**

Additional information has been furnished by Captain Lee in personal letters and in con- versation.

LetterBook [*L. B.***].** (The letter book of the Indian Office containing, among other things, letters bearing on the Ghost dance, supplementary to the documents in the "Ghost dance files.")

1—Belt, October 3 and October 20, 205–287; 206–211; 2—Belt, November 15, 207–237; 3— Noble, 208–245.

Lewis and Clark. Explorations. Washington, 1806. 12°.

The edition used is the earliest printed ac- count, in the form of a message to Congress from the President, Thomas Jefferson, commu- nicated February 19, 1806.

McCullough, J. *See* **Pritts, J.**

McKenney, T. L., and Hall, J. History of the Indian tribes of North America, with biographical sketches and anec- dotes of the principal chiefs. Embel- ished with one hundred and twenty portraits from the Indian gallery in the Department of War at Washington. In three volumes. Philadelphia, 1858. 8°.

1—vol. I, 64, 65.

MacMurray, *Major* **J. W.** [*MacMurray MS.*]. The Dreamers of the Columbia River valley in Washington Territory. A revised manuscript copy, with notes and other additions of an article origi- nally read before the Albany Institute January 19, 1886, and published in the

MacMurray, *Major* **J. W.**—Continued. Transactions of the Albany Institute, XI, Albany, 1887, pages 240–248.

Under instructions from General Miles, com- manding the Department of the Columbia, Major MacMurray, in 1884, made an official investigation of the Smohalla religion, with special reference to the Indian land grievances in that section, and his report on the subject contains a large body of valuable informa- tion.

Mallery, *Colonel* **Garrick.** Picture writ- ing of the American Indians. (Tenth Annual Report of the Bureau of Eth- nology (1888–89), 1–822. Washington, 1893. 8°.)

1—290.

Matthews, *Dr* **Washington.** Ethnogra- phy and philology of the Hidatsa In- dians. Washington, 1877. 8°. (Pub- lished as No. 7 of Miscellaneous pub- lications of the United States Geolog- ical Survey.)

—— (Personal letters and oral informa- tion.)

Dr Matthews, surgeon in the United States Army, lately retired, formerly stationed on the upper Missouri and afterward for several years at Fort Wingate, New Mexico, is the authority on the Navaho and Hidatsa Indians.

1—Letter of October 23, 1891; 2—ibid.

Merrick, J. L. Life and religion of Mo- hammed, as contained in the Sheeah tradition of the Hyat-ul-Kuloob; trans- lated from the Persian. Boston, 1850. 8°.

Minnesota Historical Collections. *See* **Warren.**

Mormons. The Mormons have stepped down and out of celestial government; the American Indians have stepped up and into celestial government. 8°. 4 pages. (n. d.)

An anonymous leaflet, published apparently at Salt Lake City, Utah, about July, 1892, ad- vertising a series of lectures on the fulfillment of Mormon prophecies through the Indian messiah movement and the Sioux outbreak.

Nebraska Historical Society. *See* **Allis; Colby; Hamilton.**

Overland Monthly. *See* **Huggins.**

Parker, Z. A. *See* **Commissioner and Journal of American Folk-lore.**

Parkman, Francis. The conspiracy of Pontiac, and the Indian war after the conquest of Canada. Two volumes. Boston, 1886. 8°.

1—II, 328; 2—I, 207; 3—I, 183; 4—I, 187; 5—I, 255; 6—II, 311.

Parr, Harriet. The life and death of Jeanne d'Arc, called the Maid, etc. Two volumes, London, 1866. 12°.

Phister, *Lieut.* N. P. The Indian Messiah. (American Anthropologist, Washington, IV, No. 2, April, 1891.)

A statement by Lieutenant Phister is also appended to the report of Captain Lee on the abandonment of Fort Bidwell. *See* Adjutant-General's Office.

1—American Anthropologist, IV, No. 2, 105–7; 2—ibid; 3—ibid.

Powers, Stephen. Tribes of California. (Vol. III of Contributions to North American Ethnology; U. S. Geographical and Geological Survey of the Rocky Mountain Region.) Washington, 1877. 4°.

Prescott, W. H. History of the Conquest of Mexico. Edited by John Foster Kirk. Three volumes. (1873?) Philadelphia. 12°.

1—I, 61; 2—I, 346; 3—I, 309.

Pritts, J. Incidents of border life, illustrative of the times and condition of the first settlements in parts of the middle and western states, etc. Chambersburg, Pennsylvania, 1839. 8°.

1—98 (McCullough's narrative).

Remy, J., and Brenchley, J. A Journey to Great Salt Lake City, with a sketch of the history, religion, and customs of the Mormons, and an introduction on the religious movement in the United States. Two vols., London, 1861. 8°.

Roosevelt, T. In cowboy land. (Century Magazine, XLVI, No. 2, New York, June, 1893.)

1—283 (Century).

Schaff, Philip. A Religious Encyclopedia; or, dictionary of biblical, historical, doctrinal, and practical theology. Based on the Real-Encyklopädie of Herzog, Plitt, and Hauck. Edited by Philip Schaff, D. D., LL. D., professor in the Union Theological Seminary, New York, etc. Three volumes. Vol. I, New York, 1882. Large 8°.

Schoolcraft, H. R. Historical and statistical information respecting the history, condition, and prospects of the Indian tribes of the United States. Collected and prepared under the direction of the Bureau of Indian Affairs, etc. Published by authority of Congress. Six volumes, 4°. Philadelphia, 1851–1857.

1—IV, 240 (Fletcher); 2—IV, 259.

Science. *See* Dutton.

Scott, *Capt.* H. L. The Messiah dance in the Indian Territory. Essay for the Fort Sill lyceum, March, 1892 (manuscript).

Additional valuable information has been obtained from Captain Scott's official reports on the Ghost dance (*see* Ghost Dance and Adjutant-General's Office) and from personal letters and conversations.

Scribner's Magazine. *See* Welsh.

Shea, J. G. History of the Catholic missions among the Indian tribes of the United States, 1529–1854. New York, (1855?). 12°.

Contains references to the Columbia river missions.

Short Bull. Sermon delivered at the Red Leaf camp, October 31, 1890. Copy kindly furnished by George Bartlett, formerly of Pine Ridge agency, South Dakota. It appears also in the report of General Miles, in Report of the Secretary of War, Vol. I, 1891, 142.

Sickels, *Miss* E. C. (Notes and oral information in regard to the dance and songs at Pine Ridge.)

The author is also indebted to the kindness of Miss Sickels for the manuscript copy of Sword's account of the Ghost dance.

Snyder, *Colonel* Simon. (Personal letter concerning the Sword-bearer outbreak of 1887.)

Southey, Robert. The life of Wesley and rise and progress of Methodism. By Robert Southey. Second American edition with notes, etc, by the Reverend David Curry, A. M. Two volumes, New York, 1847. 12°.

Stenhouse, *Mrs* T. B. H. Tell it all: The story of a life's experience in Mormonism. Hartford, Connecticut, 1874.

Contains particular reference to the endowment robe.

Stephen, A. M.   Letters and oral information.

The late Mr Stephen lived and studied for
years among the Navaho, Hopi (Moki), Cohonino, and other Indians of northern New Mexico and Arizona, and was a competent authority on these tribes, particularly the Hopi, whose
ethnology he was investigating in conjunction
with Dr J. Walter Fewkes, for the Hemenway
Archeological Expedition.

1—Letter of September 17, 1891; 2—Letter of
November 22, 1891; 3—Oral information; 4—
Letter of September 17, 1891.

Sutherland, T. A.   Howard's campaign
against the Nez Percé Indians. By
Thomas A. Sutherland, volunteer aid-
de-camp on General Howard's staff.
Portland, Oregon, 1878.   Pamphlet, 8°.

1—39.

Tanner, John.   A narrative of the cap-
tivity and adventures of John Tanner.
New York, 1830.   8°.

1—155-158.

Thompson, A. H.   (Of the United States
Geological Survey. Oral information
concerning the religious ferment among
the Paiute of Utah in 1875.)

Treaties.   A compilation of all the treaties between the United States and the
Indian tribes, now in force as laws.
Prepared under the provisions of the
act of Congress approved March 3, 1873,
etc.   Washington, 1873.   8°.

1—439.

Voth, *Rev.* H. R.   (Correspondence and
notes.)

Mr Voth, now stationed among the Hopi, at
Oraibi, Arizona, was formerly superintendent
of the Mennonite Arapaho Mission, at Darlington, Oklahoma. Being interested in the
ethnology and language of the Arapaho, he
gave close attention to the Ghost dance during
the excitement, and has furnished much valuable information, orally and by letter, in regard
to the songs and ritual of the dance.

War.   Annual report of the Secretary of
War.   Washington.   8°.   (Volumes
quoted: 1877—I; 1881—I; 1888—I;
1891—I.)

1—Colonel Carr; Brevet Major-General Will-
cox, department commander, and Major-General McDowell, division commander, in Report
1881—I, 140-154; 2—Report of Brigadier-General Ruger and of Special Agent Howard, with
other papers in the same connection, 1888—I;
3a—General Howard in Report, 1877, I, 630;
3b—(Referred to) Report of scout Arthur Chapman, 1891—I, 191-194; 4—Short Bull's sermon,
1891—I, 142-143; 5—Report of General Brooke,
ibid, 135-126; 6—Report of General Miles,
ibid, 147-148; 7—Miles, ibid, 145; 8—Miles,
ibid, 146-147; General Ruger, 182-183; Lieutenant-Colonel Drum, 194-197; Captain Fechét,
197-199; 9—Miles, ibid, 147; 10—Miles, ibid, 147
and 153; 11—Miles, ibid, 147; Ruger, 184; Lieutenant Hale, 200-201; Captain Hurst, 201-202;
Lieutenant-Colonel Sumner, 224; 12—Miles, ibid,
147; Lieutenant-Colonel Sumner, etc, 209-238;
13—Miles, ibid, 150; 14—Miles, ibid, 150; 15—
Ruger, ibid, 185; Maus, ibid, 214; 16—Miles, ib'd,
130; 17—Miles, ibid, 130; 18—Miles, ibid, 150; 19—
Miles, ibid, 154; 20—Miles, ibid, 151; 21—Miles
ibid, 151; 22—Miles, ibid, 152; 23—Miles, ibid,
152-153; 24—Report of Lieutenant Getty, ibid,
250-251; 25—Reports of Colonel Merriam, Lieutenant Marshall, et al., ibid, 220-223; 26—Miles,
ibid, 154; 27—Miles, ibid, 154.

Warren, W. W.   History of the Ojib-
ways, based upon traditions and oral
statements.   (In collections of the Minnesota Historical Society, V. St. Paul,
1885.)   8°.

1—321-324; 2—321-324.

Welsh, Herbert.   The meaning of the
Dakota outbreak. (Scribner's Magazine, IX, No. 4; New York, April, 1891,
pages 429-452.)

Mr Welsh is president of the Indian Rights
Association, and a close and competent observer of Indian affairs.

1—445; 2—450; 3—452.

Index

Index

DeSoto, Caddo encountered by, 322
Detsăna'yuka, a Comanche band, 281
Detsekayaa, Caddo name of Arapaho, 201
Devil, Indian idea of, 271
De Vreede, Jan, killed at Wounded Knee, 121
Dice game of Arapaho, 255–56
Diggers: application of term, 285; Ghost dance among, 48
Disease, cured by Ghost dance, 28
Ditsä'kăna, a Comanche band, 281
Doctrine of Ghost dance, 19
Do'gu'at, Kiowa name of Wichita, 324
Dog men, a Cheyenne division, 266; an Arapaho warrior order, 238
Dog soldiers: insignia of, 237; sketch of, 236
Do'kănă, Comanche name for Wichita, 324
Dorsey, J. O.: on Omaha game, 279; scarification as a result of, 154; on Siouan camping circles, 294; on Siouan names of Sioux, 293
Dream, see Hypnotism; Trances; Vision
Drexel mission, during Wounded Knee trouble, 124
Drum: in Caddo mythology, 322; in Crow dance, 187
Drum, Col.: Indian police praised by, 107; ordered to arrest Sitting Bull, 102
Dubois, Cora, on 1870 Ghost dance, x
Duck, in Arapaho mythology, 207
Dull Knife, a Cheyenne leader, 265
Dunlap, Robert, acknowledgments to, xv
Dunmoi, Laura, Äpiatañ's letters read by, 169
Dunn, ——, in Sioux outbreak, 112
Dyer, A. C., killed at Wounded Knee, 121
Dyer, D. B.: acknowledgments to, xv; guide on visit to Wovoka, 9; interpreter on visit to Wovoka, 13
Dzĭtsĭstäs, a synonym of Cheyenne, 263

Eagle; represented on Ghost shirts, 42, 68; sacred regard for, 184, 232, 243, 307, 329; vision of, in Ghost dance, 181; when killed by Caddo, 322, 329
Eagle-bone whistle, used by medicine man, 115
Eagle feathers: in Cohonino ceremony, 57; on Ghost shirts, 42; sacred use of, 243; song pertaining to, 329; use of, by Wovoka, 18; used in Ghost dance, 179, 228, 328, 330; used in hypnotism, 188, 198
Eagle Pipe, flight of, to Bad Lands, 138
Eagles: how trapped by Arapaho, 244; kept by pueblo tribes, 243
Earth: personification of, 325, 328; regeneration of, 207, 291, 308; sacred regard for, 182; turtle as a symbol of, 225

Earth Lodge, post–Ghost-dance religious cult, xii
Earthquake: myth concerning, 225; reference to, in Cheyenne song, 268
Eater, see Biäñk'i
Eaters, a Cheyenne division, 266
Eclipse: Paiute notion of, 16; Wovoka entranced during, 16
Eclipses, calendar of, in Nevada, 16
Edson, Casper: Arapaho delegate to Wovoka, 157; Wovoka's letter written by, 22
Education, how regarded by Sioux, 82
Eells, Myron, acknowledgments to, xv
Elliott, George, killed at Wounded Knee, 121
Emankina, Biäñk'i's vision of, 168
Endowment robe, of Mormons, 34
E'pea, Biäñk'i's vision of, 168
Epidemics, among Sioux, 75, 85
Estakéwach, a Pit River band, 289
Etsitü'biwat, a Comanche band, 282
Evĭ'sts-unĭ''pahĭs, a Cheyenne division, 265
Ewers, Capt. E. P.: ordered to arrest Hump, 146; Sitting Bull's fugitives surrendered to, 321
Eyeish, a Caddo division, 321

Facial painting: by Arapaho, 220; ceremonial, 277
Fall Indians, a synonym of Gros Ventres, 203
Fast Thunder: conduct of, in Sioux outbreak, 89; on Sioux outbreak, 84
Fasting: during eagle trapping, 244; preliminary to Ghost dance, 66
Feast: Ghost dance accompanied by, 278; sacred, in Sioux ceremony, 69
Feather, Ghost-dance ceremony of, 167, 184
Feathers: attached to amulet, 161; ceremonial use, 250; crow, Indians defrauded with, 157; crow, sacred regard for, 274; eagle, attached to Ghost shirts, 42; eagle, Caddo sacred use of, 322; eagle, in Cohonino ceremony, 57; eagle, sacred use of, 243; eagle, song pertaining to, 329; eagle, used in hypnotism, 188, 190; eagle, used in Ghost dance, 179, 228, 328, 330; eagle, used in war bonnets; 307; head, of Arapaho, 213, 214; Kiowa robe of, 163; magpie, ceremonial use of, 250; magpie, presented by Wovoka, 242; magpie, prized by Paiute, 17; as medium of exchange, 243; as protecting "medicine," 34; sacred use of, by Wovoka, 18; symbolism of, in Ghost dance, 31; turkey, on Cheyenne arrows, 264; use of, in Ghost dance, 28, 184, 316; used in Crow dance, 187
Fechét, Capt. E. G.: at arrest of Sitting Bull, 103, 104; pursuit of Sitting Bull's warriors by, 105

Howard, Henry, killed at Wounded Knee, 121

Howling Bull, hypnotism produced by, 150

Hubbub, game of, 255

Huggins, Capt. E. L., acknowlegments to, xv

Huma'whi, a Pit River band, 289

Hummer of the Arapaho, 223, 224

Hump: arrest of, 109; Ghost dance at camp of, 92; participation of, in Sioux outbreak, 108; removal of, recommended, 93; surrender of, 107; surrender of band of, 120; at surrender of Sitting Bull fugitives, 110

Hunkpapa, a Teton division, 294

Hurst, Capt. J. H.; appointed Indian agent, 141; at arrest of Sitting Bull's band, 110; arrest of Sitting Bull's band ordered by, 109; on causes of Sioux trouble, 81; on character of Sioux rations, 72

Hyde, Charles L., notification by, of Sioux outbreak, 88

Hypnotism: among Caddo, 161; among Cohonino, 57; in Crow dance, 187; in Ghost dance, 43, 44, 150, 156, 179, 181, 184, 187–89, 198–99, 221, 279, 315, 326, 327; in Indian ceremonies, 187; in Navaho ceremonies, 55; practiced by Wovoka, 18, 62, 158; see also Dream; Trance

Iätä-go, Kiowa name of Ute, 280

Iatan, a synonym of Comanche, 280

Ibids'ii, a Paiute goddess, 288

Idahi, Kiowa Apache name of Comanche, 280

Ietan, a synonym of Comanche, 280

Ietau, a synonym of Comanche, 280

Igiagyähona, acknowledgments to, xv

Ihanktoñwañ, a Sioux division, 294

Ilma'wi, a Pit River band, 289

I'mäha, a Caddo division, 321

Immortality, in Ghost-dance doctrine, 28

Incense, in Sioux ceremony, 68

Indian Office, acknowledgments to, xv

Indian Sam, on Ghost-dance doctrine, 26

In-the-middle, see Pa-iñgya

Inûna-ina, a synonym of Arapaho, 201

Ioni, a Caddo division, 321

Iowa, absence of Ghost dance among, 71; Ghost dance among, 159

Isañati, a Santee synonym, 294

Isium-itä'niuw', a Cheyenne division, 265

Itahatski, Hidatsa name of Sioux, 293

Itǎsupuzi, Hidatsa name of Cheyenne, 263

Itazipko, a Teton division, 294

Jerked beef, how prepared, 301

Jetan, a synonym of Comanche, 280

Jicarilla, absence of Ghost dance among, 49

Joan of Arc, compared to Wovoka, xi

Jocko Reserve, Indians on, 49

John Day Indians, present habitat of, 49

Johnson, G. P., killed at Wounded Knee, 121

Johnson, John, name applied to Wovoka, 6

Josephus, description of Wovoka's inspiration, 14

Jutz, Father John: interview with, 309; Sioux conference effected by, 114; at Wounded Knee, 121, 130

Kä'dohǎdä'cho, a Caddo synonym, 269; account of, 322; early encountered by French, 323

Ká'igwǔ, proper name of the Kiowa, 310; a Kiowa division, 311

Kai-wǎ, a Kiowa synonym, 310

Kanaheǎwastsǐk, Cree name of Cheyenne, 263; adherents to doctrine of, 159

Kaninahoic, Ojibwa name of Arapaho, 201

Kaninǎvish, Ojibwa name of Arapaho, 201

Kansa: Ghost dance among, 159; name of Comanche, 280; name of Sioux, 293

Ka'ntsi, Caddo name of Kiowa Apache, 313

Kataka, name of Kiowa Apache, 313

Kawinahan, an Arapaho division, 205

Keam, T. V.: acknowledgments to, xv; on Cohonino Ghost dance, 57

Keechies, a synonym of Kichai, 324

Keeps-his-name-always, see Da'tekañ

Kelley, James E., killed at Wounded Knee, 121

Kellner, August, killed at Wounded Knee, 121

Kerr, Capt., attacked by hostile Sioux, 136

Kewa'tsǎna, a Comanche band, 282

Kichai, acknowledgments to, xv

Kichai Indians: account of, 324; Ghost dance introduced among, 159; name of Cheyenne, 263; name of Comanche, 280; name of Kiowa Apache, 313; name of Sioux, 293; name of Wichita, 324; status of, 322

Kickapoo, absence of Ghost dance among, 60; Ghost dance among, 157, 159

Kicking Bear: Cheyenne scouts attacked by, 114; continued retreat of, 114; delegate to Wovoka, 64, 148; flight of, to Bad Lands, 95, 98; a Ghost-dance leader, 92; Ghost dance led by, 100; Ghost-dance mission of, 61; operations of, in Sioux outbreak, 135; Pine Ridge agency attacked by, 123; portrait of, 99; surrender of, 115; surrender of, demanded, 141

Kiñep, a Kiowa division, 311

Kiowa: absence of clans among, 204; account of, 310; cedar used in Ghost dance of, 53; confederation of Comanche with, 281; Ghost dance among, 28, 46, 150, 154,

Pit River Indians: account of, 289; Ghost dance among, 27, 48

Piute, a synonym of Paiute, 285

Pleasant men, an Arapaho division, 205

Plenty Horses, Lieut. Casey killed by, 142

Plumb, Agent, account of Ghost dance by, 52

Pa'hoi, a Comanche band, 282

Poland, Col., troops under at Rosebud, 95

Polänyup, a Kiowa warrior order, 240

Pole, sacrifice in Sioux ceremony, 68

Police, Sioux: arrest of Sitting Bull by, 103, 105; bravery of, 107; moderation of, 118

Pollock, Oscar, killed at Wounded Knee, 120, 121

Poloi, Henry, acknowledgments to, xv

Ponca, Ghost dance among, 60, 159

Poor Buffalo: a Ghost-dance leader, 165; Kiowa messiah delegation under, 164; portrait of, 165

Porcupine: account of messiah by, 37; effect of messiah visit of, 62; Ghost song composed by, 268; statement of, concerning messiah, 63; visit of, to Wovoka, 3, 26, 61, 147, 148

Potawatomi: absence of Ghost dance among, 58; Ghost dance among, 159

Potrero, prophecy of Indians of, 48

Powder, sacred: on dance ground, 182; use of, in battle, 34

Powell, J. W., quoted on Paiute, 316

Powers, Stephen, on Pit River Indians, 281

Prather, W. H., Sioux campaign song by, 136, 137

Prayer, Lord's, Arapaho equivalent of, 215, 226

Preston, Lieut. Guy, at battle of Wounded Knee, 123

Pretty Back, on Sioux outbreak, 84

Primeau, Louis: guide in attack of Sitting Bull, 103; interpreter for Sioux delegation, 145

Principal dogs, a Kiowa warrior order, 240

Pueblos, absence of Ghost dance among, 49, 199; see also Hopi; Taos

Pumpkin seed, in Caddo mythology, 322

Putchi, information concerning Cohonino from, 57

Pyramid Lake, battle of, in 1860, 13

Quanah, see Parker Quanah

Quapaw, name of Comanche, 280

Quirt, of Dog soldiers, 237

Quoit-tsow, another name of Wovoka, 3

Quoitze Ow, name applied to Wovoka, 6

Rabbits: in Paiute myth, 288; a Kiowa warrior order, 240

Rain: invoked by bull-roarer, 224; songs of Wovoka, 15

Rapid City, appearance of troops at, 95

Rapid Indians, a synonym of Gros Ventres, 203

Rations, Sioux, table of, 84; see also Sioux outbreak

Rattle: of the Dog soldiers, 237; used by Arapaho warriors, 238

Raven, sacred regard for, 232

Real-dogs, a Kiowa warrior order, 240

Red, as sacred color, 277

Red Buffalo, song composed by, 315

Red Cloud: adherent of messiah doctrine, 93; confidence in, by agent, 77; declaration of, for Ghost-dance doctrine, 65; Ghost-dance council held by, 64; an Ogalala chief, 90, 294; operations of, in Sioux outbreak, 135; opposition of, to land cession, 90; portrait of, 91; responsibility of, for Sioux outbreak, 98; surrender of band of, 136; thwarted by McGillycuddy, 90

Red Cloud, Jack, conduct of, in Sioux outbreak, 138

Red Feather, name of Paul Boynton, 220

Red-lodges, a Cheyenne division, 266

Red Tail, in Ghost dance, 317

Red Tomahawk, a Sioux policeman, 103; portrait of, 103; Sitting Bull shot by, 104

Red Wolf, delegate to Wovoka, 157

Regan, Michael, killed at Wounded Knee, 121

Regeneration: of earth, 207, 270, 291, 308; in Ghost-dance doctrine, 27, 40; idea of, ridiculed by southern Ute, 50; Indian belief in, 62; power of, attributed to Wovoka, 65

Reinecky, T. T., killed at Wounded Knee, 121

Relander, Chick, on Smohalla cult, xii

Resurrection, see Regeneration

Return-from-scout, vision of wife of, 179

Revitalization movements, theory of, xi–xii

Richard, Louis, interpreter for Sioux delegation, 145

Ridge people, a Cheyenne division, 265

Rivers, reference to, in Ghost song, 314

Roberts, J., Arapaho sacred pine seen by, 209

Robinson, Lieut., scouts under, in Sioux outbreak, 95

Rose, wild, use of seeds of, 227

Rosebud Agency: changes in land boundaries of, 75; delegates from, to Washington, 145; delegates from, to Wovoka, 64; flight of Indians of, to Bad Lands, 95; Ghost dance at, 92; number of Sioux at, 91; outbreak of Indians of, predicted, 44

remained in the circle, and set up the most fearful, heart-piercing wails I ever heard—crying, moaning, groaning, and shrieking out their grief, and naming over their departed friends and relatives, at the same time taking up handfuls of dust at their feet, washing their hands in it, and throwing it over their heads. Finally, they raised their eyes to heaven, their hands clasped high above their heads, and stood straight and perfectly still, invoking the power of the Great Spirit to allow them to see and talk with their people who had died. This ceremony lasted about fifteen minutes, when they all sat down where they were and listened to another address, which I did not understand, but which I afterwards learned were words of encouragement and assurance of the coming messiah.

When they arose again, they enlarged the circle by facing toward the center, taking hold of hands, and moving around in the manner of school children in their play of "needle's eye." And now the most intense excitement began. They would go as fast as they could, their hands moving from side to side, their bodies swaying, their arms, with hands gripped tightly in their neighbors', swinging back and forth with all their might. If one, more weak and frail, came near falling, he would be jerked up and into position until tired nature gave way. The ground had been worked and worn by many feet, until the fine, flour-like dust lay light and loose to the depth of two or three inches. The wind, which had increased, would sometimes take it up, enveloping the dancers and hiding them from view. In the ring were men, women, and children; the strong and the robust, the weak consumptive, and those near to death's door. They believed those who were sick would be cured by joining in the dance and losing consciousness. From the beginning they chanted, to a monotonous tune. the words—

> Father, I come;
> Mother, I come;
> Brother, I come;
> Father, give us back our arrows.

All of which they would repeat over and over again until first one and then another would break from the ring and stagger away and fall down. One woman fell a few feet from me. She came toward us, her hair flying over her face, which was purple, looking as if the blood would burst through; her hands and arms moving wildly; every breath a pant and a groan; and she fell on her back, and went down like a log. I stepped up to her as she lay there motionless, but with every muscle twitching and quivering. She seemed to be perfectly unconscious. Some of the men and a few of the women would run, stepping high and pawing the air in a frightful manner. Some told me afterwards that they had a sensation as if the ground were rising toward them and would strike them in the face. Others would drop where they stood. One woman fell directly into the ring, and her husband stepped out and stood over her to prevent them from trampling upon her. No one ever disturbed those who fell or took any notice of them except to keep the crowd away.

They kept up dancing until fully 100 persons were lying unconscious. Then they stopped and seated themselves in a circle, and as each one recovered from his trance he was brought to the center of the ring to relate his experience. Each told his story to the medicine-man and he shouted it to the crowd. Not one in ten claimed that he saw anything. I asked one Indian—a tall, strong fellow, straight as an arrow—what his experience was. He said he saw an eagle coming toward him. It flew round and round, drawing nearer and nearer until he put out his hand to take it, when it was gone. I asked him what he thought of it. "Big lie," he replied. I found by talking to them that not one in twenty believed it. After resting for a time they would go through the same performance, perhaps three times a day. They practiced fasting, and every morning those who joined in the dance were obliged to immerse themselves in the creek. (*Comr.*, 44.)

SONG REHEARSALS

As with church choirs, the leaders, both men and women, frequently assembled privately in a tipi to rehearse the new or old songs for the next dance. During the first winter spent among the Arapaho I had frequent opportunity of being present at these rehearsals, as for a long time the snow was too deep to permit dancing outside. After having obtained their confidence the Arapaho police invited me to come up to their camp at night to hear them practice the songs in anticipation of better weather for dancing. Thenceforth rehearsals were held in Black Coyote's tipi almost every night until the snow melted, each session usually lasting about three hours.

On these occasions from eight to twelve persons were present, sitting in a circle on the low beds around the fire in the center. Black Coyote acted as master of ceremonies and opened proceedings by filling and lighting the redstone pipe, offering the first whiff to the sun, then reversing the stem in offering to the earth, next presenting the pipe to the fire, and then to each of the four cardinal points. He then took a few puffs himself, after which he passed the pipe to his next neighbor, who went through the same preliminaries before smoking, and thus the pipe went round the circle, each one taking only a few puffs before passing it on. The pipe was then put back into its pouch, and Black Coyote, standing with his face toward the northwest, the messiah's country, with eyes closed and arms outstretched, made a fervent prayer for help and prosperity to his tribe, closing with an earnest petition to the messiah to hasten his coming. The others listened in silence with bowed heads. The prayer ended, they consulted as to the song to be sung first, which Black Coyote then started in a clear musical bass, the others joining. From time to time explanations were made where the meaning of the song was not clear. They invited me to call for whatever songs I wished to hear, and these songs were repeated over and over again to give me an opportunity to write them down, but they waived extended discussion until another time. Usually the men alone were the singers, but sometimes Black Coyote's wives or other women who were present joined in the songs. It was noticeable that even in these rehearsals the women easily fell under the excitement of the dance. Finally, about 10 oclock, all rose together and sang the closing song, *Ni'ninitubi'na Huhu*, "The Crow has given the signal," and the rehearsal was at an end. On one occasion, before I had obtained this song, I called for it in order that I might write it down, but they explained that we must wait awhile, as it was the closing song, and if they sung it then they must quit for the night.

PREPARATIONS FOR THE DANCE

On several occasions the dance ground was consecrated before the performance, one of the leaders going all about the place, sprinkling some kind of sacred powder over the ground and praying the while.

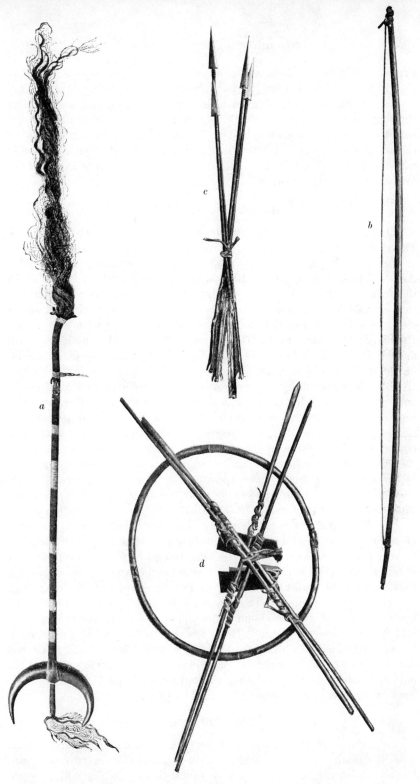

Fig. 39.—Sacred objects from the Sioux Ghost dance: *a*, staff; *b*, *c*, bow and bone-head arrows; *d*, gaming wheel and sticks.

Frequently in the dance one or more of the leaders while sitting within the circle would beat upon the earth with his extended palm, then lay his hand upon his head, afterward blow into his hand, and then repeat the operation, praying all the time. Sometimes the hypnotist would beat the ground in the same way and then lay his hand on the head of the subject (Fig. 43).　　No satisfactory explanation of this ceremony was obtained beyond the general idea that the earth, like the sun, the fire, and the water, is sacred.

GIVING THE FEATHER

The ceremony of "giving the feather" has been already noticed. This was an official ordination of the priests in the dance, conferred on them by the apostle who first brought the ceremony to the tribe. Among the Arapaho, Caddo, Kiowa, and adjoining tribes in the south the feather was conferred by Sitting Bull himself. The feather was thus given to seven leaders, or sometimes to fourteen, that is, seven men and seven women, the number seven being sacred with most tribes and more particularly in the Ghost dance. The feather, which was worn upon the head of the dancers, was either that of the crow, the sacred bird of the Ghost dance, or of the eagle, sacred in all Indian religions. If from the crow, two feathers were used, being attached at a slight angle to a small stick which was thrust into the hair. (See Arapaho song 8.) The feathers were previously consecrated by the priest with prayer and ceremony. The chosen ones usually reciprocated with presents of ponies, blankets, or other property. After having thus received the feather the tribe began to make songs of its own, having previously used those taught them by the apostle from his own language.

Besides the seven leaders who wear the sacred crow feathers as emblems of their leadership, nearly all the dancers wear feathers variously painted and ornamented, and the preparation of these is a matter of much concern. The dancer who desires instruction on this point usually takes with him six friends, so as to make up the sacred number of seven, and goes with them to one who has been in a trance and has thus learned the exact method in vogue in the spirit world. At their request this man prepares for each one a feather, according to what he has seen in some trance vision, for which they return thanks, usually with a small present. The feathers are painted in several colors, each larger feather usually being tipped with a small down feather painted in a different color. On certain occasions a special day is set apart for publicly painting and preparing the feathers for all the dancers, the work being done by the appointed leaders of the ceremony.

THE PAINTING OF THE DANCERS

The painting of the dancers is done with the same ceremonial exactness of detail, each design being an inspiration from a trance vision. Usually the dancer adopts the particular style of painting which, while

Tilford, Col., troops under, in Sioux outbreak, 95

Time, reckoning among Indians, 16

Tipi: of Arapaho, 205; a Sioux word, 295

Titoñwañ, a Sioux division, 294; *see also* Teton

Tivis, William, acknowledgments to, xv

Tlinkit, sacred regard of, for crow, 232

Tobacco, offering by Sioux, 66

To'ngyä-gu'adal, Kiowa name of Red Tail, 317

Toñkoñ'ko, a Kiowa warrior order, 240

Tops, used by Arapaho boys, 257

Towakoni Jim, acknowledgments to, xv

Trances, of Wovoka, 13; *see also* Dream; Hypnotism; Vision

Transformation in Ghost-dance doctrine, 303

Treaty: Caddo, of 1835, 323; Comanche, of 1835, 281; effect of, on Sioux, 74; failure of government to fulfill, 72, 76, 79, 81, 85; Kiowa, of 1837, 313; of Medicine Lodge in 1867, 205, 281; Sioux, of 1868, 69, 84; Sioux, of 1876, 70; Sioux, of 1877, 83

Tree: sacred in Ghost-dance symbolism, 33; used in Cohonino ceremony, 57; used in Ghost dance, 46, 67, 179, 228, 316; *see also* Cedar; Cottonwood; Pole

Troops: appearance of, among Sioux, 92, 95; conduct of, at Wounded Knee, 127; effect of, on Ghost dance, 99; effect on Sioux of appearance of, 98; formed of Indians, 145; killed at Wounded Knee, 126; necessity for, in Sioux outbreak, 77; number of, in Sioux outbreak, 95, 113

Tsabakosh, Caddo name of Sioux, 293

Tsäñ'yui, a Kiowa warrior order, 240

Tseñtä'nmo, a Kiowa warrior order, 240

Tupper, Maj., pursuit of Sioux by, 98

Turkey feathers, on Cheyenne arrows, 264

Turning Bear, flight of, to Bad Lands, 138

Turning Hawk, delegate to Washington, 145; on Wounded Knee massacre, 138, 139, 140

Turtle: in Arapaho mythology, 207; in primitive mythology, 225

Turtle River, identification of, 269

Twohig, Daniel, killed at Wounded Knee, 121

Two kettles, a Teton division, 294

Two Strike: at battle of Wounded Knee, 123; flight of, to Bad Lands, 138; Ghost dance led by, 92; operations of, in Sioux outbreak, 135; Pine River agency attacked by, 123, 126; surrender of, 114, 115

Ugly Face Woman, trance experience of, 210

U'mañhañ, meaning of word, 322

Umatilla reserve, Indians on, 39; visit of Sioux delegates to, 64

Ute; and Arapaho warfare, 202; attendance of, at Ghost dance, 46; Ghost dance among, 49; present habitat of, 50; reception of, into Mormon church, 34; southern, absence of Ghost dance among, 49, 50

Utensils of the Paiute, 12

Utley, Robert M., on Sioux history and Ghost dance, xi

Vestal, Stanley, on Sioux history and Ghost dance, xi

Viroqua, account of, 147

Vision of Biäñk'i, 168; *see also* Dream; Hypnotism; Trances

Voth, H. R., on Cheyenne sacred paint, 269; on figurative use of shell, 252

Wa-ai'h, a Comanche band, 282

Waco, a Wichita subtribe, 324

Wahpacoota, a Sioux division, 294

Wahpeton, a Sioux division, 294

Walapai, Ghost dance among, 28, 49, 58, 186

Wallace, Capt., killed at Wounded Knee, 120

Wallace, Anthony F. C.: on James Mooney and study of Ghost dance, vii–xii; on revitalization movements, xii

Wallawalla, present habitat of, 49

Wallis, Wilson D., on messiahs, xii

Wana'ghi Wa'chipi, Sioux name of Ghost dance, 35

Wand, use of, in Sioux ceremony, 68

Waqpekute, a Sioux division, 294

Waqpetoñwañ, a Sioux division, 294

Waqui'si, native name of Ugly Face Woman, 210

Wa'quithi, an Arapaho division, 205

War: bonnets, eagle feathers used in, 307; Department, acknowledgments to, xv; forbidden by Ghost-dance doctrine, 25, 40; signal of Sioux, 118

Warden, Clever, acknowledgments to, xv

Warmspring Indians, present habitat of, 49; *see also* Tenino

Warmspring reserve, Indians on, 49

Warner, C. C., letter of, to Wovoka, 8

Warner, Maj., Sioux commissioner, 84

Warrior: order of Kiowa, 240; society of Arapaho, 236

Warriors: Cheyenne renowned as, 267; Sioux, number of, 98

Wasco, present habitat of, 49

Washee, a delegate to Wovoka, 148, 158

Washo: account of, 288; Ghost dance among, 48; name of Paiute, 285